Chinese Aesthetics

Chinese Aesthetics

● ● ● ● ● ● ● ● ● ● ● ● ● ● ● ● ● ●

The Ordering of Literature, the Arts,
and the Universe in the Six Dynasties

Edited by Zong-qi Cai

 University of Hawai'i Press
HONOLULU

Library of Congress Cataloging-in-Publication Data

Chinese aesthetics : the ordering of literature, the arts, and the
universe in the Six Dynasties / edited by Zong-qi Cai.
   p.   cm.
  Includes index.
  ISBN 0-8248-2791-0 (alk. paper)
  1. Aesthetics.   2. Chinese literature—220–589—History and
criticism.
I. Cai, Zongqi.
BH39.C5268   2004
111'.85'0931—dc22   2004004777

Designed by University of Hawai'i Press production staff

Printed by The Maple-Vail Book Publishing Group

Contents

Acknowledgments

The ten essays collected in this volume are revised versions of papers presented at an international conference on Six Dynasties aesthetics held at the University of Illinois, Urbana-Champaign, November 3–4, 2000. This conference was a sequel to a conference on Liu Xie's *Wenxin diaolong* (The Literary Mind and the Carving of Dragons) held three years earlier, as it sought to address various theoretic questions raised at that conference in the broader contexts of Six Dynasties aesthetics and culture. The conference was generously funded by the College of Liberal Arts and Sciences, the Center for East Asian and Pacific Studies, and the Department of East Asian Languages and Cultures, University of Illinois. The Research Board of the University of Illinois provided a grant for hiring a graduate student to assist in the preparation of this volume, as well as a publication subvention grant. In addition to acknowledging the financial support of these institutions, I must express my gratitude to my colleagues, students, and the staff at Illinois. In particular, I wish to thank Professor George T. Yu, the Center Director, for his valuable guidance and support. To my wife, Jing Liao, I am immensely grateful for her indispensable help during the conference. The conference also benefited from the participation of Professors Douglas A. Kibbee of the University of Illinois, Wolfgang Kubin of the University of Bonn, Bernhard Fuehrer of the University of London, Ts'ai Tsung-yang of National Taiwan Normal University, and other scholars.

All contributors to this volume wish to thank Robert Ford Campany of Indiana University and an anonymous reader for their insightful comments and suggestions. We are particularly indebted to Patricia Crosby, executive editor of the University of Hawai'i Press, for her enthusiastic support and professional guidance.

Prologue

· ·

A Historical Overview of Six Dynasties Aesthetics

Zong-qi Cai

After centuries in which it played at best a subordinate role to historiography, sociopolitical theory, and philosophy, aesthetic inquiry finally emerged in the Six Dynasties (220–589) as a distinct, independent concern.[1] Although Chinese literati did not begin to discuss literature and the arts in their own right until early in the third century, by the end of the sixth century their reflections would evolve into a sophisticated system of aesthetic discourse characterized by its own rhetoric, concepts, and evaluative criteria.

Like Western aesthetics, that of the Six Dynasties is often silent about the ethical, sociopolitical, and utilitarian.[2] Yet it was precisely these factors that made its birth and rapid growth possible. In particular, the rise of an aristocratic literati culture after the collapse of the Han dynasty (206 B.C.–220 A.D.) was crucial. The evolution of such a culture would more or less shape the trajectory of Six Dynasties aesthetics. For that reason, it seems useful to look at how aristocratic culture influenced the Wei-Jin, (Liu) Song, and Qi-Liang periods, especially as exemplified by works discussed in the ten essays assembled here.[3] As I examine the common concerns and themes in these works, I will address the larger issue of aesthetic ideals for these periods and consider how those ideals may be traced to different philosophical sources.

Wei-Jin Aesthetics

The Wei-Jin period witnessed an unprecedented explosion of interest in aesthetic matters. This reflected a profound transformation of the intelligentsia (*shi* 士) from important players in the political arena to detached artists, connoisseurs, and theorists of literature and the arts.

In the Han dynasty, the intelligentsia had emerged as a class powerful enough to rival the eunuchs (*huanguan* 宦官) and the relatives of imperial consorts (*waiqi* 外戚). The ascendancy of the intelligentsia came about from Han court policy, which worked to promote Confucian scholarship and even to secure high official posts for Confucian scholars. For the Han intelligentsia, power and influence were obtainable in two ways. Some capitalized on the lack of public education to make their own households exclusive centers for Confucian study. In that fashion, they tried to monopolize Confucian scholarship and hence entry into officialdom. Over time, these households became de facto aristocratic as high official positions were passed on from one generation to the next. Others, especially those associated with the imperial academy, gained influence from their reputation in Pure Critique (qingyi 清議), a late Han forum designed to expose political corruption and assess the moral stature of court officials. The Pure Critique members—often called *mingshi* 名士, or famous scholars—won praise as the "pure stream" (*qingliu* 清流) for their moral courage, while the "intelligentsia clans" (*shizu* 士族) earned the name "turgid stream" (*zhuoliu* 濁流) because of their political opportunism and corrupt practices.[4]

The end of the Han dynasty profoundly transformed both groups. As a result of the Great Proscriptions (*danggu* 党錮), most of the major voices in the Pure Critique were silenced, as political discussion turned into a perilous affair. The suppression of dissent by the Jin rulers only made matters worse. Yet the lofty ideal of the Han *mingshi* refused to die. During the Zhengshi reign (240–248), a new group of *mingshi*, led by He Yan 何晏 (ca. 190–249) and Wang Bi 王弼 (226–249), founded the Pure Conversation (qingtan 清談) movement. Avoiding contemporary politics, the Zhengshi *mingshi* focused on abstract cosmological questions and established Xuanxue 玄學 (Abstruse Learning) based on three texts: the *Lao Zi* 老子, the *Zhuang Zi* 莊子, and the *Yi jing* 易經 (Book of Changes). Toward the end of the Zhengshi period, a new group of *mingshi*, known as the Seven Sages of the Bamboo Grove, transformed Abstruse Learning into a counterculture movement.[5]

Unlike their predecessors, they openly flouted Confucian morality and indulged in unrestrained emotion, drugs, and wine; a disinterested pursuit of the arts; and a quest for physical immortality, as well as spiritual communion with the Dao. To the people of their time (not least the Jin rulers), all of their outlandish behavior seemed a calculated protest against state-sponsored Confucian ritualism. Predictably, the Jin rulers quickly moved to suppress the Bamboo Grove *mingshi* (*Zhulin mingshi* 竹林名士). The execution of their leader, Ji Kang 嵇康 (223–262), and the submission of Xiang Xiu 向秀 (ca. 221–ca. 300) to the Jin court in the same year mark not only the end of their rebellion, but also the end of any public moral conscience as well. For the next several hundred years, there would be no more *mingshi* like Ji Kang who dared to confront a corrupt, repressive government and provide moral leadership for society. Instead, the Jin intelligentsia clans became dominant until superseded by a new intelligentsia who had risen from the "humble clans" (*hanzu* 寒族) to become the royal families of Song, Qi, and Liang. Together, these groups would foster an aristocratic literati culture that was, for all its moral defects, particularly favorable to aesthetics.

To see how the intelligentsia clans virtually monopolized the arts during the Jin, we need only to look at the Wang clan of Langye 瑯琊 (Shandong). Thanks to the political accomplishments of Wang Dao 王導 (276–339), his family became preeminent along with the Xie 謝 family of Chen Commandery 陳郡 in Henan during the Eastern Jin. A quick look at the Wang genealogy traced by Susan Bush reveals a long line of noted calligraphers.[6] In effect, the Wangs practically made calligraphy an exclusive family enterprise. Even when their political power diminished after the fall of the Jin, they continued to wield cultural influence up through the Liang dynasty. Of the later generation, the most prominent are Wang Wei 王微 (415–453), Wang Sengqian 王僧虔 (427–485), and Wang Rong 王融 (468–494). Significantly, they are better known for what they wrote about painting, calligraphy, music, and poetry than for their accomplishments in these arts.[7]

As shaped by the Wangs, Xies, and other powerful clans, Jin culture represents a superficial imitation of the counterculture of Bamboo Grove *mingshi*. But whereas the Bamboo Grove *mingshi* like Ji Kang and Ruan Ji represented the "pure stream," these clans certainly belonged to the "turgid stream" of the *mingshi* tradition, criticized for various moral weaknesses.[8] Some even participated in the brutal repressions of the Jin court in return for protection of their clan privileges.[9] If the Bamboo Grove *mingshi* sought to create an iconoclastic movement, the Jin *mingshi* imitation of it was little more than a flamboyant performance in manners, dress, deportment, verbal flair, and, above all, detachment—a performance designed to enhance social distinction.

From a sociopolitical perspective, Jin *mingshi* culture looks trivial, self-absorbed, and indulgent. But for the development of aesthetics, it was profoundly significant. Essentially, the Jin *mingshi* placed abstruse learning, literature, and the arts at the center of their life. These pursuits involved the Jin *mingshi* in a double role as performers and spectators. By observation of one another's "life performances," they cultivated an aesthetic appreciation that would later be applied to literature and the arts. Moreover, this mutual observation and appreciation gave rise to the *mingshi* coteries or "salons" to whom theoretical reflections on literature and the arts would be addressed.

Of all the texts about the Wei-Jin period, the *Shishuo xinyu* 世説新 語 (A New Account of Tales of the World), compiled around 430 by Liu Yiqing 劉義慶 (403–444), provides the most complete picture of the Jin *mingshi's* life performances. Most of its thirty-six chapters depict prominent members of the Jin *mingshi*, with the remainder devoted to famous figures of the Han, Wei, and (Liu) Song. Most entries in each chapter follow a common format: a quotation of conversational remarks by *mingshi* figures framed by a pithy and impressionistic evaluation of the central actor.

Focusing on the Jin *mingshi* entries, Wai-yee Li demonstrates the debt of the *Shishuo xinyu* to the earlier discourses of Pure Critique and Pure Conversation. Insofar as its entries focus on the observations of individual characters, this book represents a continuation of the practice of evaluating character begun by Pure Critique. But insofar as it enshrines the ideals of Daoist detachment as the basic criteria for judging behavioral performance, it is squarely in the tradition of Pure Conversation and in fact is considered by many as a later stage of this philosophical discourse. This shift from inner moral qualities to behavioral performance, Li emphasizes, corresponds to a shift in underlying principles from Confucian political activism to Daoist detachment.

Li also explains the important differences between the *Shishuo xinyu* and early discourses of Pure Critique and Pure Conversation. In the *Shishuo xinyu*, the observation and evaluation of individuals are not intended as "recommendations for offices" (*chaju* 察舉). Thus there is little interest in assessing the political accomplishments of particular individuals. Nor is there an endeavor to establish general types of human temperament and abilities as Liu Shao 劉邵 (fl. 240–250) had done in *Renwu zhi* 人物誌 (Studies on Human Abilities). Similarly, the abundant presence of Abstruse Learning ideas in the *Shishuo xinyu* does not indicate any interest on the part of either the author or the Jin *mingshi* in continuing He Yan and Wang Bi's abstruse philosophical speculation. There is in fact, Li notes, a deliberate marginalization of Wang Bi, Guo Xiang 郭象 (d. 312), and other early Pure Conversationalists in the *Shishuo xinyu*. What really interested Liu Yiqing was how the Jin *mingshi* translated Abstruse Learning ideas into unconventional modes of speech and behavior meant for aesthetic appreciation by others.

This aestheticization of Abstruse Learning ideas, Li points out, is evidenced by what the Jin *mingshi* actually said about aesthetic observation (*mu* 目 or *timu* 題目), as well as the format of the *Shishuo xinyu*. In each entry, there is either an explicit observer (the interlocutor of the framing narrative) or an implicit observer (in entries where the framing narrative is dispensed with) pleasurably watching a "pure aesthetic spectacle" unfold. Typically, such a spectacle is one of "momentary brilliance," a dazzling display of the appearance, deportment, wit, and Daoist detachment of the individual character(s) observed.

Since this heightened perception of human characters is purely aesthetic, Li maintains, it is not surprising that many of them are depicted with a string of nature images independent of moral concerns. Unlike the moralistic metaphors or *bide* 比德 (analogues of moral virtues) widely used by earlier Confucian-minded writers, these nature images do not illustrate any definite moral qualities but simply convey the ineffable beauty of manners, action, and thought. They also connote the intense aesthetic pleasure derived from observing human characters through the prism of beauty. Moreover, by conveying the ideals of detachment (*xu* 虛), purity (*qing* 清), and remoteness (*yuan* 遠), they often function to suggest what lies beyond words and images—suprasensory experience with the Dao. This use of nature imagery suggests that, to the Jin *mingshi*, the spectacle of human life and scenes of nature yield intense aesthetic experiences of a similar kind, one that culminates in the observer's "spirit transcending and his bodily form being transported (*shenchao xingyue* 神超形越)."[10] This progression from spoken words to images to suprasensory experience seems an aestheticization of Wang Bi's tripartite scheme of *yan* 言 (words), *xiang* 象 (images), and *yi* 意 (ideas).

The influence of Wang Bi's theory is even more conspicuous in Wei-Jin texts on calligraphy, music, and painting. As Ronald Egan points out, an unprecedented proliferation of nature images first occurs in calligraphy criticism. This verbal amplitude, Egan argues, is an exercise of using images to reveal what is nonverbal or supraverbal, clearly guided by the *Yi jing* notion of *xiang* as expounded by Wang Bi. The immediate model, however, is Xu Shen's 許慎 (ca. 58–ca. 147) use of the *Yi jing* notion of *xiang* to explain the sacred origin of writing. According to Xu, the earliest form of writing (trigrams and hexagrams) is born of the sages' imaging of the supraverbal cosmic order with the aid of concrete physical images (*wuxiang* 物象). For Wei-Jin calligraphy critics, calligraphy represents the reverse of this process of character creation. Divinely created, writing can enable one to leap from perceptual images (written characters) to "image" the ultimate cosmic order, especially if it is done by a great calligrapher. The verbal amplitude in calligraphy criticism, then, signifies an effort to retrace this process of imaging. The rapid move from image to image reflects a "this is it, this is not it" process in the minds of calligraphy critics. Confronting the limited usefulness of images (metaphors), critics stress that, as Egan says, "calligraphy conveys something that lies beyond images and cannot be approximated adequately by them." Since this conception of calligraphic process is inspired by Wang Bi's view on the leap from *xiang* to *yi*, it is not surprising that *yi* would eventually emerge as the calligraphic ideal in the writings of Wang Xizhi 王羲之 (303–361 or 321–379), the preeminent Jin calligrapher. "Wang Xizhi's *yi*, his calligraphic ideal," Egan notes, "is strongly reminiscent of the 'ideas' in Wang Bi's treatment of the *Yi jing* that are conveyed by images and words but also lie beyond them. But there is a crucial difference between the two. Wang Xizhi's *yi* may be, like Wang Bi's, profound and ineffable, but it is also aestheticized, as Wang Bi's 'ideas' are not."

Turning to Wei-Jin writings on music, Egan again brings our attention to the preponderance of descriptive language and the prominence of the trope of nature in it. If nature images were sparingly used to posit a cosmic analogue for the harmonies of ritual music in earlier Confucian texts, Egan notes, they appear profusely as an analogy or inspiration for all the sonorities of music in Ruan Ji's "Yue lun" 樂論 (Essay on Music) and Ji Kang's "Sheng wu aile lun" 聲無哀樂論 (Music Has No Sorrow or Joy). Moreover, they are genuinely intended to explore the idea of a cosmic origin for human music. In Ruan's and Ji's essays, there is an ultimate abstract value—called *he* 和 (harmony)—that transcends the art's affinity with nature, much like the concept of *yi* in calligraphy criticism. In the writings of Gu Kaizhi 顧愷之 (d. ca. 406) and Zong Bing 宗炳 (375–443), Egan finds similar claims of an ultimate value for portrait painting that transcends physical likeness. Called *shen* (spirit), this value is analogous to the calligraphic *yi* and the musical *he*. While formal similitude had been the ideal of painting in Han and pre-Han times, Gu and Zong strove to establish *shen* beyond formal similitude as the ideal and end of painting. In portrait painting, Gu promoted the notion of *chuanshen* 傳神, or conveying the inner life-spirit (of the subject in portraiture). In applying the term "*shen*" to landscape painting, however, Zong meant to denote the ultimate Buddhist *li* 理 (principle) that lies behind landscape and can and should be pleasurably revealed in a good landscape painting. As shown in my own contribution, the term "*shen*" is also fruitfully appropriated by other critics to facilitate their exploration of various important theoretical issues.

In Wei-Jin gardens, Shuen-fu Lin observes a similar determined quest of what lies beyond physical nature. In Chinese gardening, this quest is primarily expressed through the construction of a "paradise" or "an enclosed space of idealized existence" that affords access to the supersensible realm. Unlike Western utopias, Chinese paradises are characterized by an integration of the sacred with the ordinary, the supersensible with the sensible. As the conception of these two realms changed over time, Lin observes, so did the designs and functions of the garden. In the Shang and early Zhou, the supersensible realm was conceptualized as a world inhabited by Shangdi 上帝 (the Lord or Supreme Ruler in heaven) and royal ancestors and ancestresses who from there wielded their influence on the living. The construction of a king's park was therefore designed for ancestral worship above anything else. The center of such a park is normally an ancestral temple like the Sacred Terrace (*lingtai* 靈臺) of King Wen, a paradisal spot where the supersensible and the sensible meet and where a living king communicates with the spirits of his ancestors and ancestresses. This ancient notion of paradise as the juncture of the two worlds is also amply reflected in the depiction of the Hanging Garden or Mysterious Garden (Xuanpu 縣圃/玄圃) and the Isles of the Immortals in ancient Chinese legends and myths. In Qin and Han times, the supersensible realm was conceived to be a conscious, moral heaven embodied in the cosmic operation of yin-yang and five phases (*yinyang wuxing* 陰陽五行), while the sensible realm was seen mainly as the microcosm of this moral-cosmic ordering. Thus, to mirror the greatness and splendor of these two realms became the central theme of Han imperial parks. Masses of fauna and flora, lakes, ponds, and hills, as well as lavishly built palaces, galleries, and pavilions, were organized into a grandiose pattern aiming to match great orders of the two realms. In addition to sites of ancestral worship, the paradisal spots of Han imperial parks include the recreations of fairy mountains and isles of immortals.

Under the powerful influence of Abstruse Learning, garden construction took a drastically different direction during the Wei-Jin period. First, Wei-Jin gardens were radically "downsized," but ironically that led only to a total "paradisation" of them. Now any scene of nature in a garden, not just certain consecrated buildings or spots, would be considered capable of evoking a flight of the mind beyond the physical world. This new conception of the garden may be observed in a famous anecdote recorded in the *Shishuo xinyu:* "On entering the Flower Grove Park (*Hualin yuan* 華林園) Emperor Jianwen looked around and said to his attendants, 'the place which suits the mind-heart isn't necessarily far away. By any shady grove or stream one may naturally have such thoughts as Zhuang Zi had by the Rivers Hao and Pu, where birds and animals, fowls and fish, come of their own accord to be intimate with them.'"[11]

To strive for "such thoughts as Zhuang Zi had by the Rivers Hao and Pu"—a suprasensory experience with the Dao—is an aesthetic activity that is in essence identical to the endeavors to penetrate the innermost human spirit or to capture the calligraphic *yi*, the musical *he*, or the *shen* of painting. The major difference is that the viewers of gardens contemplate different kinds of images. The images of the garden are those of physical objects—bamboo groves, fish ponds, pavilions, meandering brooks, winding paths, and so on. Arranged into an intricate pattern of yin-yang interplay, these physical objects suggest infinite space (*xu* 虛, *wu* 無) and help the viewers to "image" and commune with the Dao. Although calligraphy, painting, music, and other arts appear in a garden, they are usually inscribed into and hence made part of these physical objects or blended into the ambience created by them.

The siting of gardens in the midst of urban life, Lin notes, is another distinguishing trait of Six Dynasties garden aesthetics. Beginning with the Wei-Jin period, gardens of modest size were increasingly constructed as parts of imperial palaces or high officials' residences located within a city. Thanks to this resiting of gardens, garden owners and their friends could daily contemplate the world of nature miniaturized in the gardens and also enjoy the amenities of urban life. This new direction in garden construction, Lin points out, attests the influence of the new theory of *ziran* 自然 (external nature and self-so-ness) developed by Guo Xiang, the chief exponent of Abstruse Learning after Wang Bi. Ingeniously reinterpreting Zhuang Zi's notion of *ziran*, Guo maintains that to follow *ziran* simply means to lead the life one is born to lead. His theory serves very well to justify and promote the popular practices of *chaoyin* 朝隱 (to be a recluse while serving at court) or *shiyin* 市隱 (to be a recluse while living in urban surroundings) during the Jin. By claiming that the courtly and urban life was what they were born to lead, the Jin officials could style themselves as detached Daoists while indulging in all kinds of worldly pursuits. The resiting of gardens is no doubt a tangible product of the vogue of *chaoyin* and *shiyin* sanctioned by Guo's theory of *ziran*.

As demonstrated by Li, Egan, Lin, and Bush, Wang Bi's cosmological-epistemological theory exerted enormous influence on Wei-Jin aesthetics. In appropriating his theory, however, Wei-Jin critics rethought the notions of *xiang* and *yi* and their relationship in the context of literature and the arts. Whereas Wang Bi conceptualized *xiang* mainly as abstract cosmic symbols of trigrams and hexagrams, they wanted to think of *xiang* as both nature images *and* cosmic symbols. On the one hand, they identified *xiang* as nature images to be contemplated and presented in diverse artistic mediums. On the other, they availed themselves of the notion of *xiang* as cosmic symbols. If cast in a proper artistic order, they believed that nature images could function as if they were trigrams and hexagrams, enabling one to "image" the cosmic order. Finally, while Wang Bi stressed the gap between trigrams and hexagrams and the ultimate *yi* 意, they earnestly explored the possibility of closing this gap. As if to repudiate Wang's idea of "obtaining *yi* and forgetting *xiang*" (*deyi wangxiang* 得意忘象), they strove to embody the cosmic ultimate in the artistic *xiang*. Such fusion of *yi* and *xiang*, aptly denoted by the term *yixiang* 意象 (a coinage of Liu Xie 劉勰 [ca. 465–ca. 520]), constitutes the aesthetic ideal that informs the Wei-Jin discussions on literature and the arts.

(Liu) Song Aesthetics

In 420, Liu Yu 劉裕 (r. 420–423), a general from a humble clan *(hanzu)* staged a successful rebellion and overthrew the Jin. The new dynasty he founded is called the Song, often referred to as the (Liu) Song to avoid confusion with the (Zhao) Song, a much longer dynasty established about five hundred years later. This dynastic change began a process that would alter the wider political and cultural landscape. From the Song onward, the old intelligentsia clans would gradually lose their political power and their long-held position as the guiding force of culture. At the same time, newly empowered clans of humble, military backgrounds would consolidate their political control, acquire the cultural trappings of new intelligentsia clans, and eventually assume the leadership role in Song culture.[12]

Much of the credit for this shift should go to Emperor Wen 文帝 (r. 424–453), who engineered it largely through peaceful means during his stable, thirty-year reign. He offered few important posts to the old intelligentsia clans, distrusting both their loyalty and their competence, and filled his court instead with officials drawn from humble clans. Keenly aware of his cultural deficiencies, however, he shrewdly courted the old intelligentsia clans by sponsoring literary-cultural activities, offering them minor official appointments, and even proposing marriages between them and members of his court. There are many stories about the difficult efforts by Wen and the imperial Lius to shed their humble origins and gain acceptance by the old elite. Strategic self-deprecation and patience would pay off as they gradually and peaceably assumed the mantle of cultural leadership.[13]

Among the important measures the Song court used to facilitate the transfer of cultural power into its own hands were the reestablishment of Confucian learning and the promotion of the Buddhist faith. They also sought to reign in Abstruse Learning by "professionalizing" it as one of the four branches of learning in the imperial academy and thus turn it from a cultural movement into a pure scholarly pursuit. These measures were calculated to achieve the same goal: to open new routes of intellectual and cultural cultivation, thereby weakening the vogue of Pure Conversation and other *mingshi* pursuits through which the old intelligentsia clans had exerted their cultural dominance.[14]

Evidence of fading interest in Pure Conversation is clearly reflected in the transition from *xuanyan shi* 玄言詩 (poetry of metaphysical words)

to *shanshui shi* 山水詩 (landscape poetry; literally the poetry of mountains and rivers). Although few examples of *xuanyan* poetry survive (a
dramatic instance of the rapid and thorough decline of a once dominant genre), they clearly testify to the Eastern Jin's intellectual preoccu-
pations. Full of dry, metaphysical language and devoid of nature and
emotion, *xuanyan* poetry reads like Pure Conversation in verse. By
stark contrast, *shanshui* poetry replaced abstraction with vivid descriptions of nature and the intense emotions of the observer. Landscapes
and the pleasures of strolling through them generated a new poetry of
aesthetic and experiential process, best represented by the works of Xie
Lingyun 謝靈運 (385–433).[15]

In his famous essay, "Xu hua" 敘畫 (Discussion of Painting), Wang
Wei presents a theory of landscape painting that corresponds to the
practice of the *shanshui* poets. He stresses a genuine appreciation of
landscape and explores the dynamic interaction between landscape and
the mind/heart within the Xuanxue cosmological framework. In her
essay, Susan Bush examines the way in which Wang Bi's philosophy
shaped Wang Wei's theory of landscape painting. A renowned practitioner of yarrow-plant divination, Wang Wei had an abiding interest in
the *Yi jing* hexagrams and was therefore very receptive to Wang Bi's
theory. He used Xuanxue terms like *wu*, explicitly compared painting
to the *Yi jing* hexagrams, and, most important, employed the "closed
interlocking parallel style," a prose style purportedly devised by Wang
Bi for probing the cosmological ultimate (*yi*) through the medium of
words (*yan*). By adapting Wang Bi's prose style, Bush observes, Wang
Wei admirably demonstrated the complex pattern of interaction between
wu and *you* 有, landscape and the mind/heart, in the process of contem-
plating landscape. Born of such intense contemplation, Wang believes,
a landscape painting can not only achieve the likeness of nature's outer
forms, but also reveal the numinous spirit (*ling* 靈) or the innermost
spirit of nature.

With the waning of the Abstruse Learning movement, calligraphy
became less concerned with the revelation of the supersensible *yi* than
with practical ends—that is, financial and sociopolitical gains. This
noteworthy change is reflected in the widespread practice of calligraphic copying during the Song. Robert E. Harrist Jr. offers an examination of the financial and sociopolitical as well as aesthetic implications of calligraphic copying. The copying of Jin calligraphic masters
became a vogue during the Song period and acquired major financial

and social significance. Collectors spent large sums to acquire elegant copies, as well as autographic works, of the Jin masters that were prized as objects of aesthetic pleasure and as sources of intangible, much coveted cultural capital. Leading this acquisition drive were none other than the royal Lius (and later the royal Xiaos of the Qi and Liang dynasties), who were themselves striving to enhance their cultural credentials. Thanks to their persistent efforts, these collectors managed to amass important holdings of works by Jin masters in their imperial libraries (*bige* 秘閣).

Calligraphic copying, though often financially or sociopolitically motivated, was an undertaking of multifaceted aesthetic significance. To begin with, it gave rise to the discussion of *zhen* 真 (true, real) and *wei* 偽 (false, unreal), an issue central and unique to calligraphy connoisseurship. In *Lunshu biao* 論書表 (Memorial on Calligraphy), by Yu He 虞龢 (fl. ca. 470), and a series of letters by Tao Hongjing 陶弘景 (456–536), the eminent Daoist master and calligraphy connoisseur, Harrist sees the emergence of "*zhen*" and "*wei*" as an important pair of terms in calligraphy connoisseurship. In these texts, the two terms ceased to denote, as they once had, dichotomous moral qualities, such as authenticity versus fakeness, genuineness versus deceitfulness, or naturalness versus hypocrisy. In calligraphy connoisseurship, Harrist points out, "*zhen*" came to mean autographic. While autographic works (*zhenji* 真跡) are always prized, copied works, labeled as "*wei*," are by no means automatically deemed undesirable. As the terms "*mo*" 摹 and "*lin*" 臨 suggest, copying is an integral part of calligraphic pursuit. During the Six Dynasties, students of calligraphy avidly copied various masters' works as a way of internalizing earlier styles and developing their own. Even talented calligraphers like Wang Xizhi and Wang Xianzhi 王獻之 engaged in copying others' calligraphic works for a wide range of reasons—mutual amusement among intimate friends, the preservation of the memory of lost works, the transmission of sacred texts and talismans of the Daoist religion, financial profit, or even a political frameup. This widespread practice of copying by known or unknown calligraphers had an enormous impact on the development of the calligraphic art at the time. The proliferation of copies and recopies of Wang Xizhi's and other Jin masters' works helped to preserve and transmit at least the perceptions, if not a close visual semblance, of them. This also helped to make these great works accessible outside small aristocratic circles and thus created a much broader viewer base for calligraphy. Moreover, a large contingent of calligraphy connoisseurs were trained who commanded a much sharper perceptual power than their contemporary evaluators of human characters, literature, and other arts.

Qi-Liang Aesthetics: The Pursuit of Literature and the Arts

The twilight of the political power and cultural influence of the old intelligentsia clans continued through the Qi, Liang, and Chen dynasties. Like Liu Yu of the Song, Xiao Daocheng 蕭道成 (r. 479–483), founder of the Qi dynasty, was of humble origins. The now imperial clan of the Xiaos, which would continue into the Liang, also had to work to consolidate its political and cultural power.

First, in the sociopolitical realm, the royal Xiaos sought to promote Confucianism, particularly the study of rituals scorned by the Jin *mingshi*. They also promoted Buddhism, claiming it as their personal faith. Whereas the Jin *mingshi* had probed the speculative *prajñā* learning in their quest for *xuan* 玄 (the mysterious), the Xiaos sponsored and participated in Buddhist activities mainly in the hope of personal salvation. Still, they by no means ignored Abstruse Learning, as many of them studied and even wrote commentaries on the three Abstruse Learning classics. For them as for the Lius, however, the study of these texts was merely a scholarly pursuit without much relevance to their sensibilities and lifestyles.

In the cultural realm, the Xiaos of the Qi and Liang dynasties indisputably exercised a leadership role. Especially fond of literature, they gathered prominent literary figures to form coteries, two of which would become particularly well known. The Eight Friends of Jingling (Jingling Bayou 竟陵八友), headed by Xiao Ziliang 蕭子良 (460–494), were very active during the Yongming reign (483–494). This coterie included the famous poets Shen Yue 沈約 (441–513) and Xie Tiao 謝朓 (464–499) and the renowned prose writers Ren Fang 任昉 (460–508) and Lu Chui 陸倕 (472–526).[16] The second literary coterie was the Donggong 東宮 (Eastern Palace) poets under the patronage of Xiao Gang 蕭綱 (503–551), the crown prince living in the Eastern Palace who later became Emperor Jianwen of the Liang 梁簡文帝 (r. 550–551).[17] This coterie was much larger than that of the Eight Friends of Jingling, and it included Shen Yue, Yu Jianwu 庾肩吾 (487–551) and his son Yu

Xin 庾信 (513–581), Xu Chi 徐摛 (474–551) and his son Xu Ling 徐陵 (507–583), and many others.[18]

Writing for courtly amusement more than self-expression, the Jing-ling and Donggong coteries developed two distinct poetic styles: the Yongming style (*Yongming ti* 永明體) and the palace style (*gongti* 宮體). The Yongming style is famous for its fondness for the description of physical objects (*yongwu* 詠物); its creation of a regulated verse (*lüshi* 律詩) prototype, marked by line reduction and the extensive use of par-allelism and tonal patterns; and its aesthetic ideal of the unadorned and refreshing (*qingxin* 清新).[19] The palace style attracts our attention for its sensuous and often erotic depiction of palace ladies, its diverse sub-jects, and its employment of rich and ornate diction. Together, the Yongming and palace styles constitute the core of the Qi-Liang poetic tradition, which is a significant departure from earlier poetic traditions —such as, for example, the lyrical-allegorical style of the *Shi jing* 詩經 (The Book of Poetry), the mythical-plaintive style of the *Chu ci* 楚辭 (Songs of the Chu), and the heroic-melancholic style of Jian'an poetry from the late Eastern Han. In short, the Qi-Liang poetic tradition may be defined by its narrow interest in cloistered courtly life, withdrawal from overt sociopolitical concerns, pursuit of sensual pleasure, and quest for formal perfection.

François Martin shows us to what extent Xiao Gang and his Dong-gong coterie transformed poetic practice into a pleasure pursuit. The poems chosen for analysis are "Four Pieces Composed by Turns about the Four Gates upon a Night of Baguanzhai," composed by Xiao Gang, Shen Yue, and six lesser figures. What deserves our special attention, Martin holds, is a series of stark incongruities. First, there is the in-congruity between the occasion and the manner in which the poems were composed. Baguanzhai 八關齋 (the Fast of the Eight Precepts) is a serious occasion for lay Buddhist believers: for one day they live the life of a monk, engaging in religious fare, meditation, and other monas-tic activities. However, Xiao Gang and the other seven participants went about composing their poems as a pleasurable game to test one another's poetic talent, especially the ability to improvise and the mas-tery of metric rules. This act of merrymaking was ostensibly incon-gruous with the serious religious occasion. In fact, one of the eight precepts explicitly forbids entertainment. An even more shocking incongruity exists between the religious occasion and the poems' con-tents. The eight participants replaced various religious figures with palace ladies and depicted their sensual beauty with a zest never seen before.

From a historical point of view, these incongruities are the natural consequence of Xiao Gang's double agenda at the Eastern Palace: the promotion of Buddhist beliefs and the advocacy of a purely aesthetic palace-style poetry. But scholars hold different opinions as to why Xiao Gang and the Donggong poets pursued these seemingly incongruous interests. Some argue that this exposes the Xiaos' sexual indulgences and hence the hypocrisy of their Buddhist faith and practice. But such accusations seem perhaps harsh and even simplistic. There is credible evidence that Xiao Yan 蕭衍 (464–549), Xiao Gang's father and Emperor Wu of the Liang, urged the cessation of sexual activities for the sake of Buddhist faith, and there is no historical account of Xiao Gang's own sexual indulgence despite the notorious debauchery within his retinue.[20] Considering this, some see the need to moderate the moral condemnation of Xiao Gang and the Donggong poets and read their depiction of palace ladies not as an indication of their depravity, but as a poetic exercise in aestheticizing sensual pleasures. Martin is apparently sympathetic to such a rereading of their palace-style works. To him, neither the sensual depiction of palace ladies nor the blending of such a depiction into a religious poem is problematic, morally or otherwise. Other scholars go even further and argue that there is hardly incongruity at all in the double agenda at the Eastern Palace. Citing the Indian Buddhist practice of depicting beautiful ladies to illustrate the evanescence of all phenomenal existences, they argue that Xiao Gang and the Donggong poets had a similar allegorical intention in their depiction of palace ladies.[21] If this is the case, they can hardly be faulted on moral grounds for their obsessive interest in palace ladies.

Qi-Liang Aesthetics: Theoretical Works on Literature and the Arts

The Qi-Liang period witnessed a full flowering of aesthetic theory. If we can speak of a common feature, it is the ambition to systematically codify all the arts. So we have a study of the entire literary and critical tradition by Liu Xie; a comprehensive anthology of poetry and rhyme prose by Xiao Tong 蕭統 (501–531); a specialized anthology of palace-style poetry by Xu Ling; a ranking of poets by Zhong Rong 鍾嶸 (ca.

469–518); and, in the visual arts, a ranking of paints by Xie He 謝赫 (fl. 500) and of calligraphers by Yu Jianwu.[22]

Of the major Qi-Liang projects of codification, the earliest and the most ambitious is Liu Xie's *Wenxin diaolong* 文心雕龍 (The Literary Mind and the Carving of Dragons). In chapters 1–3, Liu conceptualizes the origins and nature of literature as the embodiment of the Dao.[23] In chapters 4–25, he reviews thirty-six major genres of refined writing under two synchronic rubrics: a twofold division of *wen* 文 (rhymed works) and *bi* 筆 (unrhymed prose), interfaced with a fivefold pedigree from the Five Confucian Classics. In the remaining twenty-five chapters, he codifies early critical thoughts on the major issues of practical and theoretical criticism. Explaining the organization of his book, he makes clear that the fifty chapters are meant to match the *Yi jing* numerology of fifty and, implicitly, its grand scheme of codification.[24]

Neither Zhong Rong's *Shi pin* 詩品 (Grading of Poets) nor Xiao Tong's *Wenxuan* 文選 (Anthology of Refined Literature) can rival Liu's *Wenxin diaolong* in breadth and depth. However, these two works present interesting alternative models of codifying literary traditions. Zhong places his presentation of 123 major poets within a three-tier grading scheme modeled on the one used during the Han to rank human characters. This scheme also seems to be overlaid with a covert codifying scheme based on the *Yi jing*. The numbering of poets in the three ranks neatly corresponds to the important *Yi jing* numbers of 12, 39, and 72. So Zhong may have self-consciously used the *Yi jing* numbers as an organizing grid as Liu had done.

Unlike Liu, Xiao Tong does not codify the literary tradition within the pedigree of the Five Confucian Classics. While Liu holds up Confucian classics as ideal models for refined literature, Xiao excludes them altogether from his anthology. The convenient excuse he uses is that these sages' works allow none of the cutting and selecting required of an anthology.[25] But the real reason for their exclusion is his pursuit of a pure aesthetic. In the preface to the *Wenxuan*, he defines literature in purely aesthetic terms: "the depiction of events is born of deep contemplation, and the locus of principles lies in the domain of refined phrases."[26] Since Confucian classics are not valued especially for these distinctively aesthetic features, he sees fit to leave them out of his anthology.[27]

Xie He's *Hua pin* 畫品 (Grading of Painters) is probably the most important Qi-Liang text on painting. Thought to have been written between 532 and 552, the work is comparable to those of Zhong Rong and Yu Jianwu. Like these authors, Xie begins with a preface and then provides a ranked list of eminent painters interlaced with impressionistic, evaluative comments.[28] What has attracted the most interest, however, is not his list but rather his brief preface. Here, unlike Zhong and Yu, Xie offers a summary of theoretical principles—the Six Laws of painting.

Modern scholarship has focused on the *Hua pin* preface largely because of two unresolved issues: the controversy over the punctuation and hence interpretation of the Six Laws (each compressed into a brief statement) and the remarkable parallel between the Indian Six Limbs of art and the Six Laws presented by Xie.

Victor H. Mair approaches these two issues in a fresh and insightful fashion. His strategy is to see them as closely related, so that the solution of one will lead to the solution of the other. He believes that the controversy over punctuation arose largely because of Zhang Yanyuan's misinterpretation of the Six Laws as quadrinomes, or four-character phrases. Thanks to the ingenious efforts of William Acker and Qian Zhongshu, the Six Laws have finally been restored to their original syntax: a numeric + a binome + a binome + verbal judgment. Reexamining the Six Laws in the light of the restored syntax, Mair discovers ample credible internal evidence of Indian influence. First, Xie's peculiar use of numeric enumeration is distinctively Indian as no precedent in pre-Buddhist Chinese texts can be found. Second, the second binome in five of the Six Laws matches one particular "limb," while the one in the remaining law resonates with the only unmatched limb. Third, these five binomes are seldom used in Chinese aesthetic discourse, and some of them even look like neologisms. Fourth, the first binome in each of the Six Laws is a familiar term frequently used in Chinese aesthetic discourse. These four discoveries lead Mair to conclude that Xie appropriated the six limbs in a most ingenious way. He recasts the six limbs in new Chinese terms (of his own making in one case) and precedes them with familiar Chinese critical terms in order to iron out the rough edges of these new terms. So even though the first binomes are grammatically the nominal subjects, they actually serve to explain the second, foreign-inspired binomes. In unmasking the Indian origin of the Six Laws through a rigorous philological investigation, Mair shows that Indian influence is as crucial to Xie's project of artistic codification as to Shen Yue's prosodic codification.[29]

Six Dynasty Aesthetics: A Retrospective and Critique

As the product of an aristocratic literati culture, Six Dynasties aesthetics was widely criticized for its decadence by neo-Confucian critics from the Tang through the Qing dynasties. In particular, the aesthetic trends of the Qi-Liang period—often depicted as obsessed by "wind and moon, flowers and grass" (*fengyue huacao* 風月花草)—came under especially intense fire. From an early twentieth-century perspective, however, Six Dynasties aesthetics was of great value precisely because of its pure aestheticism (*weimei zhuyi* 唯美主義). To scholars who sought to establish a modern aesthetic discipline in China, that pure aestheticism was no longer a cause for moral censure. Instead, they saw how it might effectively help to legitimate art for art's sake, as well as aesthetic theory. This revisionist stance has largely determined the way Six Dynasties aesthetics has been viewed ever since.

But if we can accept the modern reassessment of Six Dynasties aesthetics on the whole, a comprehensive analysis must also recognize its weaknesses. The first of these is its narrow range of interest. Of those who produced, appreciated, and theorized about art during the Six Dynasties, nearly all came from the intelligentsia clans. Their unparalleled monopoly of the literary and artistic spheres encouraged their tendency to focus on a small number of themes and genres, all of which reflected interests of their own class exclusively. Thus if the major works of the Wei-Jin period embody the Jin *mingshi*'s "elegant interest" (*yaqu* 雅趣), those of the Qi-Liang period point to the "vulgar interest" (*suqu* 俗趣) of the new intelligentsia in sensual pleasure. As a small coterie, it was no doubt hard for the Six Dynasties literati to see beyond their own narrow circle. To an outsider, nonetheless, their work can seem rather decadent. The shallow behavioral concerns of the Jin *mingshi* often border on hypocrisy, with their narcissistic quest for an idealized *xuan* in stark contrast to their unabashed pursuit of sensual pleasure in real life.

To understand the narrowness of Six Dynasties aesthetics, we need only observe the exclusion of Tao Qian 陶潛 (365–427) from the liter-

ary canon. As Kang-i Sun Chang points out, the aristocratic literati recognized Tao merely as a hermit. Since his concerns either opposed or
were irrelevant to theirs, they felt little interest in his work. So even
though Zhong Rong sees Tao as an excellent poet, he does not admit
this anti-aristocrat into the pantheon of the great. The best he can give
him is a place in the middle rank. In a similar fashion, the aristocratic
literati excluded the *xian* 僊 (transcendents) from aesthetic discourse,
despite their prominence in popular literature and religion. The only
major Six Dynasties critic to give some attention to the *xian*, in fact,
was Liu Xie, who because of his humble background and exclusion
from the aristocratic literati circle was in a better position to appreciate
popular culture. As Rania Huntington remarks, the Six Dynasties witnessed a great increase in the portrayals of *xian* in both prose and verse.
Yet it hardly figures at all in aesthetic theory—a pity because (as Huntington makes evident) it bears on important topics: the literary imagination, allegory, and genre criteria.

The second major weakness of Six Dynasties aesthetics is its super-
ficiality. To Liu Xie, it was very evident: "When the ancient poets of
the *Book of Poetry* composed their works, they produced *wen* for the
sake of emotion. When the [later] masters of refined expressions wrote
fu and *song*, they produced emotion for the sake of *wen*."[30] As he saw it,
the lack of genuine feelings (*zhenqing* 真情) led to the degradation of
contemporary literature. From our present-day standpoint, his diag-
nosis does indeed seem accurate. Yet while Liu clearly perceived the
buzhen 不真 (falseness, disingenuousness) of literati culture, even he
failed to appreciate the *zhen* (trueness, genuineness) of Tao Qian.

By way of contrast, the life of Tao Qian can help to highlight what
Six Dynasties literati culture lacked. As Kang-i Sun Chang has shown,
it was highly insightful of Yan Yanzhi 顏延之 (386–456) and Xiao Tong
to have recognized how faithful Tao Qian was to Zhuang Zi's idea of
being true to one's simple, natural self (*renzhen* 任真). Whereas the Jin
mingshi retired to their country estates to live a life of pleasure, Tao
chose to endure the poverty and hardship of farm life. Similarly, while
the Jin *mingshi* maintained contact with the imperial court, Tao managed to extricate himself completely from all political entanglements.
The contrast between Tao and the Jin *mingshi* has led modern scholars
to suspect the "reclusiveness" of *mingshi* life as a self-conscious pose
designed to enhance their social status, while the conduct of Tao Qian
appears to exemplify a genuine return to *ziran*.

If the life of Tao Qian was expressive of *zhen*, the same was equally true of his work. His poetry revealed a complex spectrum of emotion: youthful ambition, followed by the deep disillusionment of an upright official with political corruption; the relief of retirement from political life; pleasure in the simple vocation of a farmer; moral faith in the face of poverty and hardship; the joviality of a carefree drinker; and, finally, sadness over the transience of human life. The "confessional" mode of Tao Qian's work (which extended even to the forbidden world of erotic fantasy) leaves little room for doubt about its truthfulness and takes us far away from the calculated poses and self-aggrandizement typical of most Jin *mingshi*.

Significantly, Tao Qian has now become for many scholars a pivotal figure in the assessment of Six Dynasties aesthetics.[31] Given his outsider role vis-à-vis literati culture and the lack of any theoretical utterances in his oeuvre, we might well ask why. The answer, I would argue, is twofold. On the one hand, we can think of Tao as a critical mirror that reveals the weaknesses of Six Dynasties aesthetics. On the other, we can think of his work as the fulfillment of what the Six Dynasties literati strove for but failed to attain. His finest visionary poems captured the experience of suprasensory communion with the Dao in a way that was utterly unthinkable for contemporary *xuanyan* and *shanshui* poetry, while his "Xianqing fu" 閑情賦 (Rhapsody on Calming the Passions) explored depths of erotic sentiment too elusive for the Qi-Liang court poets. In short, his work brought to fruition the promise of Six Dynasties aesthetics.

Reflections: From Aesthetic Inquiry to Aesthetic Discipline

In many ways, the Six Dynasties period can be said to have achieved a sophistication in aesthetic theory comparable to that of the West. Like their Western counterparts, Six Dynasties critics not only defined every major form, but also attempted to specify its relation to a cosmic order. Their discussion of disinterestedness in art and aesthetic judgment and of how mental images mediate between the supersensible and the sensible all strongly suggest Kant. Moreover, their complex schemes of codification seem more comprehensive and sophisticated than any proposed by Western critics. Thus we find no anthology project that can match the scope of Xiao Tong's *Wenxuan*, nor any systematizing endeavor comparable to that of Liu Xie. Indeed, no Western critic has ever explored as many literary genres or addressed as many questions of theoretical and practical criticism as Liu did in *Wenxin diaolong*. In short, by the end of the Six Dynasties, Chinese criticism had all the concepts necessary for an aesthetic discipline except the crucial one of the field itself.

The lack of a comprehensive concept like beauty is at least partly responsible for the treatment of literature and the other arts as disparate genres in the Six Dynasties and all subsequent dynasties. Although commonly translated as "aesthetics," the term "*meixue*" 美學, or "learning of beauty," becomes highly problematic when applied to the Chinese tradition. Unlike beauty, the Chinese word "*mei*" 美 refers to pleasurable impressions of order and harmony rather than to any attempt to nominalize these within some aesthetic-cosmological scheme. For proof, I need only mention the absence of a single treatise on *mei* throughout the history of traditional China. Simply put, in traditional China the word "*mei*" did not serve to integrate all the branches of art into a coherent whole. Nor did any other Chinese term do that. Even though poetry, calligraphy, and painting were much more consciously blended in China than in the West, a theoretic study of these arts never coalesced into a systematic discipline in traditional China.

The eventual establishment of an aesthetic discipline in the twentieth century, however, was quite easy and smooth. Once scholars Wang Guowei 王國維 (1877–1927) and Cai Yuanpei 蔡元培 (1868–1940) introduced Western aesthetics into China and called for a national "education in beauty" (*meiyu* 美育) an integrated study of traditional Chinese literature and the arts soon followed. The term "*meixue*" gained currency quickly. Although largely neglected from the 1950s to the late 1970s in mainland China, aesthetics has since reemerged as one of the hottest areas of scholarship. With the current explosion of books on Chinese aesthetics, from general surveys to specialized studies in a given period, and a place in the university curriculum, aesthetics has definitely arrived.

As aesthetics comes of age in China, it seems only natural for questions about its conceptual definition to arise. While earlier scholars were happy to identify "*mei*" with the Western concept of beauty, closer scrutiny has shown that for traditional Chinese critics the Chinese term never had the same broad scope. But even if neither "*mei*" nor any other term offers an exact equivalent to "beauty," that should not preclude our discovery of a concept that might allow us to organize Chinese aesthetics as a field. To that end, Ye Lang 葉朗, a prominent Chinese aesthetician, proposed "*yixiang*" 意象 (idea-image) as a possible alternative.[32] While I fully agree with Ye about the semantic inadequacy of "*mei*," the extensive studies on "*yi*" and "*xiang*" in the present volume demonstrate that either singly or together they address only the interplay between the sensible and supersensible in art without reference to its intrinsic order or its relation to a larger cosmic order. But if "*yixiang*" does not work, is there any other word in Chinese that might?

Here I would suggest "*wen*." Both in semantic scope and in history of use, "*wen*" and "beauty" seem very close. Like "beauty" in Western languages, "*wen*" has gradually acquired a broader significance. For the Zhou, it was used mainly in reference to the moral and sociopolitical order. In the Han, it was increasingly employed to describe the order of graphic signs. During the Six Dynasties, it came to signify order in words, sounds, music, and images from literature and the arts. The Tang and Song returned its emphasis to the sociopolitical, as neo-Confucian scholars habitually paired it with the (Confucian) Dao, an association that has continued into the twentieth century.[33]

Given these circumstances, we can expect some major Chinese critics to have made use of "*wen*." The most prominent of these is Liu Xie. In *Wenxin diaolong*, he deftly exploited the full range of "*wen*" as a principle of order for the cosmological, religious, sociopolitical, psychological, and artistic spheres: as coextensive with the cosmic order and hence as the source of literature (chs. 1–3); as prominent in both belletristic and nonbelletristic genres (chs. 4–25); and as vital to literary creation and reception (chs. 26–49). Thanks to its multiple significances, "*wen*" allowed Liu Xie to unify his diverse remarks into a highly coherent critical system, one that would apply not only to literature, but to all the other arts as well.[34]

Yet the potential of "*wen*" to become an organizational principle for all the arts was never realized. After Liu Xie, few literary critics would exploit "*wen*" as self-consciously and exhaustively. Those who theorized about the nonliterary arts were reluctant even to make use of "*wen*," probably because they felt it had become too closely associated with refined literature, especially prose. Since the twentieth century, that association has been reinforced (so that "*wenxue*" now refers exclusively to the study of literature), while the broader cultural resonances Confucius had in mind have been largely lost. Translation of the Western notion of "literature" as "*wenxue*" served to complete the process. The fact that "*wen*" was not essentially subjective may have played a role as well. Its lack of a prominent subjective element precluded the sort of analytical study within a cognitive or idealist framework that would help to make aesthetics a coherent discipline in eighteenth-century Europe. But even if the prospect of a unified concept for Chinese aesthetics has for the moment disappeared, the potential is still there. The history of the term "*wen*" persuasively attests to it. Clearly, the sort of creative process envisioned by those who employed the concept of "*wen*" was quite different from that of the West. Instead of a notion of creativity that went back to the concept of God as maker, we get a concept of order based on a belief in the possibility of communion with the Dao as the cosmic principle. Thus the paradigm behind "*wen*" and, more broadly, Chinese aesthetics is ultimately different from that of Western aesthetics. But that should make a comparative perspective on Chinese and Western aesthetics only more fruitful.

NOTES

I would like to thank Robert Ford Campany, Wolfgang Kubin, Rania Huntington, Shuen-fu Lin, and Victor Mair for their valuable comments. I am especially grateful to my friends Leon Chai and Cara Ryan, who meticulously read through the essay and offered extremely useful comments and suggestions for stylistic improvement.

1. The term "Six Dynasties" is generally used to refer to the Wu (222–280), Eastern Jin (317–420), (Liu) Song (420–479), Qi (479–502), Liang (502–557), and Chen (557–589) dynasties. For all of them Nanjing (then called Jiankang) was the capital. Thus defined, "Six Dynasties" covers the time span from 222 to 589, with the conspicuous omission of the Western Jin (265–317). In an effort to restore this period, some scholars use the term to mean the six successive dynasties from the Western Jin through the Chen, thereby excluding the Wu and shortening the Six Dynasties period by forty-three years. Currently most scholars use the term simply as a designation of the historical period from 220 to 589, subsuming under it all the dynasties that appeared during this period, including the Wei (220–265), Shu (221–265), and Western Jin, as well as the five Northern Dynasties that controlled northern China from 386 to 581. We have adopted this usage here.

2. Is it appropriate and advisable to apply "aesthetics," a term of Western origin, to the Chinese tradition? Can we speak of "Chinese aesthetics" and (under it) "Six Dynasties aesthetics," "Wei-Jin aesthetics," and so on? These

are questions we must answer at the very outset. Although the study of Chinese aesthetics has already come of age in China, such questions are still being raised by some scholars of Western aesthetics. For instance, writing the "aesthetics" entry for *A Dictionary of Cultural and Critical Theory,* Gregory Elliott raises doubt about the validity of applying "aesthetics" to the Chinese tradition, notwithstanding his warm praise of a famous ninth-century Chinese text on painting:

> The philosophical sophistication of such reflection in Ancient Greece is attested by Plato's *Hippias Major* and Aristotle's *Poetics,* which were formative texts for the Western tradition, but until very recently there was nothing in this tradition comparable to the level of Chinese reflection on painting reached in a text such as Chang Yen-yüan's *Li-Tai Ming-hua Chi (Records of Famous Paintings).* Yet it would be extremely imprudent to collect these and other examples of reflection on art and beauty under the title of "aesthetics." The latter is not only of modern origin, but its preoccupations, direction of analysis, and consequently its internal system of division and classification are specifically European and should not be applied to either premodern or non-European materials (in *A Dictionary of Cultural and Critical Theory,* ed. Michael Payne [Malden, Mass.: Blackwell, 1996], p. 16).

To determine whether we can speak of Chinese aesthetics depends largely on how one interprets the term "aesthetics" itself. As noted by Elliott, "aesthetics" is a term of modern European origin, coined from the Greek *aesthesis* by the eighteenth-century thinker Alexander Gottlieb Baumgarten to designate contemporary studies of art and beauty as a distinct discipline of systematic, scientific inquiry. By the late eighteenth century, aesthetics had become not only a firmly established discipline but a central part of philosophy. If "aesthetics" refers exclusively to this modern European discipline, of course, one would have to allow Elliott's disqualification of Chinese aesthetics.

However, in addition to its historical designation of a modern, philosophy-related discipline, "aesthetics" is now often used as a broad reference to all Western philosophies of art and beauty, including those developed in premodern times. This broadening of the meaning of "aesthetics" is entirely logical. After all, the establishment of the modern aesthetic discipline does not mark an abrupt departure from earlier reflections on art and beauty, but rather a culmination of them. If we use "aesthetics" in this broadly defined sense, the argument is easily made for extending it to non-Western traditions. Just as art and beauty are universal human phenomena, so reflection on them is not unique to a particular geographical or cultural sphere. As long as there are serious practices and theories of art in any given tradition, we can speak of the aesthetics of that tradition.

3. Since there are neither important literary or artistic innovations nor major theoretical works during the Chen dynasty, I shall not include the Chen in this historical overview.

4. On these two groups of the Han intelligentsia, see Qian Mu 錢穆, *Guoshi dagang* 國史大綱, 2 vols. (Beijing: Shangwu yinshuguan, 1994), vol.1, pp. 149–191.

5. On the lives and works of these two groups of *mingshi,* see Luo Zong-qiang 羅宗強, *Wei Jin Nanbeichao wenxue sixiang shi* 魏晉南北朝文學思想史 (Beijing: Zhonghua shuju, 1996), p. 74.

6. The most prominent of them are Wang Dun 王敦 (266–324), Wang Dao, Wang Yi 王異 (276–322), Wang Qia 王洽 (323–358), Wang Mi 王謐 (360–407), Wang Xizhi 王羲之 (321–379), and Wang Xianzhi 王獻之 (344–388).

7. Wang Sengqian recorded the family tradition of calligraphers, and Wang Rong studied musical harmony and the tonal rules of verse with Shen Yue 沈約 (441–513). Their senior, Wang Wei, earned his reputation through treatises on painting.

8. Members of this "turgid stream" will be collectively called "Jin *mingshi*" below.

9. On the flawed moral character of the Jin *mingshi,* see Cao Daoheng 曹道衡, *Nanchao wenxue yu Beichao wenxue yanjiu* 南朝文學與北朝文學研究 (Nanjing: Jiangsu guji chubanshe, 1999), pp. 125–144, and Luo Zongqiang, *Wei Jin Nanbeichao wenxue sixiang shi,* pp. 75–84, 126–142.

10. Liu Yiqing 劉義慶, comp., *Shishuo xinyu jiaojian* 世說新語校箋, ed. Xu Zhen'e 徐震堮 (Beijing: Zhonghua shuju, 1984), 4.76, vol. 1, p. 140.

11. Adapted by Shuen-fu Lin from Richard B. Mather, trans., *Shih-shuo Hsin-yü: A New Account of Tales of the World* (Minneapolis: University of Minnesota Press, 1976), p. 60.

12. For a case study of one such parvenu clan, see the appendix on Shen Yue and his clan in Liu Yuejin 劉躍進, *Menfa shizu yu yongming wenxue* 門閥世族與永明文學 (Beijing: Sanlian shudian, 1996), pp. 325–350.

13. See Cao Daoheng, *Nanchao wenxue yu Beichao wenxue yanjiu,* pp. 136–144.

14. On the waning of Abstruse Learning during the Song, see Luo Zongqiang, *Wei Jin Nanbeichao wenxue sixiang shi,* pp. 172–183.

15. See Kang-i Sun Chang, *Six Dynasties Poetry* (Princeton, N.J.: Princeton University Press, 1986), pp. 47–78.

16. The remaining three members were Wang Rong 王融 and two other Xiaos: Xiao Yan 蕭衍 (464–549), who later founded the Liang dynasty, and Xie Shen 蕭琛 (478–529). For an in-depth study of the Jingling coterie, see Liu Yuejin, *Menfa shizu yu yongming wenxue,* pp. 27–70.

17. For studies on Xiao Gang and his Donggong coterie, see Chang, *Six Dynasties Poetry*, pp. 153–157, and Fusheng Wu, *The Poetics of Decadence: Chinese Poetry of the Southern Dynasties and Late Tang Periods* (Albany: State University of New York Press, 1998), pp. 41–75.

18. It is noteworthy that Xie Tiao, Wang Rong, and Wang Bao 王褒 (fl. 531–560)—members of the once preeminent Xie and Wang clans—now needed the patronage of the royal Xiaos. Employed as "professional" writers at the Qi and Liang courts, they and other members of the old clans lost much of the creative freedom their *mingshi* forefathers had enjoyed. Their literary achievements now served to improve the cultural standing of the Xiaos instead of enhancing the power of their own clans as an independent cultural force. The subordinate status of Xie Tiao, Wang Rong, and Wang Bao betokens the final cultural triumph of the Xiaos over the old intelligentsia clans.

19. Interestingly, the change from *qingyuan* 清遠 (pure and remote) to *qingxin* mirrors the reorientation of poetry from the quest of *xuan* to the pursuit of pure aesthetic pleasure. On the Yongming-style poetry, see Liu Yuejin, *Menfa shizu yu yongming wenxue,* pp. 103–152.

20. See Luo Zongqiang, *Wei Jin Nanbeichao wenxue sixiang shi*, p. 418.

21. See Wang Chunhong 汪春泓, "Lun Fojiao yu Liangdai gongti shi zhi chansheng" 論佛教與梁代宮體詩之產生, *Wenxue pinglun* 文學評論 (May 1991), pp. 40–56.

22. Qi-Liang writings on calligraphy, like those on literature and painting (to be discussed below), are mostly projects of codification. Whereas their Wei-Jin predecessors had focused on calligraphic imagination and execution, Qi-Liang calligraphy critics preoccupied themselves primarily with the less sublime task of codifying the calligraphic tradition. In his *Gujin shuping* 古今書評 (Comments on Ancient and Contemporary Calligraphy), Yuan Ang 袁昂 (461–540) lists 25 prominent calligraphers; each entry is followed by pithy comments or a cluster of nature images to characterize the distinctive features of the calligrapher's works. Xiao Yan's *Gujin shuren youlie ping* 古今書人優劣評 (Comments on the Merits and Demerits of Ancient and Contemporary Calligraphers) is very similar, expanding the list to 32. In *Shu pin* 書品 (Grading of Calligraphers), however, Yu Jianwu attempts something more ambitious. He begins by tracing the history of calligraphy from the invention of characters to his own time and then presents 123 calligraphers, arranging them within nine ranks, obviously an adaptation of the nine-rank system of officialdom (*jiupin* 九品). The evaluative comments made by Yu and other Qi-Liang calligraphy critics are unmistakably modeled on the impressionistic remarks on human characters in Liu Yiqing's *Shishuo xinyu*.

23. See Kang-i Sun Chang, "Liu Xie's Idea of Canonicity," and Zong-qi Cai, "The Making of a Critical System: Concepts of Literature in *Wenxin diaolong* and Earlier Texts," both in *A Chinese Literary Mind: Culture, Creativity, and*

Rhetoric in Wenxin diaolong, ed. Zong-qi Cai (Stanford, Calif.: Stanford University Press, 2001), pp. 17–31, 33–59.

24. Among the issues thoroughly discussed are rhetoric (chs. 33–35, 37–39), general compositional principles (ch. 44), the creative process (ch. 26), and literary history (chs. 29, 45). For studies of Liu's theoretical insight into these issues, see Andrew H. Plaks, "The Bones of Parallel Rhetoric in *Wenxin diaolong*"; Ronald Egan, "Poet, Mind, and World: A Reconsideration of the 'Shen si' Chapter of *Wenxin diaolong*"; Shuen-fu Lin, "Liu Xie on Imagination"; Stephen Owen, "Liu Xie and the Discourse Machine"; and Wai-yee Li, "Between 'Literary Mind' and 'Carving Dragons': Order and Excess in *Wenxin diaolong*"—all in Cai, ed., *A Chinese Literary Mind*, pp. 163–173, 101–126, 127–160, 175–191, 193–225.

25. See Guo Shaoyu 郭紹虞 and Wang Wensheng 王文生, eds. *Zhongguo lidai wenlun xuan* 中國歷代文論選, 4 vols. (Shanghai: Shanghai guji chubanshe, 1979), vol. 1, p. 330. Cited hereafter as *ZGLD*.

26. See *ZGLD*, vol. 1, p. 330.

27. In explaining his exclusion of non-Confucian philosophical works, he is more honest and forthright: "The writings of Lao [Zi] and Zhuang [Zi] and the likes of Guan [Zi] and Mencius have the primary goal of establishing their philosophical ideas, and literary competence is not essential to them. Therefore, they are also omitted from the present anthology." See *ZGLD*, vol. 1, p. 330.

28. The scope of his ranking is quite modest—27 painters, as opposed to 123 poets in Zhong's *Shi pin* and 123 calligraphers in Yu's *Shu pin*. Arranged in six ranks, the 27 painters are all of recent times (from the Wu, Jin, Song, Qi, and Liang dynasties), while the lists of poets and calligraphers in the other two texts extend over a much wider period. Xie's six-tier ranking falls between Zhong's three-tier and Yu's nine-tier schemes.

29. See Victor H. Mair and Tsu-lin Mei, "The Sanskrit Origins of Recent Style Prosody," *Harvard Journal of Asiatic Studies* 51, no. 2 (December 1991), pp. 375–470. The authors show that the general idea of prosodic defect (*bing* 病), formulated by Buddhist-minded scholars under the leadership of Shen Yue, was inspired by the concept of *doṣa* in Indian poetry criticism. Similarly, many specific tonal infelicities in Chinese poetry were codified and named by analogy with metrical blemishes in Indian poetry. The authors also explain how Shen Yue's theory of four tones and *pingze* 平仄 (the division of the four tones into level and oblique) resulted from the reflections of Chinese scholars on Indian prosody and hymnody.

30. Zhu Yingping 朱迎平, ed., *Wenxin diaolong suoyin* 文心雕龍索引 (Shanghai: Shanghai guji chubanshe, 1987), 31/61–64 (i.e., chapter 31/sentences 61–64).

31. In most Chinese-language histories of Six Dynasties aesthetics, we can find long chapters devoted solely to him. See, for instance, Li Zehou 李澤厚

and Liu Gangji 劉綱紀, *Zhongguo meixueshi: Wei-Jin Nanbei chao pian* 中國美學史：魏晉南北朝篇, 2 vols. (Beijing: Renmin chubanshe, 1984), vol. 1, pp. 363–384, and Wu Gongzheng 吳功正, *Liuchao meixue shi* 六朝美學史 (Nanjing: Jiangsu meishu chubanshe, 1994), pp. 580–596.

32. See Ye Lang, *Zhongguo meixueshi dagang* 中國美學史大綱 (Shanghai: Shanghai renmin chubanshe, 1985), pp. 1–16.

33. I discuss the changing concepts of *"wen"* in my book, *Configurations of Comparative Poetics: Three Perspectives on Western and Chinese Literary Criticism* (Honolulu: University of Hawai'i Press, 2002), pp. 49–70.

34. Liu writes, "There are three categories involved in the creation of *wen*. The first is *xingwen* 形文 (graphic pattern), made up of the five colors. The second is *shengwen* 聲文 (sound pattern), made up of the five sounds. The third is *qingwen* 情文 (emotive pattern), made up of the five emotions. The mixing of the five colors produces brilliant beautiful embroidery. The harmonizing of the five sounds creates the Shao and Xia (music of high antiquity). The expression of the five emotions brings forth elegant works of writing. All these are concrete manifestations of the spiritual principle" (*WXDL*, 31/18–29; translation taken with modifications from Vincent Yu-chung Shih, trans., *The Literary Mind and the Carving of Dragons* [Hong Kong: Chinese University Press, 1983], p. 337).

Part I

Images and Representations
● ●
Painting, Calligraphy, and Garden Construction

Chapter 1

• •

Replication and Deception in Calligraphy of the Six Dynasties Period

Robert E. Harrist Jr.

It is within an exuberant world of copies that we arrive at our experience of originality.

The epigram that introduces this essay comes from Hillel Schwartz's freewheeling survey of the history of duplication in all its forms, *The Culture of the Copy*.[1] His memorable expression, "an exuberant world of copies," refers to contemporary life in the West; it could apply as well to the history of calligraphy in China during the Six Dynasties period, when copies and their disreputable kin, forgeries, proliferated as never before, changing the way people viewed, collected, marketed, and wrote about the visual arts. A vivid account of how one notable figure of the fourth century responded to a copy appears in Yu He's 虞龢 (fl. ca. 470) *Lunshu biao* 論書表 (Memorial on Calligraphy): "[Wang] Xizhi (303–361) himself wrote a memorial to Emperor Mu (r. 344–361). The emperor had Zhang Yi make a copy of it, which differed not by a single hair. He then wrote an answer after [the copied memorial and returned it to Wang]. At first, Xizhi did not recognize [that it was a copy]. He examined it more closely, then sighed and said: 'This fellow almost confounded the real (*zhen* 真)!'"[2]

One of the consequences of Emperor Mu's little joke was to make Wang Xizhi, later enshrined as the "Sage of Calligraphy," the first person in Chinese history known to have been fooled by a copy of his own handwriting.[3] But this amusing story has other, more significant art historical and philosophical implications. Wang's indignant statement attributes nefarious motives to the copyist, Zhang Yi, but Zhang did more than simply play a trick on a famous contemporary. In the logic of the story, which Schwartz's insights help us to grasp, Zhang's act of replication changed the status of Wang's memorial: by making a copy, Zhang transformed the document written by Wang into an original. Within a few decades of Wang Xizhi's death, so many copies of his calligraphy were in circulation that it became increasingly difficult for collectors and connoisseurs to tell the difference between these replicas and works from Wang's own brush. By the early sixth century, it was no longer possible for a well-informed viewer to look at a piece of calligraphy attributed to Wang Xizhi without asking the question that to this day bedevils so much of the study of Chinese art: Is it real?

Focusing on the case of Wang Xizhi, this essay attempts to study ideas about early copies of calligraphy and to consider how these artifacts functioned as objects of aesthetic and economic value. It will address also the seemingly paradoxical truth that calligraphy, valued for its capacity to embody in brushwork the mind and character of the individual artist, was more amenable to accurate and efficient replication than any other form of art. Finally, I will offer the suggestion that one of the reasons why calligraphy became such an important art in China was *because* it could be copied with startling faithfulness.

True or False?

The historical process through which calligraphy became the most revered of the visual arts began in the Eastern Han (25–220).[4] During this period individuals such as Zhang Zhi 張芝 (d. ca. 192) and Cai Yong 蔡邕 (132–192) began to win fame for their superb handwriting; at the same time, pieces of calligraphy began to be collected not for their literary content but for their visual qualities. The first theoretical treatise on calligraphy, Zhao Yi's 趙壹 (fl. ca. 192) famous diatribe against cursive script, *Fei caoshu* 非草書 (Against Cursive Script), also dates from the late Han. These phenomena—the emergence of calligraphers as notable figures, the formation of collections, and the writing of theoretical and critical treatises—continued during the Wei (220–265) and Western Jin (265–317) dynasties, which witnessed the careers of the master calligrapher Zhong You 鍾繇 (151–230) and the theorist of script types Wei Heng 衛恒 (d. 291). Following the removal of the Jin court to the south in 317, there took place what can reasonably be called a calligraphy boom. The Eastern Jin (317–420) was the era of Wang Xizhi, his almost equally famous son, Wang Xianzhi 王獻之 (344–388), and a galaxy of other aristocratic calligraphers living in southern China. Their works, especially in the highly expressive running and cursive scripts, eventually came to define a classical tradition of calligraphy.[5] Also under the Eastern Jin and continuing under the (Liu) Song (420–479), Qi (479–502), and Liang (502–557) dynasties, extravagant but not always discerning collectors spent large sums to acquire works of calligraphy, their choicest prizes being anything associated, however improbably, with Wang Xizhi.

Although many of these developments were paralleled in the history of painting during the Six Dynasties, calligraphy is much better documented, owing to the production of specialized texts from the fifth and sixth centuries. Most of the authors of these texts—including Yang Xin 羊欣 (370–442), Wang Sengqian 王僧虔 (427–485), Yu He, and Yu Jianwu 庾肩吾 (487–551)—were accomplished calligraphers and held government posts, sometimes serving as artistic advisers to imperial collectors. These writers addressed many of the same intellectual and aesthetic issues that engaged the authors of texts on literature: the origins and meaning of art, the effect of art on the mind and human society, and the relationship between individual character and artistic expression. Like theorists and critics of literature—most notably Liu Xie 劉勰 (ca. 465–ca. 521) and Zhong Rong 鍾嶸 (ca. 469–518)—writers on calligraphy and painting attempted to define standards of evaluation and to propose rankings of artists that paralleled contemporary assessments of personality types and government officials.[6] The close bonds between concepts of literature and those of calligraphy and painting can be seen in the way that terms such as *"yun"* 韻 (resonance) and *"qi"* 氣 (variously translated as vital essence, spirit, etc.) migrated from the critical vocabulary of one art to another. From the domains of medicine and physiology, the concepts of *"gu"* 骨 (bone) and *"rou"* 肉 (flesh), as John Hay has shown, also became permanently embedded in the vocabulary of calligraphic theory during the Six Dynasties.[7]

In spite of the permeability of boundaries separating theories of the different arts, texts on calligraphy from the Six Dynasties address a set of problems for which there are no real parallels in writings on literature and surprisingly few in writings on painting—that of copies and forgeries.[8] Any discussion of these notoriously ambiguous terms threatens to sink hopelessly into a terminological quagmire, but an attempt to define them, at least as they are used in this essay to characterize works of calligraphy, is necessary at this point.[9] Copies are works that replicate others, sometimes so closely that the differences between original and copy can be perceived only through meticulous examination, if at all. Forgeries are works intended to be taken for something they are not, and they come in two types.[10] One type of forgery might be defined as a good copy gone bad: although a copy may be made simply in order to replicate a work of calligraphy for study or aesthetic pleasure or to display the skill of the copyist—such a work has been called a bona fide copy—if the same artifact is presented as an original, it is thereby transformed into a forgery. In such cases there is no material or visual difference between a copy and a forgery; all depends on what is said, or allowed to be understood, about the artifact in question. In the case of Wang Xizhi's illicitly replicated memorial, had Emperor Mu shown the copy to Wang and said, "Look what Zhang Yi can do!," there would have been no deception and hence no forgery. A second type of forgery consists of a work not based on any preexisting model but executed in the style of another calligrapher or historical period. A letter imitating the handwriting of someone other than its true author would be a good example of this type of deception. Were such a letter simply displayed or marketed as a demonstration of calligraphic skill, however, the label of forgery would be unwarranted.

The difficulty of discussing copies and forgeries is compounded in the present discussion by the challenge of finding acceptable English renderings for Chinese terms and by the necessity of explaining ideas that are implied rather than stated explicitly in Chinese texts. One way to begin grappling with these problems is by thinking about a word that appears at the very end of the anecdote about Wang Xizhi's memorial—"zhen," which can be translated as "genuine," "real," or "authentic."[11] It is sometimes combined with the word "ji" 迹 (literally a trace), to yield the term "zhenji" 真迹, still used in modern Chinese to refer to an original work of art.[12] The word "zhen" and its cognates are paired dialectically in early texts on calligraphy with the term "wei" 偽 (translatable as fake, inauthentic, or false) and with negative expressions, including *"fei zhen"* 非真, "not authentic," or *"fei zhenji"* 非真迹, "not an authentic work."[13] In some cases the texts specify that such works were produced as forgeries; in other cases the intentions of those who made them are unknown, and it is for the former that I will reserve the term "forgery."

The key terms *"zhen"* and *"wei"* have complex philological histories in contexts unrelated to calligraphy that lie beyond the scope of this essay, but it is worth considering briefly some of the early uses of these terms in the discourses of metaphysics, morals, bureaucracy, politics, and poetics. The goal of this survey is not so much to define the qualities that *"zhen"* and *"wei"* signified as it is to raise the question, "Through what faculties could one tell the difference between the two?"

According to Roger T. Ames, the earliest occurrences of the word *"zhen"* seem to be in the *Lao Zi* 老子, where it appears three times, and in the *Zhuang Zi* 莊子, where it designates an essential philosophical concept.[14] In chapter 31 of the *Zhuang Zi*, an old fisherman explains to Confucius that *zhen* "is received from nature. What is so-of-itself cannot be altered. Thus, the sage emulates nature and values *zhen*, without being caught up in conventions."[15] The *zhenren* 真人 (translatable as genuine man, true man, or perfected man) is an ideal being, capable of infinite adaptability, his every thought and action in accord with the Dao. The *Zhuang Zi* explains "the *zhenren* of antiquity did not know pleasure for life nor displeasure for death. He embarked on life without rejoicing and passed on without resistance."[16] By the time of the lexicographer Xu Shen 許慎 (ca. 58–ca. 147) the concept of the *"zhenren"* had acquired more otherworldly connotations. Xu defines *"zhen"* as "an immortal being, changing shape and ascending to Heaven."[17] In the vocabulary of Daoism of the Six Dynasties, most significantly in texts of the Shangqing 上清 sect headquartered at Maoshan 茅山 in Jiangsu Province, *zhenren* is a transcendent "perfected being, of higher celestial rank than mere *xian* or 'immortals.'"[18] As we shall see, the concept of "the perfected" expressed by the term *"zhen"* intersects with the history of calligraphy in the editorial projects of Tao Hongjing 陶弘景 (456–536), the Daoist master and calligraphy connoisseur.

Also in the *Zhuang Zi* the terms *"zhen"* and *"wei,"* translated by A. C. Graham as "genuine" and "fake," appear as paired opposites for the first time: "By what is the Way hidden, that there should be a *zhen* and a *wei*?"[19] Elsewhere in the text, Robber Chi hurls the word "*wei*" at Confucius, calling the master a "crafty hypocrite" (*qiao weiren* 巧偽人) and accusing him of "speaking deceit and acting out hypocrisies" (*jiao yan wei xing* 矯言偽行). In the same chapter, Man Goude 滿苟德, debating Zizhang 子張, a disciple of Confucius, derides the "hypocritical speeches" (*weici* 偽辭) of the Confucianists.[20]

In the art of rulership the wisdom to sort out "*zhen*" and "*wei*" was essential at various levels of government. When Emperor Xuan 宣 (r. 74–49 B.C.) of the Western Han issued an edict in 49 B.C. intended to correct abuses in local administration, he proclaimed that "the censors will inspect the registers of accounts, and if they suspect they are not accurate they will examine them so that *zhen* and *wei* will not be confused with each other."[21] Here, the paired terms connote the results of, on the one hand, bureaucratic rectitude and, on the other, incompetence and corruption detectable through audits, interviews, and wideranging investigation. In other contexts related to government policy, "*zhen*" and "*wei*" signify true and false, as in "true-hearted" and "falsehearted." Telling them apart required that a ruler be a good judge of character. Writing in the late second century, Fu Xie 傅燮 (active ca. 184) cautioned Emperor Ling 靈 (r. 168–189) that "if there is a failure to carefully investigate *zhen* and *wei*, among loyal subjects there will again [be incidents] like the suicide at Duyou," an allusion to the forced suicide in 258 B.C. of the loyal Qin commander Bai Qi 白起, who was betrayed by envious rivals.[22]

The word "*zhen*" entered Chinese poetry and poetics through the writings of Tao Qian 陶潛 (365–427). Echoing the *Zhuang Zi*, Tao uses "*zhen*" to connote naturalness and authenticity or, as rendered in James Hightower's translations, to speak of things that are "true" or "the truth." In Tao's view, the uncorrupted men of antiquity "embraced the plain and held the true (*zhen*)." Resolving to continue his life in retirement, Tao says that "To cultivate the true (*zhen*) in my poor hut/Is perhaps the best thing I can do." And in one of the most famous lines in all his poetry, Tao surveys mountain scenery and the sight of returning birds, musing that "In these things there is a fundamental truth (*zhen yi* 真意)."[23] Though he placed Tao Qian in the second rank of poets, the critic Zhong Rong adopted the term "*zhen*," apparently for the first time in literary criticism, praising Tao for achieving *zhen gu* 真古, or "true antiquity."[24]

From the metaphysics and moral philosophy of Zhuang Zi to the uses of the terms in political or literary contexts, "*zhen*" and "*wei*" signify abstract qualities or character traits. These may be reflected in specific human actions, such as the "hypocritical deeds" of Confucius denounced by Robber Chi, detectable by persons of superior philosophical or moral insight; qualities signified by the word "*zhen*" in Tao Qian's own writings and in critical commentary they inspired were accessible to those with refined poetic sensibilities. Clarifying the difference between "*zhen*" and "*wei*" was also the goal of textual scholarship, especially in studies of spurious books and apocrypha from the Eastern Han and later periods that clogged the libraries of scholars. The literary theorist Liu Xie devoted a chapter of his *Wenxin diaolong* 文心雕龍 (The Literary Mind and the Carving of Dragons) to the subject of evaluating these works and to sorting out what was true *(zhen)* from what was false *(wei)*. The principles for detecting forgery that Liu Xie cites are intended to expose the obscurities and absurdities in the contents of texts.[25] This understanding of "*zhen*" and "*wei*" in textual scholarship also informs Pei Yin's 裴駰 (d. 425) explanation of the tasks he faced as editor and collator of the *Shi ji* 史記: "In collating this book, one finds that words and phrases are not the same, some [editions] having more, some fewer. No one has determined their accuracy, and muddled people of our age have settled on this or followed that, with the result that the accurate and inaccurate have been intermixed and the true and false (*zhen wei* 真偽) have been confused."[26]

For Pei Yin and Liu Xie, the ability to distinguish between *zhen* and *wei* depended on textual, not paleographic, evidence; their work of editing and collating was performed by the eye, but a scholar could detect spurious passages or corrupt texts no less surely by hearing them read aloud. And while vision might help one to recognize the deeds of a *zhenren* or to grasp a "fundamental truth" in the beauty of nature, these also might be discerned through other senses. Far from being a reliable source of knowledge, vision, and the perception of outward appearance it affords, could not always be trusted to reveal the difference between *zhen* and *wei*. This distrust of vision is made explicit in Zheng Xuan's 鄭玄 (127–200) commentary on ode no. 26 from the "Guofeng 國風" section of the *Shi jing* 詩經. A line from the poem reads, "My heart is not a mirror/You cannot judge me [in it]." According to Zheng's commentary, "The mirror is for investigating shapes, but [in it] one can

only know the square and the round, the white and the black; one cannot measure the true and the false *(zhen wei)*."[27] As Eugene Wang has
pointed out, the character for mirror, *jian* 鑒, originated as a graph
depicting a figure looking into a container of water; it connotes both
reflection and the act of looking itself.[28] While the mirror, understood
by Zheng Xuan as an agent of vision, can reveal shapes or colors, it
denies access to qualities of *zhen* and *wei* hidden within the character of
a human being.

It is in contexts that demanded visual acuity in the examination of
manmade artifacts that the terms "*zhen*" and "*wei*" acquired the meanings they eventually conveyed in Six Dynasties texts on calligraphy. A
good illustration of this reliance on vision appears in a story from *Han
Feizi* 韓非子 (third century B.C.) that may be the earliest known Chinese record of a forged artifact, identified in the text by the word "*yan*
贋*,*" synonymous with "*wei*":

> Qi attacked Lu and sought the Chan *ding*. Lu sent a fake (*yan* 贋). The
> people of Qi said, "It is a fake." The people of Lu said, "It is real." The
> people of Qi said, "Send Lezheng Zichun. We will listen to him." The lord
> of Lu asked Lezheng Zichun [to say it was real.] Lezheng Zichun replied,
> "Why did you not send the real one?" The lord said, "I love it." He
> replied, "Your subject also loves his trustworthiness."[29]

The people of Qi may have touched or weighed the bronze vessel
sent by the state of Lu in order to evaluate its authenticity, but it was
almost certainly after *looking* at this object that they suspected they
were being tricked.[30] This story ends with the virtuous Lezheng Zichun
refusing to authenticate the forged bronze vessel. A later incident of
forgery recorded by Sima Qian 司馬遷 (ca. 145–86 B.C.) had fatal consequences for the forger. After a man named Shaoweng 少翁 gained the
confidence of Emperor Wu 武 (r. 141–87 B.C.) through his magical arts
and was granted the title General Wencheng 文成,

> he then wrote a message on a piece of silk and fed it to an ox and,
> pretending to know nothing of the matter, announced to the emperor:
> "There appears to be some strange object in this ox's belly!" The ox was
> slaughtered and its belly opened, revealing the piece of silk, and the words
> written on it were exceedingly strange. The emperor, however, recognized
> the handwriting and, when he cross-examined (Shaoweng), discovered

that the message was in fact a forged document (*weishu* 偽書). He had
General Wencheng executed but kept the matter a secret.[31]

The formidable Emperor Wu had a keen eye. Basing his judgment of
the spurious document not on its strange text but on the appearance of
the writing, which revealed the true identity of its author, he may
deserve to be known as the first connoisseur of calligraphy.

Applied specifically to works of calligraphy, "*zhen*" and "*wei*"
appear first in anecdotes about the calligraphy of Wang Xizhi recorded
by Yu He in his *Lunshu biao*.[32] The most colorful of these anecdotes is
also the most significant for understanding the early history of copying
and forgery. Liu Yizong 劉義宗 (d. 444), who bore the noble title Marquis of Hui (Huihou 惠侯), loved calligraphy and was willing to spend
liberally to acquire outstanding works. His enthusiasm set the stage for
clever acts of deception:

> Base fellows cunningly made copies. They used the drippings from
> thatched roofs to change the color of the paper and further aged it, making
> it like old calligraphy. Authentic and fake (*zhen wei* 真偽) were mixed
> together, and no one could tell the difference. Therefore, among works
> accumulated by the Marquis of Hui, there were many that were not
> authentic (*fei zhen* 非真).[33]

Like other tales of calligraphic trickery from Six Dynasty sources,
this story is amusing and anecdotal, but there is no reason to doubt that
forgers of the fifth century were as crafty as Yu He portrays them. The
story is important also in that it clearly indicates what Yu He, a leading
authority on calligraphy of his time, understood the words "*zhen*" and
"*wei*" to mean. He records that the forgeries sold to the marquis were
made through copying (*moxue* 摹學); in this same passage he states that
these copies caused "authentic and fake" (*zhen wei*) to become mixed
together, resulting in a collection that included many works that were
"not authentic" (*fei zhen*). In the eyes of Yu He, only an autographic
manuscript, bearing characters understood to have been written with a
brush held by the person to whom a work was attributed, could be considered *zhen*. Immediately following the story of the Marquis of Hui,
Yu He records that in the collection of Emperor Xiaowu 孝武 (r. 453–
464) of the (Liu) Song dynasty, "the authentic and the fake were
confusedly jumbled" (*zhen wei hun za* 真偽混雜).[34] Describing Emperor

Ming's 明 (r. 465–472) studies of calligraphy, Yu He writes of the emperor's ability to "seek the essential and mysterious, the beauty and ugliness of characters, and the authenticity and inauthenticity *(zhen wei)* of calligraphy."[35]

Insistence on the autographic status of works labeled *zhen* or *zhenji* is clear also in the letters on calligraphy exchanged by Tao Hongjing and Emperor Wu 武 (r. 502–549) of the Liang dynasty. Expressing his doubts about the *Yue Yi lun* 樂毅論 (Essay on Yue Yi), a work of small standard script attributed to Wang Xizhi, Emperor Wu concludes that the calligraphy is "not an authentic work" *(fei zhenji)*. And in his response to this letter, Tao Hongjing confesses that he had suspected that the *Yue Yi lun* was a copy, indicated by the term *"mo"* 摹.[36] In another letter, concerning works attributed to Zhong You, Emperor Wu declares that although a certain scroll had been transmitted as authentic *(zhen)*, he believed it was a copy *(mo)*.[37] Unlike Yu He, Tao Hongjing and the emperor did not use the term *"wei"* in their correspondence, but they did share with the earlier connoisseur the understanding that only autographic originals could be labeled *zhen*; copies, at least with regard to secular works in the imperial collection, did not count.[38]

The visual skills that Tao Hongjing brought to judging calligraphy owned by Emperor Wu had been honed by his efforts to edit and authenticate handwritten texts dictated by Perfected Beings to the mystic Yang Xi 楊羲 (330–386?) at Maoshan.[39] Yang Xi had entrusted these manuscripts to Xu Mi 許謐 (303–373) and his son, Xu Hui 許翽 (341–ca. 370); father and son continued the work of copying and recopying the texts, which became the scriptural foundation of the Shangqing sect. Over time, spurious texts fabricated by would-be Daoist masters, who sold them to gullible believers, were mixed indiscriminately with texts in the hands of Yang Xi, Xu Mi, and Xu Hui, known as "the Three Lords" *(san jun* 三君). Beginning around 465, the scholar Gu Huan 顧歡 (fl. ca. 465) attempted to sort out autographic works by Yang and the two Xus from the ever-growing mass of forgeries, using calligraphy as his primary gauge of authenticity. He included those texts he believed to be from the hands of the Three Lords in a now lost collection titled *Zhenji* 真迹 (Traces of the Perfected). Although the term *"zhenji"* is the same as that used by Emperor Wu to label autographic manuscripts in his collection, Gu Huan's compilation may actually have consisted of facsimile copies in which the quality of *zhen* derived from the status of the Perfected Beings from whom the texts ultimately derived.[40]

Tao Hongjing continued the work of Gu Huan, carrying out an exhaustive visual inspection of handwritten texts. In his great editorial survey of Maoshan scriptures, *Zhen'gao* 真誥 (Declarations of the Perfected), as in his comments on secular calligraphy in letters to Emperor Wu, Tao records the impressions of his highly discerning eye, offering detailed analyses of individual characters, sometimes of individual brush strokes.[41] Although the *Zhengao* is concerned ostensibly with religion rather than aesthetics, the two domains interpenetrate. In a passage noted by Lothar Ledderose, Tao makes an explicit comparison between the calligraphy of the mystic Yang Xi and that of the two Wangs, claiming that only Yang's inferior social status kept him from being recognized as the Wangs' equal in calligraphic skill. These judgments depended on visual and stylistic evidence, on the cultivation of an educated eye capable of what Tao Hongjing refers to as *shukan* 熟看 (experienced looking).[42] Far from being a suspect agent of perception, as it had been treated earlier in other contexts, vision and vision alone made possible the connoisseurship practiced by Tao Hongjing and other experts on calligraphy during the Six Dynasties.

Varieties of Replication and Deception

One of the reasons the role of copying in the history of calligraphy is so complex is that copying permeates nearly every aspect of this art, beginning with the process of learning to write. At least since the Han dynasty, when the forms of characters still in common use today were more or less permanently fixed, student calligraphers have faced a laborious process of mastering strokes brushed in a prescribed order enforced by the pedagogy of calligraphy. As instruction begins, students must replicate as closely as possible model characters assigned by their teachers.[43] As calligraphers mature, they may select a model or style of their own. In *Cai gulai nengshu renming* 采古來能書人名 (Names of Capable Calligraphers from Antiquity Onward), by Yang Xin, we read that Liang Gu 梁鵠 "acquired the methods of Shi Yiguan 師宜官" and that Wei Furen 魏夫人 (Madam Wei) "was good at the method of Zhong You."[44] What these terse summaries of calligraphic lineages evoke are countless hours of painstaking copying, through which calligraphers mastered the styles of their predecessors.

Through the process of repeatedly copying a piece of calligraphy by another writer, a calligrapher internalizes that person's style. Some calligraphers, liked gifted mimics, were especially adept at imitating others. Zhong Hui 鍾會 (225–264), whom we will meet below as a forger, excelled at imitating the hand of his father, Zhong You.[45] According to his uncle, Wang Yi 王廙 (276–322), even while he was still a child Wang Xizhi could imitate any work of calligraphy or painting after seeing it once; in the same vein, Wang's teacher, Wei Furen (272–349), praised his ability to imitate her calligraphy in small standard script.[46] Calligraphers good at imitating the hands of others might also serve as ghost-writers. In his later years Wang Xizhi himself is said to have employed a ghostwriter whose imitations could not be distinguished from Wang's own calligraphy, though some contemporaries noticed a slight hesitancy in the writing which they attributed to Wang's advancing age.[47] If this story is true, if Wang Xizhi himself was sponsoring what can be considered forgeries of his own calligraphy, the attempts of scholars over many centuries to define a canon of his works seems futile indeed.

Calligraphers usually begin their careers by modeling their writing on one earlier master, but as they mature, they may experiment with a variety of models by copying calligraphy in different styles. Sheets of paper covered with characters written over and over by Wang Xianzhi in the styles of earlier calligraphers were in the collection of Emperor Ming.[48] According to Yu He, these practice sheets, now regrettably lost, were playfully done and of no great aesthetic value. But ephemera such as these represented the very foundations of calligraphy as an artistic practice.

In addition to making copies in order to improve their own writing, calligraphers produced copies for the sake of preserving and transmitting earlier works. Copies of this type should be distinguished from transcripts intended only to preserve the contents of texts.[49] An anecdote concerning Maoshan manuscripts recorded by Tao Hongjing makes the difference clear. Tao quotes a certain Zhang Lingmin 章靈民, who acquired autographic texts by the Three Lords; Zhang confessed, however, that at the time he "did not know enough to make tracing copies and merely transcribed the texts."[50] Unlike transcripts, calligraphic copies of the kind Zhang regretted not making preserve both texts and their visual embodiment in the hand of an individual calligrapher.

One early record of how knowledge of a calligrapher was transmitted through a copy concerns the Han dynasty master of cursive script, Cui Yuan 崔瑗 (77–142). According to Yu Jianwu, Cui Yuan was famous in northern China, but his works were rare in the south. When a copy of a piece of calligraphy by Cui Yuan turned up in southern China, it was seen by Wang Xianzhi, who praised its beauty.[51] Valued as evidence for the work of a calligrapher whose autographic originals were not accessible, the copy achieved the status of an art object and source of aesthetic pleasure in its own right. Missing, unfortunately, in Yu Jianwu's record is any comment on how southerners, presumably unfamiliar with Cui Yuan's writing, determined that the artifact they saw was in fact a copy.

Not all copies were created equal, and judging their quality and reliability became an important task for collectors and connoisseurs of the later Six Dynasties. The most extensive surviving discussion of calligraphic copies and their value is the letters on calligraphy exchanged by Emperor Wu and Tao Hongjing. Tao served the emperor as an artistic consultant and as a copyist to whom items from the imperial collection were dispatched to be studied and reproduced as tracings. Reflecting on the quality of his own copies, Tao Hongjing wrote that "in my recent outline tracings, although I've managed to roughly copy the shapes of the characters, I have not gotten the kinetic force of the use of the brush."[52] Tao arrived at this self-critical evaluation after comparing the original, unnamed works he was assigned to copy with the replicas that resulted from his labors. Able to place originals and copies side by side, to compare them stroke by stroke, he was only moderately satisfied with what he had achieved. In regard to a work attributed to Zhong You mentioned above, Emperor Wu declared it a copy "not much worth discussing," though two or three lines seemed to have captured a "bit of Zhong's style."[53] This critique does not appear to have been based on a direct comparison of the copied works and the corresponding originals by Zhong You, which probably were no longer extant; instead, the emperor's assessment seems to have been based on a more general assumption about how a piece of calligraphy by Zhong You should look. Some copies were simply messy. Evaluating copies of works by Wang Xizhi from the imperial collection, Tao Hongjing complained that some were smeared and hard to read and achieved only a vague resemblance to the original calligraphy from Wang's hand.[54]

The copies of calligraphy made for Emperor Wu by Tao Hongjing were not forgeries; nor is it certain that the various pieces of calligraphy that he and the emperor labeled as copies were ever intended to deceive: they may have been bona fide replicas misidentified at some point as originals. In the case of a letter and two other documents written by Zhong Hui, there can be no doubt: these were fabrications concocted to serve his personal interests. To spite his nephew, Xun Xu 荀勖 (d. 289), with whom he was on bad terms, Zhong forged a letter in Xun's hand in order to steal a valuable sword that Xun had entrusted to his mother, "and by this means spirited it away and never returned it."[55] During a military campaign in Sichuan, Zhong Hui concocted a palace document from the recently deceased empress dowager granting himself extraordinary powers and used this forgery to aggrandize his own status. He also rewrote a memorial to the emperor in the handwriting of his rival, Deng Ai 鄧艾 (197–264), using insubordinate and disrespectful language that resulted in Deng's arrest and execution.[56]

The letters and memorial forged by Zhong Hui closely resembled the writing of other calligraphers, but they were free inventions, not copies. Most cases of calligraphic forgery during the Six Dynasties appear to have involved the replication of preexisting works. Zhang Yi's copy of Wang Xizhi's memorial was one such forgery; another, also involving the calligraphy of Wang Xizhi, was produced by his own son: "Wang Xizhi once went to the capital, and as he was about to leave he wrote an inscription on a wall. Wang Xianzhi secretly erased it, then rewrote it in the same place, thinking to himself that it was not bad. When Wang Xizhi returned and saw it, he sighed and said: 'When I left I surely must have been very drunk.' Wang Xianzhi felt ashamed."[57] Later, Wang Xianzhi fell victim to a parallel act of deception. Kang Xin 康昕, identified in some sources as a non-Chinese, replaced with a forged copy an inscription written by Wang Xianzhi on the wall of a pavilion, imitating the original calligraphy so successfully that Wang himself could not tell at first that the writing was not from his hand.[58] Ultimately, in spite of the great skill they displayed, the forgeries by Zhang Yi, Wang Xianzhi, and Kang Xin were unsuccessful. In fact, as Leonard B. Meyer has pointed out, it is *only* unsuccessful forgeries that become known to history—a sobering thought for an art historian or connoisseur attempting to establish an authoritative catalogue raisonné of an artist's works.[59]

Meyer's observation raises an intriguing historiographic problem: if, as we often read in accounts of forgery, "no one could tell the difference," how did these deceptions come to light? Wang Xizhi was responsible for exposing two unauthorized replicas of his writing, but who revealed that his great-nephew, the poet Xie Lingyun 謝靈運 (385–433) was a skillful forger? According to Wang Sengqian, Xie removed a set of memorials written by Wang Xianzhi that had been stored carelessly in a government office, replacing them with copies so accurate that no one could have suspected they were not the originals, which Xie apparently took home for the pleasure of studying them at his leisure.[60] Wang Sengqian claims to have heard this story directly from Emperor Wen 文 (r. 424–453) of the (Liu) Song dynasty, but we never learn how the emperor discovered Xie Lingyun's trick. Perhaps Xie confessed or was caught in the act of returning the originals, which, to his credit, he eventually did. Wang Sengqian also fails to explain how other cases of forgery involving the calligraphic trickster Kang Xin were exposed. Working in league with the monk Huishi 惠式, said to be the nephew of Wang Xizhi, Kang Xin imitated (*xue* 學) Wang's cursive script so successfully that his forgeries, like Zhang Yi's copy of Wang's memorial, "almost confounded the real" when they entered the art market.[61]

By the early sixth century, misidentified copies and outright forgeries existed in such abundance that Tao Hongjing and Emperor Wu seem to have viewed as suspect nearly every work of calligraphy they encountered, and a tone of skepticism permeates their correspondence. One of Tao's longer letters to the emperor includes succinct evaluations of individual works and summarizes varieties of replication and deception prevalent in his time and in the later history of calligraphy, down to the present day.[62] In these passages Tao lists works he studied, most of them personal letters identified by their opening lines, and comments on each. Among the problematic works he encountered were the following:

> *Chen Tao yan* 臣濤言, one sheet: This calligraphy is not bad, but it is not by Youjun (Wang Xizhi) or his son. I don't recognize whose hand it is. It also seems to be a copy (*mo* 摹).
>
> *Zhi lian li, Ligu fang* 治廉瀝，狸骨方, one sheet: This is the calligraphy of Zijing (Wang Xianzhi). It also seems to be a copy (摹迹).
>
> *Huangchu san nian* 黃初三年, one sheet: This is an imitation of Youjun (Wang Xizhi) by a later person.

Wu yue shi yi ri 五月十一日, one sheet: This is a copy of calligraphy by Wang Min 王珉 (351–388). It has been oiled.[63]

Shang xiang Huang Qi 尚想黃綺, one sheet, *Sui jie di* 遂結澝, one sheet: Both items are imitations by later people, exceedingly awkward and inferior.[64]

Tao Hongjing's efforts to assist Emperor Wu in sorting out originals and copies powerfully shaped historical perceptions of the calligraphy of Wang Xizhi and other early masters by determining which works were most valued and which were most likely to be preserved and transmitted.[65] But doubts about authenticity did not necessarily slow the multiplication of suspect works. Although Emperor Wu and Tao Hongjing concluded that the *Yue Yi lun* attributed to Wang Xizhi in the imperial collection was a copy, the emperor had a duplicate of it made at his court, releasing into the stream of calligraphy attributed to Wang Xizhi a copy of a copy.[66]

The Magic of Replication

The terminology used in Six Dynasties texts to identify processes of copying raises thorny problems of interpretation; the texts are especially vague in distinguishing between different forms of freehand copying and tracing. Although they do not clarify all the problems of early usage, terms that have been more or less standardized since the Song dynasty (960–1279) make it possible to sort relationships among individual works of calligraphy into three broad categories.[67]

When a calligrapher imitates the style of another writer or period rather than replicating any particular work, he practices *fang* 倣, or "imitation."[68] This might range from closely approximating a calligrapher's habits of composing characters and shaping brushstrokes to freely evoking an earlier style, as seen in works of painting and calligraphy by Dong Qichang 董其昌 (1555–1636) and his followers. This level of relationship between the writing of two different calligraphers appears to be indicated in Six Dynasties texts by the word "*xue.*" It is used by Liu Yiqing 劉義慶 (403–444), author of *Shishuo xinyu* 世説新語 (A New Account of Tales of the World), in his account of how Zhong Hui forged a letter in the hand of Xun Xu.[69] The idea of imitating a style rather than copying a model also seems to be intended by Tao Hongjing's use of the word "*xue*" to label several of the items from the Liang imperial collection introduced above.[70]

The copying process known as *lin* 臨 (literally to lean over) signifies a close relationship between one work and another. In this process a copyist studies a piece of calligraphy, usually placing it next to the paper or silk on which the copy is to be made, and reproduces the shapes of the characters freehand, just as a student reproduces a model in order to perfect his own calligraphy.[71] This relationship between model and copy seems to be that indicated by the word "*xie*" 寫 in the earliest version of the story of Zhang Yi copying Wang Xizhi's memorial, in which Yang Xin states that Zhang was "good at imitating people's calligraphy (*shan xue ren shu* 善學人書) and copied *(xie)* Xizhi's memorial." Yu He, telling the same story, characterizes Zhang Yi's feat by using the verb "*xiexiao*" 寫效, which can be translated simply as "to copy," though the addition of the word "*xiao*" (to imitate) may be intended to suggest more strongly the idea of close imitation of a model, yielding what amounts to a facsimile of the original.[72]

An expert copyist can produce a striking likeness of a work of calligraphy through freehand copying, but this process is far less exact than tracing processes designated by the term "*mo*" 摹.[73] To make a tracing, the copyist places a sheet of paper over the original calligraphy and traces the characters stroke by stroke. It is because this method of copying is highly accurate that Tao Hongjing feared that Maoshan texts *not* replicated through tracing (*fei mo shu* 非摹書) had become corrupted.[74] The most precise and the most demanding method of tracing is known as *shuanggou kuotian* 雙鉤廓填, "outline and fill-in," also sometimes called *shuanggou motian* 雙鉤墨填, or "outline and ink fill-in." In this process, for which tracing paper coated with a thin layer of wax to make it semitransparent was sometimes used, the copyist begins by outlining the silhouettes of each character, taking care to observe even the most minute inflections of the original brush strokes.[75] After the outlining is complete, the copyist fills in the outlines of the characters with ink.

The *shuanggou kuotian* method for copying calligraphy was in use by the fifth century and may have originated specifically to reproduce the calligraphy of Wang Xizhi and Wang Xianzhi. This is suggested by a statement of Tao Hongjing, who calls the process "*guotian*" 郭填 and takes credit for using it to replicate Shangqing manuscripts:

> People today know about tracing model calligraphy by the two Wangs but have absolutely no understanding of tracing the Scriptures of the Perfected. In fact, this began with me. Furthermore, it is not always necessary to outline first and then fill in (*guotian* 郭填); one has only to use a single brush stroke to achieve a sense of kinetic force that scarcely differs from the original. As to talismans, however, regardless of whether they are large or small, they should always be outlined and then filled in.[76]

Tao Hongjing also mentions the outline and fill-in technique in his correspondence with Emperor Wu. In one letter Tao reports that a spell of bad nerves kept him from filling in the outlines of copies he had been preparing for the emperor; elsewhere, in a comment quoted above, Tao expresses his dissatisfaction with a set of his outline copies that he felt had captured the general appearance but not the dynamic brushwork of his models.

The earliest extant outlined copies, believed to have been made at the court of Emperor Taizong 太宗 (r. 626–649) during the seventh century, reproduce letters by Wang Xizhi. So meticulous are these copies that the outlines of the brushstrokes are visible only under magnification.[77] What relation, if any, these tracings had to original letters by Wang Xizhi remains an art historical mystery; all that can be said with confidence is that the tracings replicate what Tang connoisseurs accepted as autographic samples of Wang's brushwork. Nevertheless, these copies probably bring us as close as we ever will come to knowing what the calligraphy of Wang Xizhi was actually like.

Unlike rubbings, which eventually became the most common medium for reproducing works of calligraphy in large numbers, tracings require no intermediate steps of engraving or printing. Although Tao Hongjing insists that magic talismans, or *fu* 符, should be reproduced only through outline tracing, apparently in order to ensure that they retained their magical power, both this method and that of tracing calligraphy stroke by stroke may have been favored for reproducing Maoshan texts because of their unique property of bringing the original artifact into direct physical contact with the copy. The logic of tracing recalls James Frazer's formulation of how certain types of magical charms acquire their potency either by resembling or by coming into physical contact with the thing or person they are intended to enchant.[78] The principle of resemblance might be illustrated by a sorcerer casting a spell on someone by making and harming a representation of his victim, while the principle of contact might be illustrated by manipulating a piece of clothing or some other object that had touched the body of the victim. In a calligraphic tracing, the principles of resemblance and contact fuse. Even when a new tracing is made from an earlier traced copy, a material link with the original and its magical properties is maintained, like genes passed down in a family or a handshake linking an individual to "the man who shook the hand of the man who shook the hand of Chairman Mao."[79]

Thanks to the work of Qi Gong, Nakata Yūjirō, Lothar Ledderose, and other scholars, the importance of tracing in the history of Chinese calligraphy is fairly well known, but the remarkable properties of this method become most vividly apparent when considered within the context of world art. As a means of reproducing a work of art—distinguished here from mass production of identical objects such as pages printed from a single woodblock—calligraphic tracing is unique.[80] Superficially, it recalls tracing and pouncing techniques used by painters in China, Europe, and elsewhere to transfer designs from one surface to another.[81] But in these processes tracings were not finished works but merely visual guides, usually effaced as a painting was completed. In Chinese calligraphy the tracing itself is the final product.[82]

Doubts and Longings

Richard Brilliant has written that copies not only preserve lost works of art, but "their very existence also bespeaks the operation of taste."[83] Copies of calligraphy studied in this essay were made because the originals they reproduced were considered beautiful and desirable objects. That many copies were produced for deception and ill-gained profit is of secondary interest; what matters historically is the demand these copies supplied. Along with evaluations and rankings of calligraphers recorded in early texts, references to copies of works by Zhong You, Wang Xizhi, or Wang Xianzhi are vivid indexes of the critical esteem in which these artists were held.

Copies were proof of a calligrapher's stature, but they also contributed to enhancing his reputation through their multiplication and wide circulation. How, after all, could viewers in southern China have known the calligraphy of Cui Yuan without the availability of the copy seen by Wang Xianzhi? How could people outside the small circle of

Wang Xizhi's family and friends, or fortunate collectors who acquired autographic works from these sources, have learned to recognize Wang's hand without access to traced copies known for their astonishing accuracy? That all literate persons in China were potential producers and viewers of calligraphy accounts for much of the great popularity of this art. But were it not so amenable to replication or had the Chinese not invented such efficient means of making calligraphic copies, it is hard to see how calligraphy would have achieved the exalted status it still enjoys or how it would have permeated Chinese visual culture to the extent that it has.[84]

Wang Xizhi complained that the copyist who had so perfectly replicated his memorial had "almost confounded the real"; the only way Wang could tell that he had been tricked was by looking intently at the copyist's handiwork. The knowledge that such copies could be made and that the Sage of Calligraphy himself could be fooled demanded that anyone interested in the art of calligraphy learn to look with equal care. Doubt fostered visual alertness; awareness that *zhen* and *wei* were jumbled together inspired the desire to know which was which.[85] However vexing to the connoisseur or art historian they may be, copies nurtured the practice of close looking from which our ideas about art and aesthetics must grow.

NOTES

I am grateful to Susan Nelson, Michael Nylan, Jan Stuart, and Eugene Wang for their help in the preparation of this paper. I am grateful also to Victor Mair for his kind assistance in interpreting various terms concerning processes of copying mentioned in Chinese texts.

1. Hillel Schwartz, *The Culture of the Copy: Striking Likenesses, Unreasonable Facsimiles* (New York: Zone Books, 1996), p. 212. Rosalind E. Krauss makes a similar point when she writes that "harder to see or not, the notion of the copy is still fundamental to the conception of the original." See her essay, "The Originality of the Avant-Garde," in *The Originality of the Avant-Garde and Other Modernist Myths* (Cambridge, Mass.: MIT Press, 1986), p. 166.

2. Yu He 虞龢, *Lunshu biao* 論書表; in *Lidai shufa lunwen xuan* 歷代書法論文選, 2 vols., ed. Huang Jian 黃簡 (Shanghai: Shanghai shuhua chubanshe, 1979), vol. 1, pp. 53–54; cited hereafter as *LDSF*. Note that some printed editions of this passage substitute the character "嘗," which would indicate past action, for its homonym, 常, meaning "frequently," which appears in the *LDSF*

edition. The earliest extant manuscript version of the anecdote, in a handscroll by Zhao Mengfu 趙孟頫 (1254–1322), *Four Anecdotes from the Life of Wang Xizhi*, uses the character "嘗," which I have accepted in my translation. See Wen C. Fong, *Beyond Representation: Chinese Painting and Calligraphy, 8th–14th Century* (New York: Metropolitan Museum of Art, 1992), p. 423, pl. 98. For a slightly different translation, see Lothar Ledderose, *Mi Fu and the Classical Tradition of Chinese Calligraphy* (Princeton, N.J.: Princeton University Press, 1979), p. 37. The story appears also in Yang Xin 羊欣, *Cai gulai nengshu renming* 采古來能書人名, and in Wang Sengqian 王僧虔, *Lunshu* 論書, both in *LDSF*, pp. 48, 58.

3. An earlier account of one calligrapher imitating the writing of another concerns Wei Ji 衛覬 (active ca. 220–226), who copied the *Shang shu* 尚書 in the ancient script style of Handan Chun 邯鄲淳 (active ca. 220–226). When shown the copy, Handan Chun could not tell the difference between it and his own writing. See Wei Heng 衛恒, *Siti shushi* 四體書勢, in *LDSF*, p. 12. Unlike the story of Wang Xizhi's memorial, this account does not quite make clear whether or not Wei Ji was attempting to fool Handan Chun or was merely showing off his prowess as a calligrapher.

4. Among studies that consider the emergence of calligraphy as a fine art, see the following: Ledderose, *Mi Fu*; Li Zehou 李澤厚 and Liu Gangji 劉綱紀, *Zhongguo meixue shi* 中國美學史, (Tapei: Gufeng chubanshe, 1987), vol. 2, esp. pp. 466–470; Michael Nylan, "Calligraphy, the Sacred Text and Test of Culture," in *Character and Context in Chinese Calligraphy*, ed. Cary Y. Liu, Dora C. Y. Ching, and Judith Smith (Princeton, N.J.: Art Museum, Princeton University, 1999), pp. 17–77.

5. The concept of a classical tradition is explored in Ledderose, *Mi Fu*, ch. 1.

6. For an introduction to rankings and evaluations in Six Dynasties literary criticism, see John Timothy Wixted, "The Nature of Evaluation in the *Shih-p'in* (Gradings of Poets) by Chung Hung (A.D. 469–518)," in *Theories of the Arts in China*, ed. Susan Bush and Christian Murck (Princeton, N.J.: Princeton University Press, 1983), pp. 225–264. Among Six Dynasties works of painting and calligraphy criticism that adopt a system of graded rankings are the following: Yu Jianwu, *Shu pin* 書品; Xie He 謝赫 (fl. 500–535), *Guhua pinlu* 古畫品錄; Yuan Ang 袁昂 (d. 540), *Gujin shuping* 古今書評, dated 523.

7. John Hay, "The Human Body as a Microcosmic Source of Macrocosmic Values in Calligraphy," in Bush and Murck, eds., *Theories of the Arts in China*, pp. 74–102.

8. A text attributed to Gu Kaizhi 顧愷之 (ca. 345–ca. 406) gives instructions for making copies of paintings. It is quoted by Zhang Yanyuan 張彥遠 under the title *Wei Jin shengliu huazan* 魏晉勝流畫贊 in *Lidai minghua ji* 歷代名畫記 (*Zhongguo shuhua quanshu* 中國書畫全書 edition), p. 141; elsewhere Zhang mentions a text by Gu Kaizhi titled *Lunhua* 論畫, devoted to the essen-

tials of copying (p. 140). For a partial translation of the Gu Kaizhi text, see Susan Bush and Hsio-yen Shih, eds., *Early Chinese Texts on Painting* (Cambridge, Mass.: Harvard University Press, 1985), pp. 32–33. Zhang Yanyuan uses the term "*moxie* 模寫" to refer to the process of copying Gu Kaizhi discusses, but in the quoted section of Gu's text the word "*mo*" 搴 is used in a clear reference to tracing. The terms "*mo*" and "*xie*" appear in the last of Xie He's famous Six Laws—*chuan mo yi xie* 傳模移寫; in *Guhua pinlu* (*Zhongguo shuhua quanshu* edition), p. 1; also quoted in *Lidai minghua ji*, p. 124. Xie He himself mentions a painter called Liu Shaozu 劉紹祖 who specialized in copying (*chuan xie* 傳寫). See *Guhua pinlu*, p. 2. For the interpretation and correct reading of Xie He's laws, see the essay by Victor Mair in this volume. Beyond these sources, we know almost nothing about the practice of copying paintings during the Six Dynasties. I am not aware, for example, of any stories in pre-Tang texts concerning painters being fooled by copies of their own works, cases of copies of paintings being substituted clandestinely for originals, or discussions of copies and forgeries mixed together in the holdings of collectors of paintings—phenomena for which there are ample records in texts on calligraphy from the Six Dynasties, as well as in texts on painting from the Tang and later periods. Among the studies of early copies and forgeries to which this essay is most indebted are the following: Erik Zürcher, "Imitation and Forgery in Ancient Chinese Painting and Calligraphy," *Oriental Art*, n.s. 1, no. 4 (winter 1955), pp. 141–146; Wen C. Fong, "The Problem of Forgeries in Chinese Painting," *Artibus Asiae* 25 (1962), pp. 95–140; Nakata Yūjirō 中田勇次郎, *Chūgoku shoronshū* 中國書論集 (Tokyo: Nigensha, 1970), pp. 251–266; and Ledderose, *Mi Fu*, pp. 33–39.

9. Among the studies of copying and forgery in the West that I have consulted are the following: Nelson Goodman, *Languages of Art: An Approach to a Theory of Symbols* (Indianapolis: Hackett Publishing, 1976), esp. ch. 3, "Art and Authenticity"; Denis Dutton, ed. *The Forger's Art: Forgery and the Philosophy of Art* (Berkeley: University of California Press, 1983); Gregory Currie: *An Ontology of Art* (Basingstoke: Macmillan, in association with the Scots Philosophical Club, 1989), and "Artistic Forgery," in *The Routledge Encyclopedia of Philosophy* (London: Routledge, 1998).

10. Gregory Currie draws a distinction between forgery and fakery. The former consists of free invention, such as van Meegeren's "Vermeers," while the latter is based on replication, as in the case of a copy of *Mona Lisa* intended to be mistaken for the original work in the Louvre. To reduce the already excessive number of specialized terms in this essay, I use the word "forgery" to label both types of deception.

11. What may be the earliest appearance of the expression "*luan zhen*" 亂真 (to confound the real) is in the commentary of the *Heshang Gong Lao Zi* 河上公老子. See *Lao Zi zhuzi soyin* 老子逐字索引, ICS Ancient Chinese Texts Con-

cordance Series, Philosophical Works, no. 24 (Hong Kong: Commercial Press, 1996), p. 57. It was this version of the *Lao Zi* that Wang Xizhi is said to have transcribed for a Daoist master in exchange for a flock of geese. The anecdote is recorded by Yu He, *Lunshu biao*; in *LDSF*, p. 54.

12. The earliest occurrence of the term "*zhenji*" may be in the title of a collection of Daoist manuscripts from Maoshan. See note 40 below.

13. Another term in early texts that signifies forgery of various kinds includes "*yan*" 贋, used as a synonym of "*wei*" in the story from the *Han Feizi* 韓非子 translated below. In a memorial to Emperor Ling 靈 (r. 168–189), Cai Yong castigates eunuchs who employed ghost writers to do calligraphy for them, referring to this variety of forgery with the expression "*jiashou qingzi*" 假手請字. *Hou Han shu* 後漢書 (all references to the dynastic histories and the *Shi ji* cite the Zhonghua shuju editions), 77.2499; cited and translated by Martin J. Powers, *Art and Political Expression in Early China* (New Haven, Conn.: Yale University Press, 1991), 364. The word "*jiao*" 矯 also is used to indicate forgery, as in the case of a palace document forged by Zhong Hui 鍾會. See note 56 below.

14. Roger T. Ames, "The Common Ground of Self-Cultivation in Classical Taoism and Confucianism," *Tsing Hua Journal of Chinese Studies*, n.s. 17, nos. 1–2 (December 1985), p. 87. See also Daniel Coyle, "On the *Zhenren*," in *Wandering at Ease in the Zhuangzi*, ed. Roger T. Ames (Albany: State University of New York Press, 1998), pp. 197–210.

15. *Zhuang Zi yinde* 莊子引得, Harvard-Yenching Institute Sinological Series, no. 20 (Cambridge, Mass.: Harvard-Yenching Institute, 1956), 87 (31/37–38); translation in Ames, "The Common Ground," pp. 88–89 (adapted).

16. *Zhuang Zi yinde*, 15 (6/7–8); translation in Ames, "The Common Ground," p. 95.

17. Ding Fubao 丁福保, *Shuo wen jie zi gulin* 説文解字詁林, 12 vols. (reprint, Taipei: Shangwu, 1959), vol. 7, p. 3635. Cited by Coyle, "On the *Zhenren*," p. 198.

18. Michel Strickman, "The Mao Shan Revelations: Taoism and the Aristocracy," *T'oung Pao* 63, no. 1 (1977), pp. 1–64. I am grateful to Robert Ford Campany for explaining polemical implications of the term "*zhenren*" in Shangqing texts.

19. *Zhuang Zi yinde*, 4 (2/24–25); translation in A. C. Graham, *Chuang-tzu: The Inner Chapters and Other Writings from the Book Chuang-tzu* (London: George Allen and Unwin, 1981), p. 52.

20. *Zhuang Zi yinde*, 80 (29/11); 81 (29/33); 83 (29/68); translation in Burton Watson, *The Complete Works of Chuang Tzu* (New York: Columbia University Press, 1968), pp. 328, 333. In *Zhuang Zi* words and deeds to which the term "*wei*" is applied are deceitful, tricky, and untrue. In the *Xunzi* 荀子, however, "*wei*" carries positive connotations: that which is "*wei*" is the fruit of

human cultivation, artificial in the sense that it is achieved through conscious effort. This idea is developed most fully in ch. 23 of the *Xunzi,* which opens with the statement, "Man's nature is evil; his goodness is acquired only through *wei.*" *Xunzi yinde* 荀子引得, Harvard-Yenching Institute Sinological Series, supplement no. 22 (reprint, Taipei: Chinese Materials and Research Aids Service Center, 1966), pp. 86–90; translation in John Knoblock, *Xunzi: A Translation and Study of the Complete Works,* 3 vols. (Stanford, Calif.: Stanford University Press, 1994), vol. 3, pp. 150–162 and 143ff. See also Henry G. Skaja, "How to Interpret Chapter 16 of the *Zhuang Zi,*" in Ames, ed., *Wandering at Ease in the Zhuangzi,* pp. 101–102, 117, n. 6. An instance of the word "*wei*" used to label manmade artifacts appears in the *Han shu* biography of Han Yanshou 韓延壽 (d. 56 B.C.), where the term "*weiwu*" 偽物 refers to replicas of horses and carts used for burials or other rituals. *Han shu,* 76.3210. Unlike forged artifacts intended to be mistaken for something they are not, these *weiwu* were obviously *representations* of other things.

21. *Han shu,* 8.273.

22. *Hou Han shu,* 58.1874. For the story of Bai Qi, see *Shi ji* 史記, 73.2336–2337.

23. Ding Zhonghu 丁仲祜, ed., *Tao Yuanming shi jianzhu* 陶淵明詩箋注 (Taipei: Yiwen yinshu guan, 1974), pp. 30, 92, 111; translation in James Hightower, *The Poetry of T'ao Ch'ien* (Oxford: Clarendon Press, 1970), pp. 30, 103, 130.

24. *Zhong Rong shipin yizhu* 鍾嶸詩品譯注, with translations into modern Chinese and annotations by Zhao Zhongyi 趙仲邑 (Nanning: Guangxi renmin chubanshe, 1987), p. 40. I am grateful to Jonathan Chaves for this reference. For a discussion of the concepts of "*zhen*" and "*wei*" in later literary criticism, see Chaves's essay, "The Panoply of Images: A Reconsideration of the Literary Theory of the Kung-an School," in Bush and Murck, eds., *Theories of the Arts in China,* pp. 347–348.

25. Liu Xie, *Wenxin diaolong zhushi* 文心雕龍注釋, with annotations by Zhou Zhenfu 周振甫 (Beijing: Renmin wenxue chubanshe, 1981), pp. 28–29; translation in Vincent Shih, *The Literary Mind and the Carving of Dragons by Liu Hsieh: A Study of Thought and Pattern in Chinese Literature* (New York: Columbia University Press, 1957), pp. 21–25. An important article by Gu Jiegang 顧頡剛 deals with forgery in the sense of lies and false statements. See Gu Jiegang, "Zhanguo, Qin, Han jian ren de zaowei yu bianwei" 戰國秦漢間人的造偽與辨偽, *Shixue nianbao* 史學年報 2, no. 2 (1935), pp. 209–248.

26. Pei Yin, *Shi ji jijie xu* 史記集解序; appended to the Zhonghua shuju edition of *Shi ji,* pp. 3–4.

27. *Maoshi zhengyi* 毛詩正義 (Shanghai: Guji chubanshe, 1990), p. 73.

28. Eugene Yuejin Wang, "Mirror, Death, and Rhetoric: Reading Later Han Chinese Bronze Artifacts," *Art Bulletin* 84, no. 3 (September 1994), p. 511 and n. 1.

29. Zhu Shouliang 朱守亮, *Han Feizi shiping* 韓非子釋評 (Taipei: Wunan tushu chuban gongsi, 1992), p. 822.

30. This differs from the inspection of registers mandated in Emperor Xuan's edict. The registers were real; it was the information they recorded that was potentially suspect.

31. *Shi ji*, 28.1388; translation in Burton Watson, *Records of the Grand Historian of China*, 2 vols. (New York: Columbia University Press, 1961), vol. 2, p. 42.

32. The terms "*zhen*" and "*wei*" appear in Wei Heng's *Siti shushi*, but here they refer not specifically to calligraphy but more generally to ancient texts. Wei Heng, *Siti shushi*, p. 13. Zhao Yi 趙壹 uses the term "*zhen*" to signify moral rectitude. *Fei caoshu* 非草書, in *LDSF*, p. 2. Writing about cursive script, Cheng Gongsui 成公綏 (231–273) states that it "approaches artificiality" (*jin wei* 近偽). *Lishu ti* 隸書體, in *LDSF*, p. 9.

33. Yu He, *Lunshu biao*, in *LDSF*, p. 50. Cited by Ledderose, *Mi Fu*, pp. 40–41. Compare translations in Zürcher, "Imitation and Forgery," p. 142, and the partial translation in Fong, "The Problem of Forgeries," p. 96.

34. Yu He, *Lunshu biao*, in *LDSF*, pp. 50–51.

35. Ibid., p. 50.

36. *Tao Yinju yu Liang Wudi lunshu qi* 陶隱居與梁武帝論書啓, in Zhang Yanyuan, *Fashu yao lu* 法書要錄 (*Congshu jicheng chubian* 叢書集成初編 edition), 2.19–20.

37. Ibid., 2.23.

38. Tao Hongjing does use the terms "*zhen*" and "*wei*" in his *Zhen'gao* 真誥 (*Zhengtong Daozang* 正統道藏; reprint, Taipei: Yiwen yinshuguan, 1962), 19.6a. Tao states that he labeled texts he was not able to authenticate (*bu zheng zhen wei* 不証真偽) with the cyclical characters *jia* 甲, *yi* 乙, *bing* 丙, etc.

39. In addition to Strickman's "The Mao Shan Revelations," see his "On the Alchemy of T'ao Hung-ching," in *Facets of Taoism*, ed. Holmes Welch and Anna Seidel (New Haven, Conn.: Yale University Press, 1979), pp. 123–192, and Lothar Ledderose, "Some Taoist Elements in the Calligraphy of the Six Dynasties," *T'oung Pao* 70 (1984), pp. 246–278. The important relationship between Daoism and calligraphy was first discussed by Chen Yinke 陳寅恪, "Tianshi dao yu binhai diyu zhi guanxi" 天師道與濱海地域之關系, *Bulletin of the National Research Institute of History and Philology, Academic Sinica* 3, part 4 (1933), pp. 439–466.

40. The text seems to indicate that the term "*ji*," translated here as "traces," could refer to the calligraphy of the Perfected or to their deeds. Tao Hongjing, *Zhen'gao*, 19.2a.

41. Ibid., 272–273.

42. *Tao Yinju yu Liang Wudi lunshu qi*, 2.22. On the connoisseurship of Tao Hongjing, see Ledderose "Some Taoist Elements," p. 272. See also Wang

Tongshun 王同順, "Tao Hongjing 陶弘景," *Shufa yanjiu* 書法研究 63, no. 1 (1995), pp. 86–94.

43. Early evidence of the pedagogy of calligraphy consists of tables of *ganzhi* 干支 characters inscribed on Shang oracle bones, believed to be the work of student engravers practicing their craft. Guo Moruo 郭沫若 has identified one inscribed bone as the work of a student imitating characters engraved by his teacher. See David N. Keightley, *Sources of Shang History: The Oracle-Bone Inscriptions of Bronze Age China* (Berkeley: University of California Press, 1978), p. 47, nn. 99–100.

44. Yang Xin, *Cai gulai nengshu renming*, in *LDSF*, pp. 45, 47.

45. Ibid., p. 46.

46. *Lidai minghua ji*, 5.139 (translation in Bush and Shih, eds., *Early Chinese Texts on Painting*, p. 32); Li and Liu, *Zhongguo meixue shi*, p. 482.

47. *Tao Yinju yu Liang Wudi lunshu qi*, 2.23; translation in Ledderose, *Mi Fu*, p. 38.

48. Yu He, *Lunshu biao*, in *LDSF*, p. 52.

49. Jean-Pierre Drège discusses various types of copies and transcriptions in his article, "La Lecture et l'écriture en Chine et la xylographie," *Etudes chinoises* 10, nos. 1–2 (spring–autumn 1991), pp. 77–105.

50. Tao Hongjing, *Zhen'gao*, 20.3b; translation in Strickman, "The Mao Shan Revelations," p. 61. Although the character "*ta*" 搨 in this passage, a variant form of 揚, refers in later periods to calligraphic rubbings, here it refers to tracing. For a discussion of confusion generated by this word, see Nakata, *Chūgoku shoronshū*, pp. 253–256.

51. Yu Jianwu, *Shu pin*, in *LDSF*, p. 88. See also Yang Xin, *Cai gulai nengshu renming*, in *LDSF*, p. 45.

52. *Tao Yinju yu Liang Wudi lunshu qi*, 2.23.

53. Ibid., 2.21.

54. Ibid.

55. Liu Yiqing 劉義慶, *Shishuo xinyu yizhu* 世説新語譯注, with annotations by Zhang Huizhi 張撝之 (Shanghai: Shanghai guji chubanshe, 1996), p. 602; translation in Richard B. Mather, *Shih-shuo Hsin-yü: A New Account of Tales of the World* (Minneapolis: University of Minnesota Press, 1976), p. 365.

56. *Sanguo zhi* 三國志, 28.792; cited by Howard Goodman, "The Calligrapher Zhong You," *Journal of the American Oriental Society*, 1994, p. 565; Mather, *A New Account of Tales of the World*, p. 365. Mather notes that the *Zizhi tongjian* 資治通鑑 (78.2480) attributes the rewriting of Deng Ai's memorial to Wei Guan 衛瓘, not Zhong Hui.

57. Sun Guoting 孫過庭, *Shupu* 書譜, in *LDSF*, p. 125; translation in Chang Ch'ung-ho and Hans H. Frankel, *Two Chinese Treatises on Calligraphy* (New Haven, Conn.: Yale University Press, 1995), p. 3 (adapted).

58. *Lidai minghua ji*, 5.140.

59. Leonard B. Meyer, "Forgery and the Anthropology of Art," in Dutton, ed., *The Forger's Art*, p. 88.

60. Wang Sengqian, *Lunshu*, in *LDSF*, p. 59.

61. Ibid. Note that "*zan*" 贊, the final character of the text of this story in the *LDSF*, is a misprint for "*huo*" 貨. Compare the texts in the Congshu jicheng chubian edition, 1.10, and in Nakata Yūjirō, ed., *Chūgoku shoron taikei* 中國書論大系 (Tokyo: Nigensha, 1977), vol. 1, p. 210. The identification of the monk Huishi, named only as a resident of Nanzhou by Wang Sengqian, is based on Zhang Huaiguan 張懷瓘, *Shuduan* 書斷, in *LDSF*, p. 188; cited by Nakata, ed., *Chūgoku shoron taikei*, vol. 1, p. 221, n. 93.

62. In addition to his roles as consultant and copyist, Tao Hongjing acted as a kind of roving agent, ferreting out calligraphy for Emperor Wu's inspection. In this enterprise, caution was essential. When he came upon an unusual scroll in flying white (*feibai* 飛白) attributed to Wang Xizhi, Tao was impressed by the force of the brushwork but confessed that he knew nothing else like it that would allow him to judge the authenticity of the scroll. With this caveat, Tao presented the work to the emperor. *Tao Yinju yu Liang Wudi lunshu qi*, 2.20.

63. Tao Hongjing's observation may mean that the paper on which the copy was made had been treated with oil to make it translucent, thus facilitating the process of tracing. For accounts of treating tracing paper with wax in order to achieve the same effect, see Fu Shen et al., *Traces of the Brush: Studies in Chinese Calligraphy* (New Haven, Conn.: Yale University Art Gallery, 1977), p. 3, and Nakata, *Chūgoku shoronshū*, p. 256, quoting Zhang Shinan 張世南, *Youhuan jiwen* 遊宦紀聞, ch. 5, where this technique is described.

64. *Tao Yinju yu Liang Wudi lunshu qi*, 2.21.

65. According to Ledderose, other experts at the Liang court signed those pieces of calligraphy in the imperial collection they believed were authentic. *Mi Fu*, p. 42 and n. 151.

66. In his colophon for a version of *Yue Yi lun*, the calligrapher-monk Zhiyong 智永 (active ca. 515–ca. 604) mentions a copy of the work made during the Liang dynasty. *Zhiyong ti Youjun Yue Yi Lun* 智永題右軍樂毅論; in Zhang Yanyuan, *Fashu yao lu*, 2.33. This presumably was the copy bearing the signatures of calligraphy experts at the Liang court, preserved today in various rubbings. See *Shodō zenshū* 書道全集, 3d ed., 26 vols. (Tokyo: Heibonsha, 1966–1969), vol. 4, pp. 153–155.

67. This account of methods of copying is based on Nakata, *Chūgoku shoronshū*, pp. 251–264, and Fu Shen et al., *Traces of the Brush*, pp. 3–5.

68. To define this type of copy, in which "the copyist adopts the style of a master, with the intention not to reproduce but rather to create a 'new' work," Fu Shen et al. use the term "*zao*" 造 (to invent) as a subcategory of *fang*. *Traces of the Brush*, p. 4.

69. See note 56 above.

70. Wang Sengqian also uses the word "*xue*" to describe the forgeries of Kang Xin and Huishi, but I am not sure if these were copies or fabrications. *Lunshu,* 59.

71. The first use of the term "*lin*" in this sense may be in Zhiyong's colophon for *Yue Yi lun,* in which the term is combined with the word "*xue*" 學. He uses the resulting compound, it appears, to distinguish freehand copying of the scroll from the tracing copy made at the Liang court, for which he uses the character "*mo*" 模. See note 66 above.

72. Yang Xin, *Cai gulai nengshu renming,* in *LDSF,* p. 48, Yu He, *Lunshu biao,* in *LDSF,* p. 53.

73. Unlike the terms "*fang,*" which does not appear at all in Six Dynasties texts on calligraphy, or "*lin,*" which appears only in Zhiyong's colophon datable to the late sixth century, "*mo*" 摹 is used frequently to designate copies, though it is not certain that in all cases these were tracings. See Nakata, *Chūgoku shoronshū,* pp. 251–256.

74. Tao Hongjing, *Zhen'gao,* 19.6a.

75. In one refinement of this method, called *xiangta* 響搨, the original calligraphy is held up before a window in order to make the characters easier to see through the tracing paper. Fu Shen et al., *Traces of the Brush,* p. 3.

76. Tao Hongjing, *Zhen'gao,* 20.1b; translation in Strickman, "The Mao Shan Revelations," p. 56 (adapted). Strickman believes that Gu Huan used outline and fill-in tracing for his compilation of Maoshan texts, but it is unclear to me whether Gu's copies were made using this method or stroke-by-stroke tracing.

77. Ledderose, *Mi Fu,* fig. 20.

78. In his reformulation and critique of Frazer's theories, the anthropologist Michael Taussig cites things such as a horse's hoofprints, which show "imitation blending so intimately with contact that it becomes impossible to separate image from substance in the power of the final effect." The blending of imitation and contact also characterizes tracing copies of calligraphy. Michael Taussig, *Mimesis and Alterity: A Particular History of the Senses* (New York and London: Routledge, 1993), p. 53.

79. During the Cultural Revolution shaking hands with anyone who had shaken hands with Chairman Mao was considered a special honor. Weizhi Lu, personal communication, September 4, 2000.

80. The mass production of artifacts in China is studied by Lothar Ledderose in *Ten Thousand Things: Module and Mass Production in Chinese Art.* A. W. Mellon Lecture in the Fine Arts, 1998. (Princeton, N.J.: Princeton University Press, 2000). Bollingen Series 35, p. 46.

81. For tracing, pouncing, and other workshop practices in China, see Sarah Fraser: "Formulas of Creativity: Artist's Sketches and Techniques of Copying at Dunhuang," *Artibus Asiae* 59, nos. 3–4 (2000), pp. 189–224, and

"The Artist's Practice in Tang Dynasty China" (Ph.D. diss., University of California, Berkeley, 1996).

82. The closest parallels for replication through tracing outside China may be found in the history of three-dimensional media: in ancient Greece and Rome copies of statues were made through casting and, according to some authorities, through the use of pointing machines. Like tracing, these techniques could yield highly accurate copies, though original and copy never came into physical contact. For an introduction to copying sculpture in Greece and Rome, see Brunilde S. Ridgway, *Roman Copies of Greek Sculptures: The Problem of Originals* (Ann Arbor: University of Michigan Press, 1984). On doubts about the use of pointing machines in antiquity, see Miranda Marvin, "Roman Sculptural Reproductions of Ploykleitos: The Sequel," in *Sculpture and Its Reproductions*, ed. Anthony Hughes and Erich Ranfft (London: Reaktion Books, 1997), p. 8. In photography, the preferred means of accurately reproducing the appearance of works of art in modern times, light reflected from an object leaves an impression on the chemically treated surface of film. But tracing is more faithful than photography in two ways: the tracing is always the same size as the writing it replicates, and, assuming the original calligraphy is a work of ink on paper, it is always in the same medium.

83. Richard Brilliant, *My Laocoön: Alternative Claims in the Interpretation of Artworks* (Berkeley: University of California Press, 2000), p. 13.

84. While it is true that paintings were reproduced as copies and rubbings —the most notable example was Wang Wei's 王維 (ca. 699–761) *Wangchuan tu* 輞川圖—most major paintings, unlike major works of calligraphy, were simply too complex to be accurately reproduced in large numbers. This is why we read of Emperor Song Lizong 理宗 (r. 1224–1264) owning 113 copies of Wang Xizhi's *Lantingji xu* 蘭亭集序, not (let us say) 113 copies of a landscape painting by Fan Kuan 范寬 (fl. ca. 990–1030), and why, upon entering a Chinese garden, we often discover engraved reproductions of calligraphy, not paintings, lining the walls. For Lizong's collection of copies of the *Lantingji xu*, see Fong, "The Problem of Forgeries," p. 96.

85. Nelson Goodman has argued that the attempt to distinguish original from copy can constitute a kind of training in "perceptual discrimination." *Languages of Art*, p. 105. See also Currie, *An Ontology of Art*, pp. 112–113.

Chapter 2

• •

The Essay on Painting by Wang Wei 王微 (415–453) in Context

Susan Bush

The "Xu hua" 敘畫 (Discussion of Painting), by Wang Wei 王微 (415–453), has been classified with the "Hua shanshui xu" 畫山水序 (Preface on Landscape Painting), by Zong Bing 宗炳 (375–443), under the heading of "landscape Daoism." These two texts are often discussed along with a third, "Hua Yuntaishan ji" 畫雲臺山記 (The Record of Painting the Cloud Terrace Mountain), attributed to the famous contemporary artist Gu Kaizhi 顧愷之. Of the trio, the third is definitely Daoist in character since it illustrates a story about the Five Pecks of Rice sect founder Zhang Daoling 張道陵 and his disciples that takes place on the Cloud Terrace Mountain in Sichuan. Conceivably the proposal for a projected painting, the last text takes us through a magic landscape step by step in a relatively straightforward manner. By contrast, the other two essays share a strong expressive intent. In the fashion of the period, both Zong Bing and Wang Wei loved *qin* 琴 (lute music), landscape scenery, and painting. Nonetheless, their writings differ markedly in literary style and approach. Elsewhere I have argued that the Zong Bing text might better be considered under the label of "landscape Buddhism" because Zong Bing was a prominent Buddhist devotee who studied with Huiyuan 惠遠 (334–416) on Mount Lu and wrote a defense of Buddhism toward the end of his life.[1] The Wang Wei text, by contrast, was said to be

"Neo-Daoist"—that is, influenced by the tradition of philosophical Daoism current at the southern court. These labels are perhaps too simplistic to characterize the content of the two essays but can refer to different intellectual backgrounds. Another pair of headings might describe the settings of the authors' lives: "provincial" for Zong Bing versus "cultural center" for Wang Wei. Zong left Huiyuan's circle at Mount Lu to take up his duties at the endangered family property in Jiangling, another center of Buddhism further up the Yangzi. His late writings from Jiangling retain and defend Huiyuan's beliefs in such concepts as the immortality of the transmigrating spirit and the equivalence of Chinese sages with the Buddha.[2] The younger Wang Wei, whose interests by contrast were more broadly speaking those of a naturalist, remained in the region of the (Liu) Song capital, where he was in contact with such court officials in the educational establishment as Yan Yanzhi 顏延之 (384–456) and He Yan 何偃 (415–458). Thus different milieus are contributing factors to the distinctive approaches of the two texts. This chapter will attempt to place the "Xu hua" in the context of Wang Wei's time and to read the text against a background of "Neo-Daoist" thought.

A cautionary note is useful here. Earlier translators of the "Xu hua" have hailed it as a sophisticated argument for painting as a fine art but remarked that the text is abbreviated or corrupted, particularly in the central portion. As Michael Sullivan writes: "The meaning at this point is obscure ... but Wang Wei apparently conceives of three elements: nature as it is visible to the eye, the spirit that is immanent in all forms, and the power of the artist so to represent these forms that the spirit is expressed."[3] It may not be possible to put the gist of Wang's thought more concisely. Still, a fuller understanding of the essay may be developed in the context of Wang Wei's intellectual background. This chapter will first present Wang Wei's biography and then treat recent scholarship on the *Yi jing* 易經 (Changes) and its influential commentary by Wang Bi 王弼 (226–249). Finally it will discuss the three sections of the essay in the light of various interpretations.

Wang Wei's Life and Times

One word might characterize the most important influence on Wang Wei: "family." As a member of the Wang clan originally from Linyi

臨沂, Langye 郎琊 (Shandong), Wang Wei was born into an elite. In South China, the émigré Wangs were at the height of their political power during the time of Wang Dao 王導 (276–339) and his brother Wang Dun 王敦 (266–324). The family still held power later on since Wang Dao's grandson, Wang Mi 王謐 (360–407), the great-uncle of Wang Wei, survived a period of transition to serve as a (Liu) Song minister. The Wangs were also known for their religious and intellectual interests and talents. Wang Dao and his son, Wang Qia 王洽 (323–358), were prominent patrons of Buddhism, as were Wang Qia's five sons. In this generation, Wang Mi and his brother Wang Xun 王珣, Wang Wei's grandfather, also studied Daoism. Along with Wang Dun, Wang Dao, Wang Qia, and Wang Mi were noted calligraphers, as were Wang Dao's cousin, Wang Yi; his nephew, Wang Xizhi 王羲之 (321–379); and his grandnephew, Wang Xianzhi 王獻之 (344–388). Moreover, the last three men were recorded as painters in the mid-ninth-century *Lidai minghua ji* 歷代名畫記 (A Record of Famous Painters of Successive Dynasties).[4] The Wangs still retained official status and cultural prestige throughout the dynasties of Song, Qi, and Liang, which were founded by military men from families of far lesser standing. In his mid-nineties, Wang Wei's uncle, Wang Hong 王弘 (d. 432), was praised for openly weeping when Song Wendi 宋文帝 (r. 424–453) offered condolences on the death of a brother, the less accomplished thirty-six-year-old Wang Yunshou 王雲首 (d. 430). Like his famous ancestor, Wang Rong 王戎 (234–305), who mourned excessively for family members, Hong was said to show his feelings with a sage-like transparency. Wang Sengchuo 王僧綽 (424–453), Wang Yunshou's son, was Wendi's trusted adviser who searched Han and pre-Han texts for precedents at the time of the succession crisis. It was Wang Sengchuo's younger brother, Wang Sengqian 王僧虔 (427–485), a Qi official, who recorded the art of the Wang family calligraphers noted above. Toward the end of the line, Wang Hong's great-grandson, Wang Rong 王融 (468–494), was noted for his interest in musical harmony and the tonal rules of verse along with the poet Shen Yue 沈約 (441–513).[5]

Wang Wei himself exhibited talents in the areas of literary composition, calligraphy, painting, and *qin* music, and he was also accomplished in medical prescriptions, divination by yarrow stalks, and yin-yang 陰陽 studies (astrology). He spent over a decade in reclusion studying old texts and antiquities. In 450, a Northern Wei envoy inquired after him, suggesting that his reputation for technical expertise had reached Northern China.[6] On this occasion, Wang Wei's name was linked with that of the younger Xie Zhuang 謝莊 (421–466), a prodigy from the rival Xie 謝 family of Chen Commandery 陳郡 (Henan). The Xies came from a less prestigious lineage but rose to the height of political and military power by the end of the fourth century. Xie Zhuang, like Wang Wei, was skilled in literature, painting, and the *qin*, and he also wrote on painting in his "Hua qin tiexu" 畫琴帖序 (Short Introduction to Painting and the Lute). A successful official of a practical bent, he painted a ten-foot wooden map of the world to show commanderies like a jigsaw puzzle.[7] It is conceivable that Wang Wei had Xie's feat in mind when he declared that fine painting was not map making. Indeed Wang's essay might have been written in part to counter Xie's theories of painting. Moreover, one of Xie's poems was highly praised by the court poet and critic Yuan Shu 袁淑 (409–453), so Xie also gained success in another area of Wang Wei's expertise.

By contrast, Yuan Shu scornfully criticized some of Wang's writing for its expression of feeling. Wang Wei's response sheds light on his character. Conscious of a need to defend the Wang literary tradition, he wrote to his younger cousin, Wang Sengchuo, by then a court attendant married to a princess. In this letter, Wang Wei stated that his preference was for *guwen* 古文 (writing in antique style) and argued that irregular rising and falling cadences that expressed deep feelings were necessary if poetry was not to be insipid. Shen Yue's concluding comment on Wang Wei's *Song shu* 宋書 biography focuses on this incident without casting either participant in a favorable light. Shen characterized Wang as a high-minded scholar who overreacted and whose efforts thus were ultimately flawed.[8] Of course Shen's preference was for a different type of verse. The sharp contrast between Wang Wei and Yuan Shu's kind of poetry is evident in two imitations by Jiang Yan 江淹 (444–501) in *Wenxuan* 文選. A set piece on elaborate equipage represents Yuan's court position, while a mournful complaint of bodily ailments and inadequate medical remedies forcefully suggests Wang Wei's reclusive life.[9] Wei's concern with literary style and emotional expression is most evident in the lyrical conclusion of his essay on painting.

Wang Wei's adulthood took place during Song Wendi's long and initially peaceful reign. This was a time of general expansion and temple building in Jiankang, when contacts with Southeast Asia increased and imported Buddhism spread at the capital. But then, possibly linked to these contacts, plagues struck the Jiangsu region in 427, 447, 451, 457, and 460, and a major epidemic spread throughout China in 468. In some respects the (Liu) Song era became something like a Dark Age, and the later years of the Liu dynasty might be characterized as demon ridden.[10] Toward the end of Wang Wei's lifetime, Crown Prince Liu Shao 劉邵 came under the influence of a magician and a shamaness noted for using hex poison. With his brother Xun 濬, Shao organized conspiracies against his father, Song Wendi, and succeeded in assassinating him at the beginning of 453. Beforehand, Wang Wei supposedly had read the stars and tried to warn his high-placed cousin Wang Sengchuo of the forthcoming death of a ruler, but the message arrived too late. Wang Sengchuo was to die as one of Wendi's four loyal officials, martyred along with the poet Yuan Shu.[11] The sturdy stone chimeras that mark the entrance to Song Wendi's Nanjing gravesite are the only extant monuments that indicate the level of Song court art. Formerly, because of their distance from a grave and the secret undulations of the spirit path, these beasts were thought to guard the tomb of Chen Wendi 陳文帝 (d. 566).[12] Now, with only a surface overlay of fine carving, their inherent bulkiness bespeaks the earlier period of large-scale southern stonework and brings to mind Wendi's brutal end.

Thus, because of his family connections, even in reclusion outside the capital Wang Wei was affected by Song court politics. Illness was another strong influence in his life. His sickness at the age of eleven led him to take an interest in medicine, and he mentions ill health in letters to intimates, He Yan and his brother Wang Sengqian. When his father Wang Ru 王孺 became sick, Wang Wei retired from his court appointments as a member of the princes' retinue. Illness and filiality were excuses that he used to decline further posts, despite the poverty of his family. On one occasion, as an excuse he noted that his elder brother Wang Yuan 王遠 was out of office, and Wendi remedied this. Later on, the emperor sought Wang Wei's services as a diviner and sent him a famous yarrow plant. Wang in turn suggested that his younger brother Wang Sengqian 王僧謙 shared his talents and should be employed instead. Unfortunately, after serving at court, Wang Sengqian caught an illness in 453, and when Wang Wei prepared a prescription for him, Wang Sengqian drank it and died. Mourning his beloved brother's death, Wang Wei castigated himself for some possible inattention and wondered what his sin had been. And, neglecting to take care of himself, he also became ill and died some forty days later. The brothers were buried together without elaborate ceremony. A *qin* was placed on top of a plain wooden coffin, and He Yan came to play the instrument for Wang Wei as his true friend.[13]

In many ways, Wang Wei's life fits squarely into a Confucian framework. He corresponded about the hexagrams of the *Yi jing* in regard to the practice of painting with Yan Yanzhi. And Yan was a staunch Confucian under a veneer of "Neo-Daoist" eccentricity. Like Yan, Wang read both Daoist and Confucian texts while maintaining a skeptical view of Daoist and Buddhist religious beliefs. Indeed the only text that he claimed to trust was the *Bencao* 本草 (in Joseph Needham's translation, Pharmacopoeia or Pharmaceutical Natural History). The work he read was probably the early version attributed to *Shennong* 神農, an encyclopedic guide to flora, fauna, and minerals and their uses in prescriptions. It is noteworthy that a later *Bencao* was authored by the Daoist Tao Hongjing 陶弘景 (456–536), a physician, naturalist, and alchemist who concocted an immortality drug for Liang Wudi 梁武帝 (r. 502–549).[14] However, there is no indication that Wang Wei was a practicing Daoist. He spoke with scorn about people who claimed to see marvels or hoped to ascend as immortals. Instead he claimed that he could grasp the knowledge of various schools through his interest in pharmacology. As an astrologer, he had to have faith in an ordered universe. As he said, "Heaven does not cheat men."[15] As a milfoil diviner, he must have known the *Yi jing* and its various commentaries well. The four branches of study established by Song Wendi at the imperial academy in 439 comprised Xuanxue 玄學, history, literature, and Confucianism. The *Yi jing* (or *Zhouyi* 周易) was considered the Confucian classic, with the *Xici zhuan* 繫辭傳, or Great Appendix, taken to be Confucius's commentary. Separate chairs were established for the later Zheng Xuan 鄭玄 and Wang Bi commentaries, but in 454 Yan Yanzhi, then director of the Imperial Banqueting Court, determined that only the Wang Bi commentary on this text would be taught.[16] Wang Bi, who was not one of the Langye Wangs, was in many ways a highly influential writer in the Six Dynasties period. I propose to use Wang Bi's commentaries as a guide to Wang Wei's understanding of the *Yi jing* hexagrams. In doing so, I am depending on recent translations and interpretations of Wang Bi commentaried by Richard Lynn and Rudolf Wagner. Somehow it seems appropriate that interest in Wang Bi is on the rise now, when scientific theories include negative universes and indeterminate subatomic particles.

The Influence of Wang Bi's *Yi jing* Commentary

Xuanxue, the "study of the Mysterious," has indeed seemed hard to
fathom. It has also generally had a critical reception in later times. As
Richard Mather notes, "For some reason, nearly all Chinese historians,
both political and literary, have raised their voices in chorus denounc-
ing this movement as the nemesis of all creative thought or action."[17] In
Joseph Needham's judgment of the commentaries in question, "the
whole Daoist system was emasculated for continued existence in, and
adaptation to, a milieu in which Confucian conventions were dominant."[18] Wang Bi's positions on the inadequacy of words to express
ideas and on *wu* 無, fundamental nonbeing that the Sage embodied,
were particularly important in the early transmission of Buddhist
thought. But it was his philosophical reading of the *Yi jing* that was to
have enduring influence. As Richard Lynn notes, Wang Bi's commentary "as a whole focuses on the phenomenon of human existence and is
in the main a Confucian statement.... By freeing the *Changes* from
[numerical] calculations and from confusion with cosmological and calendrical considerations, [he] made it into the classic of philosophy that
so attracted the ... Neo-Confucians."[19] Presumably Yan Yanzhi was
convinced by Wang Bi's humanistic interpretations, as well as by the
brilliance of his arguments and style, when he established a chair for
Wang Bi's commentary in preference to those of others. Of course, for
Needham, reliance on the *Yi jing* was both a crutch and a straitjacket in
the development of Chinese science, and he characterizes Wang Bi's
accomplishment as undermining a less rigid, more scientific Daoist
approach. It is interesting to note that Wang Bi's "views" on the operations of the universe were grounded on contemporary astronomy, as is
evident in a passage Lynn has translated:

> That is why if one examines things from the point of view of totality, even
> though things are multitudinous, one knows that it is possible to deal with
> them by holding fast to the One, and if one views them from the point of
> view of the fundamental, even though the concepts involved are immense
> in number and scope, one knows that it is possible to cover them all with a
> single name. Thus when we use an armillary sphere to view the great
> [heavenly] movements, the actions of Heaven and Earth lose their capacity
> to amaze us, and if we keep to a single center point when viewing what is

about to come to us, then things converging from the six directions lose their capacity to overwhelm us with their number.[20]

These four linked sentences can stand as an example of how Wang Bi's parallel prose rhetoric attempts to define the known parameters of the indefinable—that is, the shifting aspects of the universe and of human existence, the changes captured by the *Changes*. In this passage, to expand on the one and the many, he emphasizes opposite points of view and extremes of size, distance, and motion—all scientific considerations. Observations of the stars were thought to underlie the images of the *Yi jing*, and astronomical instruments were among the highlights of early Chinese technology. The great Han astronomer Zhang Heng 張衡 was the first to build an armillary sphere powered by a waterwheel (ca. 132 A.D.), and the (Liu) Song astronomer royal, Qian Lezhi 錢樂之, produced a solid celestial globe in bronze by 436, as well as a series of star maps.[21] We can be sure that Wang Wei, with connections at court, was aware of the major astronomical advances of his period and that he studied contemporary star maps for his astrological calculations. As noted above, in his study of medicinal herbs Wang Wei relied on the technical expertise of the *Bencao*. And as a diviner by yarrow stalks, he would have used the *Yi jing*, including the *Great Appendix*. Thus, in general, as with the adherents of the yin-yang school, his approach to nature may have been guided by its principles: "The *Changes* is a paradigm of Heaven and Earth ... and so it shows how one can fill in and pull together the Dao of Heaven and Earth. Looking up, we use it [the *Changes*] to observe the configurations of Heaven, and looking down, we use it to examine the patterns of the Earth." The relevant lines for astrology in this text are: "Heaven hung images in the sky and revealed good fortune and bad, and the sages regarded these as meaningful signs."[22] Although Wang Wei may well have consulted a variety of *Yi jing* commentaries, even those of the yin-yang school, we may assume that he knew Wang Bi's writing, and it seems plausible that his own essay style was influenced by Wang Bi's parallel prose.

As a practitioner in the hermeneutical tradition of literary criticism, Rudolf Wagner has come up with close readings and interpretations of Wang Bi's commentaries on the *Zhouyi* and the *Lao Zi* 老子. In Wagner's analysis, Wang Bi and other Xuanxue commentators read parts of the *Lao Zi* as written in interlocking parallel style (IPS) and structured their own essays in the same manner. "Their common interest in the ability of language to deal with ultimate things prompted their attention to the means of communication used in texts such as the *Lao Zi* and the *Zhouyi.*"[23] According to Wagner, Wang Bi sought to pin down the hidden meaning of the *Lao Zi* text through its own semantic strategy. In "open interlocking parallel prose" the second pair of four phrases offers specific illustrations of the first pair, and in each set, "as a rule, a relationship of complementary opposition prevails between the core notions of parallel pairs."[24] In "closed interlocking parallel style," there are no explicit links between pairs, but there may be two parallel strains of content running through and hence structuring a passage. Again, "as a rule, the two strains are designed as complementary opposites."[25] And in Wagner's interpretation, a reader or translator should "bring out the opposition between the two strains, not the similarity within the parallel pairs."[26] He provides structured text readings of passages and labels phrases alphabetically as "a *versus* b," etc. We should be able to deconstruct Wang Bi's *Yi jing* commentary in this manner to understand the logic of his rhetoric. Here is another look at the Lynn translation given above (which should ideally be set in two columns, left a and right b).

> That is why
> 1a if one examines things from the point of view of totality, even though things are multitudinous, one knows that it is possible to deal with them by holding fast to the One,
>
> 2b and if one views them from the point of view of the fundamental, even though the concepts involved are immense in number and scope, one knows that it is possible to cover them all with a single name.
>
> 3a Thus when we use an armillary sphere to view the great [heavenly] movements, the actions of Heaven and Earth lose their capacity to amaze us,
>
> 4b and if we keep to a single center point when viewing what is about to come to us, then things converging from the six directions lose their capacity to overwhelm us with their number.

Wagner's analysis emphasizes the complementary contrasts in the logic of parallel prose. He notes that Wang Bi's long essays were written in a "highly systematized" IPS that "became the standard form for philosophical writing" used in essays, prefaces, and commentaries up through the fifth century.[27] Hence it seems legitimate to attempt Wagner's type of analysis on Wang Wei's essay on painting. Moreover, Wang Wei's text was written for Yan Yanzhi, who favored Wang Bi's commentary on the *Yi jing* and who had discussed the hexagrams in connection with writing and painting.

As quoted in the *Lidai minghua ji,* Yan Yanzhi wrote:

> The word *tu* 圖 (chart or picture; to represent) contains three concepts. The first is *tu li* 圖理, the representation of principles, that is, the images of the hexagrams. The second is *tu shi* 圖識, the representation of meaning, that is, the art of writing. The third is *tu xing* 圖形, the representation of forms, that is, painting.[28]

Although painting is the last and least important of these arts in Yan's definition, it is nonetheless linked with more prestigious types of representation devised by the sages. Mark Lewis has stressed the importance of the *Xici* commentary in developing the idea that signs epitomized the patterns of natural processes as seen in the abstract *xiang* 象 (images), features of the terrestrial world, and their astral correspondents. He notes that this interpretation also underlies the theory that writing graphs were derived from simple patterns based on nature.[29] Hence pictorial depiction would "naturally" be understood as involving conceptualization. Wang Wei's own approach to painting is similar, as noted below in the conclusion and as seen in the initial section of the "Xu hua." The text that is given below (in English and Chinese) divides into three sections: introductory statements, the main arguments, and a lyrical conclusion.

Wang Wei's "Xu hua"

> I was honored by a letter from the Imperial Household Grandee Yan to the effect that drawing pictures does not end as mere craft, since when perfected it should be in the same category as the images of the *Yi jing.* Moreover, those who occupy themselves with seal and clerical scripts naturally consider skill in calligraphy to be preeminent. I should like to discuss painting on a par with them, exploring what they have in common.

Now, critics of painting merely look for physical appearance and configurations, and nothing else. Yet, when the ancients created paintings it was not in order to lay out the boundaries of cities or delimit regions and districts, mark dominating heights, or trace watercourses.

What is based in form is infused with *ling*, and what activates transformation is *xin*. *Ling* is invisible, hence what it is entrusted to does not move. Eyesight has its limits, hence what is seen is not the whole. Therefore, with one reed brush I simulate the embodiment of the Great Void, and with fragmentary shapes I paint the intelligence of inch-wide pupils. With sweeps I render the heights of Mount Song; with a dash I create the hermit's hut. With upswept lines I mark Mount Hua, and with slanting dots show the prominent nose. The brow, forehead, chin and jaw are as if in a peaceful smile. The lonely cliffs, luxuriant and flourishing, seem to spit forth clouds. Through horizontal changes and vertical transformations, movement is produced; by being angled in front and squared off in back, [??] is brought out. After this, palaces, towers, boats, and carriages are grouped according to their kinds, and dogs, horses, birds, and fishes are differentiated according to their shapes. This is the achievement of painting.

At the sight of autumn clouds, my spirit soars on high; in the midst of spring winds, my thoughts flow swiftly. Even if I had the music of bells and chimes or a treasure of ceremonial jades, how could they compare to this? I unroll a painting and examine its inscription. It represents strange mountains and seas, verdant forests tossed by wind, white waters leaping and foaming. Ah, how could this have been accomplished easily? It must have come about through divine inspiration. This is the true feeling of painting.

辱顏光祿書：以圖畫非止藝行，成當與易象同體，而工篆隸者，自以書巧為高。欲其並辯藻繪，覈其攸同。夫言繪畫者，竟求容勢而已。且古人之作畫也，非以案城域，辨方州，標鎮阜，劃浸流。本乎形者融靈，而動變者心也。靈亡所見，故所託不動；目有所極，故所見不周。於是乎以一管之筆，擬太虛之體；以判軀之狀，畫寸眸之明。曲以為嵩高，趣以為方丈。以友之畫，齊乎太華；枉之點，表夫龍準。眉額頰輔若晏笑兮；孤巖鬱秀，若吐雲兮。橫變縱化，故動生焉；前矩後方出焉。然後宮觀舟車，器以類聚；犬馬禽魚，物以狀分。此畫之致也。望秋雲神飛揚，臨春風思浩蕩；雖有金石之樂，珪璋之琛，豈能髣髴之哉！披圖按牒，效異山海。緣林揚風，白水激澗。嗚呼！豈獨運諸指掌，亦以明神降之。此畫之情也。

As the beginning two paragraphs make clear, Wang Wei argued in response to Yan that painting was a fine art that had the same conceptual function as the hexagrams and achieved its aim through the technique of calligraphy. He underlined his main point by attacking critics who focused on placement and likeness and stressed that earlier artists, unlike Xie Zhuang, had not indulged in map making for practical purposes.

The next section, which shifts into parallel prose, is primarily concerned with the relationship between the viewed and the viewer and with the technique of depiction. There are several versions of the introductory sentence, and it has also been variously punctuated and understood.[30] Conceivably modern scholars who prefer to end the first phrase before, rather than after, "*ling*" 靈 are following Zhu Xi 朱熹 (1131–1200) in associating "*ling*," here "vitality," with "*xin*" 心, here the "viewer's mind."[31] I propose the following translation since it sets up the two polarities essential to the dialectical rhetoric of the period: "What is based in *xing* 形 (form) is infused with *ling* (the numinous, or vital, principle), and what activates transformation is *xin* (heart-mind). *Ling* is invisible, hence what it is entrusted to does not move. Eyesight has its limits, hence what is seen is not the whole."[32] While this statement may be a general proposition applicable to all things in nature, it does establish a preliminary opposition between outer and inner. It also highlights the main focus of the essay on response, whether to nature or to art, and a universal responsiveness or connection must have been an underlying assumption on the part of the *Yi jing* diviner.[33]

The Wang Bi passage cited above was also concerned with viewing and used as an illustration the observation of the stars. Another conceivable link between this occupation and the essay on painting is Wang Wei's use of the term "*ling*," since "*ling*," "spirituality" or "animating principle," also occurs in astronomical contexts. It is the "*ling*" of the *lingtai* 靈臺, the palace observatory of the ancients, and of Zhang Heng's *Lingxian* 靈憲 (Spiritual Constitution of the Universe), in Needham's translation, that discusses the *linggui* 靈軌, or "sublime tracks ... (the path of the heavenly bodies)."[34] As an astrologer, Wang Wei was likely to have read Zhang Heng's writing, where "*ling*" refers to the mysterious workings of the universe. "*Ling*" also appears in the sense of "spiritual efficacy" in *Lao Zi* section 39: "the gods have their spiritual power by having obtained the One ... if the gods had not this means to have spiritual power, they would, we fear, terminate."[35] Of

course "*ling*" commonly occurs as a noun to label the Han sets of auspicious animals and as an adjective describing supernatural Daoist
wonders such as magical fungi, spirit diagrams, and revealed scriptures.
Wang Wei, however, was not primarily interested in these matters. He
does use "*ling*" in his writings in its specific meaning as "the deceased"
to refer to his brother's ghost.[36] In Mather's translation of Shen Yue's
postface to the biography of Xie Lingyun 謝靈運, "*ling*" is consistently
given as "life" or "life principle": "People are endowed at birth with the
life principle *(ling)* of Heaven and Earth."[37] Wang Wei may have had a
similar general usage in mind.

I would avoid translating "*ling*" as "soul" because that would seem
to equate it exclusively with "*shen*" 神, "spirit," a term that Wang did
not use. If "*ling*" is associated with wilderness or mountain scenery in
both Zong Bing's text and Wang Wei's essay, it is probably best to
translate it as "the numinous," a sinological designation that evokes a
mystical aesthetic experience.[38] This rendering of "*ling*" points to the
complementary opposition between mountain and man in the main
body of the text couched in parallel prose. Here is a translation of the
central section spaced out in Rudolf Wagner's manner to emphasize
two parallel strains of thought:

What is based in form is infused
  with *ling*,

and what activates transformation is
  xin.

Ling is invisible,
  hence what it is entrusted to does
    not move

Eyesight has its limits,
  hence what is seen is not the
    whole.

Therefore with one reed brush
  I simulate the embodiment of the
    Great Void,

and with fragmentary shapes
  I paint the intelligence of inch-
    wide pupils.

With sweeps I render the heights of
  Mount Song;

With upswept lines I mark Mount
    Hua,

                    with a dash I create the hermit's
                      hut.[39]

                    and with slanting dots show the
                      prominent nose.
                  The brow, forehead, chin and jaw
                      are as if in a peaceful smile.

The lonely cliffs, luxuriant and
    flourishing, seem to spit forth
        clouds.
Through horizontal changes and
    vertical transformations, move-
        ment is produced;

                  by being angled in front and
                      squared off in back, [??] is
                      brought out.

It is unclear what is brought out by angled three-dimensionality since parallelism indicates two missing characters as marked by lacunae above. Modern scholars have suggested either "*er ling*" 而靈 or "*ze xing*" 則形 as possibilities, "[and/then spirituality/form] is brought out."[40] Both "*ling*" and "*xing*" of course occur in the initial phrase above. "*Xing*," or "form," may seem like a more logical choice, but the main thrust of Wang Wei's essay is against defining painting as a mere depiction of forms. After all, Wang's essay was written to develop Yan Yanzhi's comment on the three concepts of the word "*tu*" (depiction), which stressed the hexagrams' representations of the principles. In any case, this problematic section ends with a sentence that includes different kinds of secondary subject matter. Architecture comes first because it holds important men, rulers in their palaces and officials in their carriages; then come the useful animals and lesser fauna listed for a full coverage.

After this,
    palaces, towers, boats, and
        carriages are grouped according
            to their kinds,

and dogs, horses, birds, and fishes
are differentiated according to
their shapes.

This is the achievement of painting.[41]

My assumption is that in the body of the text Wang Wei had in mind binary oppositions between outer and inner, viewed and viewer, and mountains and recluses. Hence, rather than anthropomorphizing mountains, the right-hand phrases apply to the process of viewing and to human observers who are always present in the art of the time. The essay would seem to deal with painting as a whole and list all contemporary categories. It is *xin*, the heart-mind, that will be stimulated to experience a painted landscape in the lyrical conclusion of the essay, but the human presence is a given throughout. Just as Heaven and Earth on the one side and man on the other form the chief polarities of the *Yi jing*, the intelligent observer is assumed in Wang Wei's discourse. In the act of viewing he discerns the fundamental patterns of nature and orders chaos, whether as an astrologer or herbalist or landscape painter. By using the calligrapher's skill, he imparts movement to curving forms and brings out the liveliness that will evoke a response in an audience of viewers, their experience of painting.

> At the sight of autumn clouds, my spirit soars on high; in the midst of
> spring winds, my thoughts flow swiftly. Even if I had the music of bells
> and chimes or a treasure of ceremonial jades, how could they compare to
> this? I unroll a painting and examine its inscription. It represents strange
> mountains and seas, verdant forests tossed by wind, white waters leaping
> and foaming. Ah, how could this have been accomplished easily? It must
> have come about through divine inspiration.[42] This is the true feeling of
> painting.

Here is a summary of the main points of the sections of Wang Wei's "Xu hua" as translated above. Painting is not merely a skill but produces conceptual representations of the universe somewhat comparable to the images of the *Yi jing*. As the chief repositories of spiritual influence, mountains are the most important subjects to be depicted. Still, they are seen through the eyes of men, humanized, as it were, by their associations with sages or recluses. Furthermore, it is the mind of the artist or viewer that transforms the experience of nature and recreates it.

The concluding section of the essay is generally read as a heartfelt appreciation of nature and of the artistic process that creates an effective painting, which in turn moves the viewer. However, for William Acker, the passage indicates that a painting cannot compete with the splendors of nature.[43] Hence some interpretation of the conclusion is in order here. Again the writing places Wang Wei in a literary tradition, that of energized landscape depiction as in the "Qin fu" 琴賦 (Fu on the Lute) by Ji Kang 嵇康 (223–262).[44] In this piece, spectacular scenery provides the material for the *qin*, whose overtones both reverberate with nature and purify the mind. Kenneth DeWoskin has argued that musical concepts were fundamental to Six Dynasties aesthetics. His comments on Ji Kang's theorizing are worth noting here: "There is an overriding order of which the performer's mind, the sound, and the listener's mind are part."[45] Music was also linked to painting, as it was to poetry. The Southern Qi poet Wang Rong praised Xie Zhuang for his recognition of the harmony of sounds, and Xie wrote on both painting and the lute. In old age Zong Bing played his *qin* in front of a painted landscape to create the effect of being in natural scenery. In his final decade or so Wang Wei devoted himself to study without leaving his house, presumably because of his ill health. Thus he was obviously not a vigorous mountain climber like Zong Bing. For Wang, painting seems to have become an outlet for the shut-in recluse; hence perhaps the intensity of his imaginative projection in the concluding passage. Was the vibrant natural energy that he articulated above in the essay his conception of *ling*? Was it captured in the cadences of his response to painting? Somehow in a very simple way this passage moves us to empathy. It shows us how we should all view paintings, with the sage-like heart-mind of those Wangs who expressed their feelings openly.

Wang Wei writes of his own accomplishment in painting as a natural process in a letter to his friend He Yan. It is quoted here to reinforce the lyrical conclusion of the "Xu hua": "By disposition I understand the accomplishment of painting just as honking snow-geese have the ability to fathom the night. What is coiled and twisted in disorder must be recorded by mind and eye. Having thus combined all the beauties of landscape, when I seek them out on the spur of the moment, everything catches a likeness."[46] His description of landscape as "coiled and twisted" may bring to mind Daoist diagrams *(tu)* of "true forms" of mountains or the hidden meanders of geomancers' spirit pathways to tombs. Still he is aware that if a likeness of natural scenery emerges in his painting, it is because his mind has instinctively processed a variety of impressions, thus combining and ordering striking views. It would seem that, as in the case of the *Yi jing* images, painting for him is a manmade product that reproduces and is in turn produced by the workings of nature.

NOTES

1. Susan Bush, "Tsung Ping's Essay on Painting and the 'Landscape Buddhism' of Mount Lu," in *Theories of the Arts in China*, ed. Susan Bush and Christian Murck (Princeton, N.J.: Princeton University Press, 1983), pp. 132–164. For the label of "landscape Taoism," see William Theodore de Bary et al., *Sources of Chinese Tradition* (New York: Columbia University Press, 1960), pp. 292–293. The Zong Bing and Wang Wei texts are published together in Chen Chuanxi 陳傳席, *Hua shanshui xu* 畫山水序 (Beijing: Renmin meishu chubanshe, 1985). I am indebted to Liu Heping for this reference and for the Wang Wei bibliography in Xie Wei 謝巍, *Zhongguo huaxue zhuzuo kaolu* 中國畫學著作考錄 (Shanghai: Shanghai shuhua chubanshe, 1998), p. 23. I would like to express my appreciation to Horst and Louisa Huber for their helpful comments and suggestions.

2. For Huiyuan's Buddhist and Chinese learning, which included Daoist texts, see Erik Zürcher, *The Buddhist Conquest of China*, 2 vols. (Leiden: E. J. Brill, 1959), vol. 1, pp. 207–208, 209–219, 230–231, 239.

3. Michael Sullivan, *The Birth of Landscape Painting in China* (Berkeley: University of California Press, 1962), p. 105. For English translations of the *Xu hua*, see Shio Sakanishi, *The Spirit of the Brush*, 4th ed. (London: John Murray, 1957), pp. 42–45; Osvald Sirén, *The Chinese on the Art of Painting,* reprint 1936 (2d.) ed. (Hong Kong: Hong Kong University Press, 1963), pp. 17–18; William R. B. Acker, trans., *Some T'ang and Pre-T'ang Texts on Chinese Painting*, 2 vols. (Leiden: E. J. Brill, 1954 and 1974), vol. 2, pp. 130–131; Susan Bush and Hsio-yen Shih, eds., *Early Chinese Texts on Painting* (Cambridge, Mass.: Harvard University Press, 1985), pp. 38–39.

4. Zürcher, *Buddhist Conquest,* pp. 86, 94–97, 104, 119, 132, 155–156, 213–214. For painters in the Wang family, see Acker, *Texts*, vol. 2, pp. 37–42, 129–137.

5. See Nakamura Shigeo 中村茂夫, *Chugoku garon no tenkai* 中國畫論の展開 (The Development of Chinese Painting Theory) (Kyoto: Nakayama bunkado,

1965), pp. 81–88; note the family geneology on p. 82. Also see Richard B. Mather, *The Poet Shen Yueh (441–513): The Reticent Marquis* (Princeton, N.J.: Princeton University Press, 1988), pp. 37–39. The ancestral Wang Rong was one of the so-called Seven Sages of the Bamboo Grove. For his excessive mourning for his mother and a son, see Richard B. Mather, trans., *Shih-shuo Hsin-yü: A New Account of Tales of the World* (Minneapolis: University of Minnesota Press, 1976), pp. 10–11, 12, 324.

6. This incident, recorded in Xie Zhuang's biography and Wei's letter to Wang Sengchuo, has led editors to correct the misprints in Wei's *Song shu* biography, where his dates were given incorrectly as equivalent to 415–443. See Shen Yue, *Song shu* (Beijing: Dingwen shuju, 1998), 62:1666, 1672; 85:2167.

7. See Acker, *Texts*, vol. 2, pp. 137–138.

8. *Song shu,* 62:1666–1668, 1672.

9. See Erwin von Zach, trans., *Die Chinesische Anthologie,* 2 vols. (Cambridge, Mass.: Harvard University Press, 1958), vol. 1, pp. 601–603. In the *Shi pin* 詩品 (Classification of Poets), Zhong Rong 鍾嶸 (ca. 469–518) judged both poets to be weak and superficial but praised Wang Wei's verse on the wind and moon and noted that Jiang Yan's poetic strength came from Wei. According to Zhong, Wei's literary criticism in *Hongbao* 宏寶 (Vast Treasure) is "tightly constructed but withholds judgments"; see J. T. Wixted, "The Literary Criticism of Yuan Hao-wen (1190–1257)," 2 vols. (D. Phil. thesis, University of Oxford, 1967), vol. 2, appendix A, pp. 9, 11, 23, 25.

10. The disease or diseases may have been measles or smallpox; sometimes they were thought to be caused by internal demons. See William H. McNeill, *Plagues and People* (New York: Anchor Press/Doubleday, 1976), pp. 86–88, 132–137, 140, 295; Léon Wieger, *Textes historiques,* 2 vols. (Paris: Librairie Orientale et Americaine, n.d.), vol. 2, pp. 1339, 1342.

11. For Wang Sengchuo's biography as one of the four loyal officials, see *Song shu,* 71:1850–1852.

12. See Ann Paludan, *The Chinese Spirit Road: The Classical Tradition of Stone Tomb Statuary* (New Haven: Yale University Press, 1991), pp. 59–62. Paludan cites an article by Luo Zongzhen 羅宗真, "Nan Chao Song Wendi ling he Chen Wendi ling kao" 南朝宋文帝陵和陳文帝陵考 (An Investigation into the Tombs of Song Wendi and Chen Wendi of the Southern Dynasties), Nanjing Museum Publications (July 1984), pp. 77–80. Note that a later fifth-century date has been suggested for the Nanjing tomb at Hsi-shan-chiao, with the molded brick mural of "Seven Sages of the Bamboo Grove" usually labeled late Eastern Chin. See Sofukawa Hiroshi 曾布川寬, "Nancho teiyo no sekiju to senga" 南朝帝陵の石獸と磚畫 (Stone Animals and Tile Reliefs of the Southern Dynasties), *Toho Gakuho* 東方學報 63 (1991), pp. 225–239.

13. See *Song shu,* 62:1665–1672; Li Yanshou 李延壽, *Nan shi* 南史 (History of the Southern Dynasties) (Beijing: Dingwen shuju, 1998), vol. 21, pp. 578–579.

14. See Joseph Needham et al., *Science and Civilization in China*, vol. 2: *History of Scientific Thought* (Cambridge: Cambridge University Press, 1956), pp. 132, 136; vol. 3: *Mathematics and the Sciences of the Heavens and the Earth* (1959), pp. 595, 605, 606, 617, 621, 643–644, 648; vol. 6, pt. 1: Botany (1986), pp. 231–248.

15. *Nan shi*, 21:579; *Song shu*, 62:1669.

16. Rudolf G. Wagner, *The Craft of a Chinese Commentator: Wang Bi on the Laozi* (Albany: State University of New York Press, 2000), pp. 21, 49–50.

17. Mather, *Shen Yueh*, p. 45.

18. Needham et al., vol. 2, p. 433.

19. Richard John Lynn, trans., *The Classic of Changes: A New Translation of the I Ching as Interpreted by Wang Bi* (New York: Columbia University Press, 1994), p. 17. For extensive coverage of Wang Bi's thought in commentaries on Daoist classics, see Shuen-fu Lin's essay in this volume.

20. Lynn, *The Classic of Changes,* pp. 25–26. Note that according to Needham, the Mohists worked with pinhole and camera obscura to observe rays of reflected light coming from an object and forming an inverted image. Their interpretation of this event differed from "the Greek theory of the emission of rays from the eye in vision." See Needham et al., *Science and Civilization*, vol. 4, pt. 1: Physics (1962), p. 82.

21. Needham et al., vol. 3, pp. 264, 359, 384–385; plates xxiv, xxv.

22. Lynn, *Changes*, pp. 51, 66.

23. Wagner, *Wang Bi*, p. 113. Since these texts were thought to use a "paraverbal means of articulation" and Wang Bi held that words could not fully express ideas, one wonders whether it would be possible to substitute "inability" for "ability" in the last sentence.

24. Ibid., p. 63.

25. Ibid., p. 95.

26. Ibid., p. 82.

27. See Ibid., pp. 55, 106, 110–111.

28. *Lidai minghua ji*, I.1. See Acker, *Texts*, vol. 1, pp. 65–66.

29. See Mark Edward Lewis, *Writing and Authority in Early China* (Albany: State University of New York Press, 1999), p. 285.

30. For a discussion of paragraphing and punctuating in the Wang Wei essay, see Susan Bush, "Two Fifth-Century Texts on Landscape and the 'Landscape Buddhism' of Mount Lu," paper written for ACLS-sponsored conference on "Theories of the Arts in China," 1979. For the text used with a different punctuation of the phrase in question, see Yu Jianhua 俞劍華, comp., *Zhongguo hualun leibian* 中國畫論類編 (Chinese Painting Theory by Categories) (Beijing: Zhongguo Gudian Yishu, 1957), p. 585.

31. It is interesting to note that *"ling"* continues to be used in discussions of consciousness by Zhu Xi. But while Zhu Xi's phrases focus in on the activi-

ties of the heart-mind, Wang Wei's text is primarily concerned with the rela-tionship between the viewer and the viewed. See Needham et al., vol. 2, pp. 482, 488.

32. A variant version of the second and third phrases is 而動者變心，止靈 亡見. Here I use the *Peiwenzhai shuhuapu* 佩文齋書畫譜 version of the text as given above initially and punctuate with a comma after the first "*ling.*" For a comma placed before "*xin*" (heart-mind) to indicate that all activity takes place there, see Chen, *Hua shanshui xu*, pp. 3–4. Most English translations have pre-ferred to end the first phrase after "*ling,*" for which one early authority is Kim-bara Seigo 金原省吾, *Shina jodai garon kenkyu* 支那上代畫論研究 (A Study of Ancient Chinese Painting Theory) (Tokyo: Iwanami, 1924), p. 187; see also Acker, *Texts,* vol. 2, p. 132, n. 9.

33. See Lynn, *Changes,* pp. 9, 18.

34. Needham et al., vol. 2, pp. 556–557.

35. Richard John Lynn, trans., *The Classic of the Way and Virtue: A New Translation of the Tao-te-ching of Laozi as Interpreted by Wang Bi* (New York: Columbia University Press, 1999), p. 128. In the true Confucian commentary tradition, the Wang Bi gloss avoids any interpretation of these phrases on the spirits.

36. *Song shu,* 62:16670, 1671, 1672.

37. Mather, *Shen Yueh,* p. 40; *Song shu,* 67.

38. Note the treatments of "*ling*" in essays by Zong-qi Cai and Ronald Egan in this volume.

39. The "Great Void" has, of course, a metaphysical significance in Dao-ism, but it could also simply indicate the sky in sixth-century poetry. Mounts Song and Hua (known as Taihua) are two of the Five Sacred Peaks, and "*fangzhang*" 方丈 may refer to one of the three legendary Isles of the Immor-tals. However, here it is taken in its literal sense of "ten-yards square" as refer-ring to the hut of an ascetic or Buddhist monastic, or by extension to that of the famous Buddhist layman Vimalakirti. "*Fu*" or "*bo*" [友] (the appearance of a dog running) is usually construed with a hand radical as *ba* 拔 to pull upward (see Acker, *Texts,* vol. 2, p. 133, n. 16). Commentators diverge in their inter-pretations of this section since some, like Yu Jianhua, would have all the phrases describe mountains, whereas others, like Nakamura Shigeo, would have the phrases apply to mountains and to men alternatively, as in the transla-tion above.

40. For a recent interpretation that prefers "*xing,*" see Chen Chuanxi, comp., *Liuchao huajia shiliao* 六朝畫家史料 (Beijing: Wenwu chubanshe, 1985), pp. 176–181.

41. Two phrases in the next to last sentence are based directly on the statement near the beginning of the *Great Appendix:* "[Affairs] are arranged together according to their tendencies and things are divided according to their

classes" (Z. D. Sung, *The Text of Yi King* [New York: Paragon Book Reprints, 1969], p. 271). By implication the same conceptual ordering is evident in painting as in hexagrams. In the preceding sentence, the "horizontal changes and vertical transformations," presumably brought about by brushwork, may also recall the alterations of whole and divided lines from hexagram to hexagram that stand for temporal changes in the universe and thus capture movement.

42. Some commentators underline "*shanhai*" 山海, taking it to refer to the *Shanhai jing* 山海經 (The Classic of Mountains and Seas). "*Yun zhu zhi zhang*" 運諸指掌 has been translated as "have come about easily." "*Zhi zhang*" 指掌, "pointing to the palm," is interpreted as "easily understood/done" in *Analects*, 3/11. The second meaning parallels that of a phrase in Mencius, 1/1/7/12, "*yun yu zhang*" 運於掌, literally "to turn over on the palm." See James Legge, *The Confucian Classics* (Hong Kong: Hong Kong University Press, 1960), vol. 1, p. 159; vol. 2, p. 143. Both references seem to have been compressed in Wang's phrase. In the next phrase, "*mingshen jiang*" 明神降 might be translated as "the descending of intelligent spirits." The reference here is to *jiang shen* 降神, the spirits that were sent down from mountains to give birth to the ancestors of the Zhou dynasty; see ibid., vol. 4, p. 535 (line 3 in Ode 259, "*Song gao* 嵩高" in the *Shi jing* 詩經 [The Book of Odes]). This line is elaborated at the beginning of *Zhuang Zi* 莊子 33 as "whence does the spiritual in it come down? and whence does the intelligence in it come forth? There is that which gives birth to the Sage" (James Legge, *The Sacred Books of China: The Texts of Taoism* [New York: Dover, 1962], vol. 2, p. 214). In Wang Wei's usage the phrase would seem to imply the effective presence of the spirits of nature as conceived by the mind of the artist/viewer.

43. See Acker's annotated translation, *Texts,* vol. 2, pp. 129–137.

44. Note the introductory passage cited in J. D. Frodsham, "The Origins of Chinese Nature Poetry," *Asia Major* (1960–1961), n. s. 8, p. 77.

45. Kenneth J. DeWoskin, "Early Chinese Music and the Origins of Aesthetic Terminology," in Bush and Murck, eds., *Theories of the Arts in China,* p. 208.

46. *Song shu,* 62:1669; compare Sakanishi, *Spirit,* p. 41; Alexander C. Soper, "Early Chinese Landscape Painting," *Art Bulletin* 23 (1941), p. 164.

Chapter 3

Xie He's "Six Laws" of Painting and Their Indian Parallels

Victor H. Mair

> *The "Six Laws" [sic] of India and the "Six Laws" of Xie He are actually two unrelated theories.*
> —Jin Ronghua (1984)

> *I feel in my bones that Xie He's "Six Laws" come from India.*
> —Tsu-Lin Mei (ca. 1990)

There is universal agreement that Xie He's 謝赫 "Liu fa" 六法 (Six Laws) constitute the first systematic exposition of painting theory in China.[1] Toward the end of the Tang dynasty, the great art critic and historian Zhang Yanyuan 張彥遠 (ca. 810–880), in his enormously influential *Lidai minghua ji* 歷代名畫記 (A Record of the Famous Painters of Successive Dynasties, ca. 847) makes the Six Laws the centerpiece of his discussion of painting criticism. During the Five Dynasties, Jing Hao 荊浩 (ca. 870–ca. 930) elaborated upon the Six Laws in his "Liu yao" 六要 (Six Essentials). Guo Ruoxu 郭若虛 (eleventh century), begins the chapter entitled "Lun qiyun fei shi" 論氣韻非師 (On Vital Resonance Not Being Teachable) of his *Tuhua jianwen zhi* 圖畫見聞志 (A Record of Things Seen and Heard about Painting) with the seemingly obligatory recitation of the Six Laws. The Song landscape painter Song Zifang 宋子房 was inspired by Xie He's Six Laws to write his own "Liu fa" (Six Laws) and "Liu lun" 六論 (Six Discussions). Also in the Song period, Liu Daochun 劉道醇 (the eleventh-century painting critic) brought out another "Liu yao" (Six Essentials) and a "Liu chang" 六長 (Six Strengths), while a work under the latter title was also issued by the Qing critic Sheng Dashi 盛 大士. During the Yuan dynasty Xia Wenyan 夏文彥 begins his *Tuhui baojian* 圖繪寶鑒 (The Precious Mirror of Painting) with the words "Xie He says" and then commences immediately with the enumeration of the Six Laws. The editors of the *Qinding siku quanshu zongmu tiyao* 欽 定四庫全書總目提要 (Essentials of the General Catalog for the Imperially Commissioned Comprehensive Library in Four Divisions; completed 1781, published 1789), 112, while recognizing that nothing is known of Xie He as a person, close their notice on his *[Gu]hua pinlu* 古 畫品錄 (A Record of the Rankings of [Ancient] Painters) by stating that his book is the arbiter for discussions about painting and that the Six Laws from its preface constitute the millennial, immutable standard up to their own day. The term *liufa* was so ubiquitous in later discussions of Chinese art that right through the twentieth century it could be used to signify "painting."[2] Indeed, it would probably not be exaggerating to say, as more than one scholar has put it, that there has been an obsession with Xie He's Six Laws in the evolution of Chinese painting.

Contrasting sharply with the unanimity of opinion that the Six Laws are the fountainhead of all later Chinese art theory and criticism is the virtually universal disagreement concerning two essential matters relating to the terse formulations of Xie He: (1) how to read and understand them, and (2) whether they were based on Indian models. Through a close examination of the relevant texts, this study reveals that the solution to these two problems lies in the realization that they are tightly interwoven. The Six Laws are extremely difficult, almost impossible, to comprehend without taking into account their Indian background. Conversely, once one reads the Six Laws correctly, the one-for-one Indian influence upon them becomes obvious.

We must begin by admitting that we know next to nothing about Xie He, the formulator of the Six Laws. Biographical information concerning the father of Chinese painting theory is virtually nonexistent.[3] Xie He was himself apparently a fashionable court portrait painter of considerable skill but by no means a distinguished artist.[4] Fortunately, there is sufficient internal evidence concerning Xie He's *[Gu]hua pinlu*, in the preface to which the Six Laws appear, enabling scholars to form a broad scholarly consensus that it may be dated to between the years 532 and 549.[5] Given this dire poverty of hard facts about Xie He, it is clear that we cannot rely upon biographical information concerning him to help us solve the thorny problems surrounding his Six Laws. Instead, we will have to concentrate on the philological analysis of the Six Laws and of their Indian counterparts.

Before we embark on our philological quest, it is necessary to observe that the scholarship on the forty-two characters of the terse Six Laws (only twenty-four of which convey substantial meaning) is disproportionately large.[6] On no other subject has so much been said about so little. Considering the Six Laws' seminal importance for the entire history of painting theory and criticism in China, however, this is by no means surprising. In order to proceed as efficiently as possible, we shall not review the host of different opinions concerning the Six Laws. Instead, we shall turn directly to a philological examination of the laws themselves.

Parsing and Punctuating the Six Laws

In their raw form, with Modern Standard Mandarin transcriptions and crude word-for-word English translations, the Six Laws of Xie He are as follows:

N	R		S		D	C
一	氣	韻	生	動	是	也
yi	*qi*	*yun*	*sheng*	*dong*	*shi*	*ye*
one	breath	euphony	be born	move	this	(is)
二	骨	法	用	筆	是	也
er	*gu*	*fa*	*yong*	*bi*	*shi*	*ye*
two	bone	law	use	brush	this	(is)
三	應	物	象	形	是	也
san	*ying*	*wu*	*xiang*	*xing*	*shi*	*ye*
three	(cor)respond	thing	image	form	this	(is)

Continued on next page

Six Laws of Xie He, continued

N	R		S		D	C
四	隨	類	賦	彩	是	也
si	*sui*	*lei*	*fu*	*cai*	*shi*	*ye*
four	follow	type	spread	color	this	(is)
五	經	營	位	置	是	也
wu	*jing*	*ying*	*wei*	*zhi*	*shi*	*ye*
five	manage	administer	position	place	this	(is)
六	傳	移	模	寫	是	也
liu	*chuan*	*yi*	*mo*	*xie*	*shi*	*ye*
six	transmit	transfer	model	depict	this	(is)

The first time that I encountered these Six Laws, my immediate reaction was that they were simply unreadable. In dealing with early Chinese texts, one often encounters awkward formulations, but Xie He's Six Laws are among the most refractory forty-two characters in all of Chinese literature.

For the purpose of our grammatical analysis, let us refer to the components of each of the Six Laws as follows: N = the number that occurs in the initial position; R = the first of the two binomial members constituting the core of the law; S = the second of the two binomial members constituting the core of the law; D = the demonstrative pronoun *shi* ("this"); C = the loose copulative or judgmental particle *ye* at the end of the sentence. Thus each law consists of the following terms or components: NRSDC. (The choice of R and S as mnemonics for the first and second members of the quadrinomial core of each law will be explained below.) The problem confronting the reader of the Six Laws is how to parse their elements in such a fashion that they yield sense. If we strictly adhere to the first order analysis of the grammar as it is presented to us by Xie He, we are compelled to interpret each law as follows: N this is RS (where RS may be R+S, R by means of S, R resulting in S, etc.). Such a formulation, on the very face of it, would be rather ridiculous, for it would have Xie He saying something like N = RS! In other words, it would not make very much sense for Xie He to define a number with two linked binomials, much less to do so emphatically.

While the core quadrinomials of each law present their own difficulties (viz., determining the precise semantic content of their rarefied terms and the exact syntactic relationship between their constituent binomials), the primary hurdles that must be surmounted in coping with the very structure of the laws are N and D C. Let us first examine N.

Although the Chinese did have many numbered groupings (e.g., *shi guo* 十過 [ten errors], *shi yi* 十義 [ten moral obligations], *wu chang* 五常 [five constancies], *wu xing* 五行 [five phases; five forms of behavior], *wu biao* 五標 [five markers], *wu du* 五毒 [five vermin], *wu lun* 五倫 [five human relations], and so forth), it was rare in pre-Buddhist times to list sequentially the individual items of such groupings with bulleted numbers in front of each one, especially if they were expressed in whole sentences and not merely individual words.[7] In contrast, numbered lists are extremely common in India. The relative scarcity of numbered lists in early Chinese texts may help to account for Xie He's awkwardness in constructing his Six Laws.

The unfamiliarity of Chinese authors in dealing with numbered lists from India is borne out by their experience with *geyi* 格義 (matching concepts). While modern scholarship has overemphasized the role of *geyi* in the introduction of Buddhism to China far beyond what the available historical data concerning it will allow, a more nuanced examination of that which is actually known about it from contemporary texts is illuminating for our present investigation. Ostensibly, the purpose of *geyi* was for elucidating Buddhist terminology with the help of notions extracted from traditional Chinese thought. It is telling that *geyi* referred especially to numerical categories. Huijiao's 慧皎 (497–554) biography of Zhu Faya 竺法雅 in *Gaoseng zhuan* 高僧傳 (Biographies of Eminent Monks)[8] specifically mentions the notion of *shishu* 事數 (enumeration of items) in connection with *geyi*.[9] Buddhist authors were exceedingly fond of enumerating items relating to often abstruse doctrines, a practice that was challenging to Chinese readers and exegetes. This is vividly brought out in a passage from the fourth chapter, "Wen xue" 文學 (Letters and Scholarship), of *Shishuo xinyu* 世說新語 (New Tales of the World) by Liu Yiqing 劉義慶 (403–444):

> When Yin Hao 殷浩 (306–356) was dismissed and transferred to Dunyang he read a large number of Buddhist sutras, gaining a detailed understanding of them all. It was only when he came to places where items were enumerated (*shishu*) that he did not understand. Whenever he chanced to see a monk he would ask about the items he had noted down, and then they would become clear.[10]

Liu Jun 劉峻 (462–521), in his commentary to this passage, cites several examples of *shishu*: the five personality-components (*wu yin* 五陰, *pañcaskandha*), the twelve entrances (*shier ru* 十二入, *dvādaśāyatana*), the Four Truths (*si di* 四諦, *catvāri ārya-satyāni*), the twelvefold cycle of dependent origination (*shier yinyuan* 十二因緣, *dvādaśāṅga pratītya-samutpāda*), the five sense-organs (*wu gen* 五根, *pañcendriyāṇi*), the five powers (*wu li* 五力, *pañcabalāni*), the seven degrees of enlightenment (*qi jue* 七覺, *saptabodhyaṅga*), etc. The word *shishu* that Liu Jun is annotating here is a Buddhist technical term indicating the enumeration of affairs, matters, things. It is also referred to as *mingshu* 名數 (enumeration of terms) and *fashu* 法數 (enumeration of dharmas).[11] Many Buddhist texts are largely or almost entirely organized around numbered lists. On the one hand, these seemingly countless numerical schematizations proved extraordinarily troublesome to Chinese who were unaccustomed to them. Yet, on the other hand, various commentators have pointed out that this is one of the major Buddhist contributions to Chinese methods of analysis.[12] Once they became used to it, this manner of explaining Buddhist (and other) ideas was favored particularly by laymen in China, so it is not unexpected that Xie He might have tried his hand at it, even if he had not thoroughly mastered the technique.

Now let us turn to an examination of *shi ye*. The combination *shi ye* is to be found neither in dictionaries of particles nor in comprehensive lexicons with the presumed meaning it has in the Six Laws. Indeed, elsewhere it is uncommon to find *shi ye* occupying the final position at all, especially in sentences that begin with a number. In Sanskrit, however, it is perfectly acceptable to have sentences that end with *eso 'sti* ("this is").

Probably because he could not comprehend the Six Laws as they were originally stated by Xie He, Zhang Yanyuan rewrote them as follows in his *Lidai minghua ji*:

N	Q	R		S	
一	曰	氣	韻	生	動
yi	*yue*	*qi*	*yun*	*sheng*	*dong*
one	is called	breath	euphony	be born	move
二	曰	骨	法	用	筆
er	*yue*	*gu*	*fa*	*yong*	*bi*
two	is called	bone	law	use	brush

Six Laws by Zhang Yanyuan, continued

N	Q	R		S	
三 *san* three	曰 *yue* is called	應 *ying* (cor)respond	物 *wu* thing	象 *xiang* image	形 *xing* form
四 *si* four	曰 *yue* is called	隨 *sui* follow	類 *lei* type	賦 *fu* spread	彩 *cai* color
五 *wu* five	曰 *yue* is called	經 *jing* manage	營 *ying* administer	位 *wei* position	置 *zhi* place
六 *liu* six	曰 *yue* is called	傳 *chuan* transmit	模 *mo* model	移 *yi* transfer	寫 *xie* depict

Rewritten in this fashion, the Six Laws are relatively easy to read, if not to understand. As a result, virtually all commentators on the Six Laws after Zhang Yanyuan (mis)read them as he did. For our grammatical analysis of the Zhangian reading, we may now add Q = quotational particle. Hence, for each of the Six Laws as rewritten by Zhang Yanyuan, we have N Q R S, which may be interpreted as follows: N (i.e., the N [where N is an ordinal] law) may be stated as R S (where R S may be R + S, R by means of S, R resulting in S, etc.). Reformulated in this manner, while still challenging to the aesthetic exegete, the Six Laws no longer present the formidable obstacles of Xie He's original wording.

If Xie He had formulated each of his laws as N Q R S D C, they would have been much easier to understand: e.g., "The first is (called) R, that is [defined by] S"; and so forth. As a matter of fact, Liu Xie 劉 勰 (ca. 465–ca. 521), in the "Qing cai" 情采 (Aspiration and Embellishment) chapter (the thirty-first) of his *Wenxin diaolong* 文心雕龍 (The Literary Mind and Ornate Rhetoric), which was written not long before Xie He's *[Gu]hua pinlu,* has a numbered list of three sentences where the R binomials (textual form, textual voice, textual mood) are explained by the following S binomials: five colors, five sounds, five emotions (not individually enumerated). That is to say, Liu Xie's three sentences are constructed as N Q R S D C. The addition of the quotative particle after the numeral compels the practiced reader to parse the remaining segment correctly as R, S D C. Zhang Yanyuan must have been following some such instinct when he rewrote the Six Laws in the form N Q R S. Unfortunately, by omitting D C at the end, he unwittingly made it inevitable that readers would take R S as a single unit, thus destroying Xie He's original wording. The awkward grammar of Xie He's N R S D C must have thrown Zhang off his stride, since, in section one of the first chapter of *Lidai minghua ji*,[13] where he is discussing the multiple meanings of the word *tu* 圖 (drawing, chart), he three times in succession uses the identical formulation of Liu Xie, viz., N Q R S D C—and few would be apt to misread him here. The acceptability of N Q R S D C is reinforced by its exact recurrence in an essay on calligraphy, "Si ti shu shi" 四體書勢 (The Configuration of the Four Forms of Writing), by the Jin writer Wei Heng 衛恆 (?–291) that is quoted in his *Jin shu* 晉書 (History of the Jin), scroll 36 biography. Wei Heng is enumerating and defining the six different types of Chinese characters (*liu yi* 六義): "The first is called indicative; [the graphs for] 'above' (*shang*) and 'below' (*xia*) are such" (一曰指事上下是也). And so forth. The full complement of N Q R S D C results in a pronounced pause between R and S, such that it is entirely appropriate to mark it with a semicolon or even a period in the English translation. What is most curious (and telling) about Wei Heng's enumeration of the six different types of characters is that he has actually greatly compressed them from their original form in the "Postface" to the *Shuo wen jie zi* 説文解字 (Explanations of Simple and Compound Graphs), by Xu Shen 許慎 (fl. 100–121).[14] Xu Shen's formulation of the six different types of characters was N Q T T P E1 E2 G D C, where T is the binomial term to be defined, P is the nominalizing particle *zhe*, E1 and E2 are quadrinomials that define or explain T, and G is a binomial consisting of two example graphs of the type being defined. Hence, "The first is called 'indicative.' An indicative [is the type of character that] may be understood when seen, may be grasped when inspected. Such are [the graphs for] 'above' and 'below'" (一曰指事指事者視而可識察而可見上下是也). In Xu Shen's original, it is immediately obvious that the full formulation must be broken down into three main syntactic units, viz., N Q T_o T P E1 $E2_o$ G D C_o. Wei Heng's version, N Q R S D C, may be viewed as abbreviated thus: N Q T_o T̶ ̶P̶ ̶E̶1̶ ̶E̶2̶$_o$ G D C_o, i.e., N Q T_o G D C_o, with T and G being more semantically accurate designators for the central binomials in this particular case than R and S, but playing an identical structural role. Therefore, we have shown that Wei Heng's and Liu Xie's N Q R S D C must be parsed as N Q R_0 S D C. Similarly, although less obviously, Xie He's N R S D C should be parsed as N R_0 S D C.

Later in his essay, Wei Heng enumerates the six different styles of writing Chinese characters (*liu shu* 六書): "The first is the archaic script; [it] is the writing [that was preserved] in the wall of Confucius's house" (一曰古文孔氏壁中書也). While the structure of the E members of his formulations varies dramatically (including relative markers, conjunctions, and other types of grammatical particles) and is too complicated to discuss in detail here, the other members remain constant, viz., N Q T E C. Note that Wei Heng here omits D, probably because his E are relatively long and complex, varying from three to six characters in length. As a matter of fact, Wei Heng has also borrowed his enumerations and explanations of the *liu shu* wholesale from Xu Shen's "Postface," albeit with mistakes and changes. In Xu Shen's original formulation of the *liu shu*, the E members vary even more dramatically than they do in Wei Heng's version, ranging in length from four to fifteen (!) characters and with still more complicated internal grammar. Xu Shen once (at the end of his fourth item) omits C, perhaps through sloppiness, but this seems to indicate that when N Q are present, the C is not really necessary, as is borne out by Zhang Yanyuan's rewriting of Xie He's N R S D C as N Q R S. In any event, it is altogether natural not to have D after N Q and, since Q possesses equational qualities of its own, there is a tendency to omit final C when it is present.[15]

Still more transparent than N Q R S D C is R′ Q S′ C ("R′ is [called] S′," where R′ is a monomial and S′ is either a monomial or a binomial). This exact formulation was, in fact, used twelve times in succession by Xiao Yan 蕭衍 (464–549), a close contemporary of Xie He, at the beginning of his "Guan Zhong You shufa shier yi" 觀鍾繇書法十二意 (Twelve Thoughts on Observing the Calligraphy of Zhong You): "Level is [called] horizontal; upright is [called] vertical" (平謂橫也，直謂縱也).[16]

Another of Xie He's many successors and imitators, Liu Daochun, who was mentioned at the outset, revised the Six Laws even more radically in his "Six Essentials" than Zhang Yanyuan had in his *Lidai minghua ji*: "The first is called vital resonance and / or combined strength (alternatively: combined strength through vital resonance; vital resonance combined with strength; [instilling] vital resonance by combining strength; etc.)" (氣韻兼力一也). Liu Daochun has restructured

Xie He's N R S D C as R S N C. Bringing N next to C and omitting both D and Zhang Yanyuan's Q tightens up the syntax considerably, despite the slight oddness of equating R S so emphatically with N.

Such have been the grammatical and syntactical vicissitudes of Xie He's Six Laws during the last millennium and more. It appears that few, if any, of Xie He's successors were satisfied with what he himself had written. Zhang Yanyuan's reformulation as N Q R S, despite its manifest deficiencies, was deceptively easy to read, and it seems to have captured the imagination of art critics, both in China and abroad. Consequently, this is how art historians, theorists, and critics read them for the next twelve hundred years and more. Regrettably, aside from its being patently unfair to rewrite the words of someone who has been dead for centuries (or even the words of someone who is still alive), Zhang Yanyuan's interpretation constitutes a gross misreading of the Six Laws.

Given that Xie He would not intentionally have penned some such nonsense as "N this is R S" for the primary exposition of the aesthetic tenets of painting, he must have meant for his laws to be read differently than the strictest application of grammar would require. Relaxing our grammatical constraints somewhat, we may posit that Xie He looked upon the N members of his laws as indexical tags and that he did not think of them as entering into the grammar of the laws themselves. Hence, (N) R S D C. While R S D C by itself is still slightly unwieldy, it is completely within the realm of grammatical possibility. Naturally, if one insists on treating R S as a tightly bound quadrinomial, R S D C remains nonsensical, because that would be tantamount to saying "this is R S" or "R S is this." Once we insert a syntactical pause between R and S, however, Xie He's laws become instantly intelligible, viz.: R, S D C ("R this is S"). That is to say, R is / means S or R is defined by / as S. As we shall see below, there were sufficiently compelling psychological and linguistic grounds for Xie to adopt such a cumbersome mode for the declaration of his Six Laws. Xie's reasons for choosing inelegant phraseology to launch the aesthetics of painting in China may have been convincing to himself, but others, most notably Zhang Yanyuan, were led seriously astray.

It was only in 1954 that the traditional Zhangian misconstruing of the Six Laws began to unravel. The epochal achievement of apparently being the first person in more than a thousand years to read the Six Laws correctly belongs to William Reynolds Beal Acker.[17] To the best of my knowledge, Acker is the first scholar to go on record, and to do so in a definitive manner, as being in favor of a grammatically stringent reading of the Six Laws as they were originally stated by Xie He. I suspect, however, that Acker's discovery was prompted, or at least partly inspired, by reading the Six Laws in a Japanese fashion (*kundoku* or *kanbun kakikudashi*). He notes[18] that he began his study of the Six Laws in Kyoto as early as 1936. Acker then goes on to state explicitly that the *shi* of each law is equal to Japanese *kore* ("this," "this-like," "such," "just this," "just such," "just-such-as-it-is") and the *ye* of each law is comparable to Classical Japanese *nari* ("is," "be"). Acker's explanation of how he arrived at his new (actually the old and original) reading is both elegant and exacting.[19] It should have been convincing to anyone with a good grounding in the grammar of Literary Sinitic. In fact, Acker's reading of the Six Laws was swiftly approved by Zürcher.[20] In their 1985 collection of translations of Chinese texts dealing with painting, Bush and Shih also adopted the Ackerian interpretation of the Six Laws.[21] The earliest adoption of an Ackerian reading in China known to me occurred in the 1958 Zhonghua reprinting of Yan Kejun's 嚴可均 (1762–1843) *Quan shanggu San Dai, Qin, Han, Sanguo, Liuchao wen* 全上古三代秦漢三國六朝文 (Complete Prose from High Antiquity, the Three Dynasties, Qin, Han, the Three Kingdoms, and the Six Dynasties).[22] The editors added small round circles for punctuation as follows: N R$_o$ S D C$_o$. While the Zhonghua editors did not set off N and did not use a comma after R, in spite of the fact that they did employ commas sparingly elsewhere in Yan's gigantic collection and should have done so here, the marking of a stop after R was an enormous step forward in rectifying the millennial misreading of Xie's Six Laws.[23] The first concerted effort by a Japanese scholar to promote an Ackerian reading of the Six Laws was that of Nakamura Shigeo 中村茂夫. Nakamura not only provided detailed, extensive annotations for each of the laws, he also translated them into Japanese and offered a punctuated edition of Xie He's text, with the Six Laws being treated thus: N R, S D C$_o$.[24] Finally, although Acker parsed the Six Laws correctly nearly half a century ago, his grammatical analysis of the text has only recently and gradually begun to win acceptance in China. This is almost entirely due to the awesome reputation of Qian Zhongshu 錢鍾書 (1910–1999), who in 1979—while unleashing a barrage of caustic barbs directed against the muddleheadedness of previous explicators—punctuated the Six Laws thus: N, R, S D C; (except $_o$ instead of ; for the end of the

sixth and final one).[25] Qian's reading may be considered an improvement over previous readings in China since it not only marks the
extremely important pause between R and S, it also sets aside N. I
myself read the Six Laws with syntactic pauses after the first, third, and
fifth characters of each line when I initially began my study of them in
the late 1970s. Whether or not those who agreed with Acker in correctly dividing the central four characters of each of the Six Laws into
two syntactically separate units did so independently, it is to the great
and everlasting glory of Acker to have been the first person to have followed the dictates of grammar with regard to the Six Laws after Zhang
Yanyuan's monumental misinterpretation more than a millennium earlier. In any event, there is no longer any excuse for scholars to continue
to repeat the misreading of the Six Laws *à la* Zhang Yanyuan.[26]

Those who persist in a Zhangian reading of the Six Laws are
ineluctably ignoring the penultimate character (*shi*) of each line. And
yet so deeply entrenched is the customary misapprehension of the laws
that even modern Sinologists remain under its spell.[27]

Because art historians have fallen prey to the "standard" misinterpretation of the Six Laws, not only have they been unable to grasp what
Xie He himself meant by them, it has been impossible for them to realize that the Six Laws were not devised out of whole cloth by Xie He,
but that they have a precise set of antecedents that will be pointed out
in a later section of this chapter.

The failure to parse Xie He's Six Laws correctly has resulted in an
incredible array of semimystical gibberish and wildly discrepant translations. The most celebrated translator of Literary Sinitic texts in modern
times could come up with no better than a "Pidgin English" (his own
characterization) rendering:

(1) Spirit-harmony—Life's motion.
(2) Bone-means—use brush.
(3) According to the object depict its shape.
(4) According to species apply colour.
(5) Planning and disposing degrees and places.
(6) By handing on and copying to transmit designs.[28]

This is a rather pathetic performance, being not even literally accurate
(particularly in the last two laws), but admittedly more honest than
padding one's ignorance with fluff.

At the other extreme is this "paraphrase" by a well-known art historian who has written more extensively on the Six Laws than any other scholar during the last half century:

> Resonance initiated in the universal, macrocosmic state of energy gives birth to negentropic patterns of assonance, the coming into being of which, in a hierarchy of structural phases, is the nature of existence and life. This is reality. It is also the process by which a work of art comes into being.
>
> The initiation of activity in macrocosmic potentiality is manifested in microcosmic actuality, the inherent nature and structure of every phenomenon being pressed into its exterior manifestation as a cast vessel receives the form of the master mould. The painter's technique embodies such a process, and his brush is the patterning instrument whereby beauty in materialized form is achieved.[29]

Fortunately, the paraphraser gave up after the first two laws. What we have witnessed here is the complete breakdown of philological rigor in dealing with Xie He's Six Laws. This agonizing frustration over the intractability of the Six Laws did not begin in modern times, but has plagued scholars almost from the day they were first written down.

There is no point in regurgitating all of the turgid twaddle about the Six Laws and the abominable interpretations of them that have been put forth during the course of the last millennium and more.[30] However, for the convenience of nonspecialist readers of this chapter, we here provide a sample series of Zhangian-type mistranslations of the Six Laws:

> The first is called spirit-resonance and / or life-movement.
>   (alternatively: life movement through spirit-resonance)
>   (alternatively: [instilling] spirit-resonance in engendering vitality), etc.
> The second is called bone-method and / or the use of the brush.
>   (alternatively: use of the brush through the bone method)
>   (alternatively: [relying on] bone method in the use of the brush), etc.
> The third is called correspondence to things and / or imaging of forms.
>   (alternatively: imaging of forms through correspondence to things)
>   (alternatively: [invoking] correspondence to things in imaging of forms),
>   etc.

The fourth is called accordance to type and / or application of colors.
  (alternatively: application of colors through correspondence to type)
  (alternatively: [stipulating] accordance to types in the application of
      colors), etc.
The fifth is called layout and construction and / or placement and positioning.
  (alternatively: placement and positioning through layout and construc-
      tion)
  (alternatively: [emphasizing] layout and construction in placement and
      planning), etc.
The sixth is called transmitting of models and / or reproducing and
copying.[31]
  (alternatively: reproducing and copying through transmitting of models)
  (alternatively: [valuing] transmitting of models by reproducing and
      copying), etc.

It is clear that a great distance has been traveled from the formulations
of Xie He, who lived only a little over three hundred years before
Zhang Yanyuan.

In contrast, when we go back to Xie He's original text and force
ourselves to read it as the grammar dictates (despite the clumsy syntax), such a procedure yields the following sort of bare bones, literal
translation:

1. Vital Resonance, which is the engendering of movement.
2. Bone Method, which is the usage of the brush.
3. Correspondence to the Object, which is the imaging of form.
4. Accordance to Type, which is the application of color.
5. Arrangement and Construction, which is positioning and placement.
6. Transmission and Transfer, which is modeling and depiction.

We next move to a minimally interpretive rendering of the Six
Laws, still sticking fairly close to the Chinese text, but attempting to
convey what Xie He probably meant when he first coined them:

1. Spiritual nature is (conveyed by) instilling vitality.
2. Inner quality is (suggested through) [skillful] handling of the brush.
3. Correspondence with reality is (achieved through) the representation of forms.

4. Accordance to type is (accomplished by) [subtle] application of colors.
5. Layout and composition are (determined by) [careful] positioning and placement.
6. Similitude and accuracy are (dependent upon) [faithful] modeling and depiction.

We may note that the first pair of laws has to do with metaphysical and aesthetic matters, the second pair with technical skills, and the third pair with pictorial and representational aspects. This pairing of the laws holds an important clue about the origins of the Six Laws, so we shall return to it later in our investigation.

Finally, here are the Six Laws of Xie He as embedded in the context in which they originally appeared, the complete preface to *[Gu]hua pinlu*:

> Now, by the ranking of painters is meant the relative superiority and inferiority of all painters. As for painters, there are none who fail to illustrate admonition or show the vicissitudes of human affairs. The desolation of a millennium may be seen as in a mirror by merely spreading out a picture.
>
> Even though painting has its Six Laws, few are able to combine them completely; rather, from ancient times until now each painter has excelled in one particular branch. What are these Six Laws? First, Vital Resonance, that is, the engendering of movement; second, Bone Method, that is, the usage of the brush; third, Correspondence to the Object, that is, the imaging of form; fourth, Accordance to Type, that is, the application of color; fifth, Arrangement and Construction, that is, positioning and placement; sixth, Transmission and Transfer, that is, modeling and depiction.
>
> Only Lu Tanwei [fifth century] and Wei Xie [fl. late third–early fourth centuries] were thoroughly proficient in all of these.
>
> A painter's traces may be skillful or clumsy, but art knows no ancient or modern. Respectfully relying upon remote and recent sources and following their rankings, I have edited and completed the preface and citations. Hence, what is presented does not extend broadly. As for the origins of painting, it is merely reported that it issued from the gods and the transcendents, but none was witness to such.

Though the preface is brief, it is issued in grand, almost cosmic, tones. Xie He is writing from the vantage of a person who is confident that his pronouncements have the weight of the ages behind him.

The Ṣaḍaṅga (Six Limbs) of Indian Painting

The striking similarity between Xie He's Six Laws of painting and the Six Limbs of Indian art theory have frequently been noted during the past century, but nearly always rejected as pure coincidence, and never rigorously examined. Indeed, most scholars who raise the possibility of Indian influence on the Six Laws do so only to dismiss it.[32] Given the constant reiteration of the possibility of Indian influence upon the Six Laws, coupled with the automatic denial of any meaningful impact from the Six Limbs, the time is long overdue for the proposition to be thoroughly tested.

It was Abanindranath Tagore (1871–1951; a second cousin of the famous Indian poet and humanist, Rabindranath Tagore [1861–1941]), who not only was the first person in modern times to draw attention to the Six Limbs, but who was also apparently the first person ever to mention Xie He's Six Laws in connection with the Six Limbs.[33] Abanindranath was himself a distinguished artist whose "voluptuous mysticism" set a new trend in modern Indian painting.

While Abanindranath did cite first the Six Limbs and then immediately thereafter the Six Laws in his initial articles on this subject,[34] he did not attempt to correlate them one-for-one, nor did he attempt to fix their dates to determine priority. He merely mentioned that both dealt with rules for painting and both were six in number (not four or five or some other number). In his earliest articles on the subject, Abanindranath did provide some general information about the antiquity of the Six Limbs. He ended them by meekly opining that "our thought of six limbs of painting is purely our own, and is as important as the six Canons of Chinese mentioned by HSIEH HO." In his second set of articles on the subject,[35] Abanindranath actually spent more energy introducing Japanese art and aesthetics on the vague grounds that they preserved ancient traditions better than Chinese art and aesthetics from a comparable period. Naturally, the Japanese evidence is of little value in establishing whether or not the Six Limbs have any relevance for the Six Laws, so we will not dwell upon it. Finally, in his last article and books on the topic, Abanindranath went into erudite detail concerning the philosophical, historical, literary, and aesthetic underpinnings of the Six Limbs, but he did not take up again the question of the relationship between the Six Limbs and the Six Laws. In any event, nowhere in his writings did Abanindranath make a serious, systematic effort to demonstrate that the Six Laws were related to the Six Limbs. He must, however, be credited as the first scholar to note the overall resemblance between the two sets of principles for painting.

The next scholar to mention the Six Limbs and the Six Laws together was Percy Brown, in his popular and long-lasting *Indian Painting* in the Heritage of India series: "... besides the number of laws being the same, there is a certain resemblance in the general intention of both these codes. The Chinese canons, emerging several centuries later, suggest that these were originally borrowed from the much older system of India."[36] Since Brown's suggestion lacked specificity and his handling of dating problems was unsophisticated, his weak assertion of a connection between the Six Limbs and the Six Laws has naturally not found acceptance.

The preeminent modern authority on the philosophical foundations of Indian art theory, the Ceylonese-British scholar Ananda K. Coomaraswamy (1877–1947), who was also highly knowledgeable about the history and principles of Chinese art, rejected an Indian basis for the Six Laws: "These Six Canons have close analogies in Indian theory, but there is no good reason to suppose that they are of Indian origin."[37]

Many scholars who do recognize the possibility of Indian influence on the Six Laws assume that it must have come to China in a Buddhist guise. This is not an unreasonable assumption, considering the massive impact of Buddhism on Chinese culture during the Six Dynasties, the Sui, and the Tang. Certainly, Buddhism was the main vehicle for the transmission of all sorts of Indian cultural elements to China during this period, but it was not the sole vehicle, nor was all that it brought specifically Buddhist in nature (e.g., mathematics, medicine, linguistics, prosody, and countless stories, to name just a few important areas of Chinese culture in which fundamental changes occurred as a result of the importation of Indian ideas and techniques). Scholars who suggest possible Buddhist content in the Six Laws often mention that *suilei* ("according to class or type") refers to a kind of *upaya* ("skill-in-means" or "skillful means") whereby Buddhas and bodhisattvas reveal themselves in varying forms depending upon the need or nature of the beings whom they desire to save. But *suilei* is also used in completely non-Buddhist contexts.[38] Others maintain that the word *fa* of the title of the Six Laws (*liu fa*) derives from the Buddhist concept of *dharma*, which is translated by *fa* in Chinese, but strictly indigenous meanings of *fa* (laws, regulations, rules, methods, etc.) are actually more suitable than when it is standing in for *dharma* (moral law, doctrine, nature, duty, phenomena or elements [of the universe], truth, justice, virtue, quality, predicate, etc.). Still others invoke the celebrated wall paintings in the caves at Ajaṇṭā (in Hyderabad, northeast of Bombay) as possible sources for the Six Laws. It is true that generations of Buddhist artists worked at Ajaṇṭā, but the wall paintings date from 150 to 650, with only a few from the early period and the vast majority coming after the time of Xie He. Furthermore, even if the dating of the Ajaṇṭā caves were not a problem, it has never been shown how the principles inherent in the wall paintings there would have been transmitted to China and become known to Xie He in a discrete and codified form. Hence, it is impossible to take seriously a significant direct impact from Ajaṇṭā or other Indian Buddhist wall paintings upon Xie He. Ecke attempts to demonstrate that the sixth of the Six Laws is Buddhist by virtue of the fact that it supposedly has to do with copying, and she believes that transmission of images is an inherent part of Buddhist art.[39] Her argument, however, is exceedingly feeble, while her evidence is largely anachronistic when applied to Xie He. The only other specific claim for a Buddhist link to the Six Laws is that the celebrated layman, Zong Bing 宗炳 (375–443; N.B.: a century before Xie He), is mentioned in the *[Gu]hua pinlu* (first of two individuals in the sixth and last class of painters) as "having an understanding of the Six Laws, but not, after all, possessing the appropriate skill." Furthermore, there is indirect evidence that it may have been Zong Bing who painted an exact copy of the famous "silhouette of the Buddha" from Nāgarahāra on a wall in Master Huiyuan's 慧遠 (334–416) monastery on Mount Lu and that the painting was executed according to certain iconographic rules.[40] Even if we accept the speculative attribution of the painting of the "silhouette of the Buddha," the sum total of the evidence put forward concerning Zong Bing does not amount to a Buddhist basis for the Six Laws. Except for Zong Bing, there are no other individuals with a strong Buddhist background mentioned in the *[Gu]hua pinlu*, and Zong Bing is not the only painter in Xie He's text who is associated with the Six Laws. Aside from *fa* and *suilei*, it would be difficult to point to anything in the Six Laws themselves that might conceivably have a Buddhist connection, and, as we have seen, even *fa* and *suilei* cannot be certified as definitely Buddhist in this context. There is nothing particularly Buddhist about the Six Limbs, but that does not preclude their having been brought to China along with Buddhism as a kind of cultural baggage. The fact that the *Citralakṣaṇa* (Theory of the Arts) was included in the Tibetan *bStan-'gyur* (*Tenjur* [Translation of Teachings], the second portion of the Tibetan Buddhist canon) is proof that non-Buddhist Indian aesthetic principles could be conveyed to other cultures via Buddhist intermediaries.[41]

As things now stand, the question of whether or not the Six Limbs and the Six Laws are related is at a standstill. Every weak assertion is matched by a spirited counterassertion.

The only way to solve this scholarly impasse is to examine the Six Limbs as intensively as we have looked at the Six Laws, then combine the results of our parallel investigations. The Six Limbs are spelled out in Yaśodhara's *Jayamaṅgalā* commentary to the famous Indian text on lovemaking, the *Kāma-sūtra* of Vātsyāyana.[42] They occur as a commentarial elaboration upon the word *ālekhyam* (drawing), the fourth in a list of sixty-four arts. Vātsyāyana (also called Mallanāga), the author of the *Kāma-sūtra,* flourished about the fourth century C.E. Yaśodhara, who composed the *Jayamaṅgalā* commentary, lived during the middle of the thirteenth century.

The term *ṣaḍaṅga* itself has a very long history, dating back to the late Vedic period (ca. 800 B.C.E.), where it referred to the six ancillary "limbs" of the Vedas (the oldest sacred texts of the Indian people). From that time on, it was used with reference to all sorts of things that had six parts, six divisions, and so forth. In the tantras (religious writings concerned with mysticism and magic) and elsewhere, it referred especially to the six "active" parts of the body: the head, the two hands, the two feet, and the heart. In the *Kāma-sūtra* itself, *ṣaḍaṅga* is used in the expression *ṣaḍaṅgam amṛtam* (sixfold nectar), which is made up of six elements (butter, honey, sugar, etc.) and which "provides prolonged enjoyment of sex."

Here are the Six Limbs in Sanskrit with relevant English translations:

1. *rūpa-bhedaḥ*   diversity or variety of forms or manifestations
2. *pramāṇāni*   measurements, scales, standards, ideal
                       proportions
3. *bhāva*   becoming, being, existence, condition, state,
                       nature, object
4. *lāvaṇya*   saltiness,[43] beauty, loveliness, charm
     yojanam   joining, yoking, harnessing, embodying,
                       infusing

5. *sādṛśyaṁ*   likeness, resemblance, similarity, representation
6. *varṇikā-bhaṅga*   breaking (down) / bursting / splitting / dividing /
                       analysis of pigments

Several stylistic aspects of the structure of the Six Limbs are worthy of note: the first and last limbs are both compounds; the second and fifth (one from the first and the next to the last) are single words; the third and the fourth (the middle two) are joined by the word *yojana*, which itself means "joining"; the first pair of limbs (one and two) has to do with differentiation of forms and layout; the second pair of limbs (three and four) is concerned with aesthetic elements; and the third pair (five and six) focuses on technical skills. The division of the Six Limbs into three closely linked pairs dealing with different aspects of painting is remarkably similar to the pairing of the Six Laws mentioned above.

A better understanding of the Six Limbs may be gained through the following observations:

rūpa-bhedaḥ (literally "form-distinction") calls for a knowledge of *lakṣaṇas* (characteristic marks of a thing to be represented that distinguish it from others of the same class)

pramāṇāni ("measure") requires a knowledge of *talamāna* or canons of proportion

bhāva ("emotion") signifies the mood of a subject depicted

lāvaṇya ("charm") implies the inner qualities of a figure portrayed

sādṛśyaṁ ("resemblance") refers to visual correspondence (in rhetoric, signifies similitude or simulacrum)

varṇikā-bhaṅga ("pigment-analysis") alludes to the proper distribution of colors.

The central concept of Indian aesthetics is *rasa*. The term *rasa* literally means "juice, sap, essence" and is sometimes translated into English as "sentiment." To show how pervasive and unifying *rasa* is, not only in aesthetics, but also in metaphysics, let us examine a few of its usages in various domains. In alchemy, *rasa* basically means "liquid" and implies "element" or "primary form." Among the *rasa* employed in alchemy are various kinds of salts (*lavaṇa* [N.B.]). In ayurvedic physiology, *rasa* signifies both a bodily substance, such as alimentary juice or chyle, and the distinctive flavor or taste of things: 1. sweet (*madhura*), 2. acid (*āmla*), 3. salt (*lavaṇa*), 4. pungent (*kaṭu*), 5. bitter (*tikta*), and 6. astringent (*kaṣāya*). These are the *ṣaḍ-vidhaḥ* (the six tastes), whose metaphorical application extends to many other areas of discourse. In philosophy, *rasa* is a subtle substance (one of the *tanmātra*) and the essence of taste. In literature, *rasa* may be used to define the prevailing feeling, tone, or ethos of a work. In this sense, *rasa* is much used by critics of poetry, but it is also frequently employed in discussions of *nāṭya* (dance drama), music, and art. Perhaps the best way to grasp the overwhelming importance of *rasa* in all of the arts is through contemplation of the term *rasāsvādana*, where the latter part of the compound means "eating with relish, tasting, enjoying." Hence *rasāsvādana* is the aesthetic experience, and *rasa* is "flavor, savor, quintessence," the substance of the aesthetic experience which is knowable only in the act of "tasting" the work of art in question.

The use of *lāvaṇya* (literally "saltiness," but signifying "charm" in aesthetic terms) in the Six Limbs evokes the whole world of *rasa* in Indian aesthetics and, beyond that, in metaphysics and associated realms. Its function is analogous to that of *mādhurya* (literally "sweetness," but signifying "grace" in aesthetic terms).[44] Metaphorically speaking, *lāvaṇya* and *mādhurya* connote the aesthetic experience of possessing or sensing "charm," on the one hand and "grace," on the other. It must be pointed out that *lāvaṇya* and *mādhurya* are not surface features but existential attributes.

From this survey of the multiple applications and implications of *lāvaṇya* and *mādhurya*, the unified nature of the arts—indeed of metaphysics, aesthetics, and other realms of thought in India—becomes obvious. Certainly, we find many of the same terms used in Indian painting theory also being used in prosody.[45]

After the sublimely subtle and richly nuanced notion of *rasa*, to which the *lāvaṇya* of the Six Limbs belongs and for which it stands, the next most vital concept in Indian aesthetics is *bhāva* (psychological state, mood). Sometimes thought of as the vehicle for conveying *rasa*, *bhāva* itself is one of the Six Limbs and has already been discussed above where they are first introduced.

Although both *rasa* and *bhāva* have deep roots in earlier Indian philosophical, religious, and literary texts,[46] their theoretical and practical implications were worked out in elaborate detail by Bharatamuni in chapters 6 and 7 of his celebrated *Nāṭya-śāstra*. The *Nāṭya-śāstra*, an amazingly thorough manual covering all aspects of drama, dates roughly to sometime between about the second century B.C.E. and the second century C.E., and more likely toward the early end of that span, with parts dating still earlier.[47]

It is interesting to note that Bharatamuni, who may be thought of as the historical father of systematic aesthetics in India, uses the notion of Six Limbs. This occurs in *Nāṭya-śāstra*, 7.13, in a discussion of gestures, where he refers to the "six major limbs" (head, hands, breast, sides, waist, and feet) and the "six minor limbs" (eyes, eyebrows, nose, upper lip, lower lip, and chin). Therefore, both the name and the fundamental aesthetic concepts of the Six Limbs are present already before the third century in the *Nāṭya-śāstra*.

It behooves us now to determine whether the aesthetic criteria of the Six Limbs are spelled out in any Indian treatise devoted specifically to painting that dates from a period commensurate with that of Xie He's Six Laws.

The third *khaṇḍa* (section) of the *Viṣṇudharmottara*, one of the dozens of Indian *purāṇas* (the name literally means "ancient"; these are mostly massive collections of lore about the past), consists of the *Citra-sūtra* (Collection of Aphorisms on Painting, chapters 35–43). In his authoritative history of puranic literature, Ludo Rocher states that "the text admits being a compilation of older sources,"[48] and, in her monograph on the *Citra-sūtra*, Stella Kramrisch declares that it is the "earliest exhaustive account of the theory of painting" in India.[49] We will discuss the probable date of the *Viṣṇudharmottara* below, but must first turn our attention to its relevance for the Six Limbs.

It is encouraging to observe that, not only is the elusive term *lāvaṇya* mentioned in the *Viṣṇudharmottara*, it occurs in a context that is peculiarly appropriate for our investigation of the relationship between the Six Limbs and the Six Laws.[50] Furthermore, in the very sentence of the *Viṣṇudharmottara* in which *lāvaṇya* is found, proportionate or appropriate measurement is also mentioned as a criterion for an effective painting. Thus we find the equivalents of two of the Six Limbs (viz., *lāvaṇya* and *pramāṇāni*) in the same sentence of the *Viṣṇudharmottara*, and elsewhere in the text the concerns of the other four are also covered.[51] This lends credence to the existence of the Six Limbs of Indian painting long before Yaśodhara's commentary on the *Kāma-sūtra*.[52]

Since all of the concerns of the Six Limbs are systematically treated in the *Citra-sūtra* of the *Viṣṇudharmottara*,[53] it is essential to determine the approximate date of this crucial text. Alberuni (al-Bīrūnī, 973–1048), the famed Choresmian (Khwarazmian) scientist and scholar, repeatedly cites the *Viṣṇudharmottara* in his *India*.[54] Hence, the *Viṣṇudharmottara* must date to 1030 (when Alberuni's *India* was completed) or earlier. As to the upper limit of the *Viṣṇudharmottara*, it almost certainly falls sometime after the third century, because in *adhyāya* 63.3 mention is made of Udīcyaveṣa and of Aviyāṅga (or Viyāṅga) in the description of the image of Sūrya. These reveal Magian influence that came from Persia around the third century.[55] Thus the date of the *Viṣṇudharmottara* must fall sometime between the third century and 1030. More precise dating of the *Viṣṇudharmottara* is extremely complicated and technical, requiring reference to many relevant Indian authors and texts whose own dates are themselves sometimes difficult to ascertain. Recent scholarly opinion, however, emphasizes a close relationship between specific aspects of the canons of art enshrined in the *Viṣṇudharmottara* and the Gupta age (320–540).[56] More precisely, on the basis of sculptural features referred to in the text, Sivaramamurti detects in the *Citra-sūtra* of the *Viṣṇudharmottara* a period of transition between the art of the Kushans and the Gupta age, thus a time nearer to the fourth century.[57]

Also relevant are the *śilpa-śāstra* ("artisans' manuals") of the fourth to fourteenth centuries. These cover a wide variety of arts, crafts, architecture, and related fields. Again, much of the same aesthetic terminology as that found in the painters' manuals (such as the *Citra-sūtra*) is also employed in the artisans' manuals. In other words, we are dealing with a very old and widespread set of aesthetic standards that find their most succinct expression for painting in the *ṣaḍaṅga*. The Six Limbs are the encapsulization of a huge corpus of Indian texts on aesthetics that are securely grounded in works such as the *Nāṭya-śāstra* (before the third century) and the *Citra-sūtra* (before the sixth century) of the *Viṣṇudharmottara*. Prithvi Kumar Agrawala, who has written a splendid monograph devoted exclusively to the Six Limbs, concludes that they have their origins around the fourth or fifth century (remarking that this is near the time of Xie He) and postulates that they were fully codified sometime during the period between the fifth and the sixth century.[58]

The Six Laws and the Six Limbs Compared

We may open this section of our discussion by revealing why R and S were selected as mnemonics for the first and second binomials, respectively, of each of Xie He's Six Laws. To be blunt, R stands for "Refined" and S for "Simple." The R binomials are uniformly elegant in their diction and relatively recondite in their signification. These are the terms that have required such an enormous expenditure of erudition on the part of scholars for the last thousand and more years in order to explicate them. The S binomials, on the other hand, are straightforward and transparent. Most readers of the Six Laws, even nonspecialists, have little difficulty in apprehending what they mean. Furthermore, whereas nearly all of the R binomials can be found in much earlier literature, the S binomials were either of more recent vintage or were coined by Xie He himself.[59] Now, one may ask, why should Xie He have chosen poetic terminology for the R binomials of his laws and prosaic terminology for their S binomials? On the surface, this seems a most mysterious procedure. When we probe deeper into Xie He's *modus operandi*, his purpose for adopting such an ostensibly curious tactic becomes totally comprehensible. Namely, when Xie He encountered the Six Limbs, for which—as a group—there were no precedents in China, he was forced to come up with more or less nonce translations to convey them. Having a developed sense of *gravitas* with regard to fine writing in Literary Sinitic, he recognized that his direct, *ad hoc* renderings of the Sanskrit terms would not pass muster with the elite of his day, so he reached back into the established lexicon of the literati to find terms that would impress. Having identified six expressions of suitably dignified pedigree and elegant cachet, he proceeded to feign that they were actually the substance of his rules and that he was defining these exquisite expressions with straightforward terminology. What must have happened in reality is exactly the opposite: the substance of the Six Laws lies in the S binomials, whereas the R binomials are elaborate window dressing. Grammatically, of course, the R binomials are primary and the S binomials are secondary, whereas conceptually and derivationally the S binomials are primary and the R binomials are secondary. In other words, by the way he constructs his sentences, Xie He makes it seem as though he is equating the R binomials with the S binomials and thus, in a sense, explaining the R binomials by the S binomials. Whereas, in actuality, Xie He began with the S binomials, which were transparently translations of the Six Limbs (see below), and proceeded to prettify them with the R binomials.

As originally expressed by Xie He, the Six Laws are so notoriously difficult to comprehend that many of the best historians of Chinese art have simply thrown up their hands in despair and are reluctant to discuss them. Indeed, full sense cannot be made of the Six Laws unless they are correctly parsed and unless they are read against their Indian background. The *underlying* concepts are actually largely alien to the Chinese artistic tradition. As such, they have come to make sense in the Chinese context only through a process of reinterpretation and even outright rewriting. What the Six Laws mean now is surely not what they meant when Xie He first wrote them down (or, more cogently, just before he wrote them down in Chinese). One of the main purposes of this study is to make a dedicated effort to understand the Six Laws in the form they took before Zhang Yanyuan tampered with them.

Once we recognize Xie He's *modus operandi*, it is easy to match the S binomials of each of his laws with one of the Six Limbs. Thus, we may arrange the following two tables:

Six Laws	Six Limbs	Six Limbs	Six Laws
1	3	1	3
2	4	2	5
3	1	3	1
4	6	4	2
5	2	5	6
6	5	6	4

The following verbal table makes it easier to see the close parallels between the S binomials of the Six Laws and the Six Limbs:

Six Laws	Six Limbs
1. engendering of movement	3. being, becoming, existence
2. usage of the brush	4. charm
3. imaging of form	1. distinguishing of form
4. application of color	6. analysis of color
5. positioning and placement	2. measurements, proportion
6. modeling and depiction	5. likeness, similarity, resemblance

The identity of the first, third, fourth,[60] fifth, and sixth[61] of the Six Laws with the corresponding members of the Six Limbs is immediately obvious. Only the correspondence between the second of the Six Laws and the fourth of the Six Limbs requires explanation.

While there does seem to be a disparity between "usage of the brush" and "charm," the connection between them becomes evident upon further reflection. We have already explained *lāvaṇya*, the most elusive of the Six Limbs, in some depth above. As for *yongbi*, let us recall that it is equated with *gufa*. Translators are more or less compelled to render *gufa* as "bone method" by the surface semantics of the two constituent graphs, and learned exegetes explain that it has something to do with the quality of the lines of a painting. This may well be what it has come to mean after a thousand and more years of commentarial overlays and under the impress of the supreme role of brushwork in Chinese painting and in the even more highly esteemed realm of calligraphy. But this is not what *gufa* meant when Xie He adopted the term. *Gufa*—in its original sense—may be somewhat more interpretatively translated as "skeletal makeup / structure." The correctness of this interpretation is confirmed by the synonymous expression *guxiang* 骨相 (skeletal appearance). In other words, the term *gufa* originally referred unmistakably to the inner qualities of a person or animal as seen through their physiognomy. The practice of judging the character, worth, or quality of an individual was actually exceptionally well developed for horses during classical times in China. Applied to human beings, it is also called anthroposcopy, i.e., the art of reading a person's character or foretelling his fate and fortune from the structure of the bones of the head and body. The great Eastern Han rationalist, Wang Chong 王充 (27–ca. 90), has an entire chapter (24, "Guxiang" [On Anthroposcopy]) on this subject in his monumental *Lunheng* 論衡 (Balanced Inquiries).[62]

So what really was the relationship between *gufa* and *yongbi* when Xie He first linked them together for all eternity? Perhaps the corresponding Indian limb can aid in clarifying this perennially puzzling law. It is noteworthy that the earliest Indian treatise on painting, the *Citrasūtra* of the *Viṣṇudharmottara*, mentions *mādhurya* and *lāvaṇya* together in a discussion focussing on the bodily frame, muscles, and joints.[63] That is to say, as *yongbi* is linked to *gufa* in the Six Laws, so *lāvaṇya* is directly linked to the skeletal fundament of the body in the Six Limbs, thus removing the only possible doubt of a one-for-one correspondence between the Six Laws and the Six Limbs. Superficially, the two terms, *yongbi* and *lāvaṇya*, seem to share very little in common, yet it is possible to discern the type of link between them that Xie He must have had in mind. Because of the exalted place of calligraphy among the arts in China and the strong emphasis on brushwork in painting, it would have been hard (almost impossible) for Xie He to leave the brush out of his canons. Yet, when we take into account the direct relationship between *lāvaṇya* (one of the *rasa*) and the responsibility of the artist to capture the essential, underlying nature of the figure portrayed, that is exactly what transpires in the use of the brush (*yongbi*) to delineate the inner qualities of the person or object being painted.

It is more than curious that Liu Daochun, the eleventh-century painting critic who has twice been mentioned above, in the first of his "Six Strengths" urges the artist to "seek [the power of] the brush through brusqueness" 麤鹵求筆一也 (R S N C).[64] This is obviously a transformation of Xie He's famous second law, the core of which is *gufa yongbi*. Now, although it is almost counterintuitive, the idea that good brushwork is inherent in roughness can be apprehended upon reflection. But what is most strange about Liu Daochun's first strength is that the binomial he uses for brusqueness or roughness, *culu*, has as its second component syllable a graph that signifies saltiness. This, of course, exactly mirrors *lāvaṇya*, which, as we have already seen, corresponds to *yongbi* (brushwork). As if this were not cause enough for wonder, the second of Liu Daochun's strengths, "seek 'stuff' through eccentricity" 僻澀求才二也, employs the unusual term *pise*, the second syllable of which means astringency. Along with saltiness, astringency is one of the *ṣaḍ-vidhaḥ* (six tastes) which play a key role in the discourse of *rasa* in Indian aesthetics. It is so highly improbable for saltiness and astringency to be chosen jointly as metaphors for important elements of painting theory both in India and in China that one feels there must have been some sort of oral transmission concerning them stretching back from Xia Wenyan and Liu Daochun to Xie He and his Indian aesthetic predecessors.

Conclusion

The Six Limbs and the Six Laws are both concerned with basic aspects of painting. The fact that both of the canonical statements of art theory in India and in China are hexapartite already gives cause for suspicion that the two sets of principles may be related. By itself, of course, the hexapartiteness of the Indian and Chinese rules is insufficient to prove that they are linked. However, when we consider that there is a one-for-one correspondence between the Six Limbs and the Six Laws, the odds against their resembling each other so closely purely by coincidence is virtually nil—especially in view of the countless other variables involved in painting that might have been chosen for emphasis (e.g., shading, contrast, depth, perspective, materials, subjects, and so forth; it is not as though there were only six possible elements in the universe of painting! Why *these* six and not some other six?). Furthermore, the Six Limbs and the Six Laws date from around the same time and developed in two major cultures that were in intimate, vibrant contact with each other. Thus there are historical grounds for believing that the remarkable resemblances between the Six Limbs and the Six Laws are due to cultural exchange. Finally, it is particularly noteworthy that the Six Laws, which have been seriously misread by their own most ardent advocates, become much more intelligible when interpreted in light of the Six Limbs. As to which set, the Six Limbs or the Six Laws, is more likely to have influenced the other, the answer is plain.[65]

The Six Limbs and the Six Laws correspond closely, not just one-for-one, as we have demonstrated, but pair-for-pair. The central core of the Six Limbs is appropriately the middle pair, viz., *bhāva* (the vehicle of *rasa*, the key concept of Indian aesthetics) and *lāvaṇya* (standing for *rasa* itself). Only this pair has an extra word (*yojana* [joining, yoking]) added to it, no doubt to emphasize the paramount importance of *bhāva* and *rasa* for art. This central pair represents the purely aesthetic, philosophical, metaphysical, and spiritual aspects of art. *Bhāva* and *rasa* are concerned with the birth of the aesthetic impulse; they precisely mirror the first pair of the Six Laws (engendering of movement [i.e., bringing into being] and usage of the brush to capture the inner qualities of the object portrayed), which were undoubtedly put in the initial position by Xie He to emphasize their essential importance for the conception of art. In terms of Sanskrit stylistics, the central positioning of the key pair of the Six Limbs with the addition of *yojana* to highlight their significance is equivalent to Xie He's opening of the Six Laws with the most important pair.

Moving to the next most salient pair of the Six Limbs, we have *rūpa-bheda* (differentiation of forms) and *varṇikā-bhaṅga* (application of

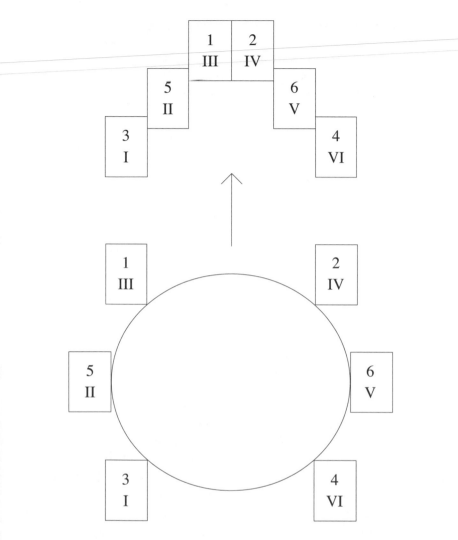

FIGURE 1. The Perfect Symmetry of the Six Limbs (Roman numerals) and the Six Laws (Arabic numerals). The central pair is at the top in both cases.

colors), the first and the sixth. This second pair has to do with the technical aspects of painting, how a painting is actually executed. Again, this second pair of the Six Limbs exactly mirrors the second pair of the Six Laws (imaging of forms and application of colors), which is also concerned with the same painterly matters.

In terms of stylistic emphasis (placed between the central core and the exposed first and sixth limbs), the third pair of the Six Limbs is *pramāṇāni* (measurements, placement, proportion) and *sādṛśyam* (visual similarity). This pair is concerned with the pictorial and representational aspects of painting. It should be noted that *pramāṇāni* and *sādṛśyam* are often closely linked in traditional Indian painting theory.[66] Once again, this third pair of the Six Limbs corresponds precisely to the third pair of the Six Laws (positioning and placement; modeling and depiction), both in content and in function. Both third pairs focus on the result or effect of the painting: does it effectively convey to the viewer the overall effect of the object or scene depicted? For both the Six Limbs and the Six Laws, the third pair is concerned with verisimilitude.

With so many precise correspondences in both the form and the content of the Six Limbs and the Six Laws, it is virtually impossible that they are unrelated. If we accept that the Six Laws were actually modeled upon the Six Limbs (and such a conclusion seems inescapable in light of the overwhelming evidence in favor of it), however, this is not to say that the Six Laws are wholly derivative. The situation with the evolution of the Six Limbs into the Six Laws is not unlike that of the transformation of portraits of itinerant Central Asian monks into the standard iconographical form of the famous Tang pilgrim, Xuanzang 玄奘 (596–664). It has been convincingly demonstrated that the early depictions of this iconographical form had nothing whatsoever to do with Xuanzang nor with any other Chinese personage.[67] Yet, for late Ming, Qing, and modern devotees of the pilgrim, the ubiquitous figure of a walking monk with a basketful of scrolls on his back has truly become Xuanzang. Similarly, in the metamorphosis of the Six Limbs into the Six Laws, the former are now only dimly visible in the latter. As they developed from the sixth century to the present day, the Six Laws truly became an integral phenomenon of Chinese culture and absorbed thoroughly Chinese characteristics. Such is the result of the intricate interplay between external influences and internal dynamics.

The Six Dynasties (220–581) witnessed a sea change in Chinese aesthetics.[68] The culmination was reached in the nearly simultaneous codification and systematization of critical and theoretical approaches to the arts enshrined in Liu Xie's *Wenxin diaolong*, Zhong Rong's 鍾嶸 (469–518) *Shi pin* 詩品 (Rankings of Poets), Yu Jianwu's 庾肩吾 (487–551) *Shu pin* 書品 (Rankings of Calligraphers), and Xie He's *[Gu]hua pinlu*. The radical transformation of theories about literature and art that took place during this period was significantly stimulated by the influx of Indian ideas that came along with the spread of Buddhism and expanding mercantile activity by land and by sea. The identical process that occurred with regard to the evolution of Sanskrit prosodic rules into the standards governing regulated verse in China[69] transpired with the transformation of the Six Limbs into the Six Laws. They started out as a product of India and became a naturalized cultural manifestation of China. Neither the rules governing prosody nor the principles regulating painting were identifiably Buddhist, but they were conveyed to China primarily by Buddhists and were certainly fostered within Chinese Buddhist circles of laymen and monks.[70]

NOTES

Although this is a relatively short paper, there are many friends and colleagues who helped me with it in one way or another. Above all, I wish to thank Ludo Rocher for going over the Sanskrit text of the *ṣaḍaṅga* with me and for providing key references. I am grateful to Michael Meister for guiding me to the excellent little book on the *ṣaḍaṅga* by Prithvi Kumar Agrawala. Daniel Boucher answered questions about Sanskrit grammar, and Fred Smith personally searched the massive lexicographical files of the Deccan College (Pune, India) archives for early occurrences of the term *ṣaḍaṅga*. Linda Chance clarified specific points about Classical Japanese grammar. Elfriede Regina Knauer answered questions about principles of Greek and Byzantine painting. Alan Berkowitz, Robert Joe Cutter, and Cynthia Chennault kindly confirmed that next to nothing is known about the life of Xie He. Robert Harrist offered valuable help with texts related to calligraphy. Guangda Zhang brought me scholarly publications from the Princeton University library. Michael Puett and Paul Rakita Goldin confirmed my hunches about the relative rarity of numbered lists of sentences in pre-Buddhist Chinese texts. Jidong Yang checked several sources and input characters into the computer. John Kieschnick consulted the Academia Sinica databases for mention of Xie He. Rosalind Bradford and Hsin-Mei Agnes Hsu tracked down bibliographical references and Internet sites. Richard Vinograd shared his perceptive views on key points, and Lothar Ledderose called significant European scholarship to my attention. Audrey Spiro posed intriguing problems raised by my reading of the Six Laws, some of which can only be answered by future research. Members of the audience who heard me deliver an earlier version of this chapter at Columbia University provided much welcome positive feedback. For the magnanimity of all those named above, I am profoundly grateful. Last, but certainly not least, I owe a deep debt to Susan Bush for her tremendous generosity in sharing with me over two decades an abundance of relevant materials and critical insights. Most recently, she helped me visualize the relationship between the Six Limbs and the Six Laws, as depicted in Figure 1. I alone am responsible for any short-comings and infelicities that remain.

Epigraphs: Jin Ronghua 金榮華, "Xie He liu fa yu Yindu gudai zhi hua lun" 謝赫六法與印度古代之畫論, *Dalu zazhi* 大陸雜誌, 68.4 (1984), 48 (194) of 47–48 (193–194); Tsu-Lin Mei, personal communication.

1. For a succinct and informative survey of Chinese painting theory and criticism, see the article by Susan Bush in *Encyclopedia of Aesthetics,* ed. Michael Kelly, 4 vols. (New York and Oxford: Oxford University Press, 1998), pp. 368–373. Xie He and his Six Laws are treated at length in the "Introduction" (vol. 1, pp. 3–8) to Osvald Sirén's massive, magisterial *Chinese Painting: Leading Masters and Principles,* 7 vols. (London: Lund Humphries; New York: Ronald Press, 1956–1958) as "the earliest still existing formulation of the essentials of Chinese painting" and "an undercurrent running through all discussions of Chinese painting." Alexander Soper, formerly doyen among historians of Chinese art, devoted an entire article to "The First Two Laws of Hsieh Ho" in *The Far Eastern Quarterly,* 8.4 (August 1949), 412–423, placing them in historical and intellectual context. An idea of how tremendously important the Six Laws are (despite their diminutive size) may be gained by considering that a small handbook covering the whole of Chinese history and culture in 1,500 entries awards Xie He's rules their own place and provides a complete (although slightly incoherent) translation. See Michael Dillon, ed. *China: A Historical and Cultural Dictionary* (Richmond, Surrey: Curzon, 1998), p. 353.

2. *Hanyu da cidian* 漢語大詞典, 2.35b.

3. In his *Zhongguo huaxue zhuzuo kaolu* 中國畫學著作考錄 (Shanghai: Shanghai shuhua chubanshe, 1998), p. 29b, Xie Wei 謝巍 states that Xie He's ancestors had lived at Yangxia 陽夏 (Chen Commandery 陳郡), i.e., (modern Taikang 太康 in Henan Province), but that, after the fall of the Western Jin (317 C.E.), the entire family had moved south where they dwelled at Guiji 會稽 (modern Shaoxing 紹興 in Zhejiang Province). If this were indeed true, it would mean that Xie He was related to the renowned Xie clan, which included among its members the great poet, scholar-official, and defender of lay Buddhism, Xie Lingyun 謝靈運 (385–433). Xie Lingyun was the grandson of the illustrious general, Xie Xuan 謝玄 (343–388), and the older cousin of the poet, Xie Huilian 謝惠連 (407–443). The Xies were the mightiest and wealthiest clan during the second half of the fourth century and the first half of the fifth century. Membership in the Yangxia Xies would have meant that Xie He would have had the sort of heritage that would have given him the opportunity to mingle with high-ranking Buddhist monks who might have communicated various

facets of Indian learning to him. Furthermore, Xie Lingyun, Xie Huilian, and two other distinguished members of the family, Xie Zhi 謝稺 (fl. 416–466) and Xie Zhuang 謝莊 (421–466, not long before Xie He's own time), were all known to be skilled artists. See Chen Chuanxi 陳傳席, *Liuchao huajia shiliao* 六朝畫家史料 (Beijing: Wenwu chubanshe, 1990), pp. 182–199. Thus, if Xie He were indeed a member of this outstanding family, which does seem quite probable, then he would not only have had the requisite Buddhist connections for contacts with eminent monks who might have been knowledgeable in the Indian Six Limbs of painting (see below), he would also have possessed the necessary painterly background to take a deep interest in the subject. However, since Xie Wei does not cite the sources for his assertion that Xie He was related to the Yangxia Xies, it would be risky to draw unwarranted conclusions from it.

4. Basic biographical information may be found in the following works: Susan Bush and Hsio-yen Shih, eds., *Early Chinese Texts on Painting* (Cambridge: Harvard University Press, 1985), pp. 23 and 308; Chen Chuanxi, *Shiliao*, p. 255; Chen Chuanxi, *Liuchao hualun yanjiu* 六朝畫論研究 (Taipei: Taiwan xuesheng, 1991), pp. 184–186, 205–206.

5. E. Zürcher, "Recent Studies on Chinese Painting, I," *T'oung Pao* 51 (1964), p. 379 (of 377–422); Wang Bomin 王伯敏, ed., *Guhua pinlu; Xu huapin* 古畫品錄；續畫品錄 (Beijing: Renmin meishu, 1959, 1962), p. 2.

6. John Hay, "Hsieh Ho revisited. Values and history in Chinese painting, II: the hierarchic evolution of structure," *Res* 7–8 (Spring–Autumn, 1984), Appendix, pp. 109–110, plus notes 136–140 (of 102–136), gives bibliographical references to more than two dozen studies of the Six Laws in Western languages, Chinese, and Japanese. See also Hay's "Values and history in Chinese painting, I: Hsieh Ho revisited," *Res* 6 (Autumn, 1983), 83ff. (of 72–111) for a review of previous scholarship on the Six Laws. Clay Lancaster, "Keys to the Understanding of Indian and Chinese Painting: The 'Six Limbs' of Yaśodhara and the 'Six Principles' of Hsieh Ho," *The Journal of Aesthetics & Art Criticism* 11, no. 2 (December 1952), 100–101, n. 17 (95–104), also provides helpful bibliographical references, especially to earlier studies and translations in Western languages. A valuable study of Xie He's criteria for ranking painters, often overlooked in the English-speaking world, is Dieter Kuhn, "Die Bewertungskriterien im *Ku Hua P'in Lu* des Hsieh Ho," *Zeitschrift der Deutschen Morgenländischen Gesellschaft* 123, no. 2 (1973), 344–358. Kuhn also provides references to the excellent work of Roger Goepper.

7. There are two such lists, one consisting of six items and the other of seven items, near the beginning of the twenty-fifth chapter ("Anwei 安危" [Security and Danger]) of the *Han Fei Zi* 韓非子 (Master Han Fei) and one such list, consisting of eight items, in the twenty-fifth chapter ("Guyue 古樂" [Ancient Music]) of the *Lüshi chunqiu* 呂氏春秋 (The Springs and Autumns of Lü Buwei). Furthermore, the sections of the *Lüshi chunqiu* demarcate the chap-

ters they contain as follows: *yi yue* 一曰 (the first says [i.e., is], *er yue* 二曰 (the second says), etc.

8. *Taishō Tripiṭaka*, no. 1059, 50.347a.

9. E. Zürcher, *The Buddhist Conquest of China: The Spread and Adaptation of Buddhism in Early Medieval China*, 2 vols. (Leiden: E. J. Brill, 1st ed. 1959; rev. ed., 1972), p. 12; Kenneth K. S. Ch'en, *Buddhism in China: A Historical Survey* (Princeton, N.J.: Princeton University Press, 1964), p. 69; Arthur F. Wright, *Buddhism in Chinese History* (Stanford: Stanford University Press; London: Oxford University Press, 1959), p. 37.

10. Richard B. Mather, trans., *Shih-shuo Hsin-yü: A New Account of Tales of the World* (Minneapolis: University of Minnesota Press, 1976), p. 123.

11. See *Foguang da cidian* 佛光大辭典, 5.4143b and 4.3421a–3422b.

12. For references, see Victor H. Mair, "Buddhism in *The Literary Mind and Ornate Rhetoric*," in *A Chinese Literary Mind: Culture, Creativity, and Rhetoric in* Wenxin diaolong, ed. Zong-qi Cai (Stanford: Stanford University Press, 2001), pp. 251–252, n. 21 (main article is on pp. 63–81).

13. William Reynolds Beal Acker, trans. and annot., *Some T'ang and Pre-T'ang Texts on Chinese Painting* (Leiden: E. J. Brill, 1954), p. 65.

14. See Göran Malmqvist, trans. and annot., "Xu Shen's Postface to the *Shuo Wen Jie Zi*," in *On Script and Writing in Ancient China*, ed. David Pankenier, Skrifter utgivna av Föreningen för Orientaliska Studier, 9 (Stockholm: University of Stockholm, 1974), p. 49 (of 48–53) and K. L. Thern, trans. and annot., "Postface to *Explanation of Simple and Compound Graphs*," in *The Columbia Anthology of Traditional Chinese Literature*, ed. Victor H. Mair (New York: Columbia University Press, 1994), p. 564 (of 562–565).

15. It is possible that Xie He, in formulating his Six Laws, received some sort of influence or inspiration from Xu Shen's lists of six types of characters and six styles of writing, especially as they were rewritten by Wei Heng. But the fact that Xie He's Six Laws have to do with painting, whereas the six types of characters and the six styles of writing are concerned with script, means that there is virtually no overlap in their contents. If we are looking for a model, we must search within the literature on painting theory. We shall pursue that path throughout the remainder of this chapter.

16. In *Lidai shufa lunwen xuan* 歷代書法論文選 (Shanghai: Shanghai shuhua chubanshe, 1979; 1983), vol. 1 of 2, p. 78.

17. See his landmark book entitled *Some T'ang and Pre-T'ang Texts on Chinese Painting*, p. 4.

18. *Ibid.*, p. xxi.

19. *Ibid.*, pp. xxi–xviii.

20. Zürcher, "Recent Studies," p. 386.

21. Bush and Shih, eds., *Early Chinese Texts on Painting* (Cambridge: Harvard University Press, 1985), p. 40.

22. *Op. cit.*, vol. 3 (of 4), p. 2931a; *Quan Qi wen* (Complete Prose of the Qi Dynasty), 25.7a.

23. The Zhonghua editors deserve special credit for this rectification because Shen Qianyi 沈乾 ，a scholar from Wujin 武進, Jiangsu Province, had refrained from marking the stop after R in his 1930 reprinting of Yan's collection, although he did add a brushed *zhu* ㇔ (dot, point), which functioned as a kind of period, after each C. See *Quan Qi wen*, 25.7a in *han* 11, *ce* 45 (from a total of sixty-six threadbound *ce* [fascicles] in sixteen *han* [cases]). Both the 1930 minimally punctuated reprinting and the 1958 partially punctuated reprinting were based on the 1894 woodblock printing by Wang Yuzao 王毓藻 of Huanggang 黃岡, Guangdong. The rough draft of Yan's collection, which was completed in 1836 but never published during his lifetime, may still be found in the Shanghai Library.

24. Nakamura Shigeo 中村茂夫, *Chūgoku garon no tenkai: Shin Tō Sō Gen hen* 中國畫論の展開：晉唐宋元篇 (Kyoto: Nakayama bunkadō, 1965), pp. 140ff.

25. Qian Zhongshu 錢鍾書, *Guanzhui bian* 管錐編, 4 vols. (Hong Kong: Zhonghua, 1979), vol. 4, p. 1353. Students of Chinese literature and art are indebted to Ronald Egan for having undertaken the difficult task of translating and annotating Qian's "'Resonance' in Criticism on the Arts," in which his discussion of the Six Laws occurs, and other learned essays from *Guanzhui bian*. See Egan's *Limited Views: Essays on Ideas and Letters by Qian Zhongshu*, Harvard-Yenching Monograph Series (Cambridge: Harvard University Asia Center, 1998), pp. 97–118, especially p. 98.

26. Seven years after Acker's announcement of the proper parsing of the Six Laws, James Cahill launched a determined rebuttal in his "The Six Laws and How to Read Them," *Ars Orientalis*, 4 (1961), 372–381. Motivated by a desire to defend the traditional Zhangian reworking of Xie He's rules, Cahill deployed an impressive array of Sinological and art historical skills. Unfortunately, even such a superlative scholar as Cahill could not rescue a fundamentally flawed reading of the Six Laws, he himself having to admit that his interpretation was fraught with ambiguity and far from definitive.

27. Supposedly authoritative reference works in China continue to treat R S D C as a single unit, being willing to go no further than to separate off the N at the beginning of each law. See, for example, Wu Mengfu 吳孟復, ed., *Zhongguo hua lun* 中國畫論, 2 vols. (Hefei: Anhui meishu chubanshe, 1995), vol. 1, p. 1.

28. Arthur Waley, *An Introduction to the Study of Chinese Painting* (London: Ernest Benn, 1923), p. 72.

29. Hay, "Values and history," p. 135. The author focuses on the first two of Xie He's Laws, but addresses issues that concern all of them.

30. Michael Sullivan, *The Birth of Landscape Painting in China* (Berkeley and Los Angeles: University of California Press, 1962), pp. 106–107, has con-

veniently assembled four relatively early and influential English translations of the Six Laws that are based on the traditional interpretation. Some of the most distinguished historians of Chinese art, who shall remain nameless, seem to revel in the presumed obscurity of the Six Laws. To be sure, the Six Laws are hard to fathom, but not so hard as they are usually made out to be.

31. One of the most respected historians of Chinese art, who shall remain unidentified, rendered this line as "Transmitting, transferring, copying, writing." Aside from the total disregard for grammar, it is particularly distressing that *xie* has been translated as "writing." *Xie* seldom means "writing" in premodern times, when it is normally interepreted as "unburden, dispel, drain (off), copy, depict," and so forth.

32. Waley, *Introduction*, p. 74: "There is very little resemblance between the two sets of Canons." Acker, *Texts*, p. xlv: "There are some resemblances, but they are not sufficient to establish any direct relation between *these* 'Six Limbs' and the Six Elements." *Zhongguo da baike quanshu; Meishu,* 2 vols. (Beijing: Zhongguo da baike quanshu chubanshe, 1991), vol. 1, p. 467a: "Some Western scholars surmise that the Six Laws of Painting included in the preface to the Chinese [critic] Xie He's *Hua pin* (Rankings of Painters) (around the fifth century) may possibly have their source in the Six Limbs of Indian Painting. At present, most Chinese scholars take an opposing view to this sort of hypothesis. The two key laws of *gufa yongbi* and *qiyun shengdong* among the Chinese Six Laws are manifestly the products of Chinese traditional painting aesthetics. As for whether or not the Indian Six Limbs and the Chinese Six Laws merely have the same number purely by chance and are mutually unrelated in terms of content, or perhaps the Chinese Six Laws influenced the Indian Six Limbs, deeper research is awaited." Charles Willemen, who is well versed in Buddhist studies, does not even mention the ṣaḍaṅga in his "The Stanza of the Six Rules of Painting," in *Studi in Onore di Lionello Lanciotti*, 3 vols., ed. S. M. Carletti., M. Sacchetti, and P. Santangelo, Dipartimento di Studi Asiatici, Series Minor, 51 (Naples: Istituto Universitario Orientale, 1996), vol. 3, pp. 1413–1429. Heretofore, the most sustained attempt to compare the Six Limbs and the Six Laws was that of Clay Lancaster, "Keys." On the last page of his article, Lancaster even matched up four of the Six Laws with four of the Six Limbs and succeeded in getting two of the pairs (Law 1 and Limb 3, Law 5 and Limb 2) correct. The overall impression one gains from reading Lancaster's article, however, is that he was not at all interested in trying to determine whether or not the two sets of rules may have been related, but only whether by chance they might have shared some of the same concerns. This accounts for his half-hearted and incomplete effort to match the individual items of the two sets. See also Thomas Munro, *Oriental Aesthetics* (Cleveland: The Press of Western Reserve University, 1965), pp. 38–41 and 50–53, who summarizes Lancaster's findings.

33. Abanindranath's rediscovery of the Six Limbs and his mention of the Six Laws were publicized in a series of articles and books published in India and Germany between 1914 and 1922: "Sadanga or the Six Limbs of Indian Painting," *The Modern Review*, 15.5; whole No. 89 (May, 1914), 580–581; the same article with the identical title was also published in *Ostasiatische Zeitschrift*, 3 (1914–1915), 103; "Philosophy of the Sadanga or the Six Limbs of Indian Painting," *The Modern Review*, 16.1; whole No. 91 (July, 1914), 102–104; the same article with the identical title was also published in *Ostasiatische Zeitschrift*, 3 (1914–1915), 375–377; "Sadanga or the Six Limbs of Painting," *The Modern Review*, 18.4; whole No. 106 (October, 1915), 337–345; *Sadanga; or The Six Limbs of Painting* (Calcutta: The Indian Society of Oriental Art, 1921); *Sadanga, ou les Six Canons de la Peinture hindoue*, translated from the English by Andrée Karpelès (Paris: Bossard, 1922).

34. "Sadanga or the Six Limbs of Indian Painting" in *The Modern Review* (May, 1914) and in *Ostasiatische Zeitschrift* (1914–1915).

35. "Philosophy of the Sadanga or the Six Limbs of Indian Painting" in *The Modern Review* (July, 1914) and in *Ostasiatische Zeitschrift* (1914–1915).

36. Percy Brown, *Indian Painting*, The Heritage of India Series (Calcutta: The Association Press; London: Oxford University Press, n.d. [probably 1918]), the edition used for this chapter (115 pages); 1927, rev. and enlarged ed.; 1930, 1947, 1953 (132 pages in the later editions).

37. Ananda K. Coomaraswamy, *The Transformation of Nature in Art* (Cambridge: Harvard University Press; New York: Dover, 1934; 1956), p. 20; see also pp. 186–189. In his abundant writings on art history, Coomaraswamy often mentioned parallels between Indian ideas and Chinese concepts. For example, he astutely observed—as have many others—that *qi* 氣 corresponds to Sanskrit *prāṇa* (immanent Breath; to which one might well add Greek *pneuma* and Phoenician and Ugaritic *rḥ*). See *Coomaraswamy: 1, Selected Papers, Traditional Art and Symbolism; 2, Selected Papers, Metaphysics*, ed. Roger Lipsey, Bollingen Series, 89 (Princeton: Princeton University Press, 1977), vol. 1, p. 315. Yet he seldom, if ever, so much as hinted at the possibility of influence from one to the other. Being more of a comparative philosopher than a historian, Coomaraswamy was simply not very concerned with the question of cultural exchange.

38. See *Peiwen yunfun* 佩文韻府 (1711), scroll 63, p. 2443b of the Commercial Press index edition.

39. Tseng Yu-ho Ecke, "A Reconsideration of 'ch'uan-mo-i-hsieh' [*sic*], the Sixth Principle of Hsieh Ho," *Proceedings of the International Symposium on Chinese Painting* (Taipei: National Palace Museum, 1970).

40. See Zürcher, "Recent Studies," p. 390 and Susan Bush, "Tsung Ping's Essay on Painting and the 'Landscape Buddhism' of Mount Lu," in *Theories of the Arts in China*, ed. Susan Bush and Christian Murck (Princeton: Princeton University Press, 1983), p. 143 (of 132–164).

41. Berthold Laufer, *Das Citralakshaṇa*, Dokumente der indischen Kunst, Erstes Heft: Malerei (Leipzig: Otto Harrassowitz, 1913), p. 3, assures us that, despite its inclusion in the *bStan-'gyur*, the *Citralakṣaṇa* "has not the slightest trace of Buddhism. Not once does it mention the name of the Buddha and it lacks all specific Buddhist terms. In the Introduction only brahmanical gods are called upon."

42. Vātsyāyana, *The Kāmasūtra*, with the *Jayamaṅgalā* of Yashodhar, ed. Gosvamī Dāmodar Shastri, Kāshi Sanskrit Series (Haridās Sanskrit Granthamālā), 29 (Benares: Chowkhamba Sanskrit Series Office, 1929), I.3.16, p. 30. There exists a complete scholarly translation into German by Richard Schmidt, *Das Kāmasūtram des Vātsyāyana; Die Indische Ars Amatoria; Nebst dem Vollständigen Kommentare (Jayamaṅgalā) des Yaśodhara* (Berlin: Hermann Barsdorf, 1907, 1922), p. 45. Unfortunately, Schmidt—apparently inadvertently—skips the third limb of the *ṣaḍaṅga* and commits a serious mistranslation of the sixth limb. Alain Daniélou's English translation of *The Complete Kāma Sūtra* (Rochester, Vermont: Park Street Press, 1994) gives only snatches of Yaśodhara's commentary. Regrettably, the *ṣaḍaṅga* is not among the parts that Daniélou offers.

43. Even specialists on Sanskrit aesthetics have been puzzled by how a word that basically means saltiness could acquire the derived meanings of beauty, charm, and loveliness. Carl Darling Buck, *A Dictionary of Selected Synonyms in the Principal Indo-European Languages: A Contribution to the History of Ideas* (Chicago and London: University of Chicago Press, 1949), p. 382 (5.81.3), offers a Sanskrit root, *lu*, "cut" (as in *lavaṅga-* the clove [tree]—i.e., something spicy, originally "cutting, sharp") for *lavana-*("salt"), but this seems forced. G. B. Palsule, "A Note on the Word *lāvaṇya*," *Annals of the Bhandarkar Oriental Research Institute*, 32.1–4 (1951), 261–262, attempts to derive *lāvaṇya* from *ramaṇa* (pleasing, charming, delightful), but Manfred Mayrhofer, the preeminent authority on Sanskrit etymology, finds his argument unconvincing. See Mayrhofer's *Kurzgefasstes etymologisches Wörterbuch des Altindischen: A Concise Etymological Sanskrit Dictionary*, 3 vols. (Heidelberg: Carl Winter, Universitätsverlag, 1953–1976), vol. 3, p. 93. In our subsequent investigations of *lāvaṇya*'s usage in various contexts, we shall find that the connection between saltiness and charm is not so far-fetched after all.

44. *Nāṭya-śāstra*, 17.100; 26.34. The *Nāṭya-śāstra* also discusses other aesthetic concepts relevant to the Six Limbs, e.g., *pramāṇa*, 5.179. See Manomohan Ghosh, trans. and annot., *The Nāṭyaśāstra (A Treatise on Ancient Indian Dramaturgy and Histrionics)*, ascribed to Bharata-muni, vol. 1 (chapters 1–27) (Calcutta: Manisha Granthalaya, 1967, rev. 2d ed.), p. 99. The first edition of the second volume is *The Nāṭyaśāstra (A Treatise on Ancient Indian Dramaturgy and Histrionics)*, ascribed to Bharata-muni, vol. 2 (Chapters 28–36), Bibliotheca Indica, Work Number 272, Issue Number 1581 (Calcutta: The Asiatic Society,

1961). See three paragraphs below for the identification and dating of the *Nāṭya-śāstra*.

45. Edwin Gerow, *A Glossary of Indian Figures of Speech* (The Hague, Paris: Mouton, 1971).

46. Prithvi Kumar Agrawala, *Aesthetic Principles of Indian Art: Their Primary Quest and Formation*, Indian Civilisation Series, 21 (Varanasi [Benares]: Prithivi Prakashan, 1980).

47. See Tarla Mehta, *Sanskrit Play Production in Ancient India*, Performing Arts Series, V (Delhi: Motilal Banarsidass, 1995); also Ghosh, *Nāṭyaśāstra*, vol. 1 (rev.), pp. lixff; vol. 2, p. 23.

48. Ludo Rocher, *The Purāṇas*, Fasc. 3 of Vol. II: *Epics and Sanskrit Religious Literature* in *A History of Indian Literature* (Wiesbaden: Otto Harrassowitz, 1986), p. 251.

49. Stella Kramrisch, "*The Vishṇudharmottara* (Part III): A Treatise on Indian Painting and Image-Making," *Journal of the Department of Letters, Calcutta University*, 17 (1924), 2–56. Issued separately as a book with the same title (Calcutta: Calcutta University Press, 1928, 2nd rev. and enlarged ed.), p. 4. For more information concerning the *Viṣṇudharmottara*, see Rocher, *Purāṇas*, p. 252 and Edwin Gerow, *Indian Poetics*, in Jan Gonda, ed., *A History of Indian Literature*, vol. 5, fasc. 3 (Wiesbaden: Otto Harrassowitz, 1977), p. 296.

50. See below at notes 62–64.

51. See, for example, Ananda K. Coomaraswamy, "Viṣṇudharmottara, Chapter XLI" *Journal of the American Oriental Society*, 52.1 (March, 1932), 13–21, esp. pp. 14, 19–20.

52. Tarapada Bhattacharyya, *The Canons of Indian Art, or A Study on Vāstuvidyā* (Calcutta: Firma KLM, 3d rev. and enlarged ed., 1986; 1st ed., 1947; 2nd ed., 1963), pp. 403–410, discusses the Six Limbs in relation to the *Citra-sūtra* of the *Viṣṇudharmottara* and other early Indian texts on painting. There can be no doubt whatsoever that Yaśodhara was not the originator of the Six Limbs, but that he was merely quoting them in his commentary on the *Kāma-sūtra*.

53. For an exhaustive thesis on the contents of the *Viṣṇudharmottara*, see Priyabala Shah, ed., *Viṣṇudharmottara-purāṇa; Third Khaṇḍa*, Vol. 2: *A Study on a Sanskrit text of Ancient Indian Arts*, Gaekwad's Oriental Series, 130, 137 (Baroda: Oriental Institute, 1961).

54. Georg Bühler, Review of Edward C. Sachau, trans. and annot., *Alberuni's India*, in *Indian Antiquary* (November, 1890), 381–410.

55. Priyabala Shah, ed., *Viṣṇudharmottara-purāṇa; Third Khaṇḍa*, Vol. 1 (Baroda: Oriental Institute, 1958), p. xxvi.

56. *Ibid.*, pp. xxvii–xxviii.

57. C. Sivaramamurti, *Chitrasūtra of the Vishṇudharmottara* (New Delhi: Kanak, 1978), p. 42.

58. Prithivi Kumar Agrawala, *On the Ṣaḍaṅga Canons of Painting*, Indian Civilisation Series, 22 (Varanasi: Prithivi Prakashan, 1981), pp. 9, 16.

59. Judging from citations in *Hanyu da cidian*, *Dai Kan-Wa jiten* 大漢和辭 典 (Morohashi), *Zhongwen da cidian* 中文大辭典, *Peiwen yunfu*, *Bianzi leibian* 駢 字類編, and other comprehensive lexicons of premodern usage, which were checked for all twelve of the binomials in the Six Laws, *qiyun* was a literary term in the Six Dynasties that was probably already in use before Xie He. Certainly *qi* and *yun* separately and in combination with other similarly elegant terms were much favored in Six Dynasties intellectual discourse, while *qi* and *yun* were often employed in the same sentence in close proximity to each other from at least the Jin period. For an extensive, illuminating discussion of *qiyun* (the main topic of the first law), see the chapter by Zong-qi Cai in this volume. There is no doubt whatsoever that *gufa* was very well established in literature by the Western Han period. For example, it is used in Song Yu's 宋玉 "Shennü fu" 神女賦 (Rhapsody on the Goddess) and in Sima Qian's 司馬遷 *Shi ji* 史記 (Records of the Grand Scribe) biography of the Marquis of Huaiyin 淮陰侯. Going back even further is *yingwu*, which was widely used in historical, literary, and philosophical texts from the Warring States and Western Han periods. The next R binomial, *suilei*, was well known in Six Dynasties Buddhism to refer to a kind of *upāya* (skillful means), whereby Buddhas and bodhisattvas reveal themselves differently and express themselves differently to various types of people, but it also occurred in non-Buddhist contexts. The fifth R binomial, *jingying*, was common in literary and historical texts already during pre-Han times for planning and construction, and was taken up by Liu Xie in his *Wenxin diaolong* during the early part of the sixth century to indicate artistic imagination. The last R binomial, *chuanyi*, is an anomaly in that it can not be found anywhere before Xie He. It is possible that *chuanyi* is a *lapsus calami* or that there has been a mistake in textual transmission. We may observe that Zhang Yanyuan has *chuanmo yixie* instead of *chuanyi moxie*, so perhaps he thought that something was wrong with the core of the sentence. On the other hand, Xie He may have fashioned *chuanyi* from many appropriate terms already in common currency, such as *chuanxin* 傳信 (transmit truth), *chuanshen* 傳神 (convey spirit), *yihua* 移畫 (copy a painting; sketch from life), and so forth. In contrast, the first S binomial, *shengdong*, is first used as an aesthetic term by Xie He. The next S binomial, *yongbi*, was already in use by the middle of the fifth century, but it was not very common and was dictionally not elevated. Although *xiangxing* was in use by the first century B.C.E. ("to represent / image a form"), it did not have a particular meaning for the arts. By the end of the first century C.E., it is used by Xu Shen in the "Preface" to *Shuo wen jie zi* to mean "pictographic" (a type of written character). Both *fucai* and *weizhi* were apparently coined by Xie He, and *moxie* seems to have come into use only slightly before him. Thus, although a couple of problematic issues remain, the overall nature of the R and S bino-

mials is that the former are older, better established in literary usage, and more refined, while the latter are newer, not common in literary usage, and simpler.

60. It is astonishing that the otherwise astute Acker, *Texts* (p. xlv) goes out of his way to deny that there is anything in the Six Laws corresponding to *varṇikā-bhaṅga* when *fucai* is such a perfect and obvious match.

61. I do not wish to enter into an extended discussion of the traditional understanding of the sixth law, for that would take us too far afield. (See the chapter in this volume by Robert Harrist for a nuanced explanation of different types of tracing and copying [the presumed subjects of the sixth law]). Early Chinese theorists did not make a large distinction between copying from life and copying from models. While recognizing that the sixth law is customarily explained as referring to the copying of ancient models, it is worth pointing out that its constituent terms (*chuanyi*, *moxie*) and related expressions (e.g., *yixie* 移寫, *yihua* 移畫, *mohua* 摹畫, and so forth) refer not only to the replication of art and calligraphy, but also—and often originally—to painting and drawing from nature. In this sense, depicting something faithfully is to copy from life, as it were. For example, *moxie* can mean either "copy, imitate" or "depict accurately." The latter meaning is clearly intended in Fan Zhen's 范鎮 (1001–1087) *Dongzhai jishi* 東齋記事 (Records of Events from the Eastern Studio), 4 (p. 27, ll. 5–6 in the *Congshu jicheng chubian* 叢書集成初編 edition of the text) where the author mentions two painters from Shu (Sichuan) surnamed Huang who were good at painting birds. From the following sentence, it is obvious that they were painting from life and not copying the works of old masters: "Their family raised many hawks and falcons. They observed the birds' spirited valor in order to accurately depict (*moxie*) it, thus capturing their excellence." Understood in this primary fashion, it is clear that the S binomial of the sixth law corresponds closely to the fifth of the Six Limbs, *sādṛśyam*.

62. See Alfred Forke, trans. and annot., *Lun-hêng; Part 1: Philosophical Essays of Wang Ch'ung; Part 2: Miscellaneous Essays of Wang Ch'ung*, Supplementary volumes to the *Mitteilungen des Seminars für Orientalische Sprachen*, 14 (1907) (New York: Paragon, 1962, rpt.), vol. 1, pp. 304–312.

63. Kramrisch, *The* Vishṇudharmottara, tr., p. 46, no. 7 (of III.39).

64. Liu Daochun's "Six Strengths" were subsequently taken up by Xia Wenyan (Yuan) in his *Tuhui baojian*, as well as by other art theorists and critics.

65. Xie He seems not to wish to take credit for the invention of the Six Laws: "But while painting has its Six Laws, few are able to combine them all together, and from ancient times until today each painter has excelled in one of the laws." Acker's comments on Xie He's wording are apposite: "The somewhat casual way in which these six elements are introduced here—'but although there are the six elements of painting'—rather tends to support the idea that Hsieh Ho is quoting from some earlier work, and is not 'enunciating the Six Canons' for the first time. If he were 'enunciating' anything here one would expect

something beginning with a *fu* (Now—) or at any rate a little more emphasis than seems to me to be implied in the *sui hua yu liu fa.*" *Texts*, p. 4, n. 2, and see also p. xli. Xie He undoubtedly was aware that his Six Laws were derivative.

66. See, for example, Coomaraswamy, *Transformation*, p. 12.

67. See Victor H. Mair, "The Origins of an Iconographical Form of the Pilgrim Hsüan-tsang," *T'ang Studies* 4 (1986), pp. 29–41, plus seven plates.

68. Mair, "Buddhism in *The Literary Mind*," p. 80.

69. Victor H. Mair and Tsu-Lin Mei, "The Sanskrit Origins of Recent Style Prosody," *Harvard Journal of Asiatic Studies* 51, no. 2 (December 1991), pp. 375–470.

70. Years after I had completed this chapter and copy-editing was finished, my good friend in Shanghai Xu Wenkan sent me two articles by the Chinese specialist on Indian philosophy and religion, Jin Kemu 金克木. The first, entitled "Yindu huajia A. Taigeer de meixue sixiang lüeshu" 印度畫家阿 · 泰戈爾的美學思想略述. In this article, Jin structures his presentation around Abinandranath's disquisitions on the Six Limbs (see note 33), but mentions nary a word about Xie He's Six Laws. The second article, entitled "Yindu de huihua liu zhi he Zhongguo de huihua liu fa" 印度的繪畫六支和中國的繪畫六法, is a superficial introduction to the two sets of rules. Jin dismisses out of hand the probability that they could be related. The most useful part of this article is Jin's discussion of several early Indian Buddhist monk painters who came to China. Both articles are collected in the author's *Yindu wenhua yulun*—Fanzhu lu ji *bubian* 印度文化餘論—《梵竺廬集》補編 (Beijing: Xueyuan chubanshe, 2002).

Chapter 4

● ●

A Good Place Need Not
Be a Nowhere

The Garden and Utopian Thought
in the Six Dynasties

Shuen-fu Lin

The following quotation, which may at first appear totally irrelevant to the topic of this essay, is from the early Daoist text *Zhuang Zi* 莊子.

> Huizi said to Zhuang Zi, "I have a big tree people call ailanthus. Its trunk is too gnarled and knotted to measure with the inked line. Its branches are too curly and twisted to fit a compass or an L-square. It stands in the road but no carpenter would even look at it. Now your talk, too, is big and useless—it will be dismissed by everyone alike!"
>
> Zhuang Zi said, "Have you never seen a wildcat or a weasel? It crouches down in wait for stray prey. It leaps and pounces east and west, not avoiding high or low, until it falls into the snare and dies in the net. Then there's the yak, big as a cloud hanging from the sky. It's certainly big, but it can't catch mice. Now you have this big tree and you're bothered by its being useless. Why don't you plant it in Not-Even-Anything Village, in the broad and open wilds, where you can while the time away and do nothing by its side, or lie down for a free and easy slumber under

it? No ax will ever cut its life short, nor will anything else ever harm it. If it's totally useless, how can it come to grief?[1]

The above is the second of two parables that conclude the "Xiaoyao-you" 逍遙遊 (Free and Easy Wandering) chapter in this great text of Daoist philosophy and literature. The title "Free and Easy Wandering" metaphorically expresses the idea of spiritual freedom, which is not only the central theme of the chapter, but also a major theme in the entire *Zhuang Zi*. In each of the two closing parables, Zhuang Zi (ca. 369–286 B.C.E.) engages his friend, the logician Hui Shi 惠施 (ca. 380–305 B.C.E.), in a lively debate on the subthemes of usefulness and uselessness. Hui Shi is here depicted as someone who has not attained spiritual freedom and is unable to roam above the artificial distinctions between usefulness and uselessness and recognize the uses of some-thing that is "big" and "useless." In Zhuang Zi's eyes, he is far from being the ideal person—that is, an ultimate person (*zhiren* 至人), a dai-monic person (*shenren* 神人), or a sage (*shengren* 聖人)—mentioned in the chapter.[2]

Zhuang Zi's remarks quoted above constitute one example of the Daoist thinker's persistent attempts to deconstruct such opposing con-cepts, distinctions, and values as large and small, long and short, beau-tiful and ugly, right and wrong, useful and useless, success and failure, dream and wakefulness, and life and death, which have structured our culture. In his response to Hui Shi's criticism, Zhuang Zi is careful not to allow his own argument to fall into any rigidly constructed category. He resorts to using "outlandish opinions, expansive discourses, and borderless words," to borrow a phrase from the "Tianxia" 天下 (All under Heaven) chapter of the *Zhuang Zi*,[3] and he creates a fantasy world named "Wuheyou zhi xiang" 無何有之鄉, which literally means "a village where there is nothing whatever."[4] This Not-Even-Anything Village is a perfect world in which one can do free and unrestricted (*xiaoyao* 逍遙) roaming or simply do nothing (*wuwei* 無為) and rest at will, free from all harm and care. It is not so much a world of literal nothingness as one that transcends all human classifications, distinc-tions, purposes, and values. The concept of "*wuwei*," which is com-monly found in both the *Daodejing* 道德經 and the *Zhuang Zi*, does not mean "doing nothing" literally but "the absence of purposive activity."[5] According to the Daoists, a person is to emulate Dao 道 in his conduct so that he can act in a manner that is natural, spontaneous, and free from human interests, judgments, and goals. The late modern intellectual historian Xu Fuguan 徐復觀 interprets the kind of life in Not-Even-Anything Village Zhuang Zi advocates in "Free and Easy Wandering" as a mode of life that embodies Dao or an artistic mode of life that is free from any utilitarian concern or practical purpose.[6] Following Xu Fuguan's interpretation, we can say that the person of the utmost spiritual attainment who can wander freely and without restriction as depicted in the *Zhuang Zi* is one who has manifested the supreme artistic spirit.[7]

It is interesting to note that the idea of "Wuheyou zhi xiang" appears virtually identical with that of "utopia" in Western cultures. Just as utopia is simultaneously a good place and nowhere, so too is Wuheyou zhi xiang at once a perfect realm and Nevernever Land, which does not seem to exist in the real world.[8] There are, of course, fundamental differences between Zhuang Zi's Not-Even-Anything Village and the Western utopia. In the first place, while a utopia is usually conceived by Western thinkers as a place of perfection, especially in its social, political, and moral aspects, Not-Even-Anything Village is a Daoist ideal realm that transcends precisely all these practical concerns of human culture. Second, a utopia is often oriented toward an attack on the social, political, and moral life within a culture, while Not-Even-Anything Village is directed toward nourishing an individual's inner life. Third, although by naming his ideal world Not-Even-Anything Village, Zhuang Zi obviously does not suggest that it exists in the real world, he nevertheless believes that the ideal spiritual state for which his parable is a metaphor can be attained by people in real life.[9] But the same thing cannot be said of the Western utopia, which is molded and nurtured by two ancient beliefs: "the Judeo-Christian faith in a paradise created with the world and destined to endure beyond it, and the Hellenic myth of an ideal, beautiful city built by men for men without the assistance and often in defiance of the gods."[10] The sense of "nowhere" is an essential part of the Western utopia because "Utopia may be conceived as a prologue or a foretaste of the absolute perfection still to be experienced."[11]

In their authoritative work *Utopian Thought in the Western World*, Frank E. Manuel and Fritzie P. Manuel observe, "Perhaps the Chinese have been too worldly and practical, and the Hindus too transcendental to recognize a tension between the Two Kingdoms [i.e., paradise in heaven and the world on earth] and to resolve it in that myth of a heaven on earth which lies at the heart of utopian fantasy."[12] Although the tension between the "Two Kingdoms" may not have existed for the Chinese, the passion for an ideal, perfect world in which to live has been as strong among them as among the people in the West. It is precisely because of the absence of this tension in their worldview that the Chinese through the ages have been able to focus their attention on life here and now. As we shall see below, this strong worldly tendency eventually results in siting Not-Even-Anything Village in the Chinese garden centuries after Zhuang Zi fantasized about it.

The Beginnings of a Paradise

The English word "paradise" is derived from the Old Persian "*paridaeza*," meaning "garden," "park," or "enclosure."[13] On the arid Persian landscape, "the Persian garden was a walled oasis divided by channels of water—a cosmological idea echoed in the biblical Eden. Symmetrically patterned by fruit trees, flowers, and verdant shrubbery, it was designed as much for philosophical contemplation as physical enjoyment."[14] The root meaning of "paradise" can perhaps be interpreted as "an enclosed space of idealized existence."

Turning to China, we find that the sense of an enclosed space is also usually relevant to the early conceptions of the garden. The words "*yuan*" 園 (flower and vegetable garden), "*you*" 囿 (walled-in park, animal park), and "*pu*" 圃 (vegetable garden), which are already found in the ancient text *Shi jing* 詩經 (The Book of Songs), all carry the implication that in building each of these things a fence, wall, or boundary marker is probably used.[15] Very early in Chinese culture the garden already appears as a special and important, if not yet exactly paradisal, place. To get a clearer picture, let us look at one of the earliest descriptions of a park/garden found in Chinese writing. The following is Song 242 in the *Shi jing*:

> He surveyed and began the Sacred Terrace,
> He surveyed it and built it,
> All the people worked at it;
> In a short time they finished it.
> He surveyed and began without goading;
> Yet the people came in their throngs.

The king was in the Sacred Park,
Where the does and stags lay down.
The does and stags were sleek;
The white birds gleamed.
The king was by the Sacred Pool;
How full it was of leaping fish!

On the upright posts and cross-beams with their spikes
Hung the big drums and bells.
Oh, well-ranged were the drums and bells,
And merry was the Moated Mound.
Oh, well-ranged were the drums and bells,
And merry was the Moated Mound.
Bang, bang went the alligator-skin drums;
The blind musicians plied their skill.[16]

In book 1, part A, section 2, of *Mencius*, it is recorded that when Mencius 孟子 (ca. 372–289 B.C.E.) went to see King Hui of the Liang 梁惠王, he quoted the first two stanzas of the above song to say that the ancient sage kings were able to share their enjoyments with the people they ruled.[17] Due to Mencius's stature as an influential Confucian thinker, scholars throughout Chinese history have generally accepted his interpretation of this song as authoritative.[18] Mencius's comment indicates that he considered the place King Wen of the Zhou 周文王 (referred to as "he" and "the king" in the song) had built as essentially a pleasure park. Terrace, pool, mound, and animals, mentioned in Song 242, are common features of the Chinese garden in later historical times. The second stanza can easily be read as describing King Wen's enjoyment of viewing the deer, birds, and fish in his park. And the playing of music in the last stanza easily brings to mind merrymaking activity.

According to the modern scholar Wang Yi 王毅, however, Song 242 is not at all about King Wen's sage efforts to share his enjoyments in the king's park with his people.[19] Rather, it records the building of the Sacred Terrace (*lingtai* 靈台), where the king in ancient China worshipped the ancestors and Di 帝 (the Lord or Supreme Ruler in heaven); entertained them with music played by blind musicians; and received the mandate of heaven. The function of the Sacred Park (*lingyou* 靈囿) is fundamentally religious. The king's Sacred Park consists of a high terrace built from earth, symbolizing a lofty mountain, which is then encircled by a moat. Animals such as deer, birds, and fish are placed in the park because of their association with auspicious portents in nature when a king receives the mandate of heaven. One can safely assume that a long tradition for a king to build a sacred park existed before the time of King Wen, father of King Wu 武王, who founded the Zhou dynasty (ca. 1122–221 B.C.E.). As Wang Yi has convincingly argued, the origin of the Chinese garden is to be found in this tradition of the construction of the king's Sacred Terrace.[20]

While the ancient king's park seems to have been originally built primarily for religious purposes, in time it acquired other functions, including that of providing the king with enjoyment. In old texts such as the *Shi jing* and the *Zuo zhuan* 左傳 a number of references can be found to the king's park as a place for hunting, fishing, boating, and entertaining state guests.[21] Historical records seem to suggest that during the Spring and Autumn period (traditionally 770–481 B.C.E.) many feudal lords and ministers increasingly built terraces, palaces, and gardens for themselves, with the chief purpose of pleasurable living in mind. Thus it seems safe to assume that the tradition of a pleasure garden had indeed been in existence long before Mencius's time so that it could serve as a good basis for him to interpret Song 242 as basically expressing a sage king's sharing his enjoyment with the people.

The shamanistic song entitled "Zhaohun" 招魂 (Summons of the Soul, perhaps written sometime in the second half of the third century B.C.E. and later collected in the anthology *Chu ci* 楚辭 [Songs of the Chu]) contains the earliest literary description of a pleasure garden.[22] In the song the shamans present invocations to the soul of a sick or dying king of the Chu state, persuading it to return to its old abode. As depicted by the shamans, the king's home features high halls, shady chambers, lattice doors, a palace garden, tiered balconies, stepped terraces, storied pavilions, covered loggias, linked galleries, ponds, meandering gullies, and rare plants and birds.[23] As Maggie Keswick points out, "the winding streams, the lotus lake, the balconied pavilion leaning out over the water, the scarlet fretwork, the terrace," etc. depicted here are characteristic of the Chinese garden in later historical times.[24] In "The Summons of the Soul," the king's garden already appears as a paradisal place, full of earthly delights, a place very different from King Wen's austere Sacred Park. To my knowledge, no other detailed description of the garden can be found in ancient Chinese texts. It seems highly unlikely that the author of the song could have derived his fantastic description solely from his imagination. There must have been a highly developed tradition of garden design to serve as the source of his inspiration.[25]

The shamans in the song are trying to persuade the soul of the king to return to its abode by appealing to the idealistic life in the palace garden. In this respect, "The Summons of the Soul" expresses a powerful affirmation of life in this world here and now. It is important to note that the garden or park also appears as the site of perfect life in early Chinese legends and myths. The *Shanhai jing* 山海經 (The Classic of Mountains and Seas), which is a major source text of early Chinese mythology, records numerous paradisal places. Although it contains written materials dating perhaps from the third century B.C.E. to the second century C.E., these materials could have come from an oral tradition that had been in existence since a much earlier time.[26] It is not at all impossible that the author of "The Summons of the Soul" might in some general way have been influenced by the same conception of the garden/park/paradise that existed in the oral tradition of ancient Chinese myths and legends. Of particular relevance to our discussion of the development of the Chinese garden is the place called Xuanpu 縣圃/玄圃 (Hanging Garden or Mysterious Garden), which emerged in ancient legends and myths.

The term "Xuanpu" does not appear in *The Classic of Mountains and Seas*, though it can be found in the songs "Li Sao" 離騷 (Encountering Sorrow) and "Tian Wen" 天問 (Heavenly Questions), which are among the earliest portions of the anthology *Songs of the Chu*.[27] In these two songs, Xuanpu is situated in the mythical Kunlun Mountains 昆侖山 in the western regions of China. In *The Classic of Mountains and Seas*, the term "Pingpu" 平圃 (Garden of Peace) is found.[28] According to Guo Pu 郭璞 (276–324 C.E.), who wrote the earliest commentary on the *Shanhai jing*, "Xuanpu" and "Pingpu" refer in fact to the same garden.[29] "Dixingxun" 地形訓, chapter 4 of the second-century B.C.E. text *Huainan Zi* 淮南子, relates that "Hanging Garden, Cold Wind [Mountain], and Fantong [Mountain] are inside the Changhe Gate of the Kunlun Mountains."[30] The chapter further notes that when an ordinary human being climbs onto Cold Wind Mountain, he/she will become immortal; when he/she climbs further up into Hanging Garden, he/she will acquire magical powers that enable him/her to command wind and rain; and when he/she ascends further up into heaven, where the Taidi

太帝 (Supreme Lord) resides, he/she will become a deity (*shen* 神).[31] The Changhe Gate is the Gate of Heaven.[32] Despite the fact that Xuanpu is not mentioned in the *Shanhai jing*, it undoubtedly exists in the Chinese imagination as a paradise in the Kunlun Mountains and also as an entrance to heaven. Below I shall present a brief general account of this paradise.[33]

Xuanpu is a very large park, some eight hundred leagues square, according to one account.[34] Within the park, there are luxurious palaces, terraces, pavilions, wells with jade banisters, and exotic plants, birds, beasts, and foods; there are plants and animals that, when eaten, can cure serious diseases; and there are coursing streams, jade-grease producing rivers, cool breezes, gigantic barley trees (which are each forty feet high and five spans wide), a variety of trees (including trees of immortality), dancing and singing phoenixes, and a kind of "looks-like-flesh creature" (*shirou* 視肉) that can never be fully consumed and will always grow back to its original size and shape (resembling the liver of an ox). The exotic objects found in the park are simply listed without being integrated into a coherent description of the features of the park as a place to live, as in the case of "The Summons of the Soul." Nevertheless, together they convey the picture of a paradise where the residents can enjoy an endless supply of exotic foods, sounds, and sights, as well as eternal life and freedom from work, hardship, illness, or any other kind of suffering. As Anne Birrell has aptly observed, "The utopian landscape [as depicted in these accounts] has as one of its functions the fulfillment of human aspirations, especially those of a rural, agricultural community, so that food, drink, and clothing are provided without toil or labour. The utopias also convey the idea of a harmony in nature, through the peaceful coexistence of wild animals and birds."[35]

Situated on top of the Kunlun Mountains between heaven and earth, Xuanpu is said to be the Lower Capital (Xiadu 下都) of Di, who is believed to be Huangdi 黃帝 (the Yellow Emperor), one of the deified ancestors of the Chinese people whose spirit is said to reside in heaven.[36] Several important points can be made concerning this conception of paradise in early Chinese myths and legends. First, Xuanpu is fully accessible to human beings. To reach Xuanpu is not easy, to be sure, and it is a feat only the strongest of human beings can accomplish, but it can be done. Once there, an ordinary human being will be able to avoid death and live forever. Second, there is no rigid dichotomy between This World and the Other World as we find in other religious traditions. Heaven and earth form one continuum in a conception of a unitary cosmos. The human world, Xuanpu, and even the Yellow Emperor's realm in heaven are all parts of the same One and Only World. There are hierarchies in the three realms, but human beings are not sinners expelled from paradise, as Adam and Eve were from the Garden of Eden. Third, as already noted above, the idea of Xuanpu represents an affirmation of life in this world. The spirit of the Yellow Emperor would even build a Lower Capital on earth, and his park is full of many earthly delights.

The late modern historian Gu Jiegang 顧頡剛 observes that two main mythological traditions existed in ancient China: the Kunlun tradition of the western plateaus and the Penglai 蓬萊 tradition of the eastern coastal regions, especially in the states of Yan 燕, Qi 齊, Wu 吳, and Yue 越.[37] According to Gu, the Kunlun tradition came first and began to spread to the Central Plain 中原, the heartland of early China, sometime during the Zhou dynasty, especially after the Warring States period (471–221 B.C.E.), stimulating the development of the eastern tradition.[38] From the middle of the Warring States period onward, the two traditions began to merge, as reflected in such texts as the *Zhuang Zi* and the *Chu ci* (in portions other than the early works of "Encountering Sorrow," "Nine Songs," and "Heavenly Questions").

In the eastern tradition, a paradise is also created for the immortals. The ocean now becomes an important feature of the paradise, which is supposed to consist of three island mountains—Penglai 蓬萊, Fangzhang 方丈, and Yingzhou 瀛洲—in the Bohai Sea 渤海. It is recorded in Sima Qian's 司馬遷 (ca. 145–86 B.C.E.) *Shi ji* 史記 (Records of the Grand Historian) that as early as the second half of the fourth century, Kings Wei and Xuan of the Qi 齊威王、齊宣王 and King Zhao of the Yan 燕昭王 had heard about the Isles of the Immortals and from time to time sent explorers there in search of elixirs.[39] As in the case of the Kunlun Mountains, there are magnificent palaces, exotic birds and animals, and precious elixirs on the three islands in the eastern ocean. Both Xuanpu and Penglai are the creations of the Chinese popular imagination, as embodied in ancient myths and legends. Nonetheless, as idealistic places they have a profound influence on later Chinese conceptions and constructions of the garden.

The Imperial Park of the Qin and Han

With the creation of the early Chinese empire, first under the Qin (221–206 B.C.E.) and soon afterward under the Han (206 B.C.E.–220 C.E.), the garden also entered a new era of development. The emperors of the Qin and early Han demonstrated an unprecedented passion for building magnificent parks of enormous size. It is recorded in Sima Qian's *Records of the Grand Historian* that whenever the First Emperor of the Qin (Qinshihuang 秦始皇, 259–210 B.C.E.) conquered feudal lords, he would build replicas of their palaces in the Qin capital, Xianyang 咸陽, undoubtedly "as trophies of his victories."[40] Ban Gu's 班固 *Han shu* 漢書 (History of the Han) notes that there were three hundred "detached palaces" (*ligong* 離宮) between Xianyang and the Qin's former capital, Yong 雍, and the famous Efang Palace 阿房宮, which the First Emperor completed, was "several tens of *ren* 仞 [seven or eight Chinese feet per *ren*] tall and spread five leagues from east to west and a thousand paces [*bu* 步, six Chinese feet each] from south to north."[41] One of the largest imperial hunting parks, Shanglinyuan 上林苑, which the Han inherited from the Qin, was more than three hundred leagues square and had seventy detached palaces within it.[42] During the early Han, hundreds of beasts were kept in Shanglinyuan for the emperor and his guests to hunt in autumn and winter, and when Emperor Wu 武帝 (156–87 B.C.E.) of the Han first began to renovate the park, officials and subjects from near and far contributed more than three thousand kinds of rare fruit trees and flowers that were planted in it.[43] Indeed, the imperial parks in Qin and Han times were well stocked with rare birds, animals, and plants, as well as lavishly built palaces, galleries, pavilions, running streams, bridges, and fish ponds.[44] Large objects in nature, such as rivers and mountains, were often integrated into these parks.[45] The imperial parks served a number of functions in Qin and Han times. They were the pleasure grounds for the emperor, his family, and other noble guests, used for hunting and other entertainments. Other practical and utilitarian purposes could also be observed.[46] Large numbers of cattle and horses were raised in the parks, and slaves were kept to labor in them as well. The animals and the slaves could also be used in times of war. The Han dynasty hunting parks were also used to perform magical ceremonies for warding off pestilences.[47]

Two main themes of the Qin and Han imperial park should be highlighted here. First, as a symbol of the splendors of the empire, the imperial park is a microcosm of the universe. The First Emperor of the Qin constructed his Xianyang Palace 咸陽宮 in such a way that it imaged the Purple Palace 紫宮 of the Lord in Heaven.[48] The Wei River 渭水 meandered through his capital city, representing an image of the Milky Way. And the forms of palaces and halls of the early Han "were patterned after heaven and earth."[49] All-inclusiveness is one important feature of the early Chinese imperial park. Second, in building an imperial park, the early emperors were also attempting to create a realm that resembled paradise for the deities and immortals—that is, a Xuanpu or an Isles of the Immortals. As mentioned briefly above, despite his brilliance as China's "Great Unifier," the First Emperor of the Qin was obsessed with the cult of immortality and sent expeditions of young men and maidens in search of elixirs on the three Isles of the Immortals in the Bohai Sea. Emperor Wu of the Han was equally taken with the cult but decided to build ravishing replicas of the fairy isles to attract the immortals to come to his palace gardens.[50] In his Jianzhang Palace 建章宮, he built two spacious lakes with islands on which simulacra of the fairy mountains made from earth were arranged in a pattern. Emperor Wu of the Han not only built numerous artificial lakes and mountains, but also made sculptures with metal or stone of fish, dragons, and other exotic birds and beasts to place on them.[51] As Maggie Keswick observes, "across the centuries Han Wu-ti's [i.e., Emperor Wu of the Han] fairy islands have spawned countless miniature mountains built in gardens all across the East."[52] In China in later historical times, fairy mountains in gardens were often represented by exotically formed rocks gathered from nature. The Chinese passion for exotic rockery was so strong that Keswick coins the term "petromania" to refer to it.[53] While the recreation of the Isles of the Immortals absorbed much of the interest of the early emperors of China, the legend of Xuanpu was still alive in the people's imagination at the time. In the "Ganquan fu" 甘泉賦 (Rhapsody on the Sweet Springs Palace), Yang Xiong 揚雄 (53 B.C.E.–18 C.E.) compared the park at the Sweet Springs Palace to the Hanging Garden: "All this befits the Hanging Garden of the Lord's abode/And images the majestic spirit of Grand Unity."[54] What deserves our special attention here is that the Hanging Garden and the Isles of the Immortals are no longer paradises in some remote, difficult-to-reach places but are right in the emperor's park. The ancient Sacred Terrace, built primarily for religious purposes, has now been transformed into the early imperial park, built for the glorification and enjoyment of everyday life, as well as for rites to the principal Han deity, Taiyi 太一.[55] The paradise is situated not on mythical mountains in the Western plateau or in the eastern ocean but right in northern China.

Wang Yi has provided good discussions of the architecture and overall construction of parks and gardens from ancient through the Qin and Han times.[56] He has made his observations mainly from literary sources and archeological finds from the sites of ancient capitals, parks, and palaces. According to his research, the garden or park before the Qin and Han usually relied on a lofty terrace as the kernel, which may involve numerous building clusters and scenic spots that were interconnected with paths and/or verandas or covered bridges. In the Qin and Han imperial park, although the previous interconnecting mechanisms continued to be used, large bodies of water such as lakes or ponds were added to become the new nuclei to integrate various clusters of buildings and scenes. The addition of bodies of water as integrative nuclei increased the complexity of the relations among hills, water, and buildings in the construction of parks and greatly enhanced their overall aesthetic effect. These new developments remained influential for later garden construction.

At this juncture, I should mention some useful observations on the distinctive orientation of traditional Chinese architecture by a leading contemporary expert in Chinese philosophy and aesthetics, Li Zehou. In his *Mei de licheng* 美的歷程 (The Path of Beauty), Li Zehou 李澤厚 offers some penetrating insights into the special features and meanings of Chinese architecture: "Chinese architecture throughout history is typified not by religious buildings isolated from the world at large and symbolizing things beyond human experience, but by palatial ancestral temples linked to actual living and the human environment."[57] In traditional China, buildings seldom exceed two stories but can extend at great length horizontally. Li Zehou further observes,

> The horizontal expansion of Chinese buildings into an organic complex virtually transforms spatial consciousness into a concept of time. Chinese complexes, with their broad horizontal dimensions, permit visitors to stroll at their leisure through an uninterrupted procession of varied and intricate

halls, balconies, pavilions, and terraces that epitomize the ease and comfort of life and evoke a feeling of mastery.... In such complexes, practical, worldly, rational, and historical elements dominate, not the supernatural awareness that is the basic aesthetic focus of many purely religious buildings.[58]

Just like Chinese architecture itself, the composition and the meandering and the interlocking parts of the early imperial park make it particularly earthbound.

During the Han dynasty, the emperors no longer had a monopoly on the construction of gardens and parks, as the aristocrats, ministers, and even some well-to-do ordinary people began to imitate them. All of the Han gardens and parks were luxuriously built for the main purpose of pleasurable living.[59]

The Infusion of the Daoist Aesthetic Spirit

The period from the fall of the Han dynasty in 220 C.E. to the founding of the Sui 隋 dynasty in 589 C.E. is known in history as either the Wei, Jin, and Southern and Northern Dynasties 魏晉南北朝 or the Six Dynasties 六朝 period. It is a period of turmoil politically and socially. But in various areas of culture—especially in intellectual, art, and literary history—the Six Dynasties period is one of great importance, richness, and vitality. Many ideas and trends formed during the Wei-Jin period (220–420 C.E.) have a far-reaching influence on cultural developments in the subsequent historical periods. A comprehensive discussion of the cultural developments of the Six Dynasties is obviously outside the scope of this chapter. I shall restrict myself to the aspects that bear special relevance to my subject of the garden.

During the reign of Emperor Wu of the Han, Confucianism was elevated to be the orthodox system of thought openly espoused by the state. Throughout the subsequent centuries of the Han dynasty, intellectual life was much given to textual and pedantic study and the acceptance of the authority of the Confucian classics and ethics, as well as of the cosmological theories of yin-yang and five phases (*yinyang wuxing* 陰陽五行).[60] Educated people put great emphasis on attaining lifelong achievements by acquiring the reputation of being an ethical person, a statesman, a general, a writer, or the like. The literature they produced was much given to didacticism and utilitarianism and was largely oriented toward the observable outside world of nature and overt actions, as seen in the rhapsodies (*fu* 賦) and biographies (*zhuan* 傳) in historical texts. With the disintegration of the Han empire in the second and third centuries, the authority of Confucian and other traditional values and beliefs began to be challenged. In place of the Confucian classics, the *Yi jing* 易經 (The Book of Changes), *Lao Zi* 老子 (i.e., *Daodejing*), and *Zhuang Zi* 莊子 became the three most respected texts.

There is no question that a qualitative change took place within Chinese culture toward the end of the Han dynasty and during the beginning of the Wei-Jin period. Previous mainstream values began to be regarded as having been imposed upon human beings, and the intrinsic meaning and value of the human person and human existence itself were instead asserted. This shift of focus has been described as "the awakening of man" (*ren de zijue* 人的自覺), which was accomplished through a rejection, questioning, and destruction of the old beliefs, values, and customs.[61]

Two texts from the Wei-Jin period can be mentioned to illustrate this new "awakening of man" in Chinese intellectual history: the *Renwu zhi* 人物志 (Studies on Human Abilities), by Liu Shao 劉邵 of the Wei dynasty (220–265 C.E.), and the *Shishuo xinyu* 世説新語 (A New Account of Tales of the World), by Liu Yiqing 劉義慶 (403–444 C.E.) of the Jin (265–420 C.E.) and early (Liu) Song 劉宋 (420–479 C.E.) periods.[62] In the *Renwu zhi*, the judging of human character and ability was no longer restricted by the previous Confucian concerns of ethics, integrity, classical learning, and moral courage, but was dependent on categories such as natural endowments, temperament, bearing, deportment, and ability. The highest criterion and principle was not a person's outward actions or conduct but the manifestation of his inner spirit.[63] The *Shishuo xinyu* is a text that contains nothing but a mixed assortment of witty expressions and brief anecdotes of the unusual behavior of people. The characters recorded in this book all gave greater attention to making their conversations appear metaphysical and their behavior unconventional and liberal than to the observance of personal integrity and ethical correctness. The new ideal of the Wei-Jin era is the ability to manifest the spirit of freedom and detachment from vulgarity and restrictive conventions in momentary expressions in words or deeds. A person who had this ability was called a *mingshi* 名士, or "famous scholar." What a famous scholar valued highly were inner wisdom, lofty spirit, unconventional speech and conduct, and beautiful appearance and deportment—and beauty here referred to the manifestation of a person's inner wisdom and character in outward appearance, which was as beautiful as natural scenery.[64] If the records of people of worth in previous historical writings emphasized lifelong achievements, the accounts of famous scholars of the Wei-Jin period stressed the demonstration of momentary brilliance. The modern intellectual historian Mou Zongsan 牟宗三 has called this new approach to the character, talent, personality, and worth of people an aesthetic approach, in contrast to the previous moral approach found in Confucian-dominated texts.[65]

Since the focus of this paper is on idealistic living, I should like now to examine the conceptions of the sage (*shengren* 聖人), the person of the highest spiritual attainment whom the Chinese educated elite in the past emulated, as set forth in the two intellectual movements in the Wei-Jin—namely, Xuanxue 玄學 (Abstruse Learning) and Qingtan 清談 (Pure Conversation). It is interesting to note that the sages revered by such leading thinkers in the intellectual movements as He Yan 何晏 (ca. 190–249 C.E.), Wang Bi 王弼 (226–249 C.E.), and Guo Xiang 郭象 (ca. 253–312 C.E.) were Confucius 孔子 (551–479 B.C.E.) and the sage-kings of antiquity admired by Confucius and his followers.[66] It seems that since Confucianism had been made the orthodox system of thought in the early Han, Confucius's prestige as a sage remained unchallenged throughout the Wei-Jin era, despite the fact that the Daoist texts *Daodejing* and *Zhuang Zi* had risen to surpass the Confucian classics in importance.

The conceptions of the idealized human being as presented in Wei-Jin intellectual discourses actually reflect a tendency to amalgamate Confucian and Daoist ideas. He Yan makes the argument that a sage does not have the feelings of joy, anger, sorrow, and happiness that ordinary people have, an argument that resembles Zhuang Zi's opinion that a perfect human being can be free from the feelings of joy, grief, like and dislike, love for life and hatred for death, etc.[67] Wang Bi disagrees with He Yan and offers the following description of the sage:

> The sage surpasses ordinary people in his abundant daimonic brightness, and what he has in common with them are the five emotions. Because his daimonic brightness is abundant, the sage is able to embody the vital forces of heaven and earth and be in communion with nonbeing. Because

he has the same five emotions, the sage cannot but respond to things with
grief and happiness. However, the sage's emotions are such that he can
respond to things without being entangled by them. It is a great mistake
for one to say now that the sage no longer responds to things because he
shows no entanglement.[68]

The five emotions Wang Bi talks about are joy, anger, grief, happiness,
and resentment. According to Wang Bi, the sage possesses human
emotions as do ordinary people. In saying so, Wang Bi is reiterating a
common Confucian belief. The sage differs from ordinary people in
having possessed an abundance of daimonic brightness (*shenming* 神
明), which enables him to embody the vital forces of the cosmos and
to open himself up to nonbeing (*wu* 無), which is ultimate reality. Thus
it is the daimonic brightness the sage possesses that enables him to
respond to things with the common human emotions while remaining
detached from any entanglements with things.

Recorded in the *Shishuo xinyu* is the following conversation, which
also touches on Wang Bi's ideas about the issues of sagehood, nonbeing, and being (*you* 有):

> When Wang Bi was barely twenty he went to visit Pei Hui 裴徽. Hui
> asked him, "Nonbeing is indeed that by which all things are sustained, yet
> the sage (Confucius) was unwilling to vouchsafe any words on the subject.
> Lao Zi, on the other hand, expatiated on it without end. Why?"
>
> Wang Bi replied, "The sage embodied nonbeing. But since nonbeing
> cannot be explained, his words must relate to being. Lao Zi and Zhuang
> Zi, not yet free from being, were constantly talking about that in which
> they felt a deficiency."[69]

Looking at the above two quotations together, we can say that according to Wang Bi, the sage is not simply "in communion with nonbeing"
or "conterminous with nonbeing"; he is in fact himself an embodiment
of nonbeing. Since Lao Zi and Zhuang Zi still have deficiencies (that is,
they are still not yet embodiments of nonbeing), they are not sages.

What is "*wu*," or nonbeing? In his commentary on chapter 1 of the
Daodejing, Wang Bi says, "All beings originate in nonbeing. Thus the
time before there is any form or name is the beginning of myriad
things.... The Dao (道, the Way), by being without form and name,
originates and brings the myriad things to completion."[70] Again in his

commentary on chapter 14 of this Daoist classic, he says, "You might wish to say that it (i.e., Dao) does not exist, but things achieve existence because of it, and then you might wish to say that it does exist, but we do not see its form. This is why the text refers to it as 'the shape of that which has no shape, the image of that which has no physical existence (as an object 物).'"[71] As the noumenon (benti 本體, original substance) of the cosmos, Dao, the way, or nonbeing, is shapeless and imageless. But it is not nothingness. Otherwise, how can it originate the myriad things? It is not something in the ordinary sense of the word because it lacks all sensory qualities and cannot be seen, heard, smelled, or touched.[72] What Wang Bi is saying here is similar to the passage in the "Tiandi" 天地 (Heaven and Earth) chapter of the *Zhuang Zi*: "In the great beginning, there was nonbeing; there was no being, no name."[73] Nonbeing, the state that exists at the beginning of the cosmos and originates all beings, is here defined as that which has no name and no attribute that human beings ascribe to being.[74] Perhaps nonbeing can thus be described as a pure, absolute state of "being" that transcends all forms and values, including the distinctions between being and nothingness.

In Wang Bi's thought the relation between nonbeing and being is that between substance (ti 體) and function or functionality (yong 用). This point can be illustrated by his commentary on chapter 11 of the *Daodejing*. The main point of this chapter is that when people make a cart wheel, a vessel, or a room, what is useful is not the wood, the clay, or the wall from which they are made, but the nothing—that is, the empty space within each of them.[75] Wang Bi's commentary: "That wood, clay, and wall can form these three things [wheel, vessel, room] depends in each case on achieving functionality [yong] through the nothing [wu] [embodied therein]. In other words, that what is there can be of benefit always depends on its achievement of functionality through what is not there."[76] Wood, clay, and wall are transformed in such a way that they "embody" (ti) nothing or nonbeing in order to achieve the three useful functions. One can say that according to Wang Bi, nonbeing, which has no form or name, is the substance of Dao, and being, which has form and name, is its functionality.

Being an embodiment of Dao or nonbeing, the sage can accomplish great tasks. At the same time, as already touched upon above, he will be able to accomplish them without any entanglements with things. A few remarks from Wang Bi's commentary on chapter 29 of the

Daodejing can be cited here to further illustrate this point: "The sage thoroughly understands the inherent character (*xing* 性) of nature (*ziran* 自然) and allows the innate tendencies (*qing* 情) of the myriad things full expression. Thus he follows and does not act, complies and does not implement. He eliminates what leads things astray and gets rid of what confuses them. Therefore, his mind-heart (*xin* 心) is free from chaos, and the natures of things are allowed to fulfill themselves."[77]

This passage contains the term "*ziran*," which is a key concept in Daoism, as well as in Wei-Jin thought. Literally meaning "self-so" or "so of itself," "*ziran*" is also used to convey the senses of "nature," "the natural world," "natural," "spontaneity," "spontaneous," "at ease," etc. Although perhaps not immediately explicit, the issues of "nonpurposive action," "communion with nature," "expressions of feelings/emotions," and "nonbeing" touched upon previously are relevant to the philosophy in the above passage. It is obvious that only a sage person, who has a perfect communion with the myriad things in nature, is able to allow them to give full expression to their innate tendencies and to help them fulfill their natures, without imposing human values upon them and causing them harm, or to get himself entangled by things. One can say that this passage is about the perfect state of being and existence, in which the sage can respond to being with nonbeing (*yi wu ying you* 以無應有) because, as we have discussed above, he himself is an embodiment of nonbeing.[78] The responses to being constitute, of course, the functionality of the sage's mind-heart. The sage's overall mode of action can be described as *ziran*—that is, natural, spontaneous, nonpurposive, noninterfering—allowing himself and other things to be "so of themselves."[79] This overall mode is essentially Daoistic. Nonetheless, the ideas of "allowing the myriad things to fully express their innate tendencies," "eliminating what leads them astray," and "getting rid of what confuses them" have a Confucian ring to them. Even though Wang Bi is here writing a commentary on the *Daodejing*, the sage to whom he is referring is Confucius, not Lao Zi. But the Confucius as depicted in the commentary is unmistakably a Daoist type of ideal personality.[80]

Let us now turn to the key issues of being, nonbeing, *ziran*, and the sage in the thought of another major Wei-Jin thinker, Guo Xiang, who came right after Wang Bi. Guo Xiang's contribution to Chinese intellectual history rests entirely on his *Zhuang Zi zhu* 莊子注 (Commentary on the *Zhuang Zi*). As is common in the Chinese commentary tradition, Guo Xiang's *Commentary on the Zhuang Zi* says more about his own philosophy than about the philosophy in the early Daoist text.[81]

Guo Xiang is one of the important thinkers in the Wei-Jin period who uphold being (*chongyou* 崇有), in sharp contrast with He Yan and Wang Bi, who highly value nonbeing (*guiwu* 貴無).[82] For Guo Xiang, the concept of "*wu*" simply means "nothing," "nothingness," and "nonexistence." Since "*wu*" is nothing (i.e., not something that exists), it cannot generate *you*, or being. In a commentary on the idea of the "music of heaven" (*tianlai* 天籟) in the "Qiwulun" 齊物論 (Making All Things Equal) chapter in the *Zhuang Zi*, Guo Xiang says,

> Since nonbeing is nothing, it cannot generate being. If being is not yet gen-
> erated, it cannot generate other things either. Who, then, generates things?
> Spontaneously things generate themselves. Things generate themselves; I
> do not generate them. Since I cannot generate things and things cannot
> generate me, I am so of myself (*ze wo ziran yi* 則我自然矣). That every-
> thing is so of itself is called natural (*tianran* 天然). Everything is naturally
> so, not made to be so by any conscious act (*wei* 為). Therefore, [Zhuang
> Zi] spoke of [the music of] heaven (i.e., nature) in order to make clear that
> things are so of themselves. He was not talking about the blue sky.[83]

In the *Daodejing*, Dao, the embodiment of nonbeing, is described as that which is without form and name. As noted above, Zhuang Zi and Wang Bi further add the qualification that nonbeing is that which lacks any attributes associated with being. In the thought of these earlier texts and thinkers, therefore, nonbeing is not nothing at all but a state of being that transcends the polarized oppositions of being and nonbeing constructed in human culture. This sense of "*wu*" is completely different from that taken by Guo Xiang. In one note in his commentary on the "Renjianshi" 人間世 (The Human World) chapter, Guo Xiang says, "*Wu* is [like] a perfectly empty house. There is no reason for it to have the functionality of originating things."[84] According to Guo Xiang, then, there has always been being, which is not preceded or produced by a certain nonbeing. Given this denial of nonbeing as ultimate reality, the concept of "*ziran*" that appears in the above quoted remark on the music of heaven becomes exceedingly important in Guo Xiang's thought.[85]

A remark from Guo Xiang's commentary on the "Zaiyou" 在宥 (Let It Be, Leave It Alone) chapter reads, "Why is it that Zhuang Zi and Lao Zi frequently talk about *wu* (nothingness)? This is because

they wish to make clear that things are not generated by anything else
but themselves. What is meant by self-generation is that things generate
themselves not for any particular [external] reason. So why should anything wish to take any conscious action toward other things that are
already in existence?"[86] It goes without saying that the ideas of "self-
generation" (zisheng 自生) and "being so of oneself" (ziran) are related.
Since things generate themselves, they are naturally so of themselves.
In the passage quoted above, self-generation is further linked to the
absence of conscious, purposive action. Guo Xiang's last remark in his
commentary on the "Dazongshi" 大宗師 (The Great and Venerable
Teacher) chapter goes as follows: "Things are all so of themselves, and
there is nothing that acts [behind] them."[87] In his commentary on the
"Free and Easy Wandering" chapter, Guo Xiang says, "Heaven and
earth have the myriad things as their substance, and the myriad things
must rely on 'being so of themselves' as their correct path. 'Being so of
themselves' means that things are naturally so without having to engage
in any purposive action."[88] Thus "wuwei," or "to have no purposive
action" means "to let everything act at will in accordance with what is
natural to it."[89]

As one would expect a person well versed in Daoist philosophy to
do, Guo Xiang also extends the principle of nonpurposive action to the
art of government. His comment on the chapter title of "Yingdiwang"
應帝王 (Fit for Emperors and Kings) is, "Those who are without mind-
hearts, letting things transform themselves at will, are fit to be emperors
and kings."[90] Of course, Guo Xiang is not saying that people who are
good enough to be emperors and kings should literally be without
mind-hearts. Rather, he is saying that rulers should not act in accordance with the guidance provided by human mind-hearts but allow the
myriad things to produce, live, and change by themselves.[91] Guo Xiang
still holds that the world should be governed, but it should be governed
in the mode of nonpurposive action. In Guo Xiang's view, only the
sage-kings are able to govern the world with nonpurposive action.

In Guo Xiang's commentary on the Zhuang Zi, the sage-kings refer
to Yao 堯, Shun 舜, Wu 武, Tang 湯, etc.—the same rulers of antiquity idealized in Confucian texts. But these sage-kings do not govern
the world by ethical means. In a commentary on a passage about Yao
and Xu You 許由, Guo Xiang says, "He who can cause the world to be
governed is one who does not govern it. Thus Yao governs the world
without governing it; he does not govern it by governing it.... By

'governing the world without governing it' is meant 'acting from non-purposive action.'"[92] As depicted here, Yao behaves like a Daoist, not a Confucian sage-ruler. It should be noted that Yao, Shun, Tang, and Wu are not represented as idealistic characters in the *Zhuang Zi* text itself. As mentioned in the beginning section of this chapter, Zhuang Zi's ideal human beings are called the "ultimate person," the "true person," the "daimonic person," and, in the appropriate context, the "sage." Guo Xiang's ideal human beings include Confucius and the above sage-kings. Let us get a clearer picture of Guo Xiang's conception of the sage because, as we shall see below, it is relevant to the development of the garden in the Six Dynasties.

In one parable in "The Great and Venerable Teacher" chapter, Zhuang Zi has Confucius make a distinction between himself and three Daoist ideal persons who have transcended ordinary concerns with matters such as etiquette and life and death: "Such men as they wander beyond the realm; men like me wander within it. Beyond and within can never meet."[93] For Zhuang Zi, the ultimate human beings are those who are roaming beyond the realm (of ordinary concerns and customs). It can be said that this realm beyond is actually where Zhuang Zi's Not-Even-Anything Village is to be found. However, Guo Xiang interprets this parable as follows:

> When the principle [of things] reaches the limit, beyond (*wai* 外) and within (*nei* 內) obliterate the boundary between them (*xiangming* 相冥). There is no one who can wander beyond the realm to the limit but cannot obliterate the boundary marking the realm within. There is no one who can obliterate the boundary marking the realm within but cannot roam beyond it. Therefore, the sage often wanders beyond the realm in order to magnify what is within the realm and eliminates his mind-heart in order to comply with beings. As a consequence, even though all day long he throws his body about, his vital spirit does not change, and he tackles ten thousand matters, he still appears calm and composed.
>
> To see his external form without getting to his spirit is a constant drag on people. Thus when people see the sage walk side by side with the various things, they are unable to say that he has left things and people behind. When they see the sage embodies a transformation to respond to affairs, they are unable to say that he has found joy in his life by sitting down and forgetting everything.... If [Zhuang Zi] explicitly says that Confucius does this (i.e., wanders beyond the realm in order to magnify what is within it),

those who are confused will reject him [Confucius] on the basis of what they see. Therefore, Zhuang Zi goes beyond the sage's traces within the realm and implies the idea about wandering beyond the realm in the several masters.[94]

As Guo Xiang sees it, at the ultimate level of spiritual attainment, wandering beyond the realm and wandering within it are fundamentally the same.[95] The sage who can wander to the limit beyond the realm must be able to wander to the limit within it as well. Guo Xiang directly mentions Confucius as a sage who often wanders beyond the realm in order to magnify what lies within it. He takes great pains to argue that Zhuang Zi purposely makes a distinction between wandering beyond and within the realm in order to prevent those lacking a clear understanding from rejecting the opinion that Confucius can wander perfectly both within and beyond the realm.

Brilliant as it is, Guo Xiang's argument constitutes a creative misreading of Zhuang Zi's conception of the ideal human being. Zhuang Zi's ideal person is one who finds "ruling the world to be of no use to him,"[96] does not work at any affairs, "does not lean towards benefit or shun harm, does not delight in seeking, does not fix a route by a Way, in saying nothing says something and in saying something says nothing, and roams beyond the dust and grime."[97] Zhuang Zi never explicitly calls Confucius a sage in this Daoist sense of the term, even though he uses him numerous times as a mask to voice his own philosophy. For Zhuang Zi, the Confucian "sage" or "sage-king" and the Daoist "ultimate person," "daimonic person," or "true person" are two completely different types of human beings, and the former is inferior to the latter. Yet Guo Xiang blends the two into one ideal type. In one passage in his commentary on "Free and Easy Wandering," he says, "The daimonic person is what people today call 'the sage.' Although the sage is in his ancestral hall in person, he is, in his mind-heart, no different from being in the mountains and forests. How could the world understand this?"[98] The "sage" in this remark refers to the "(sage-)king" because the term "ancestral hall" (*miaotang* 廟堂) often stands for the king's court. Thus Guo Xiang equates "the daimonic person" not only with "the sage," but also with "the sage-king."

The term "in the mountains and forests" in the remark is important because it refers to where a recluse dwells. In the "Tiandao" 天道

(The Way of Heaven) chapter, we find the statement: "Retire with them [i.e., the virtues of emptiness, stillness, limpidity, silence, and nonpurposive action] to a life of idle wandering and you will command first place among the recluses of the rivers and seas, the hills and forests."[99] So Guo Xiang's sage combines the qualities of a king and a recluse, living in a world in which the ordinary and the spiritual blend into one harmonious whole. As long as the sage-king does not exercise his deliberate, evaluating, and purposive mind-heart, whatever he does, including any action of a king, is naturally so of itself. The physical location of the sage person is not important. The main thing is for him to have a mind-heart that is always detached from entanglements by affairs and things. It should be noted that despite their attempts to amalgamate Confucian and Daoist ideas, both Wang Bi and Guo Xiang regard the ability to respond to affairs and things without being entangled by them as the most important defining quality of the sage. In this respect, we can say that these two Wei-Jin thinkers have given an edge to Daoist ideas in their synthesis of the two ancient Chinese constructions of the ideal human being.[100]

The new conceptions of the sage observable in the philosophy of Wang Bi and Guo Xiang have significant influence on the development of the life-patterns of *chaoyin* 朝隱, or "to be a recluse while one is serving at court," and *shiyin* 市隱, or "to be a recluse while one is living in urban surroundings," which developed during the Eastern Jin (317–420 C.E.) and (Liu) Song periods.[101] Recluses have always existed in Chinese history since ancient times. The motives for the educated elite to become recluses (*yimin* 逸民 or *yinyi* 隱逸) can vary: preserving one's principles and integrity, calming one's impetuous nature, avoiding danger in times of crisis, condemning corrupt customs, or finding fault with the world.[102] But one fact about recluses in ancient China remains the same: they voluntarily withdraw from a life of public service, usually in a more urban setting, into a private life, usually in a more rural setting. Since they withdraw from the world on their own initiative, it can be said that they do not find it congenial and are thus escaping from it.[103] From the standpoint of this original meaning of reclusion in the Chinese context, "*chaoyin*" and "*shiyin*" are essentially self-contradictory and paradoxical terms. They represent the attempts of scholars of the Eastern Jin and (Liu) Song periods to reconcile ways of life that had previously been regarded as incompatible.

Theoretical justifications for eremitism in early Chinese thought fall under two categories. In the Confucian *Analects* and *The Book of Changes*, reclusion is usually seen as a matter of timeliness and fate with regard to participation in or withdrawal from public life.[104] There are good times and bad times in which cultivated scholars live. When the fate of the times is against the scholars and brings them hardship in the world, they should withdraw from it to deepen their roots, rest in perfection, and wait for the good times to arrive.[105] For the Daoists, however, reclusion can not only help scholars escape potential danger from involvement in public service, but can also offer them a life of individual freedom and leisurely enjoyments. A story in the "Qiushui" 秋水 (Autumn Floods) chapter in the *Zhuang Zi* has it that once the king of Chu sent two officials to court Zhuang Zi's service while the philosopher was fishing in the Pu River.[106] Zhuang Zi told the officials to get lost because he would rather be like a tortoise dragging its tail in the mud alive than being dead and having its bones left behind and honored in the king's ancestral temple. A passage in the "Keyi" 刻意 (Constrained in Will) chapter in the *Zhuang Zi* contains a fuller and even more positive description of recluses: "To repair to the thickets and marshes, living idly in the wilderness, angling for fish in solitary places, 'doing nothing' (*wuwei*) their only concern—such is the life favored by the scholars of the rivers and seas, who withdraw from the world, the unhurried idlers."[107] In this passage, escaping the dangers of the world is no longer a relevant issue; reclusion is an attractive and positive value in itself—it is a way of life to be enjoyed for its own sake. In the end, to become a recluse, either in the Confucian fashion of resting in personal perfection while waiting for the right time to return to public life or in the Daoist fashion of enjoying individual freedom and leisure in a private life, is considered a lofty-minded thing for an educated person to do.

Both the Confucian and Daoist types of reclusion began with the motive to escape the world and preserve one's life, and without exception both types implied a retreat to a rural, more natural, but usually austere environment. Dongfang Shuo 東方朔 (154–93 B.C.E.), a minion of Emperor Wu of the Han, found that the court was a good place to hide if one's purpose for hiding was to escape the world for self-preservation.[108] He argued that to retreat to the mountains and forests was in fact an inferior way to escape the world for self-preservation. He admonished his sons:

> For a discerning person to live in the world, nothing is more important
> than the ability to tolerate. He lives a life of ease and leisure in compliance
> with the Dao (Way). To be a starving recluse beneath Shouyang Hill (like
> Boyi 伯夷 and Shuqi 叔齊) is stupid, but to work as an Archivist (like Lao
> Zi) is smart. He substitutes farming with public service to keep his body
> well fed and his walk in peace. Relying on "hiding" to play in the world,
> he never encounters any times of trouble.... The Way of the sage is to
> reveal one's physical form but hide the spirit, now a dragon, now a snake,
> changing with things, in accordance with the appropriateness of the times,
> without a permanent home.[109]

This is the very first theoretical statement about *chaoyin* found in Chinese history. Dongfang Shuo was able to combine the material comfort of an official's life with the freedom from care and harm of a recluse's life. The tension between participation in public service and reclusion was resolved. He also referred to Lao Zi and "the Way of the sage" (who seems to embody the Daoist, rather than the Confucian, ideal) in his description of his unique way "to be a recluse while serving as an official at court."[110] But Dongfang Shuo's "Way of the sage" is more the great skill of those good at self-preservation and survival than the Daoist sage's supreme ability to practice nonpurposive action in a position of political and social prominence. Also lacking in Dongfang Shuo's mode of reclusion at court is the sense of communion with nature. In other words, Dongfang Shuo has not embodied in his pattern of life the Daoist aesthetic spirit discussed above. The embodiment of the Daoist aesthetic spirit is accomplished in the *chaoyin* and *shiyin* forms of reclusion during the fourth and fifth centuries.

As noted, the period from the end of the Han through the Wei-Jin was one of social and political turmoil, when the conditions of public service were unattractive or even impossible. In these difficult times, the lifestyle of the recluse increasingly became an ideal alternative for scholars whose education prepared them mainly for public service. Indeed, eremitic aspirations are frequently expressed in the writings of the Wei-Jin period, even in works by those who actively participated in official service.[111] After Xuanxue became popular, the association of reclusion with untrammeled high-mindedness also began to hold sway over the educated elite. The ability to rise above the vulgar and ordinary, to remain free from entanglements by things, and to achieve communion with nature are essential parts of this high-mindedness. And this ability is expected to be demonstrated in the conduct of scholars. In his "Preface to 'Song on Thoughts of Return'" 思歸引序, the wealthy and extravagant Shi Chong 石崇 (249–300 C.E.), a favorite of Emperor Wu of the Jin 晉武帝 (r. 265–290 C.E.), says, "Late in life I am even more fond of letting myself go free and cherish a deep love for forests and marshes. Consequently, I live as a wealthy recluse in my country retreat in Heyang.... Whenever I go out, I take sightseeing, hunting, and fishing as my work; whenever I come home, I abandon myself to playing the lute and reading books."[112] One of the most prominent men of the Six Dynasties, Xie An 謝安 (320–385 C.E.), spent his early years in comfortable reclusion:

> While he was living in Kuaiji, he used to wander about with Wang Xizhi, Xu Xun of Gaoyang, and Zhi Dun of Sangmen. Outdoors they would hunt and fish in the hills and streams; and indoors they would talk, chant poetry, or compose essays, without ever showing the slightest intention of living in the world.... He often went into the mountains in Lin'an where he sat in a rock cave, beside a deep valley, heaving a long sigh, saying, "Can this be far from the way Boyi lived?"[113]

From these two accounts we can see that the vogue of the life-pattern of the recluse was so prevalent in the late third and fourth centuries that both the most ostentatious and the genuinely cultivated scholars felt the need to realize it in their own lives. Xie An did not get involved in official service until he was forty years of age.[114] His eremitic aspirations noted in the above passage were thus genuine.

The phrase "without ever showing the slightest intention of living in the world" deserves some attention here. The original Chinese phrase is "wu chushi yi" 無處世意, which can more literally be rendered as "without showing anything that means that they would live in the world." The phrase actually touches on a significant aspect of the theory about "obtaining the meaning" (deyi 得意) of something in the Xuanxue of the Wei-Jin period.[115] The idea of "obtaining the meaning" comes from the concluding passage of the "Waiwu" 外物 (External Things) chapter of the Zhuang Zi: "The fish trap exists because of the fish; once you've gotten the fish, you can forget the trap. The rabbit snare exists because of the rabbit; once you've gotten the rabbit, you can forget the snare. Words exist because of meaning; once you've gotten the meaning, you can forget the words."[116] The original meaning of the *Zhuang Zi* passage is that one can forget the means by which an end is attained. As the idea is applied by Xuanxue thinkers to the context of human action and conduct, it leads to an emphasis on obtaining the meaning of the mental or spiritual state governing a certain overt act (*xingji* 形跡, or form and trace). Since the spiritual state constituting the meaning of an overt act is all important, the overt act itself can then actually be forgotten. By the fourth century, it was believed that the most important thing that defined a recluse was his lofty and untrammeled mind-heart and his sense of harmony with nature. If a person had a grasp of this essential meaning of the recluse, then he could become one without having to set himself apart and retreat to the mountains and forests.

While Xie An spent much of his early life in reclusion in the traditional way of staying away from office and residing in a more rural setting, many scholars of his time were arguing that one could just as well become a recluse while serving at court and living in an urban area. Deng Can 鄧粲 said, "The way of reclusion can be realized while one is serving at court or living in the marketplace. Reclusion originally rests with me, not with external things."[117] What Deng Can is saying here is that the thing that determines whether a person is a genuine recluse or not is his inner self and not external things such as a hermitage. With the right spiritual cultivation, one can physically be at the court or in the city without losing one's status as a high-minded recluse. Zhou Xuzhi 周續之, an eremitist of the (Liu) Song period, was once asked why he frequently visited a king's court. He replied, "When my mind-heart wanders to the tall palace gate-towers, I regard the rivers and lakes as dried up. When my emotions and interest for things are both forgotten, the city and the court are no different from rock caves."[118] What we see here is the same kind of mental detachment with which the sage in Wang Bi's and Guo Xiang's conceptions deals with things. Since to obtain the meaning of reclusion concerns basically a person's spiritual state, which may be manifested in some momentary acts, the role he plays and the place where he resides are indeed of secondary importance. Wang Kangju 王康琚 goes even a step further to offer a new definition of the recluse in this opening couplet of a poem entitled "Refuting 'Invitation to Reclusion'" 反招隱詩: "Small hiders hide in the hills and marshes/Big hiders hide in the court and the marketplace."[119] According to this fourth-century poet, the touchstone of the level of a person's spiritual attainment as a recluse lies precisely in the places where he works and lives. Wang Kangju would certainly agree that the greatest recluse is the sage as defined by Wang Bi and Guo Xiang, even though he has not said so in his poem.

We have seen that in the early Six Dynasties theories about ideal human beings—the sage and the recluse—supreme emphasis was placed on the cultivation of a free and untrammeled mind-heart, which functioned just like the processes of nature that are so of themselves. The mind-heart of these ideal human beings is detached from things, especially from human affairs, but in communion with nature. It is essentially an ideal mind-heart as constructed by the Daoists. In theory, Six Dynasties intellectuals believed that a person could integrate Confucian and Daoist ideas into one mode of life while cultivating this ideal mind-heart, which could be realized wherever he went about his business. In practice, however, as Xu Fuguan has correctly observed, it is most difficult to carry out the Daoist ideal mode of life—which he calls the "artistic mode of life," as I mentioned in the beginning of the chapter—in the ordinary human world.[120] The Daoist ideal mode of life can best be realized in nature, relatively free from the interferences of human culture. It is always difficult for a scholar to pass up the opportunity to accept an office, since holding an office provides him with a means of livelihood and the satisfaction of fulfilling the Confucian ideology of public service, and living in the urban environment allows him to enjoy the many amenities it offers. With the development of the small garden attached to a house and the large country retreat, Six Dynasties educated elite found a way to have the best of both worlds: the comfort and convenience of an official's life in the city and the opportunity to pursue mystical communion with "nature" in an idealized paradisal space.

Siting Not-Even-Anything Village

The Chinese garden underwent a significant period of development during the Six Dynasties. In addition to the continuation of the imperial park, the private garden (in the form of either a retreat in a sizable country estate or a scholar's small garden attached to a residence) and the garden that was part of a Buddhist or a Daoist temple also greatly flourished in this period. The scholar's garden, which developed from the Eastern Jin period onward, was particularly significant as its aesthetics influenced both the imperial and the temple gardens. The art of garden design and construction became increasingly sophisticated. And the functions of the garden went through some significant changes as well. The Six Dynasties period was indeed important in the history of the Chinese garden because it witnessed a number of developments that remained conventional throughout the subsequent imperial dynasties. Let us now turn to the most important developments in the garden during the Six Dynasties that bear special relevance to the topic of this chapter.

First, Six Dynasties people moved away from building a garden or a park mainly for the previous utilitarian purposes of hunting, raising cattle and horses, or producing other kinds of goods. Increasingly a garden or park was built for enjoyment, recreation, rest, and the pursuit of other aesthetic interests.[121] These functions could be found in the previous imperial park as well, but they were subsumed under the utilitarian purposes there.

Second, the size of the garden, including the emperor's park, was greatly reduced. I noted above that the imperial parks in Qin and Han times were each often several hundred leagues square. The trend to reduce the size of parks and gardens had already started in the late Han. Emperor Ling of the Han 漢靈帝 (168–189 C.E.) built two parks outside of the capital city of Luoyang 洛陽 with a circumference of only several leagues each.[122] With the exception of retreats, which formed parts of country estates that included farmland, both the imperial parks and private gardens in the Six Dynasties were small.[123] The palace park of Emperor Taizong of the Northern Wei 北魏太宗, for instance, was surrounded by a wall that was only twenty leagues in circumference. The reduction in size, however, was easily compensated by advances in the art of garden building, specifically in the construction of artificial hills and varieties of bodies of water; a careful selection of exotic rocks, plants, birds, and animals; and the overall integration of the various components into an organic whole.[124] The vastness of the microcosmic Qin and Han imperial parks was replaced by the skillful management of woods, hills, water, halls, pavilions, and the like within a much smaller area to achieve the impression of an endless stretch of winding space.[125] In other words, vastness was replaced by compositional intricacy and an atmosphere of mystery. Techniques of appropriating scenes (*jiejing* 借景) from nature outside the garden were used to extend the ideal space beyond the confines of the walls. The poetry, calligraphy, and

painting of the literati were absorbed into the garden as well.[126] During
the Six Dynasties, the garden became a truly magnificent place, full of
beautiful sounds, sights, and colors throughout the four seasons.[127]

Third, in building a garden, Six Dynasties artists employed an
approach that was both realistic and suggestive at the same time, rather
than slavishly representational.[128] They used artificial lakes, ponds,
hills, and stalagmites to symbolize mountains and water in nature.
Their approach is similar to the painting technique of *xieyi* 寫意, or
"depicting the idea or inner meaning of things," advocated by some
literati of the Northern Song dynasty (960–1126).[129] As a technique,
xieyi designates an attempt to depart from mere surface likeness toward
a depiction implied by rich meaning in a condensed and economical
artistic image.[130] This approach to representing nature can already be
seen in the garden aesthetics of the Six Dynasties and is very different
from that used in the Qin and Han imperial parks.[131] Ge Hong 葛洪
(284–364) wrote in the fourth chapter of his *Baopu zi waipian* 抱朴子
外篇, "Pile up earth to make a quasi Mt. Song or Mt. Huo" (起土以準
嵩霍).[132] In describing the building of a garden attached to his residence, Liu Mian 劉勔 (fl. mid-fifth century) noted, "Assemble stones
and store up water to make the garden look as if it is in a mountain."[133]
Xiao Tong 蕭統 (501–531) added in his "Xuanpu jiang" 玄圃講 (A
Discourse on the Mysterious Garden), "Dig a pond to give the appearance of vastness; build a peak to create a form of loftiness" (穿池狀浩
翰；築峰形崒岌). "Quasi," "as if," "give an appearance of," and
"create a form of" indicate an attempt to express an idea or meaning
(*shiyi* 示意) through an imitation of nature.[134] Indeed, the Six Dynasties
approach to representing nature in the garden is vastly different from
the Qin and Han's attempts to "pattern the imperial park after heaven
and earth" in a scale that is humanly possible.

Finally and most important, the Six Dynasties garden can be seen
as a realization of its builder's desire to return to *ziran* in both the sense
of nature and of "being naturally itself." I have devoted considerable
space above to discussing the importance for Six Dynasties scholars of
experiencing a communion with nature and conducting themselves in a
way that resembled the processes of nature. A well-constructed garden
that was not simply a slavish imitation of nature could provide a scholar
a congenial environment to accomplish both of these lofty goals. In the
biography of the recluse artist Dai Yong 戴顒 (378–441 c.e.) in the

Song shu 宋書 (History of the Song), there is this passage: "When Yong came out of reclusion to live in Suzhou, scholars got together to build a residence for him. They assembled stones, channeled water, planted trees, and dug a stream. Soon the place became dense with things, looking just like nature."[135] In a biography of Xie Ju 謝舉 of the Liang dynasty (502–557 C.E.), the following is recorded: "In Ju's residence, his rustic studio was turned into a temple. The beauty of springs and rocks there resembled those in nature."[136] Sometimes cultural objects were used to bring about an atmosphere of nature in a garden. A story recorded in the biography of Liu Yao 劉杳 in the *Liang shu* 梁書 (History of the Liang) can be cited here to illustrate this point. When Shen Yue 沈約 (441–513 C.E.) built a new studio in his country home, Liu Yao composed two poems of praise and presented them to him. Shen Yue immediately asked a good calligrapher to write the poems on a wall and then sent a letter to Liu Yao:

> What I crave in life is usually not to be found among people. My enjoyment of forests and valleys often competes for my attention with affairs that I have to deal with.... The two poems you so graciously gave me contain very rich rhetorical flourishes and a complete account of the occasion and its significance. The scenery and the poems' lines and resonances reflect upon each other, making me feel that this place is ten times more natural (than before).[137]

Shen Yue's remark reminds one of what Jia Zheng 賈政 said when he visited Daguanyuan 大觀園 for the first time in the eighteenth-century novel *Shitouji* 石頭記 (The Story of the Stone): "All those prospects and pavilions—even the rocks and trees and flowers will seem somehow incomplete without that touch of poetry which only the written word can lend a scene."[138] Shen Yue's concern is not with a sense of scenery in his garden but of *ziran* (nature) itself as perceived by a sensitive human mind. Nonetheless, both remarks indicate that poetry has the capacity to bring to light the quality of nature in a garden.

The realization of one's residence as nature to which one can return is important to Six Dynasties scholars, as Tao Qian 陶潛 (365–427 C.E.), one of China's greatest recluse-poets, has powerfully described in the first of his poem sequence, entitled "Returning to My Home in the Country" (Guiyuantianju 歸園田居):

少無適俗韻	In youth I couldn't tune myself to the vulgar tone,
性本愛丘山	My nature was to love the hills and mountains.
誤落塵網中	By mistake I fell into that dusty net,
一去三十年	Once gone it was thirty years.[139]
羈鳥戀舊林	The migrant bird longs for its old woods,
池魚思故淵	The fish in the pond thinks of its former depths.
開荒南野際	I've cleared some wasteland in the southern fields,
守拙歸園田	Keeping to simplicity, I've come back to the farm.
方宅十餘畝	My land and house measure ten *mou* or more,
草屋八九間	A thatched roof covers eight or nine spans.
榆柳蔭後簷	Elms and willows shade the back eaves,
桃李羅堂前	Peach and plum trees range before the hall.
曖曖遠人村	Dim dim, a village in the distance,
依依墟裡煙	Lingering lingering, the smoke from the houses.
狗吠深巷中	Dogs bark in the deep lanes,
雞鳴桑樹巔	Cocks crow from the tops of mulberry trees.
戶庭無塵雜	No dust or clutter within my doors and courtyard,
虛室有餘閑	In the empty rooms, more than enough leisure.
久在樊籠裡	So long was I kept in that cage,
復得返自然	I've now returned to things as they are.[140]

In the above, the original Chinese for the phrase "things as they are" is "*ziran*," which, as noted numerous times before, also means "nature." The concluding line of the poem expresses the aspiration of the age in which Tao Qian lived: to return to nature, to things (including oneself) being as they are. Because of his distaste for the official life, Tao Qian left his post as a magistrate after an official career that spanned some twelve years and returned to live on his farm. As we can see from the poem, his farm-garden was very modest: it did not have any luxury items such as pavilions, kiosks, or artificial mountains. But for him it was as ideal a place as it could ever be. It can be argued that by using the images of "dogs barking" and "cocks crowing," Tao Qian alluded to chapter 80 of the *Daodejing*, in which a utopia is presented. Since both this poem and his story about "Peach Blossom Spring" contain these images, Tao Qian actually regarded his own farm as a utopia, an ideal space as depicted in the *Daodejing*.[141] From our perspective, Tao Qian's home in the country actually came much closer to Zhuang Zi's Not-Even-Anything Village than did the extravagant pleasure gardens of his time, given the rustic simplicity, the openness to the surroundings, the absence of dust and clutter, and the abundance of leisure that Tao Qian found there. However, the ideal of the farm and the Peach Blossom Spring that Tao Qian had created on the basis of Lao Zi's perfect agrarian society did not gain popularity and influence in his time.[142]

The educated elite in the Six Dynasties did not need to be as stubborn or as poor as Tao Qian to retire from official careers in order to live in Zhuang Zi's Not-Even-Anything Village. Indeed, many prominent people found that they had a perfect world to which to retreat as well. Let us look at three examples. Recorded in the *Shishuo xinyu* is the following informative anecdote: "On entering the Flower Grove Park (Hualinyuan 華林園), Emperor Jianwen looked around and said to his attendants, 'The place which suits the mind-heart isn't necessarily far away. By any shady grove or stream one may naturally have such thoughts as Zhuang Zi had by the Rivers Hao and Pu, where birds and animals, fowls and fish, come of their own accord to be intimate with them.'"[143] Emperor Jianwen 簡文帝 refers to Sima Yu 司馬昱 (320–372 C.E.), who ruled the Eastern Jin dynasty from 371 to 372. Flower Grove Park was one of the most magnificent imperial parks in the Six Dynasties. His remark is concerned with the experience of a communion with nature, an experience that can be compared to that of Zhuang Zi. The phrase "come of their own accord" (*zilai* 自來) was carefully chosen by Emperor Jianwen to indicate that the birds, animals, and fish behave in a way completely free from human purposive action. The state described here is thus *ziran*.

The biography of Yuan Can 袁粲 (420–477 C.E.) contains the following passage: "Can was a man of talent and valued lofty spirit. He was fond of the empty and remote, and so, even though he occupied an important position, he did not allow affairs to rule his mind-heart. He often strolled alone in his garden, satisfying himself with poetry and wine. His residence was near the city wall. Whenever he carried a staff to wander about freely and felt that his wish had been met, he would feel so carefree and leisurely that he would forget to return to his house."[144] Zhuang Zi is not directly mentioned in this passage, but the phrase "to wander about freely" (*xiaoyao*) unmistakably alludes to him. Although Yuan Can was a prominent official and lived in the city, he was able to enjoy Zhuang Zi's "free and easy wandering" during his leisure time because he possessed a garden.

Xu Mian 徐勉 (466–535 C.E.), an imperial secretary in the court of
the Liang dynasty, wrote about his garden in a letter to his son:

> I have planned and worked on this garden for years. It is now roughly
> complete. Peach and plum trees are luxuriant and dense, paulownia trees
> and bamboos form nice shade, tracks and paths crisscross, and ditches and
> channels interconnect—there is much beauty for me to view from fine
> storied buildings and tall pavilions on terraces. There is no lack of delight
> for me in seeing the mingling of a solitary peak among dense brush. The
> ditches are full of wild rice and grass, and the lakes are rich with water
> chestnuts and lotuses. Although the garden is away from people, the city
> gates are close by. . . . Whenever there are good moments or beautiful
> scenery, or whenever I am free from the work at my desk, I carry a staff,
> wear walking shoes, and wander leisurely to a rustic lodge; watch fish by a
> pond; brush through woods to listen to the birds; and play a tune on the
> lute in order to seek the temporary happiness of a few moments, so that I
> can live out my days in this ordinary manner. I should not be bothered
> with inquiries about family affairs or other trivial matters.[145]

This letter was probably written late in Xu Mian's life, but it is clear
that he had not retired from office yet. He was able to combine the life
of a high official living in the city with that of a recluse, thanks to his
financial security, which enabled him to build a garden. The two
phrases "wander leisurely" and "watch fish by a pond" allude to the
Zhuang Zi text, the latter referring to the famous ending section of the
"Autumn Floods" chapter, in which Zhuang Zi debates with Hui Shi
about his assertion that he knows that the fish in the Hao River are
happy. As clearly stated in the letter, the life of a recluse, which is free
from official business, family matters, and other practical purposes, was
what Xu Mian really enjoyed.

From the above three examples, we can see that in the Six Dynasties the ultimate purpose of building a garden was not for meeting
material needs but for spiritual and aesthetic gratification.[146] The garden was the place where Six Dynasties scholars found peace and freedom for their bodies and spirits. It was the place in which they found
that they had returned to nature, to "things as they are," and to an
opportunity to roam freely and easily within an ideal space. Numerous
emperors from Jin to Liang times called their gardens "Xuanpu" 玄圃,
or Mysterious Garden. But the Xuanpu, also called Xuanpu 懸圃, or

Hanging Garden, in the past, was no longer a paradise filled with exotic plants, birds and beasts, food, elixirs, and immortals. Nor was it something amazingly grand and magnificent that builders constructed for their emperors as a counterpart to heaven and earth. Further, it was not a paradise on earth that was so beautiful and perfect that even the immortals could be lured. It was simply a paradise where from time to time the educated elite enjoyed peace, freedom from care, and communion with beautiful nature. The ideal world in which Zhuang Zi wandered was situated in nowhere—that is, in the Not-Even-Anything Village, in the broad and open wilds. For the Six Dynasties scholars, both rich and poor, paradise was sited in the garden right here in this world.

NOTES

In the winter of 1993, Professor Li Zehou 李澤厚 and I held a Global Partnership fellowship at the Institute for the Humanities at the University of Michigan. The theme for the 1992–1993 academic year at the institute was utopia. It was during my residence at the institute that winter that I began to do some serious work on the Chinese garden and utopia. To James Winn, who was then director of the Institute for the Humanities, I wish to express my thanks for providing us fellows a most congenial and stimulating environment in which to work. To Professor Li Zehou, I wish to express my thanks for giving me unlimited opportunities to learn from his vast expertise in the Chinese humanities. In revising this paper, I have also benefited from Victor Mair's insightful comments at the conference.

1. Wang Shumin 王叔岷, *Zhuang Zi jiaoquan* 莊子校詮 (Taipei: Zhongyang yanjiuyuan, 1988), vol. 1, pp. 35–38. In rendering the quoted passages, I have consulted the following excellent translations: Burton Watson, trans., *The Complete Works of Chuang Tzu* (New York: Columbia University Press, 1968), p. 35; A. C. Graham, trans., *Chuang-tzu: The Inner Chapters, A Classic of Tao* (London: Mandala, 1981), p. 47; Victor H. Mair, trans., *Wandering on the Way: Early Taoist Tales and Parables of Chuang Tzu* (Honolulu: University of Hawai'i Press, 1994), pp. 8–9.

2. I am following A. C. Graham in rendering "*shen*" as "daemonic," but I use the spelling of "daimonic." Graham says, "'Daemonic' seems to me to be the modern word closest to *shen*, but I use it with the warning that its restless, anguished quality is foreign to the Chinese word, not to mention the malign associations which it tends to collect by confusion with 'demoniac.'" See Graham, *Chuang-tzu*, p. 35.

3. The original Chinese phrase is "謬悠之説，荒唐之言，無端崖之辭."
See Wang Shumin, *Zhuang Zi jiaoquan*, vol. 3, p. 1344.

4. "無何有之鄉" has been rendered "Not-Even-Anything Village" by Watson (*The Complete Works of Chuang Tzu*, p. 35), "the realm of Nothingwhatever" by Graham (*Chuang-tzu*, p. 47), "Nevernever Land" by Mair (*Wandering on the Way*, p. 8), "the domain of nonexistence" by Yu-lan Fung (*Chuang-tzu: A New Selected Translation with an Exposition of the Philosophy of Kuo Hsiang* [New York: Paragon Book Reprints, 1964], p. 40), and "a village where there's nothing at all" by David Hinton (*Chuang Tzu: The Inner Chapters* [Washington, D.C.: Counterpoint, 1997], p. 12).

5. Donald Munro has an excellent discussion on the concept of "*wuwei*" or "nonpurposive action" in Daoist thought. See *The Concept of Man in Ancient China* (Stanford, Calif.: Stanford University Press, 1969), pp. 141–144.

6. Influenced by the ideas of Immanuel Kant and other Western thinkers concerning aesthetic appreciation and experience, Xu Fuguan argues that the concept of Dao, as Lao Zi and Zhuang Zi use it in the context of human life and experience, is best understood as a kind of artistic spirit (*yishu jingshen* 藝術精神) because it is conceived as completely separate from all intellectual concepts and practical interests. See Xu Fuguan, *Zhongguo yishu jingshen* 中國藝術精神 (Taipei: Xuesheng shuju, 1974), pp. 45–143. His comments on Not-Even-Anything Village can be found on p. 65 of this book.

7. Ibid., pp. 63–64.

8. For a good brief discussion of the etymology of the word "utopia," see Frank E. Manuel and Fritzie P. Manuel, *Utopian Thought in the Western World* (Cambridge, Mass.: Belknap Press, 1979), pp. 1–4.

9. There is no dearth of utopias in Chinese literature that are concerned with social, political, and moral issues. "Peach Blossom Spring," by Tao Qian (365–427), is one good example. Yet unlike Zhuang Zi's Not-Even-Anything Village, which does not exist in the real world, Peach Blossom Spring is not conceived by Tao Qian as a "nowhere." Rather, it is depicted as a perfect agrarian society hidden somewhere deep in the mountains. I believe Tao Qian's Peach Blossom Spring is modeled upon the small ideal state advocated in chapter 80 of the *Daodejing*. Tao Qian uses the auditory images of dogs barking and cocks crowing as textual allusions to refer to the Daoist text. The Chinese construction of such an ideal, perfect place as realizable in the real world is very different from the Western construction of utopia.

10. Manuel and Manuel, *Utopian Thought*, pp. 16–17.

11. Ibid., p. 17.

12. Ibid., p. 1.

13. *Utopian Visions*, ed. Time-Life Books (Alexandria, Va: Time-Life Books, 1990), p. 6. "*Pari*" means "around" and "*daeza*," "wall." See the *American Heritage College Dictionary* (Boston: Houghton Mifflin, 1993), p. 989. Dur-

ing his travels in the region of Mazandaran near the Caspian Sea one February in the 1670s, Sir John Chardin remarked, "the whole Country is nothing but one continued Garden, or a perfect kind of Paradise, as the Persians call it." Quoted in Norah Titley and Frances Wood, *Oriental Gardens* (London: British Library, 1991), p. 38.

14. *Utopian Visions*, p. 6.

15. In Song 76 in the *Shi jing*, there is the line, "Do not climb into our garden" 無踰我園, and in Song 100, there is the line, "He breaks the willows in a fenced vegetable garden" 折柳樊圃. For these lines in Chinese, see Qu Wanli 屈萬里, *Shi jing quanshi* 詩經詮釋 (Taipei: Lianjing chuban shiye gongsi, 1983), pp. 135 and 169. As we can see in these two lines, there is a wall or fence implied in the words "*yuan*" and "*pu.*"

16. This is a modified version of the translations by Arthur Waley and D.C. Lau. See Arthur Waley, trans. *The Book of Songs* (New York: Grove Press, 1960), pp. 259–260, and D. C. Lau, trans. *Mencius* (London: Penguin Books, 1970), p. 50. Since Mencius quoted only the first two stanzas, Lau has not translated the last stanza.

17. See Lau, *Mencius*, p. 50. In book 1, part B, section 2, of this text, Mencius is recorded as again talking about King Wen's park, this time with King Xuan of Qi 齊宣王. Mencius mentions that King Wen's park was seventy *li* square and was open to woodcutters as well as to hunters of pheasants and hares. The theme of the king's sharing the enjoyments of the park with the people is continued here.

18. Wang Yi 王毅 mentions that Mao Heng 毛亨, Zheng Xuan 鄭玄, Su Ce 蘇轍, Zhu Xi 朱熹, and others all followed Mencius's interpretation. See Wang Yi, *Yuanlin yu zhongguo wenhua* 園林與中國文化 (Shanghai: Renmin chubanshe, 1990), p. 3.

19. Ibid., pp. 2–26. My discussion of the religious function and the construction of the king's park in ancient China is largely drawn from this section of the book.

20. Ibid.

21. For a brief review of these references, see Hou Naihui 侯迺慧, *Shiqing yu youjing—tangdai wenren de yuanlin shenghuo* 詩情與幽境—唐代文人的園林生活 (Taipei: Dongda tushu youxiangongsi, 1991), pp. 19–21.

22. I am here following David Hawkes's speculation regarding the date of this poem. See David Hawkes, trans., *The Songs of the South: An Anthology of Ancient Chinese Poems by Qu Yuan and Other Poets* (Middlesex: Penguin Books, 1985), p. 223. In her book *The Chinese Garden: History, Art and Architecture* (London: Academic Editions, 1986), Maggie Keswick mentions this song as presenting the earliest description of a "true pleasure garden" (p. 31).

23. The shamans' description of the king's palace and garden can be found in Hawkes, *Songs of the South*, pp. 226–228.

24. Keswick, *The Chinese Garden,* p. 32.

25. Here I completely agree with Keswick's argument. See ibid., p. 31.

26. Here I am following the dating of materials as given in Anne Birrell, trans., *The Classic of Mountains and Seas* (London: Penguin Books, 1999), p. xl.

27. The *Chu ci* is generally regarded by modern scholars as an earlier text than the *Shanhai jing.*

28. The term appears in book 2, chapter 3, of *The Classic of Mountains and Seas.* See Birrell, *The Classic of Mountains and Seas,* p. 22.

29. For Guo Pu's comments, see Yuan Ke 袁柯, *Shanhai jing jiaozhu* 山海經校注 (Taipei: Hongshi chubanshe, 1981), p. 46.

30. Chen Guangzhong 陳廣中, *Huainanzi yizhu* 淮南子譯注 (Changchun: Jilin wenshi chubanshe, 1990), pp. 184–185. The Chinese text is "懸圃、涼風、樊桐，在昆侖閶闔之中."

31. Ibid., p. 187.

32. John S. Major, "Notes on the Nomenclature of Winds and Directions in the Early Han," *T'oung Pao* 65, nos. 1–3, pp. 66–80.

33. Hou Naihui has done an excellent review of the brief accounts of the Pingpu or the Xuanpu as presented in the *Shanhai jing* and the *Huainan Zi.* See *Shiqing yu youjing,* pp. 15–18. I generally follow her interpretation in my description.

34. See Birrell, *The Classic of Mountains and Seas,* book 11, p. 140. For the details summarized here, the reader can also look at book 2, chapter 3, pp. 22–24; book 11, p. 140; and book 16, pp. 174–175.

35. Birrell, *The Classic of Mountains and Seas,* p. 267.

36. Yuan Ke observes that in the *Shanhai jing,* Shangdi 上帝 (Lord on High), Tiandi 天帝 (Lord of Heaven), and those lords who are equal to these two in status are often referred to simply as "Di." Depending on the context, therefore, "Di" can refer to Di Jun 帝俊, Di Yao 帝堯, or Huangdi. Since the Kunlun Mountains are said to occupy the center of the cosmos and Huangdi is the mythical ruler of the central realm, the "Di" in the passages about the Kunlun Mountains refers to the Yellow Emperor. See the entry on Tiandi in Yuan Ke, *Zhongguo shenhua chuanshuo cidian* 中國神話傳說辭典 (Taipei: Huashi chubanshe, 1987), p. 46.

37. Gu Jiegang, "Zhuang Zi he chuci zhong kunlun he penglai liangge shenhua xitong de ronghe" 莊子和楚辭中昆侖和蓬萊兩個神話系統的融合, *Zhonghua wenshi luncong* 中華文史論叢 (Shanghai: Guji chubanshe), vol. 10 (1979), pp. 31–57.

38. Ibid., p. 31.

39. Burton Watson, *Records of the Grand Historian of China* (New York: Columbia University Press, 1961), vol. 2, p. 26.

40. Wang Yi, *Yuanlin yu zhongguo wenhua,* p. 47; quote from Keswick, *The Chinese Garden,* p. 34.

41. Wang Yi, *Yuanlin yu zhongguo wenhua,* p. 49.

42. Chen Zhi 陳直, *Sanfu huangtu jiaozheng* 三輔黃圖校證 (Xi'an: Shaanxi renmin chubanshe, 1980), p. 83.

43. Ibid. Also see a brief discussion of this in Keswick, *The Chinese Garden,* p. 34.

44. The *fu* 賦 (rhapsodies) on the capitals and imperial parks of the Han dynasty contain very detailed descriptions of these features. See, for instance, "Two Capitals Rhapsody" 兩都賦, by Ban Gu, and "Rhapsody on the Imperial Park" 上林賦, by Sima Xiangru 司馬相如 in David Knechtges, trans., *Wenxuan, or Selections of Refined Literature,* (Princeton, N.J.: Princeton University Press, 1982), vol. 1, pp. 93–180, and vol. 2 (1987), pp. 73–114.

45. Wang Yi, *Yuanlin yu zhongguo wenhua,* p. 48.

46. See Murakami Yoshimi's 村木嘉實 brief discussion of these features in "Rikucho no teiyin" 六朝の庭園 in his book *Rikucho shiso shi kenkyu* 六朝思想史研究 (Kyoto: Heirakuji Shoten, 1974), pp. 361–364.

47. Keswick, *The Chinese Garden,* p. 33.

48. For this detail and the next, see Chen Zhi, *Sanfu huangtu jiaozheng,* p. 6.

49. This is noted in Ban Gu's "Western Capital Rhapsody." See Knechtges, *Wenxuan,* p. 115. "Eastern Capital Rhapsody" 東京賦, by Zhang Heng 張衡, and "Rhapsody on Lulingguang Palace" 魯靈光殿賦 contain similar references. See Wang Yi, *Yuanlin yu zhongguo wenhua,* p. 55.

50. For details about Emperor Wu's pursuits, see Keswick, *The Chinese Garden,* p. 40. According to *Sanqinji* 三秦記, a text that no longer exists, the First Emperor of the Qin built a long lake that spread two hundred leagues from east to west and twenty leagues from south to north and guided water from the Wei River to fill it. In the lake, he built Penglai Mountain with earth and carved a stone whale that was sixty-six meters long. If this account is true, the First Emperor of the Qin would have been the first person in Chinese history to build a large artificial lake and create an artificial mountain with earth. See Hou Naihui, *Shiqing yu youjing,* pp. 21–22.

51. Hou Naihui, *Shiqing yu youjing,* pp. 23–24.

52. Keswick, *The Chinese Garden,* p. 40.

53. Ibid., p. 53.

54. Knechtges, *Wenxuan,* p. 25. "The Lord," of course, refers to the Lord of Heaven. "Grand Unity," or Taiyi 太一, is considered another name for the Lord of Heaven, who resides in the Purple Palace.

55. See Wang Yi, *Yuanlin yu zhongguo wenhua,* p. 68.

56. For Wang Yi's discussions in this paragraph, see ibid., pp. 61–68.

57. Li Zehou 李澤厚, *Mei de licheng* 美的歷程 (Beijing: Wenwu chubanshe, 1981), p. 63. The quotation is a modified version of the rendering in Gong Lizeng, trans., *The Path of Beauty: A Study of Chinese Aesthetics* (Beijing: Morning Glory Publishers, 1988), p. 83.

58. Li Zehou, *Mei de licheng,* pp. 63–64. The quotation is from Gong Lizeng, *The Path of Beauty,* p. 83.

59. Hou Naihui, *Shiqing yu youjing,* pp. 23–27.

60. For general observations about Han intellectual life, see Li Zehou, *Mei de licheng,* pp. 85–92.

61. Ibid., pp. 87 and 91. The late intellectual historian Qian Mu 錢穆 made a similar observation in his *Guoxue gailun* 國學概論: "The learning and thought of the Wei, Jin and Northern and Southern Dynasties period can be summed up in one phrase: the awakening of the individual's self." Quoted in Lin Lizhen 林麗真, *Wang Bi* 王弼 (Taipei: Dongda tushu gufen youxian gongsi, 1988), p. 27.

62. A complete translation of the *Shishuo xinyu* is available. See Richard B. Mather, trans., *Shih-shuo Hsin-yü: A New Account of Tales of the World* (Minneapolis: University of Minnesota Press, 1976).

63. Li Zehou, *Mei de licheng,* p. 92. Wai-yee Li has offered a more comprehensive treatment of, and new insights into, these changes in "Evaluating Characters and the Emergence of Aesthetic Self-Consciousness in the Six Dynasties," in the present volume.

64. Li Zehou, *Mei de licheng,* p. 92.

65. Mou Zongsan 牟宗三, *Weijin xuanxue* 魏晉玄學 (Taichung: Tunghai University, 1962), p. 4.

66. Zhou Yong 周顒 of the Southern Qi 南齊 (479–502) once remarked that both He Yan and Wang Bi had indicated, "Lao Zi is inferior to Confucius." See Lin Lizhen, *Wang Bi,* p. 58.

67. He Yan's comment comes from He Shao's "Wang Bi zhuan" 王弼傳. See Lin Lizhen, *Wang Bi,* p. 34. For Zhuang Zi's opinion, see the story about Lao Dan's death in chapter 3, the debate between Zhuang Zi and Huizi about whether a man can be without feelings in chapter 5, and the lack of ordinary feelings in a True Man in chapter 6 in Watson, *The Complete Works of Chuang Tzu,* pp. 52–53, 75–76, 77–80.

68. Quoted in Lin Lizhen, *Wang Bi,* p. 34. Details of He Yan's full argument are unfortunately not recorded in extant texts.

69. This is adapted from Mather, *A New Account of Tales of the World,* p. 96.

70. Adapted from Richard John Lynn, trans., *The Classic of the Way and Virtue: A New Translation of the Tao-te-ching of Laozi as Interpreted by Wang Bi* (New York: Columbia University Press, 1999), p. 51.

71. This is a slightly modified version of Lynn's translation. See ibid., p. 73.

72. See Lin Lizhen, *Wang Bi,* p. 43, for a helpful discussion of this.

73. Watson, *The Complete Works of Chuang Tzu,* p. 131. I have removed the capital letters from the terms "Great Beginning" and "Nonbeing" in Watson's rendering to be consistent with my own use of the term. The similarity between Wang Bi's conception of non-being and the passage in the *Zhuang Zi*

has been pointed out by Tang Yijie 湯一介 in his recent book, *Guo Xiang* (Taipei: Dongda tushu gongsi, 1999), p. 62.

74. Tang Yijie, *Guo Xiang*, p. 62.

75. For a translation of the chapter, see D. C. Lau, trans., *Lau Tau: Tao Te Ching* (Middlesex: Penguin Books, 1963), p. 67.

76. This is a slightly modified version of Lynn's rendering of the commentary. See *The Classic of the Way and Virtue*, p. 69.

77. This is modified from Lynn's translation. See *The Classic of the Way and Virtue*, p. 105.

78. See Lin Lizhen, *Wang Bi*, p. 36.

79. A. C. Graham defines "*ziran*" as follows: "*Wei* is ordinary human action, deliberated for a purpose, in contrast with the spontaneous processes of nature which are 'so of themselves.'" See *Disputers of the Tao: Philosophical Argument in Ancient China* (La Salle: Open Court Publishing, 1989), p. 232. Graham's definition of "*wei*" clearly shows the influence of Donald Munro's interpretation of "*wuwei*" as "nonpurposive action."

80. Lin Lizhen has observed that the picture of Confucius that Wang Bi has painted is Daoism-tainted ideal personality. See Lin Lizhen, *Wang Bi*, p. 36.

81. See Tang Yijie, *Guo Xiang*, p. 45.

82. Ibid., p. 31.

83. Guo Qingfan 郭慶藩, *Zhuang Zi jishi* 莊子集釋 (Taipei: Shijie shuju, 1962), vol. 1, p. 50.

84. Guo Xiang's comment can be found in ibid., p. 150. I follow Tang Yijie's reading of the remark to make my rendering of it into English. See Tang Yijie, *Guo Xiang*, p. 63.

85. Tang Yijie regards "letting everything be naturally what it is" (*renziran* 任自然) as the foundation of Guo Xiang's thought. See *Guo Xiang*, p. 40. I should like to mention that Brook Ziporyn has offered a penetrating discussion on the concept of "*ziran*" in the philosophy of Guo Xiang in "The Self-So and Its Traces in the Thought of Guo Xiang," *Philosophy East and West* 43, no. 3 (July 1993), pp. 511–539.

86. Guo Xiang's comment can be found in Guo Qingfan, *Zhuang Zi jishi*, vol. 1, pp. 381–382. Again, I follow Tang Yijie's reading in translating the passage. See *Guo Xiang*, p. 63.

87. Guo Qingfan, *Zhuang Zi jishi*, vol. 1, p. 286.

88. Ibid., p. 20.

89. Tang Yijie, *Guo Xiang*, p. 40.

90. Guo Qingfan, *Zhuang Zi jishi*, vol. 1, p. 287.

91. The Confucians especially hold the view that our mind-hearts perform the important function of evaluating nature, seeking ethical qualities and relationships inherent there for the sake of guiding conduct. See Munro, *The Concept of Man in Ancient China*, pp. 47–49.

92. Guo Qingfan, *Zhuang Zi jishi*, vol. 1, p. 24.

93. Watson, *The Complete Works of Chuang Tzu*, pp. 86–87.

94. Guo Qingfan, *Zhuang Zi jishi*, vol. 1, p. 268.

95. I am following Tang Yijie's excellent interpretation of this commentary of Guo Xiang. See *Guo Xiang*, pp. 56–59.

96. This appears in Xu You's response to Yao in "Free and Easy Wandering." See Guo Qingfan, *Zhuang Zi jishi*, vol. 1, p. 24.

97. Graham, *Chuang-tzu*, p. 59.

98. Guo Qingfan, *Zhuang Zi jishi*, vol. 1, p. 28.

99. Watson, *The Complete Works of Chuang Tzu*, p. 143. In the Inner Chapters (Neipian 內篇) of the *Zhuang Zi*, which are generally regarded by scholars as the works of Zhuang Zhou 莊周 (better known as Zhuang Zi), there is no clear reference to recluses who live "in the mountains and forests." Nevertheless, the daimonic man in "Free and Easy Wandering" lives on Guye Mountain, north of the Fen River. And all of the idealistic characters in the Inner Chapters do not reside in places of political and social prominence.

100. As noted in note 80, Lin Lizhen has observed that the picture Wang Bi has painted of Confucius, the sage, is a Daoism-tainted ideal personality. See *Wang Bi*, p. 36. I think Guo Xiang's picture of Confucius falls under the same category.

101. These life-patterns are the subject of discussion in an article by Wang Yao 王瑤 entitled "Lun xiqi yinyi zhi feng" 論希企隱逸之風, in Wang Yao, *Zhonggu wenren shenghuo* 中古文人生活, reprint (Shanghai: Guji chubanshe, 1982), pp. 49–68. I have briefly touched on the development of these life-patterns and the intellectual context in my book, *The Transformation of the Chinese Lyrical Tradition: Chiang K'uei and Southern Sung Tz'u Poetry* (Princeton, N.J.: Princeton University Press, 1978), pp. 17–24.

102. These motives are listed in the "Biographies of Recluses" 逸民傳 in the *History of the Later Han* 後漢書, by Fan Ye 范曄 (398–445). See Wang Yao, *Zhonggu wenren shenghuo*, p. 49.

103. See Wang Yao, *Zhongguo wenren shenghuo*, p. 49.

104. In a footnote explaining the philosophy about reclusion as expressed in the "Shanxing" 繕性 (Mending the Inborn Nature) chapter of the *Zhuang Zi*, Watson mentions that the Japanese scholar Fukunaga Mitsuji points out that the philosophy in this passage is contrary to that expressed in the Inner Chapters and closer to that expressed in the Confucian *Analects* and *The Book of Changes*. See Watson, *The Complete Works of Chuang Tzu*, p. 173.

105. See the passage about the "so-called scholars in hiding of ancient times" in "Mending the Inborn Nature" in Watson, *The Complete Works of Chuang Tzu*, p. 173.

106. See ibid., pp. 187–188.

107. Adapted from ibid., p. 167.

108. Wang Yao, *Zhonggu wenren shenghuo*, p. 52.

109. This is quoted and discussed in ibid.

110. Dongfang Shuo's expression of "now a dragon, now a snake, changing with things, in accordance with the appropriateness of the times" reminds one of a similar statement in the "Shanmu" 山木 (The Mountain Tree) chapter of the *Zhuang Zi*. See Watson, *The Complete Works of Chuang Tzu*, p. 209.

111. Wang Yao, *Zhonggu wenren shenghuo*, pp. 53–61.

112. Ibid., pp. 57–58.

113. Ibid., p. 58. Richard Mather has translated the first part (to "living in the world") of the passage quoted here. My rendering of this first part is adapted from Mather's translation. See Mather, *A New Account of Tales of the World*, p. 190.

114. See Richard Mather's biographical note of Xie An in *A New Account of Tales of the World*, p. 526.

115. Wang Yao, *Zhonggu wenren shenghuo*, p. 61.

116. Watson, *The Complete Works of Chuang Tzu*, p. 302.

117. Quoted in Wang Yao, *Zhonggu wenren shenghuo*, p. 61.

118. Ibid.

119. Wang Kangju 王康琚, "Fan zhaoyin shi" 反招隱詩, in *Wenxuan* 文選, ed. Xiao Tong 蕭統 (Hong Kong: Shangwu yinshuguan, 1960), p. 467. For a complete translation and interpretation of the poem, see Burton Watson, *Chinese Lyricism: Shih Poetry from the Second to the Twelfth Century* (New York: Columbia University Press, 1971), pp. 75–76.

120. Xu Fuguan, *Zhongguo yishu jingshen*, p. 133.

121. Hou Naihui, *Shiqing yu youjing*, pp. 34–35.

122. Wang Yi, *Yuanlin yu zhongguo wenhua*, p. 79.

123. Kong Jigong 孔季恭 of the (Liu) Song period had a sizable retreat that had a circumference of thirty-two leagues, covering an area of some 4,009 acres. See Hou Naihui, *Shiqing yu youjing*, p. 30.

124. Wang Yi, *Yuanlin yu zhongguo wenhua*, pp. 76–96.

125. Ibid., pp. 97–99.

126. Ibid., pp. 99–102. Wang Yi also observes that in poetry, painting, and the garden, Six Dynasties artists shared a common goal of creating within a limited physical space (i.e., size of paper, length of poem, area of land) an artistic space that was vast and deep, capable of embracing many variations. See pp. 138–139.

127. Wu Gongzheng 吳功正, *Liuchao meixue shi* 六朝美學史 (Nanjing: Jiangsu meishu chubanshe, 1994), pp. 561–562.

128. Ibid., p. 559.

129. This is a painting method advocated by such literati of the Song dynasty as Zhong Ren 仲仁, Wen Tong 文同 (1018–1079), and Su Shi 蘇軾 (1037–1101). See Wang Yi, *Yuanlin yu zhongguo wenhua*, pp. 428–429.

130. Ibid., 429.

131. Ibid. and Wu Gongzheng, *Liuchao meixue shi*, p. 559.

132. The remarks of Ge Hong and Xiao Tong (below) are quoted in ibid.

133. Quoted in Wang Yi, *Yuanlin yu zhongguo wenhua*, p. 429.

134. Ibid.

135. Quoted in Wu Gongzheng, *Liuchao meixueshi*, p. 560.

136. Ibid.

137. The story about Shen Yue and Liu Yao is mentioned by Wang Yi in *Yuanlin yu zhongguo wenhua*, p. 101.

138. David Hawkes, trans., *The Story of the Stone* (London: Penguin Books, 1973), vol. 1, pp. 324–325.

139. Tao Qian first became an official in 393 and retired as a magistrate in 405, so he was involved in official service for a total of twelve (thirteen in the Chinese way of counting) years. Although various early editions of Tao Qian's collected poetry say "thirty years" in this line, modern scholars generally prefer to emend the text to read "thirteen years." I believe "thirty years" is the correct reading. The word "*shao*" 少 in line 1, "少無適俗韻," can mean "in youth," "when young," "when very young," or "when small." It can be argued that Tao Qian said that he had fallen into the dusty net when he started seriously preparing himself for an official career. If this line of reasoning is correct, "that cage of mine" can cover a span of roughly thirty years, from the time the poet was ten to the time he was forty. Thirty is a neat number because it constitutes one generation (*yishi* 一世) in Chinese. For a discussion of the problems in the phrase "thirty years," see Gong Bin 龔斌, *Tao yuanming ji jiaojian* 陶淵明集校箋 (Shanghai: Guji chubanshe, 1966), p. 74.

140. In rendering this poem, I am indebted to the translations by Burton Watson (*The Columbia Book of Chinese Poetry: From Early Times to the Thirteenth Century* [New York: Columbia University Press, 1984], pp. 129–130); James Hightower (*The Poetry of T'ao Ch'ien* [Oxford: Clarendon Press, 1970], p. 50); and William Acker (*Tao the Hermit: Sixty Poems by T'ao Ch'ien* [London: Thames and Hudson, 1959], pp. 52–53). Watson notes that Tao's house plot was probably about one and a half acres and that a span is the distance between two pillars in a Chinese-style house.

141. See note 9 for my comments on "Peach Blossom Spring."

142. This fact clearly parallels the slow reception of Tao Qian's literary works in Chinese history, the topic of Kang-i Sun Chang's paper in this volume.

143. Adapted from Mather, *A New Account of Tales of the World*, p. 60.

144. Quoted in Wang Yao, *Zhonggu wenren shenghuo*, pp. 61–62.

145. Quoted in Wu Gongzheng, *Liuchao meixue shi*, p. 510.

146. Ibid., pp. 505–511.

Part II

Words and Patterns
● ● ● ● ● ● ● ● ● ● ● ● ● ● ●
Poetry and Prose

Chapter 5

• •

The Unmasking of Tao Qian and the Indeterminacy of Interpretation

Kang-i Sun Chang

$\mathbf{T}$his chapter will examine the history of the reception of Tao Qian 陶潛 (365?–427), a Six Dynasties poet who became one of the greatest figures in the Chinese literary canon—surprisingly, since in his own time Tao Qian was practically unknown as a poet, and it was only a succession of readers over the centuries who eventually canonized him. Such a dramatic case of historic reception has ramifications that go far beyond the literary position of a single poet, as it touches on all the cultural and aesthetic questions that are implicit in the act of reading and rereading.

When we consider the relatively few works Tao Qian produced (approximately 150 poems and 10 essays and rhyme-prose pieces in all) and the emphatically marginal literary position he had in his lifetime, his eventual canonical position in Chinese literature is truly striking. A key moment in his canonization occurred during the Song dynasty, when Su Shi 蘇軾 declared Tao Qian to be the greatest poet ever, and Fang Hui 方回 (1227–1306) praised Tao Qian (along with Du Fu) as one of the two foremost masters in the Chinese literary tradition.[1] During the Qing dynasty Wang Shizhen 王士禎 (1634–1711) claimed that Tao Qian's accomplishments "cannot be rivaled by his predecessors and successors and cannot be assessed within the confines of a single age."[2] Early in the twentieth century Liang Qichao 梁啟超 (1873–1929)

singled out Tao Qian and Qu Yuan 屈原 (China's first poet known by name) as the two literary giants whose poetic voices were the most powerful, a view that Wang Guowei 王國維 (1877–1927) simultaneously held.[3] Indeed, whomever the list comprises, the inclusion of Tao Qian's name now seems inevitable. The total aggregate of Tao Qian scholarship over the centuries is now so overwhelming that a special term, "*Tao xue*" 陶學 (Taology), has been coined, comparable to terms used for the scholarship on the *Shi jing* (*Shi jing xue* 詩經學), *Chu ci* (*Chu ci xue* 楚辭學), and *The Dream of the Red Chamber* (*Hong xue* 紅學 or Redology).[4] To this day, readers continue to read Tao Qian with a consistent enthusiasm, all claiming to have found the true voice of the poet anew.

One aspect of the image of Tao Qian that has been perennially appealing to readers is Tao's honesty with himself, the idea that despite all his anxiety and self-questioning he would not go against himself— even if he had to suffer the very real physical consequences of poverty: "Why, you ask. Because my instinct is all for freedom, and will not brook discipline or restraint. Hunger and cold may be sharp, but this going against myself really sickens me."[5]

It is with the exploration of this selfhood as revealed in his works that Tao's readers found so easy to identify. Thus, it is not surprising that many readers turned to Tao Qian's poetry for help during times of duress, seeking to find a satisfactory explanation, even a remedy, for their personal suffering. For example, during his illness Liang Qichao read nothing but Tao Qian's poetry and consequently produced his famous "Chronology of Tao Yuanming" (Tao Yuanming nianpu).[6] Li Chendong 李辰冬 studied Tao's poetry diligently on a farm during the Sino-Japanese War in the 1930s and as a result completed his thought-provoking work on Tao Qian.[7] More recently the famous literary critic Liu Zaifu 劉再復 claimed that Tao Qian was one of two great authors —the other being Goethe—whose works gave him strength in his days of exile after leaving China.[8] And, of course, there have been readers who simply enjoyed reading Tao's works as a pastime, such as Ding Fubao 丁福保, who found happiness in reading and reciting Tao's poems daily. Ding collected more than twenty editions of Tao's works and eventually became known as the commentator who wrote *Tao Yuanming shi jianzhu*, which was based on a rare edition from the Song dynasty.[9] Indeed, one would agree with the Song dynasty poet Xin Qiji 辛棄疾, who once wrote the following in "Shui long yin" 水龍吟: "We must believe that Tao has not died/Even to this day he is full of vigor and vitality" (須信此翁未死，到如今凜然生氣).[10]

But what accounts for the immortality of Tao Qian when in fact very little is actually known about the poet? Even today, we are still not certain of so basic a fact as his original given name. Unfortunately, the early biographies of Tao gave different names—Tao Qian with the courtesy name Yuanming 淵明; or Yuanming with the courtesy name Yuanliang 元亮; or simply Yuanliang, also known as Shenming 深明. Most interesting of all, the biographer for the *Jin shu* 晉書 (History of the Jin) simply dropped the name "Yuanming," the very name by which Tao Qian would be best known to posterity. As for Tao's birth date, it remains an unresolved puzzle, as is demonstrated by the opening chapter of a book published in 1996 that asks, "When, in which year, was Tao Yuanming born?"[11] Despite the fact that most scholars tend to agree with the A.D. 365 birth date, there are others who insist (as did Liang Qichao) on A.D. 372.[12] Yet other scholars give alternative dates such as A.D. 376 and A.D. 369, all claiming to have based their theories on serious research.[13] Ironically, it is because of the lack of definite dates for most of the events in Tao's life that scholars have created so many chronologies (*nianpu* 年譜) throughout the centuries, all meant to give a sense of "precision" to Tao's life and works. Regarding the proliferation of these ongoing *nianpu* publications, A. R. Davis (one of the most well-known experts in Tao Qian studies) notes the following: "This peculiarly Chinese form of presentation has an inherent tendency to over-precision.... My own repeated contention is that this is false and I believe that it may be of some service to Tao Yuan-ming studies to demonstrate the weakness of many accepted arguments and the probable impossibility in many cases of achieving any definiteness of date."[14]

In any case, this lack of "definiteness of date" highlights one of the thorniest issues in Tao Qian studies: the poet's obscurity reflects his rather insignificant position in contemporary Wei-Jin society. In my book, *Six Dynasties Poetry*, I pointed out that Tao's work "was unappreciated by his age and misunderstood by critics and poets" of the Six Dynasties period mainly because of the lack of polish in his poetic diction.[15] But I think that Tao Qian's obscurity might also be due to the fact that he was regarded by his contemporaries essentially as a recluse, not a poet, and that he had a very marginal position in the political world at the time. During the Six Dynasties period, as the poet Zuo Si 左思 once put it, "scions of great houses [climbed] to high positions, while men of talent [were] buried as petty clerks."[16] Thus, those who had no aristocratic connections in the court were bound to remain unknown. Although Tao's great-grandfather Tao Kan 陶侃 was a famous official who had made a great contribution to the founding of the Eastern Jin, the family fortunes had declined long before the birth of Tao Qian. Of course, Tao Qian never rose to prominence in the court, and he eventually spent the last twenty years of his life in retirement, which would hardly add prestige to his social position. Indeed, as Tao Qian said of himself in a tone of self-mockery in his autobiographical sketch, "The Biography of Mr. Five-Willows," "We do not know where he came from, nor do we know his family or courtesy names."[17]

Unfortunately in the "Funeral Elegy" (by the poet Yan Yanzhi 顏延之 [386–456]), the only contemporary piece of writing about Tao Qian, there is little description of Tao's life involving factual data other than the fact that Tao "lived in seclusion among the southern hills" and that he died in the fourth year of the Yuanjia period.[18] Likewise, the early official biographies of Tao Qian all tend to be sketchy and anecdotal. As A. R. Davis has suggested, these character anecdotes "had acquired a greater or less degree of exaggeration and had been sometimes set for the sake of verisimilitude in particular but doubtful context."[19] Similarly Wang Kuo-ying 王國瓔 has observed that some quintessential episodes in the Tao Qian legend as recorded in the official biographies—including one referring to Tao's statement about not being willing to bow down to someone for "a measly bushel of rice"— have all been based on shaky evidence.[20] In most cases, such anecdotes might derive from mere hearsay, but Shen Yue 沈約 (441–513), author of the official biography of Tao Qian in the *Song shu* 宋書, used them mainly for dramatic effect. Later, Fang Xuanling 房玄齡 (578–648) in the *Jin shu* 晉書 and Li Yanshou 李延壽 (?–679?) in the *Nan shi* 南史 both followed suit in their biographies of Tao. In fact, they took the liberty of adding still more stories to their entries, perhaps with the intention of creating the perfect image of Tao Qian as an upright recluse.

It should be mentioned that all these biographies of Tao appear in the "Group Biography" section on "Recluses" (Yinyi 隱逸). If anything, the biographers themselves were more concerned with the public image of Tao the Recluse (to be consistent with those individuals in the same "group biography") than with the private side of Tao Qian as a poet.[21] In Shen Yue's biography of Tao, for instance, not a single word is said about Tao's literary position; the fact that Tao was a poet is somehow forgotten. Apparently Tao Qian's moral character and his political role as a recluse are the real focus of these official biographies. Known as one of the three eminent recluses of Xunyang (潯陽三隱), Tao was made to represent typical recluses, who remained constant in their refusal to participate in public service, model figures who were admired for their distaste for conventional values. Thus, reading through the group biographies of recluses in the dynastic histories, we can find numerous examples of individuals whose experiences and attitudes resemble those of Tao Qian.[22] In fact, for many generations, the regions around Tao Qian's hometown were known for high-minded recluses.[23] In particular, Liu Linzhi 劉麟之, the hermit of Nanyang mentioned in Tao Qian's "Peach Blossom Spring," appears almost as a double of Tao Qian in the Group Biography section of the *Jin shu*.[24] Like Tao, Liu would not compromise his principles and continued to turn down offers for political office. In daily living Liu practiced frugality and self-reliance, and in obscurity he managed to find peace and contentment, again very much like the Tao Qian of the dynastic histories. Such images of the perfect recluse are of particular value for the traditional Chinese because they respond to one of the key existential questions with which they are confronted—namely, how should the relationship between an upright intellectual and a troubled political world be conceived?[25] One way to resolve this problem is of course to create representative models to exemplify the virtues of historical figures who all managed to find inner peace in the midst of a troubled world. Thus, the Tao Qian we find in the historical records conveniently serves as an exemplary person whose individuality corresponds perfectly with the characteristics of traditional recluses. As Yan Yanzhi says in his "Funeral Elegy" for Tao Qian, Tao's "honesty was deep, his simplicity pure/His truth was tranquil, his purity gentle."[26] All this explains why Tao Qian was conceived as a part of only the moral, rather than the literary, canon at first, and very little was known of his literary merits until at least a century after his death.

When one begins to read Tao's poetry, however, one finds a somewhat different Tao Qian who was by no means the simple or consistent figure presented by the traditional biographers. Several modern scholars have pointed this out. For example, A. R. Davis mentions that one generally gets "an impression from [Tao's] writings very different from the anecdotes related in the early biographers," where the poet's own "ironic poses" have often become distorted.[27] Stephen Owen notes that Tao's poetry "is filled with contradictions, the contradictions that come from a sophisticated, self-conscious man who yearns to be unsophisticated and unself-conscious."[28] Similarly, Wang Kuo-ying "discovers" (based on close readings) a more "complicated and interesting personality" in Tao Qian than was formerly perceived. She further observes that although Tao took pride in his deliberate choice of becoming a recluse-farmer, he was by no means free from occasional self-doubt.[29] Most notably, in his important letter to his "Sons, Yan and Others" 與子儼等書 (assumed by some to be Tao's final will), Tao Qian expresses considerable regret about causing his sons to suffer hunger and cold in their childhood. The poet also grieves that his wife could not be as virtuous as Lao Laizi's legendary wife, who apparently supported her husband's ideals of hermitage wholeheartedly and once even dissuaded her husband from taking office.[30] Tao Qian's confession here of course gives a rather different picture from Xiao Tong's biography of Tao, in which Tao's wife is portrayed as an ideal soulmate for the poet.[31] But such insightful comparisons have not been noted until recently, when scholars have begun to do closer readings of Tao's work. Indeed, these new readings have encouraged us to explore newer and deeper layers of meaning in Tao's poetry and to discover a more complex human being with whom we ourselves can identify. We have found that, contrary to the rather simple portrait of Tao in the conventional biographies, Tao Qian himself intended to convey to his readers a great deal of information about himself—including specific dates of important events in his life, the names of his friends, his motives for freeing himself from public service, his anxieties and frustrations, his self-mocking tendencies, and the like. Most important, the richness of the poet's inner life, as captured in his poetry, has continued to lead us into an "indeterminacy of interpretation" concerning Tao Qian. When the modern scholar Zhong Youmin 鍾優民 said, "We can never stop talking about Tao Qian," he referred precisely to this indeterminacy of interpretation characteristic of Tao studies.[32] But such a realization came only after a long time of reading, a reading that signified the culmination of a gradual progression from mere moral considerations to a more literary and overall appreciation of Tao's works, including aesthetic, moral, and political readings.

In this sense we can say that Tao Qian has been invented by his readers, or perhaps, if we follow Harold Bloom's theory concerning the

power of great authors, we might even say that to a certain extent Tao
Qian has "invented" the Chinese.[33] The Chinese over the last several
centuries so shaped themselves through their readings of Tao that they
often took Tao's voice to be their own. Moreover, there was so much
"Chineseness" in Tao Qian—and especially in the extremely long historic reception of Tao's literary works—that we can claim that Tao's
total impact upon Chinese culture is immeasurable.[34] Needless to say,
it is beyond the scope of this chapter to trace the long history of the
canonization of Tao Qian and the role that Tao as a canonized poet has
played in Chinese culture. Here I wish only to highlight the few areas in
the historic reception of Tao that have significantly contributed to the
gradual "unmasking" of the poet. Indeed, if we consider the early biographers' works as a kind of "masking"—in the sense that they were
inclined to overemphasize Tao's simplicity as a recluse-farmer—then
we can perhaps say that later readers of Tao's poetry were at their most
original in their unmasking of Tao.

The first critical text to mention Tao Qian's stature as a poet was
Zhong Rong's 鍾嶸 (ca. 469–518) *Shi pin* 詩品 (Grading of Poets).
Unlike Yan Yanzhi, who could see Tao Qian only as a recluse (and
nothing else), Zhong Rong was able to recognize Tao's role as both a
recluse and a poet, thus granting him the eminent title of "paramount
recluse-poet of all time" (古今隱逸詩人之宗). In an age when Tao Qian
was not yet perceived as a poet, Zhong Rong's was indeed quite an
innovative methodological step, one that greatly enlarged reader perceptions. However, in the long history of Chinese criticism, Zhong
Rong has repeatedly been faulted for placing Tao Qian in the second,
rather than the first rank. Modern scholars such as Wang Shumin 王叔
岷 and Bernhard Fuehrer came strongly to Zhong Rong's defense; in
their view, the fact that Zhong Rong was able to include Tao Qian in
his *Shi pin* at all (as compared to Liu Xie, who had completely neglected Tao Qian in his *Wenxin diaolong*) was already an accomplishment.[35] However, due to Zhong Rong's special criteria for evaluating
poetry—such as his preference for *yuan* 怨 (grief) in poetry, a quality
for which Tao Qian was not especially known—it was simply not possible for him to place Tao Qian in the first rank.[36] In fact, it was typical of Six Dynasties readers to feel a greater admiration for poetry that
was characterized by emotions that expressed deep grief and bitter-
ness caused by political injustice and punishment.[37] But what is really
admirable about Zhong Rong is his ability to see beyond Tao Qian's

generally plain style (which Six Dynasties readers disliked) and discover a beauty and elegance in his poetry that most of his contemporaries had missed: "The world at large criticized his plain and straightforward (質直) style. But how about such lines as 'Happily I pour the spring-brewed wine' (歡言酌春酒), and 'At sunset the sky is cloudless' (日暮天無雲)? Aren't these also characterized by graceful elegance and pure refinement (風華清靡)? Who can say that Tao used only rustic language?"[38]

It is obvious that Zhong Rong's remarks greatly influenced the views of later readers. For example, in his famous anthology, *Wenxuan* 文選, the Liang prince Xiao Tong 蕭統 (501–531) made sure to include the two poems by Tao Qian to which Zhong Rong had referred in the *Shi pin* (see quotation from *Shi pin* above).[39] Moreover, in his preface to *The Collected Works of Tao Qian*, which he compiled, Xiao Tong praised Tao Qian for his unusual literary style and especially for his skillful and outstanding poetic diction (辭采精拔)—a judgment that is the exact opposite of Yang Xiuzhi's 楊休之 (509–582) famous comment on Tao Qian's "lack of verbal ornament" (辭采未優).[40] It is easy to understand that under the influence of his brother Xiao Tong, Xiao Gang 蕭綱 (503–551) also enjoyed reading the works of Tao Qian, although Xiao Gang's own ornate style of writing was quite different from Tao's. And the great palace-style poet Yu Xin 庾信 (513–581), while living the life of an exile in the north, began to compose poems in imitation of Tao Qian's works.[41] All this proves that Xiao Tong's promotion of Tao Qian's literary position was certainly influential in changing the general view of Tao Qian as a poet. In a way, all the important Tang readers of Tao Qian—including Wang Wei 王維, Li Bai 李白, Du Fu 杜甫, and Bai Juyi 白居易—were inspired by Xiao Tong's example. But it should be emphasized that despite their appreciation of Tao Qian's poetry, these Tang readers (perhaps with the exception of Bai Juyi) are still remembered as poet-critics who were somewhat unsympathetic to Tao's views and actions. For example, Li Bai criticized Tao for passively remaining a lifelong recluse, and Wang Wei blamed Tao for his "unwillingness to bend his waist" before a local inspector, a stance that led to a lifetime of hardship.[42] As Ronald Egan aptly puts it, "The real Tao Qian peeked out at them from behind, but they [the Tang readers] did not necessarily approve fully of what they saw."[43]

One thing that almost all Tao scholars have overlooked—until recently, when we were reminded by Li Hua 李華—is the fact that as early as the Tang dynasty the poet Du Fu was already perceptive enough as a reader to see through the "mask" of Tao Qian as a completely happy recluse.[44] Unfortunately Du Fu's words were misread for many centuries, and hence his views on Tao were also misunderstood. The misunderstanding concerns Du Fu's poem "Qianxing 遣興," which, according to Li Hua, should be translated as follows:

陶潛避俗翁	Although Tao Qian was a recluse in retreat,
未必能達道	He had not quite achieved the ideal state of Dao.
觀其著詩集	Looking through Tao's collection of poems, one feels that
頗亦恨枯槁	Tao Qian had regretted his impoverished life [kugao].[45]

Thus, unlike traditional readers, who often took the term "kugao" 枯槁 in Du Fu's poem to mean "stylistic plainness," Li Hua for the first time read it as "poverty." This new reading is very convincing because, as Li Hua explains, Tao Qian once in one of his own poems ("Drinking Wine," no. 11) used the same term, "kugao," to refer to the financial destitution of Confucius's favorite disciple, Yan Hui:

顏生稱為仁	Master Yan they praise for being good
榮公言有道	And old man Rong is said to have been a sage:
屢空不獲年	The one was often empty—he died young,
長飢至于老	The other always hungry his whole life long.
雖留後世名	They may have left behind an honored name
一生亦枯槁	But it cost a lifetime of deprivation [kugao].[46]

In suggesting that Yan Hui had paid too high a price for his posthumous fame, Tao Qian was perhaps mocking his own state of deprivation. By extension, one may argue that Du Fu, in his reference to Tao Qian's suffering, was also creating an ironic pose for himself. While Du Fu was trying to unmask Tao Qian—the ideal recluse who took comfort in all life's circumstances—Du Fu was, in fact, also performing an act of self-revelation. Certainly, as someone who had often lived through difficult conditions in his lifetime, Du Fu had legitimate grounds for comparing himself to Tao Qian. Thus, in his commentary on Du Fu's poem "Qianxing," the Qing scholar Pu Qilong 浦起龍 suggested that "by mocking Tao Yuanming, Du Fu was in fact laughing at himself, because Du was using Tao Yuanming as a role model for himself" (嘲淵明，自嘲也。假一淵明為本身象贊).[47]

But the problem is, as Li Hua has pointed out, that critics over the last several centuries have continued to misread Du Fu—in effect, it is a case of misreading Du Fu's reading of Tao Qian. As has been noted above, critics often misread the word *"kugao,"* and thus they simply assumed that Du Fu was criticizing Tao Qian for his overly plain poetic style. This misunderstanding led the Ming scholar Hu Yinglin 胡應麟 to claim in his book *Shi sou* (詩藪) that "Du Fu disliked Tao's poems because of their 'withered and plain' quality."[48] It was not until 1992, when Li Hua first published his book on Tao Qian (literally titled "New Thoughts on Tao Qian"), that scholars began to reread the Du Fu poem in question. This interesting case of misreading confirms our idea that a canonical author is always the product of reader responses in progress.

Still Du Fu was not fully responsible for the eventual canonization of Tao Qian. It was the Song dynasty readers who elevated Tao Qian to his supreme position as a perfect poet who was universally admired and worshipped. It is interesting to observe that the reason that kept Six Dynasties readers from granting Tao Qian full status as a first-rate poet was also the very reason that made Tao an all-powerful model poet six hundred years later. During the Six Dynasties period Tao was faulted for using "rustic language" in his poetry, and his marginal social and political position prevented him from being thought of as a poet. But during the Song dynasty it was Tao's use of "easy and plain" (*pingdan* 平淡) diction that appealed most to his readers. For *pingdan* represents authenticity (*zhen* 真), and according to Su Shi, it was this quality that made it possible for Tao Qian to be true to himself and to be able to choose freely between office and retirement. If Tao Qian could be a contented farmer and poet on the slopes of Lushan, they themselves should be able to do the same during times of personal political setbacks. Thus, that was precisely what Su Shi did. During his exile in Huangzhou, Su Shi worked as a farmer on the East Slope and progressively convinced himself that he was indeed another Tao Qian.[49] This idealization of Tao Qian was like a masking all over again, but it was in this context that Tao Qian's utopian ideal of the Peach Blossom Spring was given a reality that captured the imagination of Song readers. It is interesting to note that whereas Tao Qian's kind of utopia was marginalized in his own times—when extravagant pleasure gardens were considered the true land of utopia—his farm ideal finally rose to prominence in the Song dynasty.[50] This is because for Song readers true freedom meant a place of rustic seclusion, a community of self-preservation that was away from political danger but was at the same time perfectly attainable in the real world. Thus, it should not come as a surprise that Wang Anshi 王安石 would deconstruct the Tang poet Wang Wei's version of a mystical Peach Blossom Spring that existed only in the immortal world.[51] In his poem "Taoyuan xing" 桃源行, Wang Anshi brings back the realistic dimension of Tao Qian's utopia by depicting the Peach Blossom Spring as a place for refugees who had run away from war and political unrest. In this peaceful farm community called Peach Blossom Spring people are satisfied by simple agricultural life without the need for exploring beyond the confines of their own village.[52] Thus, many Song readers (including Su Shi and Hong Mai 洪邁) claimed that Tao's Peach Blossom Spring represented some hidden communities that actually existed during the Six Dynasties, a view with which the renowned modern scholar Chen Yinke agreed.[53]

Closely related to this myth of the Peach Blossom Spring is that of a content recluse who was perfectly happy with his small farm and country life. But did Tao Qian ever regret his decision to retire from public service? Did he from time to time wish his circumstances were otherwise? Such questions appeared especially often after the Ming-Qing transition, as critics began to wonder about the real Tao Qian. For example, the nineteenth-century poet Gong Zizhen 龔自珍 (1792–1841) considered Tao a person of great chivalry with many worldly ambitions, someone who could be compared to the wise minister Zhuge Liang in the Three Kingdoms period.[54] Clearly Gong Zizhen did not think that Tao Qian was a contented recluse. To Gong and many of his contemporaries, Tao Qian represented a typical Chinese intellectual who had high ideals of public service but had to give them up because of the ills of the times. Thus they believed there was a sense of helplessness, though quite subtle, in Tao Qian that was characteristic of the frustrated scholar in traditional China. And this subtle sense of dissatisfaction was precisely the quality that the modern writer Lu Xun found so attractive in Tao Qian.

Parallel to this "unmasking" of Tao was an even more powerful tradition of allegorical interpretation concerning Tao's perennial image as a wine lover. As early as the Six Dynasties period Xiao Tong had suggested that "although Tao's poems were filled with descriptions of wine, Tao's real intent was to convey something other than wine."[55] Xiao Tong did not specify what the "other" meanings were, but under Xiao's influence later scholars began to view Tao not as a poet who simply drank, but as someone who used drinking as a mask for something deeper. Indeed, Tao's famous "Drinking Wine" poems (twenty poems) were not really about wine drinking but were perhaps meant as something political, as conveyed by the ending lines of this poem series:

終日馳車走	All day the hurried carriages dash by
不見所問津	But no one comes to ask about the ford.
若復不快飲	If I fail to drink to my heart's content
空負頭上巾	I will be untrue to the cap I wear.
但恨多謬誤	Still I regret the stupid things I've said
君當恕醉人	And hope you will forgive a man in his cups.[56]

Here the poet is obviously using drunkenness as an excuse for conveying something serious. As James Hightower has noted, these lines have become the "delight of Confucian commentators," for the poet claims that if he abandons himself to drink, "it is clearly in despair at the bad times, not a rejection of the proprieties."[57] Judging by the fact that Chinese commentators often have an urge to contextualize, one can imagine that they would try every means to make Tao Qian's "Drinking Wine" poems historically referential.[58] To many commentators, the so-called "bad times" implied in Tao Qian's poems must refer to the government of (Liu) Song, a new dynasty that Tao refused to serve. In one sense, this reading can be seen as an extension of Shen Yue's classic reading of Tao as a conscious loyalist of the Jin dynasty. In his *Song shu*, Shen Yue makes the point that although Tao put down the Jin year designation for his poems before the Yixi period (405–418), he used only the cyclical sign (*jiazi* 甲子) from the beginning of the (Liu) Song dynasty—a device that seems to bear witness to the poet's loyalist position.[59] Although Shen Yue's statement involves his own bias and ideology and has therefore been regarded by some commentators as unreliable, it has nonetheless served since the Song dynasty as the fundamental basis by which to interpret Tao's works. For Chinese critics, no other mode of interpretation seemed more convincing. Indeed, later this kind of allegorical reading became an especially effective mode of interpretation for loyalists who resisted the pressures from a new dynasty. One of the most telling examples was the Song dynasty patriot Wen Tianxiang 文天祥 (1236–1283), who praised Tao Qian for using his drunkenness as a guise for his loyalist sentiments (陶潛豈醉人)—at a time when Wen himself was threatened by a similar problem of dynastic transition.[60] To Wen Tianxiang, Tao Qian's drinking represents an ideal device or mask for saying one thing while meaning another. What Xiao Tong said about the "other" meaning of Tao's drinking thus found a perfect answer in Wen Tianxiang's response. Of course, not all critics agreed with such allegorical readings, but the general attempt to look for hidden meanings regarding Tao's drinking has encouraged many generations of scholars to view Tao Qian as a person of greater complexity who knew how to choose between self-revelation or concealment in his poetry. For example, in his famous article on wine and medicine among Six Dynasties literati, Lu Xun emphasized both the sense of peaceful transcendence and active political concern on the part of Tao Qian.[61] Similarly, the famous aesthetician Zhu Guangqian 朱光潛 considered Tao's wine drinking as both an escape from and a protest against corrupt contemporary politics.[62] But in the meantime, many modern scholars—such as Liang Qichao and Zhu Ziqing 朱自清—began to question the validity of political readings contextualizing Tao as a Jin loyalist.[63] Some scholars even emphasized that Tao Qian took office under Liu Yu 劉裕 (the founder of the [Liu] Song dynasty), a fact that would rule out the possibility of Tao's being a true loyalist to the Jin house.[64] And others discovered that the poems that had been read as political allegories were in fact written long before the fall of the Jin and thus could not possibly count as loyalist writings.[65] All these new readings of Tao illuminate both the complexity of the human condition and the necessary gap between art and reality.

One other myth about Tao Qian is that of an upright Confucian who would never concern himself with a romantic passion for women. Perhaps for this reason, Tao's "Xianqing fu" 閒情賦 (The Fu on Calming the Passions), exploring the theme of romantic love, has been a problem for many traditional as well as modern scholars. One problem is that Xiao Tong, the first anthologist to bring together Tao Qian's works, was also the first critic to denounce "Xianqing fu" as a "minor flaw in the white jade."[66] Although moral considerations certainly played a great part in Xiao Tong's negative evaluation, the fact that the piece also contains some feminizing discourse typical of "decadent" palace-style poetry might have also contributed to his assessment.[67] Or as Wolfgang Kubin has pointed out, "Xianqing fu" represents an "amorous offence against the etiquette," although at the end of the poem the persona is able to overcome his emotions and observe the rules of etiquette.[68] At any rate, because of Xiao Tong's criticism, for as long as several centuries no critic dared to take a different view regarding this controversial poem until the Song dynasty, when Su Shi (considered by many to be Tao Qian's greatest follower ever) began to take a closer look at this long-neglected work. Unlike Xiao Tong, who must have wished that "Xianqing fu" had never existed, Su Shi considered Tao's poem a brilliant piece of literature whose value was as great as the *Shi jing* and the works of Qu Yuan. Thus, in his inscription on the *Wenxuan*, Su Shi writes: "The 'Xianqing fu' is like poems in the 'Guofeng' section of the Odes; it appears to be sensual but not excessively so (好色而不淫). But even if it cannot be compared to 'Zhou Nan' [the opening section of the Odes], shouldn't we still say it's at least as good as the works of Qu Yuan and Song Yu? However, Xiao Tong was making fun of it. This was like little children trying to understand something when they couldn't."[69] This statement by Su Shi was later endorsed by the well-known Qing scholar Chen Hang 陳沆 (1785–1825), who claimed that Tao's "Xianqing fu" was the single greatest piece of literature during the Jin.[70] What Su Shi found most admirable in "Xianqing fu" was again the quality of *zhen*, which Su took to be the secret of Tao Qian's art.[71] To be *zhen* in poetry means the ability to speak one's mind, even though it is done through the manipulation of a persona. Precisely because of this *zhen*, Tao's poem is able to introduce emotions that are at once true and bewildering, quiet and turbulent. Indeed, with "Xianqing fu" Tao Qian seems to have moved up to a new level of sophistication and hence a new level of difficulty and achievement that includes the successful intermingling of various themes and stylistic experiments. Perhaps that was why Su Shi said that Tao Qian's poetry "looks plain but is in fact extravagantly beautiful" (質而實綺),[72] a perfect rebuttal to the often carping remarks about the "plainness" of Tao's poetic style.[73] It is important that many modern scholars have been able to learn from Su Shi's revaluation of "Xianqing fu" and have continued to provide new readings of the poem. For example, Liang Qichao praised Tao Qian's description of his ten wishes related to the beloved woman (longing to be a collar on her dress, etc.) as one of the most moving passages in literature.[74] Zhu Guangqian expressed his admiration for Tao Qian's ability to capture the intimate feelings of a human being, "one who possesses the flesh and blood of a real person."[75] Similarly, Lu Xun applauded Tao's courage to explore various aspects of sensual love that read almost like a confession (*zibai* 白白).[76] Such comments by modern scholars represent a progression away from the allegorical interpretation—which includes Su Shi's invoking the moral authority of *Shi jing* in his interpretation of "Xian-qing fu"—toward a richer, more down-to-earth reading that is less predictable and more penetrating into the human condition. As a result, a more human and more believable image of Tao Qian emerges from our encounter with the text itself. But I should add that as early as the Ming dynasty, critics such as Zhong Xing 鍾惺 (1574–1624) had already begun to look into the complexity of Tao Qian's art.[77] In particular, Sun Yuefeng 孫月峰 claimed that Tao's "easy and plain" *(pingdan)* style was the result of tremendous hard work and artistry, and thus its impression of easiness was no more than an impression.[78]

From what we know, Tao Qian seems to have been someone who would care very much about a reader's response. As he said in the preface to his "Drinking Wine" poems, he had a friend make a copy of his verses (聊命故人書之). Although Tao Qian said this in a tone of ostensible modesty—that he had no more in mind than to provide "pleasure and laughter" for his friends—there is no doubt that he cared about the transmission of his works.[79] Moreover, as A. R. Davis has pointed out, Tao Qian shared with many other Chinese poets "the creation of the self-image."[80] Interestingly it is perhaps largely in Tao's death pieces that readers found a real correspondence between the early biographers' descriptions of the poet and Tao Qian's own self-descriptions.

Most readers are fascinated by Tao's contemplation of his own death. The truth is that no writer has been as self-consciously concerned with the reality and acceptance of death as Tao Qian—as may be demonstrated by his "Burial Songs" and his last sacrificial piece, "In Sacrifice for Myself" 自祭文. The following words, supposedly written shortly before Tao's death, can belong only to someone who has not only questioned, but has also found ultimate answers to, the problem of finite existence:

樂天委分	I rejoiced in my destiny, accepted my lot,
以至百年	And so lived out my "hundred years."
. . .	
識運知命	I understand my destiny, I knew my fate,

疇能罔眷	But who can be quite unconcerned?
余今斯化	Yet now I am thus to be transformed,
可以無恨	I can take it without regret.[81]

Words like these, written as an elegy for oneself, were simply without precedent in Chinese literature before Tao Qian's time. As Liang Qichao has said, "There is not a single author aside from Tao Yuanming who has created so many pieces of work on his deathbed that contain so much inspirational wisdom [*li qu* 理趣]."[82] Of course, one cannot be sure that Tao literally wrote these works on his deathbed. But there is no doubt that many readers believe that he did. Supposedly under the influence of Tao Qian, the Japanese anthology of poetry, the *Man'yoshu* (萬葉集), included sections called the "Burial Songs" (輓歌), as well as other songs, which seemed to echo Tao's anticipation of his own death.[83]

The idea that Tao Qian "regarded death as returning to his native home," as is described in the "Funeral Elegy" by Yan Yanzhi, indeed echoes Tao's own description of himself.[84] That certainly is the self-image by which Tao wished to be remembered, although he could not help sharing his sense of helplessness with the reader at the end of his last sacrificial piece:

人生實難	Man's life is truly hard;
死如之何	What can he do about death?
嗚呼哀哉	Oh! Alas![85]

This last utterance of Tao's remains a public acknowledgment of a canonical poet's rather complex private self. But readings of great poets like Tao Qian will always imply a continuing process of masking and unmasking and even remasking. Perhaps we could borrow from another enigmatic Chinese classic, one surely congenial to Tao Qian—namely, the *Lao Zi*—and suggest that the person(a) that you can understand is not the constant person(a).

NOTES

1. See Fang Hui's poem series entitled "Thoughts of Poetry" (詩思), in which he mentioned both Tao Qian and Du Fu.

2. See Zong-qi Cai, *The Matrix of Lyric Transformation: Poetic Modes and Self-Presentation in Early Chinese Pentasyllabic Poetry* (Ann Arbor: Center for Chinese Studies, University of Michigan, 1996), p. 13. Wang Shizhen's original passage can be found in his *Gushi jian* 古詩箋 (Shanghai: Guji chubanshe, 1990), p. 2.

3. Liang Qichao 梁啟超, *Tao Yuanming* 陶淵明 (1923; reprint, Taipei: Shangwu yinshu guan, 1996), p. 1; Wang Guowei 王國維, "Wenxue xiaoyan" 文學小言; as cited in Zhong Youmin 鍾優民, *Tao xue shi hua* 陶學史話 (Taipei: Yunchen, 1991), p. 202. Recently, Yeh Chia-ying 葉嘉瑩 has also echoed this view. See Yeh Chia-ying, *Tao Yuanming yinjiu shi jianglu* 陶淵明飲酒詩講錄 (Taipei: Guiguan, 2000), p. 137.

4. See Zhong Youmin, *Tao xue shi hua*, p. 7.

5. See Tao Qian, "Guiqu lai xi ci"; translation taken from James Hightower, *The Poetry of T'ao Ch'ien* (Oxford: Clarendon Press, 1970), p. 268. Martin Powers elaborated on this point in "'Privacy' and Related Terms in Classical and Early Modern China," paper presented at Academia Sinica, Taipei, June 24, 2000, p. 6.

6. Liang Qichao, "Tao Yuanming nianpu," in *Tao Yuanming*, pp. 39–77.

7. Li Chendong, *Tao Yuanming pinglun* 陶淵明評論, rev. ed. (Taipei: Dongda tushu gongsi, 1991).

8. Liu Zaifu 劉再復, "Liangge gei wo liliang de mingzi" 兩個給我力量的名字, in *Manbu gaoyuan* 漫步高原, vol. 5 of his *Piaoliu shouji* 飄流手記 (Hong Kong: Cosmos Books, 2000), pp. 15–16.

9. Ding Fubao 丁福保, preface to *Tao Yuanming shi jianzhu* 陶淵明詩箋注 (1927; reprint, Taipei: Yiwen yinshu guan, 1989), p. 3.

10. For an insightful discussion of this poem, see Wang Kuo-ying, "Shi zhuan zhong de Tao Yuanming" 史傳中的陶淵明, *Taida zhongwen xuebao* 台大中文學報 12 (May 2000), p. 200.

11. Wang Dingzhang 王定璋, *Tao Yuanming Xuan an jiemi* 陶淵明懸案揭秘 (Chengdu: Sichuan daxue chubanshe, 1996), pp. 3–6.

12. See Liang Qichao, "Tao Yuanming nianpu" 陶淵明年譜, in *Tao Yuanming*, pp. 45–77. In his "Tao Yuanming zuopin xi nian" 陶淵明作品繫年 (in *Tao Yuanming pinglun*, pp. 1–30), Li Chendong follows Liang Qichao's chronology of Tao Qian. Zong-qi Cai also follows this chronology; see *The Matrix of Lyric Transformation*, pp. 10, 230.

13. According to Gu Zhi 古直, Tao Qian was born in A.D. 376 and died at the age of fifty-two *sui*. See Gu Zhi, "Tao Yuanming de nianji wenti" 陶淵明的年紀問題, *Lingnan wenshi* 嶺南文史 1 (1983).

14. A. R. Davis, *Tao Yuan-ming (A.D. 365–427): His Works and Their Meanings* (Cambridge: Cambridge University Press, 1983), vol. 1, p. 2.

15. Kang-i Sun Chang, *Six Dynasties Poetry* (Princeton, N.J.: Princeton University Press, 1986), pp. 3–14.

16. Quoted in J. D. Frodsham, trans., *An Anthology of Chinese Verse: Han Wei Chin and the Northern and Southern Dynasties* (Oxford: Clarendon Press, 1967), p. 95.

17. See David Hinton, trans., *The Selected Poems of T'ao Ch'ien* (Port Townsend, Wash.: Copper Canyon Press, 1993), p. 13; Davis, *Tao Yuan-ming*, vol. 1, p. 208; Hightower, *The Poetry of T'ao Ch'ien*, p. 4.

18. In Davis, *Tao Yuan-ming*, vol. 1, pp. 243–245.

19. Ibid., vol. 1, p. 2.

20. Wang Kuo-ying, "Shi zhuan zhong de Tao Yuanming," pp. 207–208. For a translation of the bushel of rice episode, see Hinton, *The Selected Poems of T'ao Ch'ien*, p. 12.

21. See Wang Kuo-ying, "Shi zhuan zhong de Tao Yuanming," pp. 216–228; Davis, *Tao Yuan-ming*, vol. 1, p. 4.

22. See Wang Kuo-ying, "Shi zhuan zhong de Tao Yuanming," pp. 216–118.

23. See Cao Daoheng 曹道衡, *Nanchao wenxue yu Beichao wenxue yanjiu* 南朝文學與北朝文學研究 (Nanjing: Jiangsu guji chubanshe, 1999), pp. 151–155.

24. Fang Xuanling 房玄齡 (Tang dynasty), *Jin shu* 晉書, *juan* 94 (Beijing: Zhonghua shuju, 1974), vol. 8, p. 2447.

25. Karl Joachim Weintraub asks a similar question in *The Value of the Individual: Self and Circumstance in Autobiography* (Chicago: University of Chicago Press, 1978), p. 295.

26. See translation in Davis, *Tao Yuan-ming*, vol. 1, p. 246.

27. Ibid., vol. 1, p. 4.

28. Stephen Owen, "The Self's Perfect Mirror: Poetry as Autobiography," in *The Vitality of the Lyric Voice: Shih Poetry from the Late Han to the T'ang*, ed. Shuen-fu Lin and Stephen Owen (Princeton: Princeton University Press, 1986).

29. Wang Kuo-ying, "Shi zhuan zhong de Tao Yuanming," p. 4.

30. Wang Kuo-ying 王國瓔, *Gujin yinyi shiren zhi zong: Tao Yuanming lunxi* 古今隱逸詩人之宗：陶淵明論析 (Taipei: Yunchen, 1999), pp. 245–264, 323–350. See also Chen Yongming 陳永明, *Mo xin shiren jing pindan: Tao Yuanming xinlu licheng xintan* 莫信詩人竟平澹：陶淵明心路歷程新探 (Taipei: Taiwan shudian, 1998), p. 75.

31. Xiao Tong 蕭統, "Tao Yuanming zhuan" 陶淵明傳, in *Tao Jingjie ji zhu* 陶靖節集注, commentary by Tao Shu 陶澍 [Qing dynasty] (Taipei: Shijie shuju, 1999), p. 17.

32. Zhong Youmin, *Tao shi shi hua*, p. 382.

33. See Harold Bloom, *Shakespeare: The Invention of the Human* (New York: Riverhead Books, 1998), in which Bloom says that in part Shakespeare "has invented us" (p. xviii).

34. Commenting on the cultural function of Tao's literary works, Charles Kwong says: "The function of literature as a cultural conveyor is especially clear from the often aesthetic-cum-spiritual response of later readers to Tao's poetry, since the artistic ideal and model of wisdom it excmplifies are essentially similar. In this light, our appreciation of the total significance of Tao's art does depend on our understanding of the poet's entire culture." Charles Kwong, *Tao Qian and the Chinese Poetic Tradition: The Quest for Cultural Identity* (Ann Arbor: University of Michigan, 1994), p. 5.

35. See Wang Shumin 王叔岷, *Zhong Rong Shi pin jianzheng gao* 鍾嶸詩品箋證稿 (Taipei: Academia Sinica Press, 1992), pp. 264–266. For the system of Zhong Rong's categorization, see Bernhard Fuehrer, "High Wind and True Bond, Defying Ice and Frost: Illustrative Remarks on the *Shipin* of Zhong Hong," *Bochumer Jahrbuch zur Ostasienforschung,* Band 19 (1995), pp. 51–70. Regarding Zhong Rong's rationale for his placement of Tao Qian in the second rank, I have benefited greatly from conversations with Bernhard Fuehrer.

36. I owe this point to Ronald Egan, who gave very detailed and insightful comments on an earlier version of this chapter, presented as a paper at the conference on "Chinese Aesthetics: The Orderings of Word, Image, and the World in the Six Dynasties," University of Illinois, November 3–4, 2000. For Zhong Rong's assessment of poetry based on his aesthetics of *yuan,* see Bernhard Fuehrer, "Apotheosis of Poets: Two *Modi Operandi* of the Reasoned Exercise of Literary Taste," *Tamkang Review* 24, no. 2 (winter 1993), p. 73.

37. Liao Dongliang 廖棟樑, "Tong yinjiu, shudu 'Li sao'—jianlun Liuchao shiren dui Qu Yuan de du jie" 痛飲酒、熟讀離騷—簡論六朝士人對屈原的讀解, *Zhongguo wenzhe yanjiu tongxun* 中國文哲通訊, December 1998, pp. 67–78.

38. See Wang Shumin, *Zhong Rong Shi pin jianzheng gao,* p. 260.

39. See *juan* 30 of *Zhaoming wenxuan,* commentary by Li Shan (reprint, Taipei: He luo tushi chubanshe, 1975), vol. 1, pp. 659, 679.

40. Xiao Tong 蕭統, "Tao Yuanming ji xu" 陶淵明集序, reprinted in Lu Qinli 逯欽立, *Tao Yuanming ji* 陶淵明集 (Beijing: Zhonghua shuju, 1979), p. 10.

41. See Chang, *Six Dynasties Poetry,* pp. 170–171.

42. See examples cited in Zhong Youmin, *Tao xue shi hua,* pp. 25–26. I am indebted to Ronald Egan for a reminder of this point.

43. Ronald Egan, unpublished notes presented at University of Illinois conference, November 4, 2000.

44. Li Hua 李華, *Tao Yuanming xinlun* 陶淵明新論 (Beijing: Beijing Shifan Xueyuan chubanshe, 1992).

45. Ibid., pp. 227–228.

46. Translation taken from Hightower, *The Poetry of T'ao Ch'ien,* p. 140, with minor modifications.

47. Pu Qilong 浦起龍, *Du Du xin jie* 讀杜心解, (Beijing: Zhonghua shuju, 1961), p. 69.

48. Hu Yinglin 胡應麟, *Shi sou* 詩藪, *juan* 2 [*Waibian*] (Shanghai: Zhonghua shuju, 1958), p. 146. See also Li Hua, *Tao Yuanming xinlun*, p. 227.

49. Ronald Egan, *Word, Image, and Deed in the Life of Su Shi* (Cambridge, Mass.: Council on East Asian Studies, Harvard University, 1994), pp. 229–237.

50. I am indebted to Shuen-fu Lin for an ongoing discussion regarding Six Dynasties garden aesthetics and Tao Qian's farm ideal. See Shuen-fu Lin's essay in this volume.

51. For a translation of Wang Wei's "Song of Peach Blossom Spring," see Pauline Yu, *The Poetry of Wang Wei* (Bloomington: Indiana University Press, 1980), pp. 59–60.

52. Note Lao Zi's formative passage on such a utopia: "Let there be a small state with few people, where military devices find no use.... Though they may gaze across at a neighboring state, and hear the sounds of its dogs and chickens, the people will never travel back and forth, till they die of old age" (Lao Zi, *Daodejing*, ch. 80; translation by Victor H. Mair in *The Columbia Anthology of Traditional Chinese Literature*, ed. Victor H. Mair [New York: Columbia University Press, 1994], p. 59).

53. See Zhong Youmin, *Tao xue shi hua*, p. 58. See also Chen Yinke 陳寅恪, "Taohua yuan ji pangzheng" 桃花源記旁證, in *Chen Yinke xiansheng wenshi lunji* 陳寅恪先生文史論集 (Hong Kong: Wen Wen Publications, 1973), vol. 1, pp. 185–191. For a discussion of this view, see Yang Yucheng 楊玉成, "Shiji mo de xingsi: 'Taohua yuan ji bing xu' de wenhua yu shehui" 世紀末的省思：〈桃花源記并詩〉的文化與社會, *Zhongguo wenzhe yanjiu tongxun* 中國文哲研究通訊 8, no. 4 (December 1998), pp. 85–93.

54. Gong Zizhen 龔自珍, "Zhou zhong du Tao shi" 舟中讀陶詩, in *Gong Zizhen quanji* (Shanghai: Shanghai guji chubanshe, 1999), pp. 521–522.

55. Xiao Tong 蕭統, "Tao Yuanming ji xu" 陶淵明集序, in *Jianzhu Tao Yuanming ji* 箋注陶淵明集, commentary by Li Gonghuan 李公煥 [Song dynasty] (facsimile reprint; Taipei: National Palace Museum, 1991), p. 4.

56. In Hightower, *The Poetry of T'ao Ch'ien*, p. 155.

57. Ibid. For a discussion of these lines, see Yeh Chia-ying, *Tao Yuanming yinjiu shi jianglu*, pp. 225–233.

58. For the Chinese urge to contextualize, see Pauline Yu, *The Reading of Imagery in the Chinese Poetic Tradition* (Princeton, N.J.: Princeton University Press, 1987), p. 85.

59. In *Tao Jingjie ji zhu*, commentary by Tao Shu, p. 16.

60. See Wen Tianxiang's poem, "Hai shang" 海上, in *Wenshan quanchi* 文山全集 (rpt., Changsha: Shangwu yinshu guan, 1939), 14.4a–4b.

61. Lu Xun 魯迅, "Wei-Jin fengdu ji wenzhang yu yao ji jiu zhi guanxi" 魏晉風度及文章與藥及酒之關係, in his *Eryi ji* 而已集, vol. 17 of *Lu Xun sanshi nian ji* 魯迅三十年集 (Hong Kong: Xinyi chubanshe, 1967).

62. Zhu Guangqian 朱光潛, "Tao Yuanming" 陶淵明, in his *Shilun* 詩論, ch. 13 (Shanghai: Shanghai guji chubanshe, 2001), pp. 205–206.

63. Liang Qichao, *Tao Yuanming*, pp. 5–6.

64. See, for example, Song Yunbin 宋雲彬, "Tao Yuanming nianpu zhong de jige wenti" 陶淵明年譜中的幾個問題, in *Xin Zhonghua* 新中華 *[fukan]* 6, no. 3 (February 1948); cited in Zhong Youmin, *Tao xue shi hua*, p. 183.

65. See, for example, Li Chendong, *Tao Yuanming pinglun*, p. 2.

66. In *Jianzhu Tao Yuanming ji*, commentary by Li Gonghuan, pp. 4–5.

67. I am indebted to Nicholas Tustin for this point. See his paper, "'The White Jade's Flaw'? An Exploration of the Xianqing fu" (term paper, Yale University, 1999), pp. 9, 23.

68. Wolfgang Kubin, "The Rise of an Aesthetic Consciousness in China," paper presented at the University of Illinois conference, pp. 11–12.

69. Su Shi, "Ti *Wenxuan*" 題文選, in *Shu Shi quanji* 蘇軾全集, *juan* 67 (Shanghai: Shanghai guji chubanshe, 2000), p. 2114. See also Zhong Youmin, *Tao xue shi hua*, p. 61.

70. Chen Hang 陳沆, *Shi bi xing jian* 詩比興箋, (reprint, Beijing: Zhonghua, 1965). See also Zhong Youmin, *Tao xue shi hua*, p. 151.

71. Su Shi 蘇軾, "Shu Li Jianfu shiji hou" 書李簡夫詩集后, in *Shu Shi quanji, juan* 68, p. 2148. See also Zhong Youmin, *Tao xue shi hua*, p. 46.

72. Su Shi 蘇軾, "Yu Su Che shu" 與蘇轍書, as cited in Li Hua, *Tao Yuanming xinlun*, p. 231.

73. According to Zhong Rong, Six Dynasties readers complained about the plainness of Tao's poetic style. See Zhong Rong 鍾嶸, *Shipin* 詩品, entry on Tao Qian, in *Shipin zhu* 詩品注, notes by Chen Yanjie 陳延傑 (Beijing: Renmin wenxue chubanshe, 1980), p. 41.

74. Liang Qichao, *Tao Yuanming*, p. 13.

75. Zhu Guangqian, "Tao Yuanming," in his *Shilun*, ch. 13.

76. Lu Xun 魯迅, "Ti Weiding cao" 題未定草, section 6, in his *Qie jie ting zawen erji* 且介亭雜文二集. See *Lu Xun quanji* 魯迅全集 (Beijing: Renmin wenxue chubanshe, 1981), 6:422.

77. See Zhong Xing's comments on Tao's poem "In Early Spring of the Year 403, Thinking of the Ancients on My Farm" (癸卯歲始春懷古田舍). In Zhong Xing, *Gushi gui* 古詩歸, *juan* 9, 1617 ed.; collected in *Siku quanshu cunmu congshu* 四庫全書存目叢書, *ji* 337; (rpt., Tainan: Zhuangyan wenhua shiye youxian gongsi, 1997), 9:13b.

78. See Sun Yuefeng's comments on Tao's "Drinking Wine," poem 5, in Sun Yuefeng 孫月峰, *Wenxuan yuezhu* 文選瀹註, *juan* 13; as cited in Zhong youmin, *Tao xue shi hua*, p. 105.

79. See Chen Wenzhong's 陳文忠 comments in his *Zhongguo gudian shige jieshou shi yanjiu* 中國古典詩歌接受史研究 (Hefei: Anhui daxue chubanshe, 1998), p. 276.

80. Davis, *Tao Yuan-ming,* vol. 1, p. 3.

81. Translation taken from ibid., vol. 1, pp. 241–242, with minor modifications.

82. Liang Qichao, *Tao Yuanming,* p. 38.

83. See Wang Dingzhang, *Tao Yuanming xuan an jiemi,* p. 244. For the possible influence of Tao Qian on the *Man'yoshu,* see Songs 481–486 of the *Man'yoshu.* I am indebted to Wang Dingzhang for this idea. For Songs 481–486, see Susuma S. Nakanishi 中西 進, ed., *Man'yoshu* (Tokyo: Kadokawa shoten, 1995), pp. 68–70. I would like to express my thanks to Charles Exley for discussing the *Man'yoshu* songs with me.

84. Wang Kuo-ying 王國瓔, "Letian weifen, yizhi bainian: Tao Yuanming 'Zi ji wen' zhi zihua xiang" 樂天委分，以至百年：陶淵明＂自祭文＂之自畫像, *Zhongguo yuwen xue* 中國語文學 34 (December 1999). See also Davis, *Tao Yuanming,* vol. 1, p. 3.

85. Translation taken from ibid., vol. 1, p. 243.

Chapter 6

• •

Crossing Boundaries

Transcendents and Aesthetics in the Six Dynasties

Rania Huntington

$\mathbf{A}$t the same time as the establishment of aesthetics, *xian* 仙 (transcendents) became an important literary topic. Although literary portrayal of transcendents began before the Han, during the Six Dynasties the range of portrayals in poetry, prose, and philosophical and scriptural texts expanded greatly.[1] However, the relevance of this topic to aesthetics has generally been neglected. This chapter will explore two aspects of that relevance: first, it will consider the relationship between concepts of transcendents and theoretical ideas about literature, and second, it will analyze the aesthetic value of various portrayals of transcendents.

As Zong-qi Cai argues in the prologue, aesthetics is concerned with cosmological questions—how human patterning in the arts relates to the patterns of the world. In Chinese cosmology, *xian* take up a unique place. They are defined by movement between different states of being and their simultaneous accessibility and elusiveness to ordinary mortals. Thus they stand between the abstract philosophical speculations of *Xuanxue* 玄學 (Abstruse Learning), so important to Wei-Jin aesthetics, and the sensory world, by embodying philosophical ideals of transcendence of the known in sensually vivid imagery. They stand also between two different concepts of the imagination that are associated with two distinct ways of reading portrayals of otherworldly beings: one that sees imagination as the journey of a writer's spirit and other worlds as allegories, and another that allows for the possibility of possession by actual alien beings and actual experiences of alien realms.

In this chapter I shall compare the poetic portrayals of transcendents that were granted aesthetic status in anthologies and literary criticism, particularly *youxian shi* 遊仙詩 (poems on wandering in transcendence) with others that were excluded, particularly passages in Daoist revelatory texts. The two central poets in my study are Guo Pu 郭璞 (276–324) and Yang Xi 楊羲 (330–386?). These two bodies of texts, while sharing a great deal of language and imagery, delineate differing concepts of the otherworldly that simultaneously establish and question the borderlines between the aesthetic and the utilitarian, the self-expressive and the didactic, and personal imagination as opposed to divine revelation. Although transcendents are a unique species because of their appearance in both prose and poetry, a thorough comparison of the poetic and the prose traditions, particularly the *zhiguai* 志怪 (tales of the strange) tradition, falls beyond the scope of this chapter.

The Heritage of Marvel

Wenxin diaolong, one of the core texts of this volume, lays out the framework for reception of the two different ways of writing about transcendents. For Liu Xie, the frame for the reception of writing on the world beyond the human is set by the *wei* 緯 (apocrypha) and, even more important, the *Chu ci* 楚辭 (Songs of Chu), which he explores in the fourth and fifth chapters of *Wenxin diaolong*. These chapters mark the point when Liu Xie turns away from the orthodox classics to more dubious territory, where the literary imagination is given potentially perilous free rein.

Liu endeavors to discredit the identification of the apocrypha with the classics but offers literary value as a substitute for philosophical validity. He accepts the authenticity of ancient *wei* but doubts more recent additions. The *wei* are "of no advantage to the classics but benefit literary composition."[2] Although he labors to reject works that are not genuine divine revelations, the divine origin of these works is not crucial to their use; rather the apocrypha are useful to later writers for their impressive range of marvelous events and the wealth of gorgeous language. At the same time as imagination is disparaged as a source of the *wei*, imagination is its only acceptable use. Even if, as Stephen Owen argues, this chapter is here only to provide a parallel to the chapter on the classics, it still expands the range of relationship between literary antecedents and current inspiration, offering a less awesome and more arcane model than the classics.[3] Zong-qi Cai has argued that the *wei* are the source of the idea of language as potentially divine, equivalent to the Dao, and thus crucial to an evolution that would allow for the rise of serious literary criticism.[4] The *wei* are thus important yet often denied and disparaged ancestors of literature, standing outside the patrilineal line that begins with the classics.

The next genre to occupy Liu Xie's attention, the *Chu ci*, fulfills this suggested use of the imagination. While for the *wei* Liu's task was to debunk a spurious association with the classics, for the *Chu ci*, comparison with the classics is scrupulously established. Enumeration of their similarities with and differences from the classics results in an exploration of the virtues and flaws of otherworldly imagery of the kind gleaned from the *wei* and later to appear in *youxian shi*. Some of *Chu ci*'s imagery—dragons representing gentlemen, and the rainbows as false flatterers—is accepted as continuing the *Shi jing's* 詩經 practice of *bi* 比 (comparison) and *xing* 興 (affective image). On the other hand, some similar imagery goes too far: the pursuit of divine women with the mediation of fantastic matchmakers in "Li sao" 離騷 (Encountering Sorrow), the fragments of mythical narratives in the "Tianwen" 天問 (Asking Heaven), and the specters of terrifying beasts in the "Zhao-hun" 招魂 (The Summons of the Soul) are criticized as excessively strange.[5] This tendency to judge strangeness as most acceptable when deployed as an allegorical means of making moral and political points continues in the interpretation of *youxian shi*.

The extravagant imagery of the *Chu ci* is moreover justified by the presence of an impassioned poet, whether Qu Yuan or one of his later imitators, at its core. Qu Yuan provides the model, explored further in the "Ming shi" chapter, of a genius who can rise alone beyond the literary conventions of the time and the man who can make appropriate secularized use of divine inspiration.[6] He provides a pattern that later poets can productively follow. The presence of the poet's own persona remains crucial in the interpretation of *youxian shi*.

The distinction between the two forms of problematic marvel, the *wei* and the *Chu ci*, is between an anonymous voice of revelation and a particular poet's voice, between an inspiration for the imagination and a display of its powers. This foreshadows the distinction between the transcendents' own poems and *youxian shi*. In Liu Xie's judgments, the perils of marvel are falseness and excessive strangeness. The promise of proper use of the imagination is seen as primarily secular rather than divinely inspired, the work of a poet who can use spectacular images to express his grief or frustration without literally believing them.

The Place of *Xian* in Poetic Creation

When Liu Xie turns from these uses of the imagination to a discussion of poetry, *xian* have an ambivalent place: on the one hand, in the Zhengshi 正始 reign (240–248), the declining years of the Wei, poetry became mixed up with "thoughts of the transcendents" (詩雜仙心), which resulted, in the works of He Yan 何晏 (c. 190–249) and his followers, in shallowness.[7] On the other hand, in the context of a generation in which poetry was dominated by *xuan* 玄 (metaphysical discussion), Guo Pu's poems on transcendents single him out in a positive sense. Critical opinion about whether this means he was the best example of a poet of mystical words (玄言詩) or that he differed from such poetry seems divided.[8] Interest in transcendents is seen as a negative influence on an entire generation but a topic of inspired use for a particular poet. The flaws of the false *wei* seem linked to the general literary decline of periods of excessive mass interest in *xuan* or transcendents, the virtues of the *Chu ci* to the individual poets who use the same topic to rise above their surroundings; thus Guo Pu and his poems are representative of the proper use of, narrowly, transcendents, and more broadly, the imagination.

According to Liu Xie, in his own day poetry had distanced itself from the philosophy of Lao Zi and Zhuang Zi and replaced it with the landscape.[9] Transcendents have an anomalous position in this transition: they are associatively linked to the abstract philosophical ideas of Daoism, but they have a presence in popular religion and folklore that renders them distinct from Abstruse Learning or mysticism. The world of the transcendents has its own landscapes, which like terrestrial landscapes are described in terms of appeals to the senses, but they are extreme landscapes, defined by remoteness and inaccessibility to the one who reads. Within portrayals of transcendents the same two elements that were in tension and transition in the poetic tradition as a whole, abstraction and the particular, struggle to be reconciled.

Beyond Liu Xie's judgments, the connection between the place of transcendents in theoretical statements on literature and the practice of poetry on transcendents lies in the spirit journey as a conception of the poetic imagination. Lu Ji 陸機 (261–303) presents the literary imagination in terms of the spirit journey in his *Wen fu* 文賦 (Poetic Exposition on Literature), and Liu Xie continues this train of thought in his chapter on "Spirit and Thought" (神思).[10] The dominant conception of the literary imagination and the practice of *youxian shi* are literary cousins, both descendents of the "Yuan you" 遠遊 (Far Roaming) of the *Chu ci*.[11] The inherent motions of the literary imagination and *youxian shi* are the same: literary composition is also a process of wandering, emphasizing sudden transitions and lack of limitation. If in any composition the mind of the writer transcends time and space, *youxian shi* differs from other poetry only by making that transcendence its explicit subject. However, although the *Wen fu* describes the mind reaching the heights of heaven and the eight edges of the world, and the "Spirit and Thought" chapter describes traveling ten thousand leagues and seeing the clouds, the explicit geography of another world is missing. This is the motion of the "Yuan you," but in contrast to that work, it goes to the fringes of a vast world but does not leave. The world of *xian* is surely within the range of the traveling mind that these descriptions claim as without limits. Yet at the same time, Liu Xie puts an emphasis on the mountains and oceans of this world that seems to make the world of the transcendents, at the limits of the physical world, marginal to the tradition. A further difference between the two kinds of journey seems to be, as Zong-qi Cai points out, that the traveling spirit of literary composition always returns, while in the journey within *youxian shi*, the emphasis is on departure.[12]

If all poetic creation involves a spirit journey, how does that affect the categorization of the experiences in *youxian shi*? How does one distinguish between flights of literary fancy and religious visions? How can the reader decide whether the clouds at the edge of the world are a literal description of the poet's visions or a metaphor for other desires? With the spirit journey as the model of the imagination, is there a discernible difference between the two? Furthermore, how is the literal or allegorical nature of *youxian shi* journeys relevant to the critical assessment of poetry?

The sources of these questions lie in the uneasy coexistence of religious devotion and political allegory in the *Chu ci*. According to Wang Yi's 王逸 (d. A.D. 158) interpretation, the "Jiu ge" 九歌 (Nine Songs) were based on genuine, possibly licentious devotional songs but were adapted by Qu Yuan to use their original devotion to the gods to express his loyalty to king and country, while the "Li sao" was Qu Yuan's allegorical address of his ruler.[13] The spirit journey and the allegorical tradition founded by "Li sao" are the part of the heritage of the *Chu ci* that the dominant poetic tradition assimilates. The other possible model of inspiration is possession aroused by religious devotion. This may be exemplified by some of the "Jiu ge," where the divisions between devotion and allegory, as well as who is seeking and who is sought, are not clear. In the mainstream poetic tradition, the idea of the Other coming to take over the body from one's own spirit is absent, but in the tradition of revealed verse, possession remains important, as we will see in Yang Xi's work below. In both revealed verse and at the edges of the predominant tradition, the Goddess and the metaphor of the romance are the means to talk about possession, longing for loss of control, and fear of that loss. The female muse who is not enthroned at the center of the poetic tradition keeps appearing in many other places.[14] In the later tradition, this "underground" tradition of poetic inspiration through possession remains alive in the large volumes of poems granted to the planchette, often by disembodied female transcendents or ghosts.

Because some degree of world rejection is a prerequisite for the pursuit of transcendence, *jituo* 寄托 (entrusting feelings to writing), often in a veiled or allegorical way, and devotion cannot be easily separated.[15] Li Fengmao discusses the entire subgenre of *youxian shi* in terms of *you* 遊, wandering, inspired by *you* 憂, sorrow.[16] Judgment about whether transcendent-related content is a vision or a metaphor seems determined by which world occupies the bulk of the poem's attention. Yet more than any feature within the poems themselves, *jituo* and devotion are distinguished by the context in which poetry is preserved. These contexts are also those that shape the differences between religious and secular verse: *youxian shi* are preserved in anthologies including verse on other topics, but in scriptural contexts virtually all the poetry will have some association with transcendence. "Religious" and "secular" are imperfect terms because the division is not absolute: it is the context of "secular" poetry that allows for readings of *jituo*, which the context of revelation precludes, but "secular" anthologies do not exclude the possibility of devotion.

Guo Pu and *Youxian Shi*

Although I take *youxian shi* as representing the mainstream of aesthetic practice in depicting transcendents, the history of their portrayal in poetry is larger than the history of *youxian shi* and predates the Six Dynasties. As Li Fengmao argues, the subgeneric title is not exclusive: not all poems about journeys to the realm of the transcendents are labeled as such.[17] The tradition can be traced as beginning with the "Yuan you" and continuing through some Han *yuefu* (music bureau poems), and, most famously, several poems under various titles by Cao Zhi.[18] The flexibility of titles is a symptom of the permeability between longing for transcendence and other poetic topics, like reclusion and lament for the brevity of life. The *Wenxuan*'s 文選 (Anthology of Refined Literature) placement of *youxian shi* immediately before *zhaoyin shi* 招隱詩 (poems on summoning recluses) seems particularly suggestive of this overlap. Yet even if the title does not determine content, labeling poems with the phrase "*youxian shi*" seems a significant move, as it includes the transcendents even in poems where they might otherwise seem absent.

Guo Pu is the poet who is most strongly associated with *youxian shi*. Not only are his *youxian shi* singled out as representative of his poetry, but he is also the representative poet in the *Wenxuan*'s selections in the *youxian* category. Yet at the same time as he is representative, he is a transitional and controversial figure, at the heart of the question of whether the proper task of *youxian shi* is the portrayal of genuine desire for pursuit of immortality or use of the imagery of transcendence for self-expression. The debate about whether he was himself a poet of mystical words or a man who transformed that tradition for the better is complex.[19] Zhong Rong 鍾嶸 (ca. 469–518) faults him for using the language of frustration, deviating from the authentic tradition of writing about the pleasure of immortality,[20] yet those who rebut him argue that precisely this creative use of *youxian shi* is Guo Pu's virtue. In his notes on the *Wenxuan*, Li Shan 李善 (630–689) noted that in contrast with other *youxian shi*, Guo Pu's poems told of himself, and he expressed approval for this departure from convention.[21] Shen

Deqian 沈德潛 (1673–1769) goes so far as to say that *jituo* and expression of frustration is fundamental to the genre.[22] Allegorical readings of the genre evidently became dominant.

Guo Pu's role as the central figure in the debate about *jituo* may have in part been shaped by the selection standards of later anthologies; Stephen Owen argues that the *Wenxuan*'s selections of Guo Pu's works are skewed in favor of poems of reclusion, while the fragments preserved elsewhere reveal more pure pleasure in the fantastic spectacle of transcendents.[23] Yet even if the Guo Pu I discuss below is a historical construction, that construction is still crucial to the history of the *youxian shi* subgenre and its connection to aesthetics.

Although *youxian shi* are made up of sets of recurring gestures, there is a great deal of flexibility about their order and the amount of focus on each. In contrast with the anecdote that argues that painting ghosts is easy while painting horses and dogs is hard (assuming that one has more freedom painting the unseen), the world of the transcendents has its own highly conventional body of places and figures.[24] In the annotations of the *Wenxuan*, Li Shan lists these features: "As for pieces on *youxian*, they all, despising the pollution of the dusty world, as well as negligible gain and the entanglements of office, turn to eating the mists at the peak of the heavens, and tasting jade in the Dark Capital."[25] The legacy of the *Chu ci* spirit journey takes the form of gestures relating the traveler to the enchanted landscape: consuming it, putting on the celestial trappings of *xian*, and touching the edges of the world. The gestures coexist with the spectacle of scenes along the journey, both the landscape of the edges of the world and the heavens and the assembly of established *xian*, who can either form static tableaus or interact with the journeying mortal.

In Guo Pu, movement between the worlds is seldom linear. From the beginning, "Li sao" and the spirit journey bestow a complex legacy of the alternating motions of frustrated and fulfilled desire. As the portrayal of transcendents develops, the distinction between linear and nonlinear journeys seems crucial. As Zong-qi Cai argues, Cao Zhi reshaped what had, in folk *yuefu*, been a relatively linear journey into a dynamic comparison of the celestial and terrestrial worlds that reveals the poet's personal feelings.[26] Influenced partially by a growing focus on each couplet as a separate unit, Guo Pu continues this move away from linear narrative, allowing for a different kind of reading of *jituo*, as the poet's persona fills the gaps between couplets.

Guo Pu's *youxian shi* contain recurring elements, but each follows a distinct trajectory. Their content is very diverse, raising the question of whether, for Guo Pu, "*youxian*" is simply a general title under which he groups all of his poetic concerns, just as Ruan Ji 阮籍 (210–263) uses the title "*yong huai*" 詠懷 (writing about one's feelings). If one were to group them simply, there are poems that waver between concerns of this world and display of *xian*, those that concentrate purely on this world, and those that focus on the other.[27] It is this variation that gives him his unique place.

His first two poems are explorations of the pursuit of transcendence and reclusion as linked but not entirely interchangeable worlds: it is the relationship of the traveler to the landscape, and to figures that traveled that landscape in the past, that differs. His first poem plays with different levels of metaphor and historical allusion in constructing the space between the literal experience of transcendents and *jituo*.

其一	Poem of wandering in transcendence, The First[28]
京華遊俠窟	The capital is the lodging of wandering heroes,
山林隱遯棲	The mountain forests are roosting places for recluses.
朱門何足榮	How could the crimson gates of the wealthy be worthy of glory?
未若託蓬萊	Far better to lodge on Penglai.
臨源挹清波	Facing the source, I scoop up the clear waves,
陵岡掇丹荑	Nearing the ridge, I pluck the red sprouts.
靈谿可潛盤	At Spirit Brook I can retreat from the world,
安事登雲梯	What need to ascend the cloud staircase?
漆園有傲吏	In the Lacquer Garden there is a proud officer,[29]
萊氏有逸妻	Mr. Lai has a recluse wife.[30]
進則保龍見	If I advance, then I assure the dragon will be revealed.
退則觸藩羝	If I turn back, then I will be trapped as the ram on the hedge.
高蹈風塵外	I step high beyond the wind and dust of the world,
長揖謝夷齊	Bowing low, I bid farewell to Bo Yi and Shu Qi.[31]

Couplets can be divided into those that mark direct progress in the journey and relatively stable tableaus whose relationship to the journey the reader must infer. The division between these two kinds of couplets is not absolute: a certain flexibility about the link of the journey to the traveler is the hallmark of *youxian shi*. After an introduction of lesser retreats from the world in the first couplet and resolve to depart in the second, he consumes the landscape of the edges of the world in the third couplet and travels further in that landscape in the fourth.[32] There is a move from a general to a more specific geography. He seems to reject a more spectacular vision of becoming a transcendent, climbing the cloud staircase, in favor of terrestrial reclusion.

In the second half of the poem, there is a shift from landscapes to figures. The last three couplets place the whole in the realm of metaphor by use of allusions, which do not seem to be physically present in the same way as the parts of the landscape that are consumed. The move to less physical images throws the concreteness of the earlier lines into question. The fifth couplet also provides a pause in the movement of the individual traveler. It evokes two past figures, Zhuang Zi and Laizi's wife, but in a relatively static fashion; such people exist, but the individual traveler does not interact with them. The link between the two is proud rejection of solicitation of government service. The figures evoked are all recluses rather than transcendents as such. The sixth couplet presents fantastic animals as abstract images of success and failure, but at the same time they, especially the dragon, suggest the marvelous denizens of the transcendent realm. The reading of these images of advance and retreat is ambiguous: the dragon revealed could be either success in pursuit of immortality or career success.[33] The final couplet is departure, but here he bids farewell to figures of historical allusion rather than any other embodiment of the dusty world. In contrast with the figures in the fifth couplet, he directly addresses Bo Yi and Shu Qi. These figures appear in a couplet of motion rather than a pause, but still all the figures are static, and only the traveler moves. The mention of Bo Yi and Shu Qi ties *xian* to politically motivated reclusion (which was also evoked in the opening couplet), but he both pays respect and rejects it, in the same way as he rejected the cloud staircase.

The different ways figures of allusion function reveal both the role of allusion in *youxian shi* and how Guo Pu's poems can be read as an encoded venting of feelings. Because of their longevity, transcendents are accessible to immediate contact in a way that other historical figures are not, granting more potential flexibility to allusions; but here that quality seems to have been transferred to Bo Yi and Shu Qi. Bo Yi and Shu Qi might be at a liminal position between recluse and transcendent because of their dietary choices, refusing to eat the grain of Zhou and living on pine seeds. Recluses and transcendents are similar in the way that they form both absences and lingering presences in the landscape; both are figures who have departed and need to be sought. The recluse is more embedded in a terrestrial landscape than the *xian* in his celestial one (transcendents are quite often in motion), but in some ways the recluse is less accessible. The poetic tradition focuses more on the recluse who cannot be found, as opposed to the transcendent who is finally glimpsed in a successful flight to the heavens. The presence of Bo Yi and Shu Qi marks this poem as a venting of frustration rather than a spiritual quest both because of the specific weight of the allusion and by drawing into question the immediacy of the fantastic figures encountered on the journey. The indeterminacy between allusions as abstract images and allusions as vivid inhabitants of a transcendent world is the mark of Guo Pu's *youxian shi*.

The second poem reveals a different way of interacting with the divine figures encountered upon the journey. There are paired objects of desire in the poem, one male in the opening and one female in the end. The male transcendent, presented with a semi-narrative description as viewed from the outside, is a different kind of presence than the figures of allusion that appear paired in couplets, each in a single line.[34] The gaze of the poem lingers on this single spot, making this figure more tangible.

The next couplet puts the questing "I" in relationship with other recluse or *xian* figures who have left their traces in the landscape. Xu You is an allusion in the more contained and conventional sense, like Zhuang Zi and Laizi's wife in the previous poem. The line "Nearing the river, I long to wash my ears" is a variation on ingesting the landscape that, by imitating the actions of earlier recluses/transcendents, makes allusion to something that can be enacted. Transcendence and reclusion seem fundamentally similar in the way that they are poses and attitudes of the body, to be put on or off. Both reclusion and transcendence are simultaneously individual journeys and established tracks on which one can strive to follow others.

As the male figure in a distant valley motivates the initial quest, a female figure is the tantalizing suggestion of consummation. At this point in the poem there is also a transition from the realm in which transcendent and recluse overlap to that where they do not: gender provides an absolute marker of this division, for the envied recluse is virtually never female.[35] She is placed after a couplet of broad vistas of the journey, and the focus of attention narrows down to her white teeth.[36] She looks back at the narrator in contrast to the self-contained male. But as is usual in visions of the divine woman, the final couplet regrets the absence of a matchmaker, with an allusion present only to be negated, leaving the poet again longing, gazing across distance. Again, transcendents are both compelling presences and absences. This final failure is pure "Li sao," suggesting that one should read the unattainable divine woman as a figure of political frustration, but she is capable of being both that metaphor and a dazzling vision.[37]

In contrast with these poems that waver between worlds, the fourth and the fifth poems remain rooted in concerns of this world, demonstrating the interpenetration between *youxian shi* and general Six Dynasties poetic concerns. These poems might also be labeled *yong huai*. The attempt to read a journey in them becomes untenable. The fourth poem broods on the passing of time and the fifth on frustrated human ambition. Both are more consistent in tone than the others: in the fourth, it is reiterated what the poet cannot do and that time cannot stop. Cloud-soaring beasts are present only not to be ridden.[38] Such feelings are more likely to be confined to a couplet in other poems.

其五	The Fifth
逸翩思拂霄	The swift-winged bird longs to brush the clouds,
迅足羨遠游	The fine steed desires distant journeys.
清源無增瀾	The clear source lacks deep-layered billows,
安得運吞舟	How could it transport the boat-swallowing fish?
珪璋雖特達	Although the jade tablet is resplendent,
明月難闇投	It is hard to accept the moonbright pearl given in obscurity.[39]
潛穎怨青陽	The sprouts resent the late arrival of spring,
陵苕哀素秋	The reeds lament the early arrival of fall.
悲來惻丹心	Sorrow comes and rends my heart,
零淚緣纓流	My tears fall, flowing along my hatstrings.[40]

This poem is more constant in tone and register than the poems in which actual journeys take place. As a whole it remains on the level of metaphor from beginning to end. The transcendents are overtly present only in the title. Li Shan's *Wenxuan* annotations, apparently trying to justify the subgeneric title, are more insistent than in other cases that each of these metaphors is to be read as referring to the world of the transcendents, but they could easily be read as referring to worldly frustration. In the former reading, the first couplet expresses desire for transcendence, the second the mundane world's inability to support transcendence, and the third ordinary mortals' inability to accept the wonders of transcendence when revealed to them. Even the fourth couplet's resentment of the passage of time is put in the context of the mundane world's inability to accept transcendence. In the alternate reading, the transcendents are utterly absent: the first couplet is the poet's unfulfilled career ambitions, the second the world's inability to support him, the third his unappreciated talent, and the fourth simply resentment at the passage of time. There are two kinds of images present in the poem. The terrestrial natural images in the first and fourth couplet seem more to resemble older poetic conventions rather than having any direct tie to the transcendents. In contrast, in other couplets, the language evokes the sensually vivid world of the transcendents by distant echo: there are marvelous animals, deep streams, and brilliant gemstones.

As with the fourth poem, here the journey is merely contemplated. The first couplet presents the desire for departure, but the second frustrates it: the landscape is inadequate for the traveler. The huge beasts of Zhuang Zi's world are evoked only to be denied. The jade and pearls of the third couplet are present in order to be rejected, rather than adorning a landscape through which a traveler moves. The fourth couplet has plants as passive victims of time, in contrast with the horse and bird of the first couplet who are victims of limitations in space. The final couplet finally casts aside metaphor to focus on the body and emotional core of the poet; rather than being engaged with a world of recluses, *xian*, and fantastic landscapes, the poet weeps alone. It seems to me that the fourth and fifth poems are motivation for departure rather than departure itself. The presence of poems like these in the sequence strengthens the impression that the *youxian shi* as a whole are venting worldly frustration; even if the *Wenxuan*'s selection is biased, this element was present in the original corpus.

The sixth poem, in stark contrast to the fourth and fifth, offers an exuberant display of the world of *xian*; the *Wenxuan* also includes this poem within its range. Because of this sense of spectacle, it is closer to the transcendents' own songs, which will be discussed below, than are Guo Pu's other poems. *Youxian shi* is defined by the extremes of frustration and fulfillment present in the various poems.

其六	The Sixth
雜縣寓魯門	The *zaxian* bird lodges at the gates of Lu,
風暖將為災	The warm wind is about to become a plague.[41]
吞舟涌海底	The boat-swallowing fish looms up from the bottom of the sea,
高浪駕蓬萊	The high waves race on to Penglai.
神仙排雲出	Gods and transcendents pushing aside the clouds emerge,
但見金銀臺	I only see the towers of silver and gold.
陵陽挹丹溜	Lingyang scoops up the cinnabar waves,
容成揮玉杯	Rongcheng lifts the jade cup.[42]
姮娥揚妙音	Huan'e raises her splendid tones,
洪崖頷其頤	Hong Yai moves his jaw.[43]
升降隨長煙	(I or they) rise and fall following the long plumes of smoke,
飄颻戲九垓	Drifting and playing in the nine regions of the world.
奇齡邁五龍	(My or their) marvelous age approaches that of the five dragon-faced immortals,
千歲方嬰孩	At a thousand years, still a child.
燕昭無靈氣	King Zhao of Yan had no marvelous *qi*,
漢武非仙才	Han Wudi was not of transcendent stuff.[44]

The opening animal images seem ominous, like an archaeological fragment of the terrifying outer world presented in the "Zhaohun." Perhaps these vast or strange animals, reminiscent also of Zhuang Zi's creatures, out of place and unable to be contained in mundane landscapes, represent the traveler out of place in the workaday world. The wind and the waves give a sense of swift motion, preparing for the appearance of all the transcendents. All of the sensual pleasures of the world of the transcendents—eating, drinking, and music—are enacted by named figures. Here it is the transcendents, rather than the traveler, who consume the landscape. Such a gallery of immortals seems related to the assembly presented in a prose collection like *Shenxian zhuan* 神仙傳 (Biographies of Gods and Transcendents). Each transcendent here is making a single gesture. The individual traveler exists entirely as an observer of this spectacle. The penultimate couplets describe freedom of limitation first in space and then in time: in space, there is emphasis on playful freedom of motion and direction, whereas time is expressed simply in terms of constancy. This contrast between the description of space and time seems inherent in the poetic definition of the transcendent state.

Only these, the sixth and seventh couplets, might introduce the figure of the once mortal voyager, but the referent is ambiguous: these proud claims of immortality might instead apply to the transcendent figures evoked earlier. But even this expansive poem seems to need to include some limitation, this time not of the poet, but of two monarchs who had pursued immortality in vain. The images of their glamorous failure are seen from a lofty perspective, but in a different way than in narrative, that reveals royal limitations. The transcendents are vital, active presences, while the historical monarchs are absent, and passive, again revealing the different function of various kinds of allusions. The contrast between this exuberant poem and the two solemn ones preceding it may be an artifact of the *Wenxuan*'s editorial selections rather than Guo Pu's intentions, but reading the poems in sequence has the same effect as the alternating couplets of elation and despair in a single poem.

Another poem (not chosen for the *Wenxuan*) is entirely ascent, wasting no time in the mortal world; this makes the final gesture, turning back to look at the mortal world, all the more dramatic.[45] The elements of the ascent—eating, drinking, the dragon chariots, and the spectacular clothes—are arrayed together in a relatively linear way, all the way to the door of heaven. The last four lines are, "The Eastern Ocean is like a puddle in a hoofprint, Kunlun is like an anthill. In the vague distance, looking down makes one despair" 東海猶蹄涔，崑崙螻蟻堆。遐邈冥茫中，俯視令人哀.[46] That linear pursuit is reversed in a dazzling perspective by looking down, as the vast landscape becomes miniature. The final moment is pure Qu Yuan: after all of the joy of ascent, looking back causes grief, displaying again the contrast of fulfilled and unfulfilled desire that seems necessary to *youxian shi*.[47]

Guo Pu, as presented by the *Wenxuan*, straddles the space between the two worlds of transcendence and self-reference. More broadly, his poems reveal that the transcendents are a unique topic because poetry can describe a process of becoming. The difference between wandering to the world of the transcendents and wandering among the mountains is that the wanderer may in the process become a transcendent himself. Free wandering is an inherent part of both becoming and being a transcendent, which creates a certain ambiguity in the subgenre's title: is it the poet or the transcendents who travel? Thus transcendents are described from both the inside and the outside, as marvels viewed by a mortal outsider and as gestures the mortal himself takes on. A reading of *jituo* implies confidence that the poet does eventually come back from the journey and remains mortal, while a literal reading allows for the possibility of departure and transformation.

Later Voices: Containing *Xian* in the Moment

After Guo Pu, no other poet of the Six Dynasties is considered representative of *youxian shi*, although the genre continues to be written. In *youxian shi* after Guo Pu, there is a tendency to abandon the trajectory for the sake of focus on a particular moment, which can also serve to contain the poem in a finite, mundane landscape. This is tied to the rise of regulated verse, which condenses the experience. I examine first Tao Qian 陶潛 (365–427), who made his own unique interpretation of the *youxian* tradition, and then later poets of the Qi and Liang who reinterpreted *youxian shi* in a manner typical of their generation. Guo Pu and this later generation are also distinguished from one another by their inclusion in two successive anthologies, the *Wenxuan* and the *Wenyuan yinghua* 文苑英華 (Finest Flowers of the Preserve of Letters).

A cousin of sorts to *youxian shi*, Tao Qian's "Du *Shanhai jing*" 讀山海經 (Reading *The Classic of Mountains and Seas*) is both typical of the subgenre's evolution and exceptional because it creates a moment of the external circumstances of reading rather than the internal progress of the mind. This poem series dramatizes the connection between the spirit journey and reading already suggested in the *Wen fu*. The first poem in the group, as preparation for departure on the spirit journey, presents an image of seclusion, but secluded bliss rather than rejection of the world. The moment of departure, after the couplet on reading, is the upward and downward glance that encompasses the universe, one of the fixed gestures of the spirit journey and the *youxian shi*. The gaze of reading and, in the case of the *Shanhai jing*, looking at illustrations, leaps beyond the limits of the domestic isolation he has just established. The sense of an established geography and pantheon for *youxian shi* is presented in a different light here: there actually is a set map and pantheon, contained within the covers of a book. In the rest of the poems, scenes of *xian* as tableaus, perhaps to be expected from reading, and moments of the voyager interacting with them in relatively conventional ways alternate.[48] In some ways Tao covers a similar range of emotional territory as Guo Pu's series, including communing with transcendents, lamenting the brevity of life, and using the *Shanhai jing* creatures as political allegories, but the frame of reading and a universe in a book sets it apart.

Tao Qian reveals a highly original individual reading of the *youxian* tradition, but later poets reveal more generational change. Emperor Wu of the Liang 梁武帝 (r. 502–549), in a poem chosen for the *xian* category in *Wenyuan yinghua*, also lingers at a particular moment in the trajectory rather than describing the broad swath of the journey.[49] As of the second couplet of the poem, he possesses the elixir that will allow him to ascend to the heavens once he swallows it, but he does not. This stage in a transcendent's progress is more commonly given attention in narrative than in poetry: several figures in *Shenxian zhuan* spend the bulk of the narrative in this situation, only taking their promised exit in the final lines.[50] This poem ends in rejecting departure, rather than with departure.[51] Zhan Shichuang explains this uncharacteristic reluctance as Emperor Wu's reluctance to give up his luxurious life on earth, but it seems instead related to his tendency to focus on glamorous moments.[52]

Shen Yue's 沈約 (441–513) *youxian shi* are tightly constructed: parallelism, which has played a role in the often nonlinear progress of *youxian shi* throughout its history, has become more artful, sensually vivid without abstractions. In his two "He Jingling Wang youxian shi" 和竟陵王遊仙詩 (Poems of Wandering in Transcendence Matching Rhymes with the Prince of Jingling), the first of which also suits the aesthetic standards of *Wenyuan yinghua*,[53] a sense of dizzying motion and continuity in the middle couplets ("The wind at the jasper tower never stills, the ripples flow at the Red Water," or "The bluebirds depart and return again, the clouds at Gaotang have not dispersed") is followed by final physical gestures making a personal link to the *xian* landscape rather than the usual eating and drinking: plucking a branch from the alabaster tree or drying one's hair at the edge of the world.[54] The gesture is dramatized because it stands alone rather than in a series of moves consuming the world.

Some of Shen Yue's other poems, not entitled *youxian shi*, are important because they show how transcendents can be subsumed into the landscape. His poem on Chi Songzi's waterfall makes it clear that all that remains of the *xian* is the landscape and that the poet's journeys anywhere beyond that landscape are purely in his mind. Just as Emperor Wu of the Liang's poem expanded on a single moment in the pursuit of *xian*, this poem could almost be read as an expansion of a single couplet in Guo Pu's second *youxian shi*, when he stands by the river longing to wash his ears. Absence of the *xian* creates the same longing for departure as in other poems, but the poem closes with the poet merely patiently waiting for the *xian*'s return.[55] Zhan describes this as a stage in the conversion of *youxian shi* to the landscape, but it seems also, like Emperor Wu of the Liang's poem, to be an attempt to focus the various emotions of the journey into a single place and moment.[56] It also marks a further confluence, already latent in Guo Pu, of transcendent material with the "Summoning the Recluse" tradition.

As poetry changes from Guo Pu's generation to later poets, *xian* subject matter is transformed in turn, following the shift from *qingyuan* 清遠 (pure and remote) to *qingxin* 清新 (unadorned and refreshing) observed by Zong-qi Cai in the prologue to this volume. When the trajectory is condensed in a single moment, the persona of the poet is more firmly in control. That single moment can be either fulfillment or frustration or most suggestively the single moment that is neither, as the elixir of immortality is held unswallowed in the mouth.

The Songs of the Transcendents

The contrast between *youxian shi* and the transcendents' own songs reveals related but distinctive forms of aesthetic practice, with different underlying assumptions about the nature of the imagination. The transcendents' own songs raise a different expressive question than *youxian shi*, not how to create a world beyond common human experience as seen through (at least temporarily) mortal eyes, but instead how to render the voice of an alien being describing that other world. Presented as actual divine revelations, they are beyond the attention of Liu Xie, heirs to the aspects of the *wei* he minimalizes. Nonetheless, the transcendents' songs catered to an elite audience, whose expectations were formed by the aesthetics of worldly poetry.[57] I refer to these texts as songs because of the emphasis on performance, which distinguishes them from *youxian shi*, but Yang Xi's works are referred to in the *Zhen'gao* 真誥 (Declarations of the Perfected) as poems.[58]

The contrast between poems aspiring to transcendence and the transcendents' own words involves a shift in genre as well as the identity of the poetic persona. The divine nature of the transcendents' own songs is established by many kinds of framing. The mortality of the speaker can be assumed in a freestanding poem, with the author's biography providing the unspoken frame, but immortality must be established by a prose frame. Thus the songs of the transcendents involve their paratextual context in a different way than mortals' poems. Unlike *youxian shi*, the transcendents' songs must be framed by an audience, as transcendents perform before mortals who preserve their words. The songs of *xian* are close to being scripture, for which transmission is a vital issue.[59]

Closely related to framing, the keys to the difference between transcendents' own songs and mortal poets' words are instruction and performance. *Youxian shi* may persuade readers of the desirability of pursuing immortality, but they rarely tell them how to get there. The transcendents' own works often seem longer and more discursive because they provide more information. *Youxian shi* trajectories are anything but a map. The transcendents' own song is itself like the promised elixir of immortality, offered to a listening mortal. *Youxian shi* dramatizes an internal journey, so remains at some essential level private, while the songs of the transcendents, in both their frames and their own content, are tied to crowded feasts and music before an audience. Even if only one mortal receives revelation, the transcendents often appear in groups.[60]

In many of the songs of the transcendents, the aspect of the text as performance becomes more pronounced because the relation between the speaking transcendent and the listening mortal is further complicated by gender: female transcendents often offer revelations to male mortals. I will contrast two such performances, one in a historical fantasy at the margins of the *zhiguai* genre, depicting the experiences of Emperor Wu of the Han, and the other revelations to Yang Xi, recorded by himself and edited by Tao Hongjing 陶弘景 (456–536) in the *Zhen'gao*.[61]

With these examples, we see texts about the transcendents crossing the boundaries between *zhiguai* and devotional literature, differences again established by the context of their preservation. The *Han Wudi neizhuan* 漢武帝內傳 (The Inside Chronicle of Emperor Wu of the Han) is preserved both in a *zhiguai* context, *Taiping guangji* 太平廣記 (Broad Gleanings from the Era of Great Peace), and in Daoist contexts; Yang Xi's work is entirely in Daoist contexts.[62] Current scholarly consensus holds that the text might date to the Eastern Jin or to the

Liang, so either contemporary or later than Guo Pu.[63] Although the relative dating of this poem and Yang Xi's poems is problematic, I discuss
them in this order for thematic reasons.

In the *Han Wudi neizhuan*, the emperor has prepared, by fasting
and meticulous arrangements, to receive a visit from Xi Wang Mu on
the seventh day of the seventh month. When she descends with her
throng of attendants, she both treats him to celestial delicacies and bids
her followers to perform for him.[64] This is the first of their songs:

大象雖寥廓	Although the Great Way is deep and distant,
我把天地戶	I grasp the door of heaven and earth.
披雲沉靈輿	Draping myself in clouds, the numinous chariot descends,
倏忽適下土	In an instant, I reach the ground below.
空洞成玄音	The empty cave makes a mystic music,[65]
至精不容冶	Perfect essence, in no way indulgent.
太真噓中唱	Taizhen sings in the middle of her sighing,[66]
始知風塵苦	Only now do I know the bitterness of the dusty world.
頤神三田中	I cultivate my spirit in the midst of the Three Fields,[67]
納精六闕下	And concentrate my essence below the Six Gates.
遂乘萬龍輈	Then I mount the myriad dragon chariot,
馳騁眄九野	And race away, glancing down at the Nine Wilds.[68]

Compared to *youxian shi*, the frame transforms the motion of the song
in several ways: a transcendent descends rather than a mortal ascending, and the voice is that of the object of desire rather than the desiring
mortal. Many of the couplets do frame an individual journey, however.
The opening couplet underlines both similarity and difference: the vastness of the universe comes down to a single figure, but the gesture is
one of bravado and control, sometimes present in *youxian shi*, but
rarely at the beginning. The quick motion, and especially the racing
and looking outward of the final couplet, are gestures shared with mortals' journeys. The presentation is more linear than Guo Pu's *youxian
shi* because it is a performance of certainty and security, without the
doubts and doubling back of a wandering mortal. Nevertheless she
descends to rise again in the end. It is still not entirely linear, with variation in both direction of motion and emotional tone. The perfection of
the third couplet, embodied in musical performance, contrasts with the
flaws of the mortal world in the fourth couplet, which interrupts that
performance. These physical and emotional movements illustrate the

difference between transcendent and mortal rather than blurring those boundaries.

The inclusion of singing within the text, a recursion common in the transcendents' own songs (note that the female singer also appears in Guo Pu's sixth poem, his purest display of the wonders of transcendence), lays further stress on the nature of this song as performance. The framing of the song as a command performance by a servant, which might reflect either her own experience or her mistress's, undermines the reading of the couplets of individual experience. The second song is much more clearly in Xi Wang Mu's voice, closing with self-reference to the song that is presently being performed; it thus situates itself very differently in time than do *youxian shi*, which do not include the poem's own performance as the final destination of the journey.

In general, the transcendents' own songs are denser with the abstract vocabulary of self-improvement, as seen in the third and fifth couplets here, than are *youxian shi*. In the same way that some of Guo Pu's imagery can have a double life as metaphor and adornment of a dazzling cosmos, some of the Daoist terms can be read as both abstractions and physical places. A turn inward to the body in the fields or gates is also, on the surface, a gesture toward expansive space.

Although the songs in *Han Wudi neizhuan* are also instruction, they seem more disposable than the prose instruction of the emperor; some editions include the songs and some do not. It matters more that the performance took place at all. The poems are relatively independent of their context, although there are some differences between the opening songs and those presented after the attempt to transmit the Way. Indeed Li Fengmao argues that they may well be borrowed and reused from other sources, suggesting a body of conventions in the dialogue between transcendent and aspiring mortal.[69] The later songs also contain elements of landscape and journey but open, instead of with self-reference, with straightforward statements about the project of pursuit of immortality that would not be out of place in *youxian shi*: "Who says that one's lifespan has a limit? Fusang is not blocked off."[70]

Much like Han Wudi, the medium Yang Xi is visited by night by female divinities offering songs.[71] Poetry is an important feature of Shangqing Daoist scriptures in general, and the *Zhen'gao* in particular preserves a large number of poems from a varied group of transcendent informants.[72] Yang Xi has more than eighty extant poems, most of them attributed to various female transcendents. However, he is ex-

cluded from the *Wenxuan*, and even in modern anthologies his poems
are included in a specific category for Daoists.[73] The erotic element
suggested in Han Wudi's story is more explicit here, as the divinities
come to propose a spirit marriage. As Stephen Bokenkamp points out,
the erotic is all the stronger for the passage's vehement denigration of
physical love, for by this point description of the female transcendent
has become the language of the erotic.[74]

Yang Xi's revealed poems raise the specter of an alternate understanding of the poetic imagination, particularly as it relates to encounters with transcendents, based on possession and revelation. The
secular *youxian shi* follows the path of the "Li sao," with a male figure
pursuing reluctant goddesses, but usually eschews the ecstatic blurring
between divinity and worshipper of some of the "Jiu ge." Performance
is also essential to the distinction between the "Li sao" and the "Jiu
ge": "Li sao," if a performance at all, is a solo performance for a possibly absent audience, whether a neglectful monarch or a posterity who
would deplore Qu Yuan's fate; but some of the "Jiu ge" feature mortals
performing for both throngs of other mortals and for the gods; sometimes gods perform before mortals, and sometimes mortals perform as
gods.

Yang Xi's depiction of possession in the prose frames of the poems
presented to him is dry; unlike the narrative about the Emperor Wu,
there is no elaboration on the circumstances of performance, and the
marvel is concentrated in their words. In contrast with the blurring of
the "Jiu ge," Yang Xi's revelations delineate the distinction between
Perfected and mortal, but through silence rather than words. Yang Xi
is presented as both scribe and addressed object of some of the poems,
but his own voice is repressed. Tao Hongjing's claims about Yang Xi's
skills as a calligrapher, cited by Robert Harrist, further raise the question of authorship: can Yang Xi's calligraphic hand be his own if the
words are not? Does the calligraphic skill rightfully belong to the transcendent? In a sense, by excluding him from consideration as a serious,
prolific poet, the literary tradition takes Yang Xi's denial of authorship
seriously.

Here is the first poem proposing spirit marriage, with Stephen
Bokemkamp's translation. As with Han Wudi, I have chosen the first
poem as an example rather arbitrarily, as many other poems in the
Zhen'gao would illustrate the same point.

Then the Perfected Consort commanded me, saying: "I wish to present you with a page of writing, so I must trouble you to take up the brush to convey my humble sentiments. Is this possible?"

"I obey your commands," I responded. Forthwith, I smoothed out a sheet of paper, dipped my brush, and copied verbatim the following poem:

雲闕豎空上	A cloud-swathed gate stands above in the emptiness,
瓊臺聳鬱羅	Then red-gem tower rises into the densecloud Net.
紫宮乘綠景	The Purple Palace rides on green phosphors,
靈觀藹嵯峨	Its spirit-observatories shadowed among jagged peaks.
琅軒朱房內	With vermilion chambers roofed in malachite,
上德煥絳霞	Upper potencies flash their scarlet auroras.
俯漱雲瓶津	Looking down, I rinse my mouth with liquid from a cloudvase;
仰掇碧柰花	Looking up, I pluck a deep-blue blossom from a crabapple tree.
濯足玉女池	Bathing my feet in heaven's jade pool,
鼓枻牽牛河	Striking oars in the ox-herder's river.
遂策景雲駕	I urge on the carriage of effulgent clouds,
落龍轡玄阿	And rein in the descending dragons on the Slopes of Mystery.
振衣塵滓際	Shaking out my garments on the borders of this world of dust and dregs,
褰裳步濁波	I lift my skirts and stride over the turbid waves.
原為山澤結	My desire is to make a bond between mountain and marsh,
剛柔順以和	To let the rigid and the yielding conform to one another in harmony.
相攜雙清內	Hand in hand, paired in matched purity:
上真道不邪	Our way of supreme perfection will not be depraved.
紫微會良謀	In Purple Tenuity we have met a fine matchmaker,
唱納享福多	I sing that we may receive blessings in abundance.[75]

The colorful scenes of splendor in the first lines of this poem could also grace *youxian shi*, although it is a more detailed and extensive landscape than Guo Pu would usually construct; one couplet of the opening three probably would have sufficed in secular *youxian shi*. Perhaps even Yang Xi, marginalized as he was, took part in his generation's shift toward the landscape. Here it is the transcendent, rather than the traveling mortal, who consumes and is submerged in the landscape. Again, the motion is descent rather than ascent. The dramatized presentation of clothing coming in contact with the filth of the world is a reversal of the traveling mortal, who drapes himself with the colors of the clouds. The poem moves in a more linear way toward a final resolve than most *youxian shi* because the wishes expressed are propositions to a mortal listener rather than mortals' grandiose and self-doubting desires. As in the song performed for Han Wudi, here there can be no doubt. Although earlier *youxian shi* also had a social aspect, related to congratulatory banquet songs wishing for long life, Guo Pu moved them to a more private, less situational context.[76] In contrast, like most performance of *xian* songs, these poems are at the most social end of the spectrum between solitary flights of the mind and social performances because here transcendent flight is combined with betrothal and wedding songs. In the divine bride's wedding song a few days later, her proposal of a joined spirit journey, "together pluck scarlet fruit in the groves of jade; together pick cinnabar blossoms in Wildwind Garden," reveals by contrast the solitude of the mortal poets' journeys.[77] The ending here is a triumphant reversal of Qu Yuan's flawed matchmakers and failed courtship. Only in songs of revelation and devotion could the Goddess be actually attainable, and it is only the divine voice that can promise such consummation.

Although Li Fengmao argues that the exchange of poetry is an essential motif in legends of mortal encounters with divine women, whether in scriptural or in *zhiguai* contexts,[78] these similar poems and frames differ in the amount of emphasis placed on the poetry: the divine revelations are the heart of Yang Xi's text, while the songs in the versions of the Han Wudi story are elements that can be added and discarded by the textual tradition. This in turn is related to the differences between first- and third-person revelations: in the case of Han Wudi, more of the focus is on the famous person receiving the transcendents' words than the words themselves, while Yang Xi is notable only as medium, the recipient of the transcendents' words. These differences place the transcendents' words and their mortal recipients in differing frameworks of desire: in the Han Wudi cycle, the reader observes the emperor's thwarted desire, drawn by both nostalgia for historical glamor and envy of his proximity to the divine and certain in the knowledge of his eventual failure. Although both narrative frames show the mortal men humbling themselves before superior divinities, the reader of Han Wudi's story is privy to the divinities' disparagement of the ruler's prospects. Ruler and transcendent are equally remote. Yang Xi's success and the possibility that it could be duplicated tantalize the reader of the *Zhen'gao*.

The songs of female transcendents' advances to mortal males change the structure of desire, compared with *youxian shi* and the older spirit journey: the transcendents long for a companion and envision a shared journey, but they are confident of consummation. They are in contrast to the tradition of male poets' descriptions of mortal female desire, which presume female helplessness and containment in the boudoir. Thus they present another alternative for writing poems beyond the self and personal *zhi* 志.

Conclusion

Looking at the literary depictions of *xian* reveals the place of the otherworldly and divine in Chinese literary history. The otherworldly was linked to the workings of the human imagination, for good and ill: for Liu Xie, it was regarded as a potential topic of inappropriate fabrication, but also for creative allegory. If one views the Chinese literary tradition as a lineage, the orthodox, paternal-side ancestors are for prose, the classics, and for poetry, the *Shi jing*; and the heterodox, maternal-side ancestors are the *wei* and the *Chu ci*. As aesthetic thought was formulated in the Six Dynasties, the paternal heritage was acknowledged and established, but the maternal heritage, although it remained influential, required taming. The spirit journey, originating in the more marginal tradition, was claimed by the orthodox tradition as the accepted vision of the poetic imagination. Inspiration through possession was absent but remained a powerful force in marginal genres. Allegory and *jituo* were the acceptable orthodox use of otherworldly imagery, while divine revelation was restricted to genres that were not considered literary. Transcendents waver between uses of the imagination that the dominant literary tradition considered acceptable and those that were marginalized. To put it another way, transcendents are in between two distinct ways of reading otherworldly imagery, one that always turns its eyes back to this world and one that remains looking outward.

Transcendents are a border-crossing species by their inherent definition. As they develop in various textual traditions in the Six Dynasties, the number of borders they cross increases, and considering their dual nature is key to understanding their aesthetic nature. Some portrayals of transcendents are accepted in the central works of aesthetic criticism and anthologies, but many others are left outside. Transcendents are between the expression of personal *zhi* and projecting the voice of another. In poetry they can be viewed from both the inside and the outside, as an object of marvel and a state the poet, or a singing transcendent, achieves. In poetic practice, transcendents are in between abstraction and the sensual. Both *youxian shi* and the songs of the transcendents strike a balance between the sensory beauty of the world of the transcendents—its colors, sounds, and most of all the sense of movement—and abstract statements of principle. If, as Campany says, the essence of the transcendents is freedom from limitation, poems, regardless whether of mortals seeking transcendents or transcendents addressing mortals, must concentrate on both drawing limits and crossing over them.[79] The difference is on which side of these divisions poetic persona and reader are left at the end of the poem. In emotional terms, transcendents are between frustrated and fulfilled desire, but the balances of desire work out very differently between *youxian shi* and the transcendents' own songs.

The Six Dynasties poetic depictions of transcendents formed an important basis for the later evolution of the species in both poetry and other genres. The transcendents remain important to both the literary and the religious imagination and raise the question of where the two diverge and converge again.

NOTES

1. For a useful general summary, see Donald Holzman, "Immortality-Seeking in Early Chinese Poetry," in *The Power of Culture: Studies in Chinese Cultural History,* ed. W. J. Peterson, et al. (Hong Kong: Chinese University Press, 1994), pp. 108–118.

2. Liu Xie, *Wenxin diao* (Hong Kong: Shangwu yinshu guan, 1964), 4/29. Cited hereafter as *WXDL*.

3. Stephen Owen, *Readings in Chinese Literary Thought* (Cambridge, Mass.: Council on East Asian Studies, Harvard University, 1992), p. 185.

4. See Zong-qi Cai, "The Polysemous Term of *Shen* in *Wenxin diaolong*," in *Recarving the Dragon: Understanding Chinese Poetics*, ed. Olga Lomová (Prague: Charles University Press, 2003).

5. *WXDL*, 5/36.

6. Ibid.

7. Ibid., 6/49.

8. See the discussion in Zhou Xunchu 周勛初, "Guo Pu shi wei Jin 'zhongxing di yi' shuo bianxi" 郭樸詩為晉'中興第一'說辨析, in *Weijin nanbei chao wenxue lunji* 魏晉南北朝文學論集 (Hong Kong: Chinese Department of the Chinese University of Hong Kong, 1994), pp. 9–28.

9. *WXDL*, 6/67.

10. Owen, *Readings in Chinese Literary Thought*, pp. 86–96.

11. Traditional Chinese critics also note the similarity between Guo Pu's *youxian shi* and the "Yuan you"; see He Zhuo 何焯 and Yao Fan 姚範, quoted in *Weijin nanbeichao wenxue shi cankao ziliao* 魏晉南北朝文學史參考資料 (Beijing: Zhonghua shuju, 1962), A. 330–331.

12. See his essay in this volume.

13. Zhu Xi 朱熹, ed., *Chu ci jizhu* 楚辭集注 (Hong Kong: Zhonghua Shuju, 1987), pp. 1–2, 29.

14. See Wai-yee Lee, *Enchantment and Disenchantment* (Princeton, N.J.: Princeton University Press, 1993).

15. "*Jituo*" in this sense originates in Wang Xizhi's 王羲之 (321–379) "Lanting ji xu" 蘭亭集序: "或因寄所託，放浪形骸之外," translated by Stephen Owen as "others invest their feelings in something external as they roam free, beyond the body's world." Stephen Owen, *An Anthology of Chinese Literature* (New York: W. W. Norton, 1996), p. 283. In this context as well, *jituo* is identified with flight beyond the mundane world.

16. Li Fengmao 李豐楙, *You yu you: Liuchao suitang youxian shi lun ji* 憂與遊：六朝隋唐遊仙詩論集 (Taibei: Xuesheng shuju, 1996), pp. 8–9.

17. Ibid., p. 10.

18. See Donald Holzman, "Ts'ao Chih and the Immortals," *Asia Major*, series 3, vol. 1 (1998), pp. 15–58.

19. Zhou Xunchu, "Guo Pu shi wei Jin 'zhongxing di yi' shuo bianxi," pp. 9–28.

20. Zhong Rong, *Shi pin*, B. 38.

21. *Wenxuan (suoyin ben)* 文選（索引本）(Kyoto: Zhongwen chubanshe, 1972), 21/293. Another critic of Zhong Rong's view of Guo Pu is Chen Zuoming 陳祚明, quoted in *Weijin nanbeichao wenxue shi cankao ziliao*, A. 331.

22. In Zhu Taimang 朱太忙, ed., *Xiangzhu gushi yuan* 詳註古詩源 (Dalian, 1935), A. 191.

23. Stephen Owen, course notes for History of Chinese Literature, Harvard University, fall 1990. *Wenxuan* includes seven complete poems; Lu Qinli

逯欽立 ed., *Xian Qin Han Wei Jin Nanbeichao shi* 先秦漢魏晉南北朝詩 (Beijing: Zhonghua shuju, 1983), collects twelve other complete poems and fragments.

24. Han Feizi, "Waichushuo shang" 韓非子：外儲説上, in *Han Feizi jishi* 韓非子集釋, ed. Chen Qiyou 陳奇猷 (Shanghai: Shanghai renmin chubanshe, 1974), B. 633.

25. *Wenxuan*, 21/292.

26. Zong-qi Cai, *The Matrix of Lyric Transformation: Poetic Modes and Self-Presentation in Early Chinese Pentasyllabic Poetry* (Ann Arbor: Center for Chinese Studies, University of Michigan, 1996), pp. 141–145.

27. A distinction between the worldly and otherworldly poems is shared among many of the readers of Guo Pu; I, however, move some of the poems others consider purely *jituo*, like the first and second, into the middle category of wavering between the worlds. See, for example, Xu Gongchi 徐公持, *Weijin wenxue shi* 魏晉文學史 (Beijing: Renmin wenxue chubanshe, 1999), p. 496.

28. The numbering of poems 1–7 is based on the order in *Wenxuan*. After that, numbering is based on the order as collected in Lu Qinli, ed., *Xian Qin Han Wei Jin Nanbeichao shi*.

29. Zhuang Zi.

30. According to *Lienü zhuan*, when the King of Chu came to solicit Laizi's service, it was his wife who first rejected the idea and left, with her husband following her into reclusion. "Chu Laolai qi" 楚老萊妻, in *Lienü zhuan jinzhu jinyi* 烈女傳今註今譯, ed. Liu Xiang 劉向 and Zhang Jing 張敬 (Taibei: Shangwu yinshu guan, 1994), B. 83–84.

31. *Xianqin han weijin nanbei chao shi*, B. 865. I am indebted to an anonymous reader for corrections to my translations. There is another translation of this poem by John Frodsham in *Classical Chinese Literature: An Anthology of Translations*, ed. John Minform and Joseph S. M. Lau (New York: Columbia University Press, 2000), vol. 1, p. 437.

32. See also Li Fengmao's reading of this poem in *You yu you*, p. 120.

33. Li Shan argues that it is pursuit of *xian*, while one of the Wuchen annotators takes it as referring to maintaining virtue. *Wenxuan* 21/293, *Jingyin songben wuchen jizhu Wenxuan* 景印宋本五臣集注文選 (Taibei, 1981), 11/10b.

34. The third poem has a similar focus on a single male recluse, who is introduced by a dazzlingly colorful opening pair of couplets. Lu Qinli, ed., *Xian Qin Han Wei Jin Nanbeichao shi*, B. 685.

35. Laizi's wife is an exception, but her reclusion is presented primarily as an inspiration for her husband's.

36. Zhang Hua uses divine women in a similar way in his *youxian shi*.

37. See, for example, the reading in Xu Gongchi, *Weijin wenxue shi*, p. 498.

38. Lu Qinli, ed., *Xian Qin Han Wei Jin Nanbeichao shi*, B. 685.

39. In other words, although I have great talent, it is not accepted in this benighted world. "珪璋特達" is a reference to the *Li ji*, which becomes an

expression for a man of exceptional talent. *Li ji:* "Pin yi" 禮記：聘義; Wang Meng'ou 王夢鷗, ed., *Liji jinzhu jinyi* 禮記今註今譯 (Taibei: Shangwu yinshu guan, 1977), B:46.827. The moonbright pearl given in secret is a reference to the *Shi ji:* "I have heard that if one gives a moonbright pearl or a night-glowing jade disk to someone on the street, he will draw his sword and glare at you." It becomes a fixed expression for something splendid that cannot be accepted under certain circumstances. *Shi ji:* "Lu Zhonglian Zou Yang liezhuan" 魯仲連鄒陽列傳; Sima Qian, *Shi ji* 史記 (Beijing: Zhonghua shuju, 1982), 8:83.2459.

40. Lu Qinli, ed., *Xian Qin Han Wei Jin Nanbeichao shi*, B. 866.

41. The *Wenxuan* annotations cite an anecdote in the *Guoyu* in which the import of this sea bird roosting at the gates is initially misinterpreted. *Wenxuan*, 21/294.

42. These figures have biographies in *Liexian zhuan* and *Shenxian zhuan* respectively. Teng Xiuzhan 滕修展 et al., eds., *Liexian zhuan shenxian zhuan zhuyi* 列仙傳神仙傳注譯 (Tianjin: Baihua wenyi chuban she, 1996), pp. 138, 333.

43. Li Shan reads his motion as approval of the song. Huan'e is another name for the moon goddess Chang'e, and Hong Yai is a minister of the Yellow Emperor, who became a transcendent. See Robert Campany, *To Live as Long as Heaven and Earth: A Translation and Study of Ge Hong's Traditions of Divine Transcendents* (Berkeley: University of California Press, 2002), p. 273.

44. Lu Qinli, ed., *Xian Qin Han Wei Jin Nanbeichao shi*, B. 866.

45. Li Fengmao, *You yu you*, p. 126.

46. Lu Qinli, ed., *Xian Qin Han Wei Jin Nanbeichao shi*, B. 866.

47. A similar gesture closes Fu Xuan's 傅玄 "Yunzhong baizi gaoxing" 雲中白子高行, in Lu Qinli, ed., *Xian Qin Han Wei Jin Nanbeichao shi*, A. 564.

48. Lu Qinli, ed., *Xian Qin Han Wei Jin Nanbeichao shi*, B. 1010–1012.

49. Li Fang 李昉 et al., eds., *Wenyuan yinghua* 文苑英華 (Taiwan: Huawen shuju, 1965), 3/225/1a.

50. For example, "Baishi sheng" 白石生, *Shenxian zhuan*, pp. 174–175; "Yinchang sheng 陰長生, *Shenxian zhuan*, pp. 263–266. Campany, *To Live as Long as Heaven and Earth*, pp. 292–294, 274–275.

51. Lu Qinli, ed., *Xian Qin Han Wei Jin Nanbeichao shi*, B. 1530.

52. Zhan Shichuang 詹石窗, *Daojiao wenxue shi* 道教文學史 (Shanghai: Shanghai Wenyi chubanshe, 1992), p. 96.

53. Li Fang et al., eds., *Wenyuan yinghua*, 3/225/1b.

54. Lu Qinli, ed., *Xian Qin Han Wei Jin Nanbeichao shi*, B. 1636–1637.

55. "Chisong jian shi" 赤松澗詩 (Poem on Chi Songzi's Waterfall), in Lu Qinli, ed., *Xian Qin Han Wei Jin Nanbeichao shi*, B. 1638–1639.

56. Zhan Shichuang, *Daojiao wenxue shi*, p. 99.

57. See Stephen Bokenkamp, *Early Daoist Scriptures* (Berkeley: University of California Press, 1997), p. 277.

58. Li Fengmao also refers to these pieces as *xian'ge* 仙歌. See *Liuchao suitang xiandao lei xiaoshuo yanjiu* 六朝隋唐仙道類研究 (Taibei: Xuesheng shuju, 1986), pp. 31–32.

59. In the Shangqing scriptures, also revealed to Yang Xi, the account of the transmission of the scripture is described in some detail. See Bokenkamp, *Early Daoist Scriptures*, pp. 275–306.

60. Although some *youxian shi* are social in that they are exchanged and match one another's rhymes, the world within the poems is relatively private.

61. Campany actually considers the *Han Wudi* cycle marginal to the *zhiguai* tradition. Robert Campany, *Strange Writing: Anomaly Accounts in Early Medieval China* (Albany: State University of New York Press, 1996), pp. 318–321.

62. Some traditional sources attribute this text to the historian Ban Gu 班固 (32–92), others to the important author of *xian*-related texts Ge Hong 葛洪 (284–364). The latter range of dates is more plausible, even if the attribution to Ge Hong is not. See Xu Yimin's 許逸民 entry on this text in Liu Shide 劉世德 et al., *Zhongguo gudai xiaoshuo baike quanshu* 中國古代小說百科全書 (Beijing: Zhongguo baike quanshu chubanshe, 1993), pp. 149–150.

63. Li Fengmao argues for a date of composition in the reign of Xiaowudi of the Jin (r. 373–396). Li Fengmao, *Liuchao suitang xiandao lei xiaoshuo yanjiu.*

64. The version of *Han Wudi neizhuan* included in *Taiping guangji* does not include the text of this song. *Taiping guangji* (Beijing: Zhonghua shuju, 1994), 3.14. The same edition, lacking the poems, is preserved in various fiction-centered compendia, such as *Wuchao xiaoshuo* 五朝小說.

65. "空洞" is a Daoist term for the vacant origins.

66. Taizhen was the young mother of Xi Wang Mu.

67. The Three Fields are spaced between the eyebrows, the heart, and the abdomen.

68. Lu Qinli, ed., *Xian Qin Han Wei Jin Nanbeichao shi*, B. 1091–1092. *Daozang* 道藏 (reprint, Taibei: Yiwen yinshu guan, 1962), *Dongzhen bu* 洞真部, *Jizhuan lei* 記傳纇, *Hai* 海 4/3b. See also Schipper's annotated French translation. E. M. Schipper, *L'Empereur Wou des Han dans la légende Taoiste* (Paris: Ecole Française d'Extrême-Orient, 1965), pp. 75–76. Li Fengmao points out that the same poems appear in *Maojun neizhuan* 毛君內傳 and argues that the reuse of this material at a different point in the supplicant's pursuit of immortality has satirical intent. Li Fengmao, *Liuchao suitang xiandao lei xiaoshuo*, p. 32.

69. Li Fengmao, *Liuchao suitang xiandao lei xiaoshuo*, p. 32.

70. Lu Qinli, ed., *Xian Qin Han Weijin Nanbeichao shi*, B. 1092–1093. I follow Schipper's translation, but he admits the line is not clear. Schipper, p. 123.

71. Strictly speaking, the divinities Yang Xi encountered were Perfected *zhenren* 真人 rather than *xian*, who in Shangqing cosmology exist on a lower level of the heavens. Although theologically significant, I do not think this distinction makes much difference in terms of literary depiction. See Bokenkamp, *Early Daoist Scriptures*, p. 276.

72. Ibid., p. 277.

73. The poems are taken out of their original context and collected in Lu Qinli, ed., *Xian Qin Han Wei Jin Nanbeichao shi*, B. 1096–1122.

74. Stephen Bokenkamp, "Declarations of the Perfected," in *Religions of China in Practice*, ed. Donald S. Lopez (Princeton, N.J.: Princeton University Press, 1996), pp. 166–179. See also Paul Kroll, "Seduction Songs of One of the Perfected," in the same volume, pp. 180–187.

75. Lu Qinli, ed., *Xian Qin Han Wei Jin Nanbeichao shi*, B. 1097. *Zhengao* 真誥, in *Xuejin taoyuan* 學津討原, *Baibu congshu jicheng*, series 46, vol. 286, 1/12a–14a. Bokenkamp, "Declarations of the Perfected," p. 173.

76. Li Fengmao, *You yu you*, p. 32.

77. Bokenkamp, "Declarations of the Perfected," p. 176. *Zhengao*, 1/16a. The poem is also discussed in Li Fengmao, "Weijin shennü chuanshuo yu daojiao shennü jiangzhen chuanshuo" 魏晉神女傳說與道教神女降真傳說, in *Weijin nanbei chao wenxue yu sixiang xueshu yantaohui lunwen ji* 魏晉南北朝文學與思想學術研討會論文集 (Taibei: Wenshizhe chubanshe, 1991), p. 497.

78. Li Fengmao, "Weijin shennü chuanshuo," p. 497.

79. Campany, *Strange Writing*, p. 303.

Chapter 7

●●

Literary Games and Religious Practice at the End of the Six Dynasties

The Baguanzhai Poems by Xiao Gang and His Followers

François Martin

Intellectual life during the latter part of the Six Dynasties period, notably from about 450 onward, may be said to be dominated by two salient cultural (and at the same time social) phenomena. One is the unprecedented development of both literary theory and practice. Among the members of the leading gentry, literary talent, especially notably poetic ability, tended to become a requisite. Literary pursuits, rarely individual, were rather a social practice with many political connotations and were centered upon the courts of emperors and princes. The core of literary life was constituted by salon activities in which literary games, especially group improvisations of poetry, played a conspicuous part. Poetic activity was thus typically linked to courtly life, with all its sensuous pleasures, encouraging the levity of themes, a tendency of which later orthodox traditions would rather disapprove.

The second phenomenon is the striking growth of Buddhism, especially lay Buddhism. It was then expected from any member of the gentry to take lay orders, vowing himself to the five precepts and generally

leading the life of a *jushi* 居士 (*upāsaka*, layman believer) modeling himself on Vimālakirti. This entailed having monasteries and stupas built,
commissioning images carved and painted, making generous gifts to the
sangha, and respecting each month the six days of Baguanzhai 八關齋,
or "the Fast of the Eight Precepts" (on the eighth, fourteenth, fifteenth,
twenty-third, twenty-ninth, and thirtieth day). This practice, which
constituted the very core of lay Buddhism, required of lay believers who
had already sworn to respect the five principles to assemble under the
conduct of a monk and swear to lead for one day the life of a monk,
partaking of religious fare, meditating, and listening to sutras and to
predications.

Therein lies a fundamental contradiction (certainly not unique to
China): how to reconcile religious practice with a public life of which
pleasurable pursuits occupied a rather important part? To answer that
perhaps some of the gentry led rather religious lives while others
devoted themselves to pleasure (and literature), though certainly true
for a number of individuals, would be globally rather naive. Certainly
the contradiction was acutely felt by many. Let us take the instance of
Shen Yue 沈約 (441–513): he was a prolific Buddhic writer and one of
the leading lay believers of his time, but he was at the same time the
very emblem of the new poetry movement and left a great amount of
somewhat frivolous poetry, some of which seems indeed to reflect his
own amorous adventures, like the very charming "Six Rememberances"
(六憶).[1] In fact, that this is no mere literature needs no effort to prove,
as he himself left us a text in which he confessed to having had carnal
relations with a very large number of girls and not a few boys. Xiao
Gang 蕭綱 (503–551), whose poetry is, if anything, more frivolous than
Shen Yue's, was a great patron of Buddhism, a prolific Buddhist writer,
and certainly a sincere believer. Nevertheless, as a prince, he had the
privilege of a populous harem and certainly made unrestrained use of
that facility; at least in a text setting the rules for Baguanzhai discipline,
he deplores the raising of sexual desire as a serious hindrance to meditation.

Let us think, then, not in terms of contradictions but of facets of
what may be termed a cultural complex. As a matter of fact, our purpose here is certainly not to solve moral issues for contemporary Chinese, but rather to search out points of contact between aesthetic
research in poetry and Buddhist faith and practice. The place to begin
our inquiry is in what has been left us of Buddhic poems by aristocrats

("Buddhic poetry" meaning here not only pieces reflecting directly religious teachings or speculation, but also any piece written on the occasion of a Buddhist festival or similar occasion). The main repositories for such poetry are chapters 76 and 77 ("Neidian" 內典) of the *Yiwen leiju* 藝文類聚 and chapter 30 ("Tonggui" 統歸) of the *Guang Hongming ji* 廣弘明集, a compilation published by the Tang high monk Daoxuan 道宣 during the year 664. Compositions by emperors (notably Liang Wudi) and princes stand out conspicuously. The amount is relatively small (all the more so for a number of overlaps), hardly more than one hundred, but it cannot be doubted that the actual corpus has suffered considerable losses.

Typically, Buddhic poetry as reflected in these two collections does not fundamentally differ from current court composition: a prince improvises a poem, requiring of his attendant followers to echo him by a similar composition on the same subject, with the same number of lines, on imposed rhymes. Thus Buddhic poetry takes the garb of poetic play, only the occasion (visits to temples, festivals) differing. In fact, much, if not all, seems to have been written not during a visit or ceremony itself, but rather on the evening of the same day, on the banqueting mats, the probably meager fare on such an occasion being perhaps the main difference with other banquets. Under such conditions, the ludic element, indeed, tends to overcome the religious one. I shall now take as a topic of discussion a set of poems in which the ludic element plays a strikingly conspicuous role. However narrow the subject may seem at first sight, its richness and liveliness as a document certainly make its study worth our while.

Chapter 30 of the *Guang hongming ji* contains a rather intriguing set of poems entitled "Four Pieces Composed by Turns about the Four Gates upon a Night of Baguanzhai" 八關齋夜賦四城門四首.[2] The title in itself needs some clarification. First, "Four Pieces" is misleading, as we have in fact thirty-two quatrains improvised "by Turns" by eight poets. It means in fact "four sets of pieces on four different rhymes." As to the subject, the "Four Gates" refer to the four occasions on which the young prince Gautama set out four times—each time from a different gate—from his father's palace toward the royal garden, seeing in succession an ill man, an old man, a dead man, and a mendicant. I have already touched upon the occasion of the improvisation, the Baguanzhai. If poetry making is to find a place in it—this indeed constitutes a problem to which we will return below—then the four outings of the future Buddha, which determined his religious career, are certainly a fitting subject.

More concretely, the whole game is organized as follows. The first poet improvises four lines on illness; the second one then composes four answering lines on the same subject, endeavoring to be congruent with the first poet's composition. The two quatrains together form an eight-line piece entitled "East Gate: Illness." The Third and fourth poets then improvise in the same way on "South Gate: Old Age." The fifth and sixth poets now do their part about "West Gate: Death," while the seventh and eighth have to deal with "North Gate: The Monk."

Each of the eight participants having thus composed one quatrain, the imposed rhyme now changes, and the poets set forth for a second turn. There will be four turns in all. The order of improvisation is changed four times, according to rules not altogether easy to understand and into which I cannot delve in this chapter. Suffice it to say that they are so devised as to ensure that each poet will compose not only one time at each turn, but also one time (and only one) on each of the four subjects.

A closer inquiry into the personality of the eight poets involved, though it gives somewhat meager results about the individual, is not altogether unrewarding as concerns the background and general circumstances of the contest. We will take a look at the poets not in order of appearance, but in decreasing order of fame (or rather perhaps in the decreasing order of the wealth of documentation available to us).

By far the most famous of all is of course Xiao Gang, son of Wudi and brother to Xiao Tong 蕭統, crown prince from 531 to 549 (he figures in the *Guang hongming ji* edition of our poems as *huang taizi* 皇太子), and Emperor Jianwen from 550 to 551. A rather poor figure in history, he is well known in the field of literature, where his name is forever associated with *gongti* 宮體 poetry ("*gong*" refers to the Eastern Palace), more often with deprecating implications. This is a somewhat reductive view, as he was also the most prolific Buddhic writer of his time, though the great majority of his works are lost. As J. Marney remarks, if his Buddhist production had survived, "Hsiao Kang might be remembered above all as a great Buddhic writer."[3] The very small part of it that has been preserved has been, still according to Marney, overlooked as "superficial literary dazzle," but it testifies to his unremitting efforts to harmonize Buddhic lore and the high Chinese literary style.[4] His most important Buddhic work—in fact probably an anthology commissioned by him—the *Fabao lianbi* 法寶連璧, is more than two hundred chapters.

Second comes Yu Jianwu 庾肩吾, father of the famous poet Yu Xin 庾信 (513–581). Up to his death a loyal servant of Xiao Gang, he is known to have been Xiao Gang's mentor, on the same footing as Xu Chi 徐摛, father of Xu Ling 徐陵 (507–583), compiler of the *Yutai xinyong* 玉臺新詠 (New Songs from a Jade Terrace). The two men, associated in the appellation Xu-Yu 徐庾 (hence the "Xu-Yu style," another name for the *gongti* style), together whith their sons, were the pillars of the Eastern Palace group. Xu Chi left behind almost one hundred poems, of which a significant number are signaled by their titles to have been written in answer to the prince. Thirteen of them are in the *Yutai xinyong*. It may be added that it is probably from Yu Jianwu's own collection of works that Daoxuan gleaned the Baguanzhai poems, as he appears in the *Guang Hongming ji* edition as "*zhongshe fu jun*" 中庶府君, probably another title for *taizi zhongshuzi* 太子中庶子, a title he held from the late thirties onward.

Then comes a group of four persons whose relations with Xiao Gang are more or less easy to determine. Xu Fang 徐防 was certainly an old retainer of the prince, as his name appears in a famous list of the "Gaozhai scholars" 高齋學士, a group assembled by Xiao Gang in Yongzhou when he was still prince of Jin'an and governor of Yongzhou in the 520s.[5] It is probably the case for Kong Dao 孔燾. Though his name is altogether ignored by historical sources, we have from him another poem in answer to the prince. Moreover, we have from the prince's own hand a text ordering a gift of money for him to enable his two daughters to marry; he hailed Kong Dao's erudition, as well as his long and faithful service, in the provinces as well as in the capital.[6]

As to Wang Taiqing 王臺卿, it is difficult to say whether he was at one time or the other in the pay of the prince. He did not need to be because he is mentioned in a historical text as an overtly rich man in connection to the calling back of a young nephew of Wudi, the emperor being quite discontented with the life he led in Yongzhou under the lead of his four prodigal friends (Wang being one of them).[7] He could have come back to the capital together with Wudi's nephew in 531. But whenever it was, then or later, he certainly was in close contact with Xiao Gang; that much we know from the many poems written in answer to the prince among the eighteen pieces that survive. That in itself is not a small amount for poets of that time. So we may infer that he occupied a not inconsiderable place on the poetic scene. Moreover, he was certainly appreciated by the prince, as suggested by the fact that two of his poems were selected in the *Yutai xinyong*; this puts him apart from the other poets here, with the exception of Yu Jianwu. Another poet, Li Jingyuan 李鏡遠, otherwise unknown, left some poems quite in the vein of the *gongti*, but whether he was a denizen of the Eastern Palace, we cannot say.

About the last two poets, Zhuge Kai 諸葛愷 and a mysterious person styled "the Jun" 君, we cannot find any scraps of information. We do not even know who hid behind the title of "the Jun." My guess is that it may well have been a woman and possibly a relative of Yu Jianwu. That could explain the absence of any personal name and the abbreviated form of the title. Our ignorance is all the more to be pitied as "the Jun" shows no small wit in our poems.

In conclusion, out of eight poets, five or even six may be related more or less directly to Xiao Gang. It is enough to conclude that the thirty-two quatrains of the Baguanzhai were very probably written in the Eastern Palace, within the circle known as the *gongti* poets, even if their authors were not all regular members. It is certainly unnecessary here to elaborate on the nature of *gongti* poetry. I shall mention only some salient points about it. Though specialists do not entirely agree upon the exact definition of the *gongti*, it is certainly not erroneous to define it as follows:

(a) a poem of preferably short form (four or eight lines) answering the new roles of tonal prosody first set down by Shen Yue and afterward improved upon by Xiao Gang, his masters, and his followers, all great admirers of the famous poet.
(b) a poem where heavy, systematic parallelism is rather to be avoided in favor of syntactic liberation and original formulation.
(c) a poem whose main theme is preferably linked with palace life and, quite typically, to the life of palace women. It seems that even when the poem is not explicitly related to women, it is expected of the poet to relate the poem in one way or another to the feminine world, often by some pun very often not devoid of humor.

Gongti poetry, historical sources tell us, became a rage at the capital in the period just following the installation of the new crown prince in the Eastern Palace, in 531. As a matter of fact, it seems that Xiao Gang, as the leader of a literary movement aiming at art for art's sake, put himself somewhat at odds with his deceased brother, Xiao Tong, a man of rather classical tastes (though quite up-to-date poetry may be found even in his own works).

I just alluded to Xiao Tong, under whose direction the illustrious anthology *Wenxuan* was compiled. A number of authors consider that it was as a counterweight to the *Wenxuan* that Xiao Gang had the young Xu Ling compile the famous anthology of love poetry, *Yutai xinyong*. I will not enter here into the problems that such an assertion raises, but it is at least undeniable that the *Yutai xinyong*, and especially the chapters of it that are devoted to contemporary poetry, may be taken as a defense and illustration of *gongti* style. With regard to the dating of the *Yutai xinyong*, it has long been considered a work compiled under the Chen dynasty—which is most certainly erroneous—or at least during the late Liang period. Anne Birrell considers it to date from ca. 545.[8] But Kōzen Hiroshi has proposed a somewhat earlier date.[9] As the date bears very much on our purpose, we must briefly discuss Kōzen's method. Having remarked that the names of the poets of the *Yutai xinyong* who were also in the list of the compilers of the *Fabao lianbi* (given in its preface by Xiao Yi) appeared in the same order in the table of the *Yutai*,[10] Kōzen inferred that the poets in the last chapters of that work had been arranged not by their date of death (as in the other chapters) but, as in the *Fabao lianbi*, by order of rank. More important, this is proof that they were living at the time of the compilation. A careful study of available data showed him that the *Yutai xinyong* could have been compiled only between 533 and 535—that is, very near the time Xiao Gang succeeded his brother. This could explain some difficulties, particularly why Xiao Gang did not put his own name on the *Yutai xinyong*. It may well be a consequence of the overt disapproval of the *gongti* expressed by Wudi. We know too that Xu Chi, possibly in an indirect connection with the matter, was the object of imperial disgrace at the time. That could explain why Xiao Gang commissioned the work not to Xu Chi but to his son Xu Ling, and why no poem of Chi's can be found in his son's anthology, neither Ling nor Xiao Gang wanting to further embarass their father and friend respectively. More important, the *Fabao lianbi* having been compiled in 534, it appears that at the very same time, duly applying the principle that "the Eastern Palace nurtures culture" 東宮養文, Xiao Gang preoccupied himself with two (if not more) important matters: the promotion of purely aesthetic poetry, on the one hand, and the promotion of Buddhist literature, on the other, for whatever may have been the contents of the *Fabao lianbi*, the very title implies that they were certainly of literary concern.

Although the poems with which we are concerned today cannot be anterior to 537, the earliest date at which Yu Jianwu became *taizi zhongshuzi*, they undoubtedly can be taken as representative of this double trend. For although the severity of the Baguanzhai does not seem easy to link with the atmosphere of palatine life, redolent with sensuous pleasures, on reading the poems, we are soon struck by the fact that the gap between Buddhist ideas and current poetic ideals is not as wide as one might have expected.

In the first place, the form of the poems is quite congruent with *gongti* requisites: they are quatrains, and a close study soon reveals the consistent respect of tonal rules. Moreover, heavy parallelism is more often than not avoided in favor of smoother diction. But more significant, although a good number of the quatrains basically do nothing other than extol the virtues of the Buddha's teachings, some of them are strikingly near to the usual themes of *gongti* poetry, centered as they are on female figures. This is typically the case for the quatrains about old age. Let us read some of them now. The first one is by Xiao Gang himself:

昔類紅蓮草	She who was once like a pink lotus,
自玩綠池邊	Moving gently on green water's margin,
今如白華樹	Today seems like a tree of white flowers,
還悲明鏡前	Full of sadness, in front of her mirror.[11]

This could easily pass as a *yange* 艷歌 (poem about love or women) in true *gongti* style. In fact, it would have passed as such if it had been preserved only in the *Yiwen leiju*, where it carries the title "On Old Age," without any mention of the Buddhic context of the composition (a fact that in itself gives food for thought).[12] The same may be said of a quatrain by Kong Dao, which is precisely the second of the two quatrains selected by the *Yiwen leiju*, also with the simple title "On Old Age":[13]

盛年歌吹日	In her beautiful years, in the time of songs and flutes,
顧步惜容儀	She watched her steps, was mindful of her looks.
一朝衰朽至	And then one morning, old age came.
星星白髮垂	And now her white hair looks like falling stars.

This, too, would not be out of place in the *Yutai xinyong*. To this poem, Xiao Gang's tutor and friend Yu Jianwu answered by the following quatrain:

已傷萬事盡	Shedding tears on the end of all things,
復念九門枝	She's now aspiring to the nine gates.[14]
垂軒意何在	How could she still hope to climb into a chariot?
獨坐鏡如斯	So she stays seated in front of her mirror.

This last, much more risky than the previous ones in spite of its orthodox Buddhic incipit, has sexual undertones since "the climb into a chariot" is a clear allusion to the story of Han Wudi and Empress Wei 衛皇后: when the emperor first fell in love with the famous dancer at the residence of one of his sisters, he had her follow him in his chariot under the pretext of helping him change clothes and made love to her right there.[15]

I will end with the theme of old age by the two quatrains of the first round. Here is the opening verse, by Zhuge Kai:

虛蕉誠易犯	The hollow plantain is so easy to break
危藤復將囓	And the fragile rattan will be gnawed away.
一隨柯已微	Even now her trunks are weakening;
當年信長訣	This very year they will leave us forever.

Plantain and rattan are allusions to two sutras.[16] There is nothing feminine in this quatrain. But let us look at the answer by "the Jun":

已同白駒去	Gone they are, like the white horse,
復類紅花熱	Just like the red flowers being burnt.
妍容一旦罷	Her nice looks (too) this morning were no more,
孤燈行自設	And she will light the lamp for herself alone.

Here, even lacking a cue from the first poet, after having begun to answer with Taoist-Buddhist images,[17] the poet chooses to bend her answer, in the second distich, in the direction of the feminine, even with the slightly erotic implication of a lamp burning for one person alone, instead of two lovers.

The aging of courtesans and favorites is a favorite theme with *gongti* poets. Not so death—hardly a thing of beauty—unless it be indirectly, through the evocation of famous beauties of past ages. Nevertheless, two poets did manage, on that Baguanzhai night, to evoke it in a more intimate way. Yu Jianwu, definitely *gongti*'s master, begins thus:

高堂信逆旅	These high halls are but a hostelry,
懷業理常牽	Our bad karma endlessly leads us away.
玉匣方委櫬	A jade box has been put in the bier:
金臺不復延	Never again will the stand be set up.

The jade box is easy to associate with women. Still easier is the mirror and its stand. This is particularly clever, as the unopened mirror box or folded mirror stand are a very frequent image among the *gongti*, where they usually mean that the woman alluded to in the poem does not care about her looks because her lover is away.

Yu Jianwu having so oriented the subject of death toward the womanly world, "the Jun" has to follow him and does so in his (or her) answering verse:

挽聲隨迾遠	On the path, the funeral dirges are dying away
蘿影帶松懸	But the moss's shadow is still clinging to the pine.
詎能留十念	How could the ten invocations be enough?
唯應逐四緣	What we must do is to chase away the four causes.

This is done most delicately but with enough clarity, as the moss clinging to the pine is a set cliché of a husband and his wife, so the dead one here can only be a woman.

Let us come to the theme of the monk. It would seem definitively impossible to feminize, until we get the very simple idea of turning the monk into a nun, like Xu Fang:

俗藺厭纏絲	Disgusted with the intertwining threads of the worldly cocoon,
因田抽善穀	She'll now get a good harvest out of the causality field.
長披忍辱鎧	She has donned forever the armor of endurance[18]
去此纖羅服	And rejected for good her silk gauze robes.

"Silk gauze robes," more evocative of women than of men, induced me to feminize my translation. Did I take a liberty here? I do not think so, for "the Jun's" answering verse is decidedly woman-oriented:

願引三塗眾	She only wants to guide the crowds of the three paths
俱令十使伏	And to vanquish the ten messengers.
珠月猶沉首	Cut off has been the head with moonlike pearls!
金鈿未挑目	The golden hairpin won't seduce any more eyes.

Here the overused image of jewels as suggestive of a beautiful woman is used in a truly original way. But in spite of the religious implications, we still can imagine a very beautiful nun!

Only on the theme of illness do we fail to find any allusion to women. In conclusion, out of thirty-two quatrains, at least one-half may be said to be woman-oriented, while the number of quatrains that can be related only to a male person is fewer, perhaps one-quarter, the remainder being difficult to determine. It is enough to conclude that the Eastern Palace poets, even on religious occasions, did not demur from following the usual trends of their inspiration.

I think we do not need to suspect a simple game of wits here. After all, evanescence of beauty, decay, and death are subjects quite consistent with Buddhist teachings. Nevertheless, we cannot but feel a little surprised at seeing such a poetic contest, which, though extolling the Buddha's doctrine, has after all the character of a game, taking place on a Baguanzhai day, especially as one of the eight precepts forbids any kind of entertainment. As a matter of fact, we have a list of ten rules for the Baguanzhai from the hand of Xiao Gang himself, setting penalties for those who doze off during sutra lectures, those who fail to chant along with the others, and so forth.[19] The reading of it gives us an impression of austerity rather different from the atmosphere of our poetic contest. For one thing, how can the same Xiao Gang on one hand point to the raising of carnal desire as something to be avoided at all costs and on the other hand let his companions make use of allusions such as we have seen, quite susceptible to letting the mind stray along sensuous paths?

I think the answer to this apparent contradiction is to be found in the fact that many yearly festivals, either indigenous or of foreign origin, fell on Baguanzhai days. It is notably the case of Shangyuan 上元, the Festival of Lanterns, held on the fifteenth of the first month and that of Buddha's birthday, held on the eighth of the second or fourth month. While devoted to festive celebrations, they still retained the appellation of "Baguanzhai"—witness a title like the "Narration of the Setting up of the Ten Kinds of Lanterns in the Emperor's Private Apartments" 皇帝後堂八關齋造十種燈記, which figures in the catalog

Fayuan zalu yuanshi ji 法苑雜錄原始記,[20] or the *Jingchu suishi ji* 荊楚歲
時記, which depicts the festivities of Buddha's birthday in central
China; on that day, the crowds take the images of the Buddha in pro-
cession all around the town, with much music and chanting, and in
every family of believers, the "lanterns of the *baguanzhai*" are taken
out.[21] On the same day, according to the somewhat later Dunhuang
texts, along with wholesale rejoicing and dances, even the drinking of
wine was permitted to monks, so a poetic contest could not be much of
a trespass. It is in fact probable that the banquet during which our
poems were improvised saw some drinking too.

It is a possibility that poetic improvisation on the Four Gates was a
fixed part of the celebrations, as was the reading in Dunhuang in the
tenth century, and probably elsewhere and before that time, of *yucheng-
wen* 踰城文, texts relating the departure of prince Gautama from his
father's palace.[22] We have some indications that our contest was by no
means a unique event: thus, the *Yiwen leiju* contains a quatrain by Shen
Yue, "Poem on the Four City Gates" 四城門詩, which most probably
corresponds to "West Gate: Old Age." Furthermore, the *Dharmic Collection of the Prince of Baling, Heir to the Prince of Jingling of the Qi* 齊竟陵
王世子撫軍巴陵王法集 contains a mention of "Poems on the Four
Gates, Four Pieces."[23] So perhaps in Xiao Gang's times, the improvisations on the Four Gates were already a well-established tradition.

Even if such improvisation represented a moment of loosening
within Buddhic discipline, the participating poets certainly did not
make light of Buddhist ideals, but on the contrary strove toward the
glorification of the Buddhist faith. At the same time, they composed a
poetry conforming to their aesthetic ideals, thus filling the gap between
the foreign religion and the indigenous literary tradition and harmonizing both spiritual and artistic research.

My conclusion is no conclusion at all. What I have discussed we all
basically knew already. I only feel that the Baguanzhai contest we have
studied is worth being acknowledged as a valuable historical document,
illustrating in a very concrete and lively fashion the actual intermingling
of aesthetics and religion.

NOTES

1. See Xu Ling 徐陵, comp., *Yutai xinyong [jianzhu]* 玉臺新詠[箋注], 2
vols. (Beijing: Zhonghua shuju, 1985), vol. 1, pp. 182–196.

2. Daoxuan 道宣, comp., *Guang Hongmingji* 廣弘明集, "Tonggui," T. 2103, vol. 52, p. 353.

3. John Marney, *Liang Chien-wen ti* (Boston: Twayne, 1976), p. 123.

4. Ibid.

5. See Li Yanshou 李延壽, comp., *Nan shi* 南史, 6 vols. (Beijing: Zhonghua shuju, 1975), vol. 4, p. 1246.

6. See "Zi qian Kong Tao er nü jiao" 資遣孔燾二女教, in Ouyang Xun 歐陽詢, comp., *Yiwen leiju* 藝文類聚, 4 vols. (Shanghai: Shanghai guji chubanshe, 1982), *juan* 40, vol. 2, p. 724.

7. Li Yanshou, *Nan shi*, vol. 4, p. 1292.

8. Anne Birrell, *New Songs from a Jade Terrace* (London: George Allen and Unwin, 1982), p. 1.

9. Kōzen Hiroshi 興膳宏, "Gyokutai-shin'ei no hensan ni tsuite," in *Tōhōgaku* 東方學 1(1982), pp. 58–73.

10. *Fabao lianbi xu*, in *Guang Hongming ji*, *juan* 20, T 2103, p. 242c.

11. All parts of the Baguanzhai poems cited in this chapter are from Lu Qinli 逯欽立, ed., *Xian Qin Han Wei Jin Nanbeichao shi* 先秦漢魏晉南北朝詩, 3 vols (Beijing: Zhonghua shuju, 1983), vol. 3, pp. 2005–2008.

12. Ouyang Xun, *Yiwen leiju*, *juan* 2, vol. 1, p. 342.

13. Ibid., *juan* 2, vol. 1, p. 343.

14. The nine gates are the nine states or conditions in which sentient beings aspire to stay.

15. See Ban Gu 班固, comp., *Han shu* 漢書, 12 vols. (Beijing: Zhonghua shuju, 1962), *juan* 97A, vol. 12, p. 3949.

16. *Dazhuangyan jing* 大莊嚴經, 12, and *Weima jing* 維摩經. The hollow plantain is one of the metaphors for illusory things. Rattan expresses vanity: while growing very high, it is unaware that at the same time two rats (the sun and the moon—that is, time) are gnawing at its roots.

17. The white horse is of course Zhuang Zi's, while the red flower is the *kuranta* (a Pali name), chosen for altars because it will endure a very long time when dried. But even it must be burned in the end.

18. A frequent metaphor for the religious robe.

19. See "Baguanzhai zhi xu" 八關齋制序, in *Guang hongming ji*, *juan* 28A, T 2103, vol. 52, p. 324c.

20. *Chu sanzang jiji* 出三藏集記, *juan* 12, T 2145, vol. 55, p. 93a.

21. See Wang Yurong 王毓榮, *Jing-Chu suishi ji jiaozhu* 荊楚歲時記校注 (Taibei: Wenjin, 1988), p. 99.

22. Françoise Wang-Toutain, "Le Sacre du printemps: Les Cérémonies bouddhiques du 8è jour du 2è mois," in *De Dunhuang au Japon: Etudes chinoises et bouddhiques offertes à Michel Soymié* (Geneva: Droz, 1966), pp. 73–92.

23. See n. 19.

Part III

The Parameters of Six Dynasties Aesthetics
● ● ● ● ● ● ● ● ● ● ● ● ● ● ● ●
Modes of Discourse

Chapter 8

●●●●●●●●●●●●●●●●●●●●●●●●●●●●●●●●●●

Shishuo xinyu and the Emergence of Aesthetic Self-Consciousness in the Chinese Tradition

Wai-yee Li

Shishuo xinyu 世説新語 (A New Account of Tales of the World, ca. 430) plunges us into a finely observed and deftly articulated world of variations on human sensations, perceptions, and actions.[1] Its dominant concern is the compass of beauty—the discernment, judgment, and delineation of physical, moral, verbal, intellectual, and spiritual beauty and the connections (or apparent lack thereof) among these categories. Lu Xun's 魯迅 statement that Wei-Jin is "the era of literary self-consciousness" is by now something of a truism.[2] Histories of Chinese literary thought never fail to note the rise of new aesthetic categories in works such as Cao Pi's 曹丕 (187–226) *Dianlun lunwen* 典論論文 (A Discourse on Literature) and Lu Ji's 陸機 (261–303) *Wen fu* 文賦 (Poetic Exposition on Literature). Yet the later fruits of Wei-Jin literary self-consciousness—notably Liu Xie's 劉勰 (ca. 465–ca. 521) *Wenxin diaolong* 文心雕龍 (The Literary Mind and the Carving of Dragons) and Zhong Rong's 鍾嶸 (ca. 469–518) *Shi pin* 詩品 (Classification of Poetry)—offer ambivalent and sometimes negative assessments of the Wei-Jin (especially Jin) literary-cultural legacy. By contrast, *Shishuo xinyu* depicts this legacy by and large sympathetically.[3] It is also interesting to note that the materials included in *Shishuo* lie outside the province of literature in the systematic classifications of genres in *Wenxuan* 文選 and *Wenxin diaolong.*[4] *Shishuo* contains only sporadic, though often insightful and evocative, judgments of specific literary works and comments on literary and artistic creation. Somewhat less tangible and coherent, but also more pervasive and influential, is the discourse of beauty that emerges from the book. Paradoxically, it is precisely because *Shishuo* is not directly or deliberately confronting the meaning of literature and its place in the Great Tradition (and is therefore not constrained by theoretical and historical systems or obliged to address the competing claims of ethics and philosophy) that an emergent aesthetic self-consciousness freely unfolds.

How did this happen? The aesthetic mode of apprehending and appreciating human existence in *Shishuo* displaces or represses political-historical categories of significance, despite the fact that many entries in *Shishuo* bear structural similarities with anecdotes in historical writings, and quite a number of them duly make their way into the *Jin shu* 晉書 (History of the Jin), compiled in the Tang dynasty.[5] Consider the phenomenon of so-called "Pure Conversation" (*qingtan* 清談, *qingyan* 清言). Many scholars have characterized *Shishuo* as a compendium of Pure Conversation. (As a record or recreation of that cultural practice, the book itself might have become "an aid to conversation.")[6] There is scholarly consensus on how Wei-Jin Pure Conversation evolved from late Han "Pure Critique" (*qingtan* 清議).[7] Of the latter FanYe 范曄 (398–445) writes in the *Hou Han shu* 後漢書:

> By the time of the reigns of Emperors Huan 桓 and Ling 靈, rulers neglected their duties and there was political decay. The fate of the country was put in the hands of eunuchs, and educated persons were ashamed to consort with them. That was why commoners protested in frustration, and scholars without official positions gloried in their arguments. Whereupon, with ever more extreme opinions, they enhanced their own names. They judged each other, evaluated the lords of the land, and sized up those deciding on policies. The mood of defiant probity thus became prevalent.[8]

Pure Critique started off as a system of local recommendations for office based on evaluations of talent and virtue; by late Han the system was corrupt and crumbling. The Pure Critique launched by the students of the Han imperial academy was a form of political intervention. It was when political life became too dangerous or apparently

futile that the intellectual elite turned to the more abstruse and philosophical Pure Conversation. Whereas the word "pure" (*qing* 清) in
"Pure Critique" has distinct moral connotations, referring to the right-
eous opinions of the "pure stream" (*qingliu* 清流) attacking the corrupt
elements in government, "pure" in the compound "Pure Conversation"
denotes philosophical speculativeness, unworldly refinement, lofty
detachment, and the ability to stay above the fray. In various early
usages, the term seems to have no particular philosophical resonance
and simply describes witty and felicitous verbal expression.[9] The word
"*qing*" also recurs in the approbation of characters in *Shishuo*, where
it conveys associations of wit, refinement, perceptiveness, and lofty
detachment.[10] (On rarer occasions, "*qing*" also refers to moral incor-
ruptibility, as in *SS* 1.27.)

However, there are also deeper continuities between Pure Critique
and Pure Conversation. Both share a keen rhetorical awareness. Pure
Conversation is obviously premised on the delight with words. Leaders
of Pure Critique are also renowned rhetoricians, sometimes noted for
their style and beauty (e.g., Guo Tai 郭泰, Fu Rong 符融).[11] (It is perhaps no accident that *Shishuo* begins with anecdotes about Chen Fan
陳藩, Li Ying 李膺 (110–169), and Guo Tai—the heroes of *qingyi* enter
the world that is to be dominated by *qingtan*.) Both participate in the
tradition of an abiding fascination with evaluating character. Like the
system of using local recommendations for office (*chaju* 察舉), based on
reputations of moral exemplarity, the vociferous protests of the students of the imperial academy focus on the proper employment of talent (*yongren* 用人) in government. One of the leaders of Pure Critique,
Guo Tai, was famous for his uncanny discernment and judgment of
people.[12] Notwithstanding the overt preoccupation with philosophical
subjects in Pure Conversation, the evaluation of characters through
their performance is always the stated or implicit concern, as Nanxiu
Qian demonstrates in her recent study of *Shishuo xinyu*.[13] (In some
cases, a person's competence in evaluating characters becomes the
venue whereby he is judged [e.g., *SS* 8.119, 9.7]). Here the criteria of
judgment rest not only on talent and moral character, but also on
appearance, eloquence, and stylistic flair. The aesthetic dimensions of
understanding language and human character in *Shishuo* thus have historical roots in political purpose. Moreover, political reality is sometimes merely masked or repressed in the aestheticized life of the Wei-Jin
elite. Chen Yinke 陳寅恪 points out, for example, that in the earlier

phase of Pure Conversation (mid- to late third century), philosophical positions were enmeshed in conflicting loyalties to the Cao 曹 and Sima 司馬 clans (and the respective ruling classes they represented) in the Wei-Jin dynastic transition.[14] More broadly, one may say that even in cases of deliberate unconcern with politics, the issue remained one of coveted membership in the cultural-intellectual elite and ranking therein.[15] (The term "one of us" [*wobei* 我輩], usually used to express approbation, best captures this sense of cultural community.) Aesthetic self-consciousness in *Shishuo* unfolds as an escape from or defiance of violent political reality and as a struggle with ethical-political categories of significance. Indeed, these are issues that not only inform the content of *Shishuo*, but might also have motivated its compilation. Shen Yue 沈約 wrote in his biography of Liu Yiqing in *Song shu* 宋書 (History of the Song): "From his youth he excelled as a horseman. By the time he was older, because of the difficulties and perils in the ways of the world (*shilu jiannan* 世路艱難), he no longer rode horses. He summoned and brought together literary men, who came from far and near." Zhou Yiliang 周一良 opines that the cryptic phrase "*shilu jiannan*" may refer to suspicions from Liu Yiqing's cousin, Emperor Wen 宋文帝 (Liu Yilong 劉義隆, r. 424–453), potential political persecution, and the general climate of distrust, danger, and insecurity in the (Liu) Song court.[16] Horsemanship suggests martial aspirations and perhaps political ambitions, and Liu Yiqing renounced it to become instead a literary patron.

At this juncture, a cursory comparison may be instructive. Terry Eagleton observes the following regarding the European tradition: "Aesthetics is born as a discourse of the body. In its original formulation by the German philosopher Alexander Baumgarten, the term refers not in the first place to art, but, as the Greek *aisthesis* would suggest, to the whole region of human perception and sensation, in contrast to the more rarefied domain of conceptual thought. The distinction which the term 'aesthetic' initially enforces in the mid-eighteenth century is not one between 'art' and 'life,' but between material and immaterial."[17] In the Chinese context, the discourse of beauty also arises from defining and refining human perception and sensation, but it registers contradistinction with the political realm rather than conceptual or metaphysical thought. It is interesting to note that in *Shishuo* abstruse philosophical discussions actually provide the occasions for dwelling on the concrete particulars of human form, speech, and behavior. One may say that the discourse of the body joins forces with rarefied conceptual thought to confront the volatility and dangers of political life. This merging becomes evident when we examine the presentation of Pure Conversation in *Shishuo*.

Surface as Meaning

Form is content and surface is meaning in accounts of Pure Conversation in *Shishuo*. Historians have combed through the book for its wealth of information on intellectual currents and philosophical debates (especially Abstruse Learning [Xuanxue 玄學], the discourse on names and principles [*mingli* 明理], and eclectic fusion of Confucianism and Daoism and of Daoism and Buddhism) and on the sociopolitical history of the period covered by the *Shishuo*. But the form of Pure Conversation is no less important. Time and again Pure Conversation is presented as an all-too-earnest mode of competition, wherein the spectacle of confrontation takes precedence over ideological differences:

> Sun Sheng 孫盛 (302–373) went to Yin Hao's 殷浩 (306–356) house, where they had a discussion (*gonglun* 共論). Going back and forth, their exchanges were hairsplitting (*jing* 精) and unrelenting (*ku* 苦). There was no interstice in the arguments between host and guest. The attendants brought in food, which grew cold and was rewarmed three or four times. Both sides in their excitement threw down their sambar-tail chowries (*zhuwei* 麈尾), whose hair completely fell off all over the food.[18] Guest and host thus went on until nightfall, forgetting to eat. Yin then said to Sun, "Don't you be a stubborn-mouthed horse, or I will pierce your nose!" Sun retorted, "Haven't you seen oxen with broken noses! People will pierce your cheeks" (*SS* 4.31)!

The fervor of the conversationalists culminates in mutual insults, comic echoes of the wit and subtlety that supposedly characterize such exchanges.[19] Both compare their opponents to animals that have to be tamed, and both spin deliberately incongruous metaphors of subjugation: thus oxen, not horses have their noses pierced, and oxen never have pierced cheeks (the idea is that particularly recalcitrant animals have to be roped in through pierced cheeks). Presentations of fierce competition are heightened by military metaphors and the comparisons of attack and defense of arguments to strategies in warfare (*SS* 2.70, 4.26, 4.34, 4.51).[20] In some other instances, participants subsume agonistic momentum to conviviality, studied informality, deliberate nonchalance, and playful seriousness (or serious playfulness), although the concern with rank and evaluation is omnipresent.

As the term itself indicates, "Pure Conversation" or "pure words" *(qingyan)* is a mode of expression, exchange, and interaction. (Other terms for "pure conversation," such as "mutual discussion" [*gonglun* 共論] and "mutual conversation" [*gongtan* 共談], also point to the sense of community and exploratory disquisition.) Late Warring States and Han genealogies of exegetical, textual, and philosophical traditions proclaim and transmit self-evident truths; master-disciple dialogues leave little doubt regarding the locus of authority. Textual authority is combined with political authority in Han scholarly debates in which the emperor presided (e.g., the discussions preserved in *Debates on Salt and Iron* [*Yantie lun* 鹽鐵論], *Comprehensive Discussions in the White Tiger Hall* [*Baihu tongde lun* 白虎通德論]). By contrast, with Pure Conversation in *Shishuo*, truth is mediated through performance, open to debate and manipulation.[21] Pure Conversation is conducted like a game—for the duration of the game hierarchies of age and rank are temporarily suspended, and mastery of the rules of the game rather than the content of an argument is the focus of attention.

Accounts of Pure Conversation in *Shishuo* dwell more on the contexts of performance; the ranking and evaluation of the participants; the speaker's style, appearance, wit, and eloquence; and the audience's reaction than on the content of arguments (which more often than not is passed over in silence.) Pure Conversation is an aesthetic spectacle. Chapter 14, "Appearance and Style" (Rongzhi 容止), contains many entries on the beauty of the conversationalists. (Indeed, *Shishuo* celebrates male beauty much more insistently than female beauty.)[22] "Wang Yan's 王衍 (256–311) appearance was impeccably beautiful, and he excelled in discoursing on abstruse matters. He constantly gripped a sambar-tail chowry with a white jade handle that was completely indistinguishable from his hand" (*SS* 14.8). Pure Conversation also aspires to the harmony of sounds and the effect of music. Wang Meng 王濛 (309–347) compares his competence in pure conversation with Liu Tan's 劉惔 (311–347): "For sheer musical effect and elegant phrasings, he's not equal to me; but when it comes to speaking out directly and hitting the mark, he surpasses me" (*SS* 9.48). Pei Xia's

裴遐 (fl. ca. 300) subtle reasoning is described as "clear and pure like the notes of the *qin* and zither 泠然若琴瑟" (see Liu Jun's 劉峻 commentary in *SS* 4.19).[23]

The primacy of form is most evident when conversationalists switch sides or take up roles.[24] The represented audience in *Shishuo* is often capable of appreciating opposed positions. On one occasion we are told that "together they [i.e., the audience] marveled and lingered over the beauty of the performance from both sides, without the slightest discrimination regarding the content of their respective arguments" (*SS* 4.40). By the same token, many anecdotes in *Shishuo* celebrate sophistry and equivocation. Chapter 2, "Speeches and Conversations" (Yanyu 言語) contains many instances of clever and witty language (*qiaoyan* 巧言), retorts of precocious children who outwit adults, skillful self-defense or self-justification (sometimes by a person obviously at fault), and artful insults. The shift from political to aesthetic concerns is obvious: the most common category of speeches in historiography, remonstrances that enumerate moral principles of good government or strategic calculations, is conspicuously absent.[25] Instead the chapter delights in clever words (often by children), which deftly defend opposite positions:

> When Zhong Yu 鍾毓 and his younger brother Zhong Hui 鍾會 were small, it happened once that as their father was taking a siesta, they used the opportunity to steal a draught of medicinal wine. At the time their father was awake, but feigned sleep in order to observe them. Yu bowed and then drank. Hui drank without bowing. Afterwards their father asked Yu why he bowed. Yu said, "Wine is used for completing the rites; I wouldn't dare not bow." He also asked Hui why he did not bow. Hui said, "Theft is basically offending ritual propriety; that was why I did not bow" (*SS* 2.12).[26]

The lighthearted, bantering tone here conceals a more fundamental and persistent concern with the wit, beauty, and internal logic of an argument rather than irrefutable truths, which also unfold in the conventions of Pure Conversation.

> He Yan 何晏 (ca. 190–249) was serving as president of the Board of Civil Office (240–249) and enjoyed both status and acclaim. Conversationalists often thronged the seats of his home. Wang Bi 王弼 (226–249), who was

not yet twenty, went to visit him. Yan had heard of Bi's name, and thus enumerated to Bi the best arguments from past conversations, saying: "These arguments I consider to be ultimate. Still can you counter (*nan* 難) them?" Bi thereupon made counter-arguments, and all present considered Yan defeated. Bi then went on, himself taking up the roles of "host" and "guest" for several rounds 自為客主數番.[27] In every case he was unequaled by anyone else in the whole company (*SS* 4.6).

Wang Bi displays his erudition and rhetorical skills by "taking up the roles of 'host' and 'guest' for several rounds." Role playing might have meant defending opposite positions with equal dexterity. Obviously the issue is not truth or conviction but compelling performance. The force of this anecdote depends on a reversal of expectations: the crowd of conversationalists (*tanke* 談客), drawn by He Yan's fame and position, end up applauding the much younger and less distinguished Wang Bi. Formal conventions of the game of words make possible the momentary abeyance of sociopolitical and generational hierarchies. Perhaps this is why *Shishuo* delights in accounts of precocity.[28]

Later instances of Pure Conversation have more in common with wine games and occasional poetry than with philosophical debates.

Zhi Dun 支遁 (314–366), Xu Xun 許詢 (fl. fourth century), Xie An 謝安 (320–385), all of exalted virtue, gathered together at Wang Meng's house. Xie looked around and said to all present, "Today is what might be called a distinguished assembly. Time of course cannot be made to stand still, and this gathering also is difficult to sustain. We should speak or intone poems to let flow what's on our mind." Xu then asked the host whether he had a copy of *Zhuang Zi* 莊子. It so happened that he had one chapter, "The Fisherman" 漁父. Xie saw that title and asked all present to write an exposition of it. Zhi Dun was the first to do so, using more than seven hundred words. The style of his disquisition was refined and beautiful, his talent and eloquence were wonderful and awe-inspiring. Everyone commended him. Thereupon each of those present told what was on their mind. Xie asked, "Have you exhausted your meanings?" They all said, "What we have said today seems not quite to have unfolded to the limit." Xie then raised a few general counter-arguments, wherewith he developed his own meanings, and wrote more than ten thousand words. The acuity of his talent is graceful and transcendent. Not only was it difficult to dispute his arguments, he had in addition put his mind and spirit in them

意氣擬托, as he reveled in free and easy expression. There was no one present who was not satisfied in his mind 饜心. Zhi said to Xie, "From beginning to end you rushed on relentlessly 一往奔詣, without any doubt you are the best" (*SS* 4.55).

Philosophical exposition answers the need for expression of thoughts and feelings (*xiehuai* 寫懷); in that sense it shares the same burden as poetry. Xie An's appeal to mutability (the ineluctable passage of time, the doubtful repeatability of the gathering of fine minds) reminds the reader of Wang Xizhi's 王羲之 (303–361 or 321–379) famous preface to "The Gathering at Orchid Pavilion" 蘭亭集序. The specification of topic or title seems to be incidental (although the choice of *Zhuang Zi* is not), comparable to the decision on a rhyme (*nianyun* 拈韻) in later poetry gatherings. Whether "words can exhaust meaning" (*yan jin yi* 言盡意) was one of the major philosophical problems of the time;[29] here the issue comes up in an affective, occasional context—Xie An asks whether the present company has managed to fully express their thoughts and feelings. Again we learn little about the content of the arguments. Instead the focus is on the style of eloquence, the flow of moods, and the reactions of the audience. The expression of ideas has a distinctly sensory and emotive dimension. Xie An excels because he revels in the pleasure of free and easy expression (*xiaoran zide* 蕭然自得). Inasmuch as his words apparently suffice as vehicles for his "mind and spirit" (*yiqi* 意氣), he is responding through performance and self-expression (rather than purely discursive modes) to the query or challenge he poses his guests: "Have you exhausted your meanings?" The approval of his guests is conveyed with a word (*yan* 饜) that also means satisfied hunger in other contexts.

Lest it be misunderstood that the present discussion trivializes the intellectual achievements of the period, I hasten to add that "formalism" denotes not paucity or irrelevance of content but heightened awareness of how ideas have expressive, affective, and almost somatic dimensions, and how formal conventions—the rules that allow free play—define intention, articulation, and perception.[30] It is interesting to note that the most important thinkers of the period, such as Wang Bi and Guo Xiang 郭象, appear only in a few entries in *Shishuo*. It is as if the *Shishuo* compilers are more interested in how ideas enter the realm of aestheticized existence; hence the more extensive coverage of lesser thinkers from later periods. (Of course availability of sources and acci-

dents of transmission may also explain why there is less material on
Wei figures such as Wang Bi than on Jin conversationalists.) The monk
Zhi Dun is an instructive example. Zhi Dun is one of the most prominent characters in *Shishuo*, appearing in about forty-eight entries.[31] We
learn little about the content of his thoughts from *Shishuo*.[32] We see
him matching wits with other worthies of the time, judging others, and
being evaluated in his turn. (Despite a by and large positive portrait, we
also have entries on how he is maligned, even as he insulted some other
characters.) Zhi Dun wins his place in center stage because he exem-
plifies how religious understanding squares with the persona of the
"unconventional gentleman" or "renowned gentleman" (*mingshi* 名士).
His contemporaries note possible incongruities:

> Wang Tanzhi 王坦之 (330–375) was not recognized by Zhi Dun, and
> accordingly composed a treatise on "Why a Sramana Is Not Capable of
> Becoming a Lofty Gentleman." Broadly, it maintained that a lofty gentle-
> man (*gaoshi* 高士) gives his mind free rein, harmonious and joyful, while
> the sramana, although claiming to be beyond earthly ties, is on the con-
> trary constrained by teachings and cannot be said to freely let feelings and
> dispositions come into their own (*SS* 26.25).

Zhi Dun's unconventional interests (e.g., in horses [*SS* 2.63] and
cranes [*SS* 2.76]), worldliness (he is teased for "buying a mountain
to become a recluse" 買山而隱 [*SS* 25.28]), perceptiveness, aesthetic
sensibility (he excels in philosophical poetry [*xuanyan shi* 玄言詩], landscape poetry [*shanshui shi* 山水詩], and calligraphy), and total immer-
sion in the game of defining and ranking characters render him less
than transcendent as a religious figure, but it is precisely such inconsis-
tencies that earn him a place in *Shishuo*.[33] In other words, *Shishuo* is
concerned less with ideas per se than with the relationship between
ideas and aestheticized existence.

Indeed, the life of an idea in *Shishuo* may sometimes be understood
as a historical process of aestheticization. We may compare two anecdotes on reconciling Confucian and Daoist thought:

> When Wang Bi was barely twenty he went to visit Pei Hui 裴徽 (fl. 230–
> 249). Hui asked him, "For non-being is indeed that which the myriad
> things draw upon, but the Sage was unwilling to give his word on it, while
> Lao Zi expounded it endlessly. Why?" Bi said, "The sage embodied non-

being. But non-being cannot be taught; his words therefore by necessity deal with being. Lao Zi and Zhuang Zi cannot escape [the realm of] being, hence they constantly teach about that in which they feel a deficiency (*SS* 4.8).[34]

Ruan Xiu 阮脩 (ca. 270–312) had an excellent reputation. The grand marshal, Wang Yan, went to visit him and asked, "Are the *Lao Zi* and *Zhuang Zi* the same as, or different from, the Sage's teachings?" He replied, "Perchance they are the same (*jiang wu tong* 將無同)?" The grand marshal liked his answer and appointed him his aide, so in his day he was known as "the Three-Word-Aide." Wei Jie 衛玠 (d. 312) teased him about this, saying, "For only one word you still would have been appointed. Why bother with three?" Ruan replied, "If one is what people in the world look up to, then for no words at all one can be appointed. Why even bother with one word?" Whereupon they became fast friends (*SS* 4.18).[35]

Wang Bi's ingenious exposition ranks Confucius (the Sage) above Lao Zi and Zhuang Zi but perversely claims that the Sage embodies nonbeing. By appealing to the concept that "words do not exhaust meaning" (*yan bu jin yi* 言不盡意), Wang Bi subsumes both Confucian and Daoist thought to primary, ineffable nonbeing. Confucius emerges as the supreme Daoist sage whose silence on the subject of "nonbeing" testifies to his higher understanding, compared to Lao Zi, whose teachings on "nonbeing" paradoxically become proof of his deficiency. Scholars have devoted much attention to analyzing Wang Bi's reply in the context of fusing or reconciling moral teaching (*mingjiao* 名教) and naturalness (*ziran* 自然).[36] This project has in turn been linked to the Cao and Sima clans' political rivalry and, more broadly, the need for champions of Daoist "naturalism" to justify holding office and pursuing ambitions. Ruan Xiu's three words also belong to the same tradition of mediating the differences between Confucian and Daoist thought (*hui tong Kong Lao* 會通孔老). But his manner of expression deserves special attention. The expression "*jiang wu tong*" laces basic affirmation of sameness with a sense of not wishing to be overhasty or too insistent.[37] Ruan is defining a philosophical position by articulating his lingering tentativeness, sense of distance, and willingness to negotiate differences. If Ruan implies the essential sameness of Confucian and Daoist thought, then indeed one word, "*tong*" 同, would have sufficed, as Wei Jie quips. Ruan counters by going beyond one word to silence—the issue is how one is perceived and respected, not the articulation of an opinion. Using gestures of uncertainty, playfulness, brevity, and silence, Ruan and Wei dramatize in their exchange the proposition of words being inadequate to meanings, the beginning premise of Wang Bi's reconciliation of Confucian and Daoist thought. In thus matching wits (both trying to go one step beyond the other), Ruan and Wei recognize their affinities as kindred spirits. In the last analysis, this anecdote is less about the philosophical implications of *jiang wu tong* than about friendship, affinities and mutual appreciation, philosophical expression as aesthetic gesture, and giving an opinion while rising above it at the same time.

More generally, the eclecticism of the period may be in part explained by the primacy of form. Arbitrators who can explore common grounds for contending viewpoints are praised (e.g., *SS* 4.9). As Han Bo 韓伯 puts it, "There is neither 'may' nor 'may not'" (*wu ke wu buke* 無可無不可) (*SS* 2.72). The ideal personality encompasses opposites. On the "free spirits" of his day who flaunt their audaciousness and unrestraint by such extreme measures as going naked, Yue Guang 樂廣 (252–304) famously comments: "There is a place for pleasure in Moral Teaching—why go to such lengths!" (*SS* 1.23). He Yan and Wang Bi, among others, are renowned for their efforts to mediate differences between Confucian and Daoist teachings. There is also important (and in some ways more expected) crossfertilization of Daoist and Buddhist thought. The monk Zhi Dun, for example, uses Buddhist doctrines to interpret *Zhuang Zi* and draws upon Daoist ideas to explain Buddhism.[38] As presented in *Shishuo*, modes of performance, techniques of debate and discussion, implicit and open competition, self-conscious and vigilant evaluation—down to the fine art of insulting and putting down one's opponents—underlie intellectual discourse of the day, irrespective of ideological content.[39] The pleasure in eloquence facilitates appreciation and mediation of differences:

> Various renowned gentlemen (of the Western Jin court) went together to the Lo River on a pleasure excursion (*xi* 戲). On their return, Yue Guang asked Wang Yan, "Was today's excursion pleasurable?" Wang said, "Pei Wei excels in discourses about Names and Principles (*mingli* 名理), his words gushed forth in a torrent, yet with a refined poise 混混有雅致; Zhang Hua 張華 (232–300) discussed the *Shi ji* 史記 (Records of the Grand Historian) and *Han shu* 漢書 (History of the Han), and, his words, gentle

and beguiling, were well-worth listening 靡靡可聽; Wang Rong 王戎 (234–305) and I talked about Ji Zha 季扎 and Zhang Liang 張良; our words too were transcendent, with an abstruse remoteness 超超玄著 (*SS* 2.23).

The philosophical positions of the participants and their subject matter are widely divergent. Pei Wei authored the treatise "In Praise of Actuality," which attacked proponents of "nonbeing" such as Wang Yan.[40] Here Wang Yan just admires how Pei's forcefulness (gushing torrent of words) is tempered by refined poise. Historical writings, usually prized for inspiring moral vigilance, are here appreciated as engrossing narratives. Wang Yan and Wang Rong dwell on historical characters famous for traversing boundaries of commitment and withdrawal.[41] There is a consistent emphasis on a disinterested appreciation of the beauty of ideas and verbal expression; perhaps this accounts for the ideal of a graceful balance between calm poise and rousing fervor, between engagement and detachment in the style of both personality and eloquence.

Perception as Action

If surface is meaning, then perception is tantamount to action. The acts and ways of seeing, often self-consciously registered in *Shishuo*, have very tangible consequences.

> When Wei Jie was going down (in 312) from Yuzhang 豫章 to the capital (Jianye 建業), people had long since heard of his reputation, and onlookers were lined up along the road like a wall. Jie had previously suffered from an emaciating illness and his body could not bear exertion. He thereupon became sick and died. At the time it was said that people had "stared Wei Jie to death 看殺衛玠" (*SS* 14.19).[42]

In another anecdote Wei Jie is said to have fallen sick and died after a particularly absorbing bout of "subtle conversation" (*weiyan* 微言) with Xie Kun 謝琨 (280–322) that lasted from evening until dawn (*SS* 4.20). One may regard Wei Jie as a kind of "aesthetic hero" whose frail frame cannot bear the burden of his beauty, excessive feelings, intellectual curiosity, and spiritual refinement.[43] In the world of *Shishuo*, Wei Jie is either being looked at (and evaluated) or is himself looking upon scenes that overwhelm him with emotions. The story about him being "stared to death" is historically implausible but aesthetically fitting.

Perception is linked to evaluating character, a pervasive and all-consuming activity in *Shishuo*. As mentioned above, *Shishuo* belongs to a long tradition of discerning and judging human character (*renlun jianshi* 人倫鑒識). What is new here is a heightened self-consciousness about the act of seeing (its nature, functions, contexts, consequences). The first four chapters of *Shishuo*—"Virtuous Conduct" (Dexing 德行), "Speeches and Conversations," "Affairs of State" (Zhengshi 政事), and "Letters and Scholarship" (Wenxue 文學)—correspond to the four branches of Confucian learning (*Kongmen sike* 孔門四科). Compared to their original meanings in the *Analects*, however, we see a much greater emphasis on perception and apprehension. The first chapter, for example, is deeply concerned with "visible virtue"—how the virtuous person is seen, appraised, understood, and sought after. For a ruler to earnestly and assiduously seek out sages (*qiuxian* 求賢) to aid in government is a recurrent topos traceable to Warring States writings. Alluding to this tradition, Chen Fan compares his desire to meet Xu Zhi 徐穉 (97–168) with King Wu's 周武王 quest for the sage Shang Rong 商容 (*SS* 1.1). But there are other examples of "quest for the sage" that have a distinctly individual dimension, where the focus is on how a person is affected by or transformed through the apprehension of virtue. In many cases, we have an interlocutor or a commentator who passes judgment on a character's virtuous conduct. There are arguments about how to compare and evaluate virtue and playful exchanges on "the worth of virtue."[44] Wang Yi 王乂 rewarded Zu Na 祖納 (late third century) with two slave girls and a minor official position for having served his mother with filial devotion. Someone teased Zu Na: "So the price of a male slave is twice that of a female slave?" Zu replied, "Must Boli Xi 百里奚 be worth less than five sheepskins?" (*SS* 1.26). Virtue is validated only through acknowledgment.

> While Ruan Yu 阮裕 (ca. 300–360) was in Shan 剡 (Zhejiang), he owned a fine carriage. For anyone who asked to borrow it he never failed to make it available. There was one man who was burying his mother and who had it in mind to borrow it but did not dare speak to him. Ruan, hearing of it later, sighed and said, "If I own a carriage and make people not dare to borrow it, what's the use of having a carriage?" Whereupon he burned it (*SS* 1.32).

Ruan Yu burns the carriage not to atone for his lack of generosity, but for the fact that it is not immediately obvious. With this extravagant and in some ways totally pointless act of destruction, Ruan demonstrates his indifference to his possessions. What was previously imperceptible has to be ostentatiously displayed as compensatory gesture. On the other side, the ability to appraise virtue or talent is itself of supreme importance, but recognition is also like a game or implicit competition.[45] To be recognized for one's superior qualities and yet to project the impression of being unfathomable is to emerge as winner in this game. Hence reticence and imperturbability are lauded—the virtues beyond understanding and language are the highest (e.g., *SS* 1.7, 1.15, 1.16, and most of the entries in chapter 6, "Depth and Tolerance" [Yaliang 雅量]).

Chapters 7, 8, and 9 are explicitly devoted to the evaluation of character. Whereas chapter 7, "Discernment and Judgment" (Shijian 識鑒), still develops the conventional topos of recognition (such as abounds in historical writings), chapters 8 and 9 ("Appreciation and Praise" [Shangyu 賞譽] and "Classification of Talent" [Pinzao 品藻]) use new vocabularies and conceptual categories to evaluate human beings.[46] Anecdotes in "Discernment and Judgment" typically describe how a judgment made at an early point in a person's life or in an unfolding situation is borne out by later developments. A prescient character makes correct predictions by reading small signs and early clues. In other words, these anecdotes are premised on duration, often bringing together two points in time. The context is often political, military, or historical, emphasizing both the role of characters in historical events and the importance of judgment in the fate of a person and of the country. By contrast, chapters 8 and 9 deal not with duration but with the moment. They present impressions of talent, virtue, and sensibility, sometimes with concrete images from other spheres of existence, and they are less concerned with the political consequences of a person's character and actions. We are squarely in the realm of aesthetic pleasure. To illustrate the differences between these categories of judgment, we turn to contrary evaluations of Wang Yan, a major figure in *Shishuo*:

When Wang Yan's father, Wang Yi, was serving as General Pacifying the North (272), there was a public affair for which he sent an envoy, whose intercessions brought no result. At the time Wang Yan was in the capital. Ordering his carriage, he went to see his uncle, the vice-president of the

Imperial Secretariat, Yang Hu 羊祜 (221–278), and the president of the
Board of Civil Office, Shan Tao 山濤 (205–283). At the time Yan was only
a young lad with his hair in tufts, but his appearance and ability were outstanding and unusual. Since the impact of his presentation was refreshing,
and the content was, moreover, well-reasoned, Shan Tao greatly marveled
at him. Even upon Yan's withdrawal, Tao did not stop gazing after him. At
last he sighed and said, "If one were to have a son, shouldn't he be like
Wang Yan?" Yang Hu rejoined, "The one who will bring about disorder in
the realm is certainly this boy" (SS 7.5).[47]

Wang Dao 王導 (276–339) characterized (mu 目) the grand marshal,
Wang Yan, as follows: "Craggy, untainted peaks, towering high like a wall
of eight thousand feet 巖巖清峙壁立千仞" (SS 8.37).

Whereas the first anecdote is concerned with Wang Yan's historical
role, takes an overview of his entire career, and credits Yang Hu with
prescience, the second one focuses on a moment of magnificence, the
style of Wang Yan's appearance and personality at the moment it is
observed by Wang Dao. The fact that Gu Kaizhi's 顧愷之 (ca. 345–ca.
406) inscription on his portrait of Wang Yan uses almost the same
wording underlines the aesthetic dimension of Wang Dao's remarks:
they focus on appearance and yet claim to proceed to essence by drawing on analogies from nature.[48] Wang Yan's beauty, wit, eloquence, and
judgment are repeatedly celebrated in Shishuo; at the same time, Yang
Hu's indictment of Wang Yan and what he stands for are sporadically
echoed in other condemnations of the presumed negligence and moral
decadence brought about by the cultural attitudes associated with Pure
Conversation.

The special term for the apprehension and appreciation typified by
Wang Dao's evaluation of Wang Yan is "mu" 目 or "timu" 題目, which,
perhaps because of its specific associations with aesthetic contemplation, recurs in chapters 8 and 9 but does not appear even once in chapter 7.[49] The term "mu" implies visual focus, deliberation, and felicitous
verbal expression that capture the essence of a person or a spectacle. In
this wealth of formulations, evaluative statements that bring together
the natural world and the human realm are among the most interesting.
Many scholars have noted how heightened awareness of the beauty
of nature and appraisal of human character are parallel developments
in this period and how each draws on the vocabulary of the other.[50]

Responses to nature are self-consciously registered and savored.[51] Some anecdotes paint a web of sympathetic resonance or stimuli-responses, bringing together nature and human beings in a harmonious continuum: "Wang Ji 王濟 and Sun Chu 孫楚 were both boasting about the beauties of his native place and the people there. Wang said, "Our land is level and plain, the rivers limpid and clear, the people modest and true." Sun responded, "Our mountains tower tall and craggy, the rivers are mud-roiled, with tossing waves, the people rock-rugged, with heroes aplenty" (*SS* 2.24).

Landscape acquires dimensions of human character. Xie Wan 謝萬 (321–361) says of the Lake of Crooked Banks: "Undoubtedly it is profoundly filled and quietly limpid, receptive and not flowing on" (*SS* 2.77). This is the natural correlative of the lauded human qualities of calmness, poise, tolerance, and imperturbability. Conversely, human character, appearance, speech, and emotions are appraised through the prism of nature. Guo Tai said of Huang Xian 黃憲 (second century): "Huang Xian is boundless, like an expanse of water of ten thousand hectares. Purify the water, and it will not become clearer; disturb it, and it will not become muddy. His capacity is deep and broad, and it is difficult to fathom" (*SS* 1.3).[52] "The world regarded Li Ying as rousing like the wind beneath indomitable pines" (*SS* 8.2). "Someone asked chancellor Wang Dao, 'How would you rate Zhou Yi 周顗 (269–322) in comparison with He Qiao 和嶠 (d. 292)?' The chancellor replied, 'He Qiao is craggier'" (*SS* 9.16). The world regarded Zhou Yi as "unscalable as a sheer cliff" (*SS* 8.56). Shan Tao said of Ji Kang 嵇康 (223–262), "Ji Shuye 嵇叔夜 carries himself majestically, like a solitary pine tree standing alone. When he is drunk, he lets go like a jade mountain about to collapse" (*SS* 14.5). Wang Yan described Pei Kai 裴楷 (237–291) in his illness: "His two twin pupils flashed like lightning beneath a cliff 閃閃如巖下電, and his spirit (*jingshen* 精神) moved vigorously 挺動" (*SS* 14.10).[53] Zhi Dun's "style and eloquence were fresh and wonderful, like flowers blooming in dazzling sunlight 花爛映發" (*SS* 4.36).[54] Gu Kaizhi describes his grief over Huan Wen's 桓溫 (312–373) death with metaphors of unruly nature:

> Gu Kaizhi bowed at Huan Wen's grave, and composed the following verse: "The mountain has crumbled, the boundless sea runs dry; / The fishes and birds—on what will they rely?" Someone asked him, "Since you esteemed and depended on Huan Wen so much, may we know of the manner of

your mourning?" Gu replied, "My nose was like the long wind over the northern plains; / My eyes like a dammed-up river bursting forth." Or (according to another source) he said, "My voice was like reverberating thunder smashing the mountains; / My tears like an overturned river flooding the sea" (*SS* 2.95).

We have here framed nature—a scene distilled through perception and imagination—what Xu Fuguan 徐復觀 terms "mediated nature" (*di'er ziran* 第二自然).[55] This mediation is more evident when metaphorical significance is subsumed under sensory perception. For example, when Zong Cheng 宗承 (d. ca. 230) refuses to befriend Cao Cao 曹操 and claims that "the intent of pines (*songbo zhi zhi* 松柏之志) still remains" (*SS* 2.5), he is simply using the pine tree as a metaphor for uncompromising integrity. But note Yu Ai's 庾敳 (262–311) characterization of He Qiao (d. 292): "Dense and imposing, like a thousand-*zhang* pine 森森如千丈松. Though gnarled and full of knots 磊砢有節目, if used for a large building, it may serve as a beam or a pillar" (*SS* 8.15). This comparison goes beyond a direct analogy between the tall pine as pillar and human integrity to an aesthetic appreciation for its imposing beauty (*sensen* 森森) and gnarled, knotted state.[56] Extended metaphors are more likely to have paraphraseable meanings subsumed under sensory impressions:

> A guest once asked Chen Chen 陳諶 (fl. ca. 130–200), "What achievements and virtues does your father (Chen Shi 陳寔 [104–187]) have that he bears such an honorable reputation throughout the realm?" Chen Chen said, "My father is like a cassia tree growing on the slopes of Mt. Tai. Above there is a height of ten thousand *ren*, and below, an unfathomable depth. Above it is sprinkled with sweet dew; below it is watered by deep springs. At such a moment, how can the cassia tree know the height of Mt. Tai or the depth of the springs? I do not know if he has any achievements and virtues or not" (*SS* 1.7).

Chen Chen manages to counter the slightly skeptical overtones of his interlocutor's question (he seems to imply that Chen's father has a reputation greater than what he deserves) by painting the image of lofty and profound virtue not fathomable by the being it nourishes. Chen Chen thus seems to be comparing himself to the cassia tree and his father to Mount Tai (matching biological filiation with botanical development). Alternatively, Chen Chen may be implying that his father's virtues and achievements are nourished by mysterious, profound resources. Inasmuch as his greatness is natural, inevitable, and unself-conscious, he cannot fathom it himself. In both cases, nature as metaphor for the impossibility of understanding becomes secondary to the grandeur and sublime resonance of the image evoked.[57]

On some occasions the aesthetic contemplation of nature shades effortlessly into an appraisal of human character. "Liu Tan said, 'In a fresh breeze under the bright moon I always think of Xu Xun'" (*SS* 2.77). A magical moment of renewal and purification in nature makes Wang Gong 王恭 (d. 398) think of his estranged clansman Wang Chen 王忱 (d. 392): "At the time clear dewdrops were gleaming in the early morning light, and the new leaves of the paulownia were just beginning to unfold 清露晨流新桐初引. Gong gazed at (*mu* 目) them and said, 'Wang Chen is surely just as cleansed and shining 濯濯!'" (*SS* 8.153). While Liu Tan's remark involves relatively straightforward analogy, Wang Gong's exclamation suggests involuntary association and the transformative powers of perception—being able to see beauty in nature allows him to overcome his negative judgment of Wang Chen.

That perception implies framing and distillation is most evident in pleasing descriptions of what is conventionally held to be ugly. Liu Tan regards Huan Wen's "temples bristling like a rolled-up hedgehog's hide, and eyebrows as pointed as the corners of amethyst stones" as signs of greatness.[58] "Liu Ling's 劉伶 (d. after 265) person was but six *chi* tall, and his appearance was extremely homely and haggard. Yet detached and carefree 悠悠忽忽, he treated his bodily frame like so much earth or wood 土木形骸" (*SS* 14.13). "Yu Ai's height was not quite seven *chi*, yet the girdle at his waist measured ten double spans (*wei*). With reckless abandon he let himself go 頹然自放" (*SS* 14.17). As with deformed transcendents in *Zhuang Zi*, physical ugliness is more than redeemed by sublime indifference and becomes the wherewithal of spiritual freedom. The burden of aesthetic creation is precisely the transcendence of mere resemblance: "Gu Kaizhi was fond of painting people's likenesses. He wanted to make a picture of Yin Zhongkan 殷仲堪 (d. 399/400), but the latter said, 'My form is ugly; just don't bother.' Gu replied, 'Your excellency said so only because of your eye. But I would brightly dot the pupil, and then with "flying white" (*feibai* 飛白) gently brush over it, making it like light clouds veiling the sun'" (*SS* 21.11).

In thus rendering Yin's physical blemish with a beautiful image (again borrowed from nature), Gu Kaizhi is claiming that a painting should express the subject's spirit or essence (*chuanshen* 傳神) rather than simply reproduce the external form and contour.[59] The focus on vision (or loss thereof) is typical. Other anecdotes on Gu Kaizhi's art in chapter 21, "Skill and Art" (Qiaoyi 巧藝)—numbering six out of four-teen—also deal mostly with vision, perception, the eyes, and the spirit:

> Gu Kaizhi painted Pei Kai, and added three hairs to his cheek. When someone asked why, Gu replied, "Pei Kai was outstanding and luminous (*junlang* 儁朗), and possessed great powers of perception (*shiju* 識具). This is precisely to show his powers of perception." Those who looked at the painting pondered this, and actually did feel that with the added three hairs the figure seemed to have spirit and illumination (*shenming* 神明), far exceeding its state before they had been applied (*SS* 21.9).

> Gu Kaizhi painted Xie Kun among crags and rocks. When someone asked why he did so, Gu replied, "Xie said, 'When it comes to a hill or a vale, I consider myself superior.' This man should be placed among hills and vales" (*SS* 21.12).[60]

> Gu Kaizhi would paint a portrait and sometimes not dot the pupils of the eyes for several years. When someone asked his reason, Gu replied, "The beauty or ugliness of the four limbs basically bears no relation to the most subtle part of a painting. What conveys the spirit and portrays the likeness (*chuanshen xiezhao* 傳神寫照) lies precisely in those dots" (*SS* 21.13).[61] Gu Kaizhi said of painting, "To paint 'the hand sweeps over the five-stringed lute' is easy; to paint 'the eyes send off the wild geese returning home' is hard" (*SS* 21.14).[62]

The spirit or essence of a person rises above literal verisimilitude, yet it is conveyed through particular details—most often the eyes' expression, but also an idiosyncratic trait (the three hairs on the cheek) or a setting that functions as an objective correlative of the person's intent and aspirations. In this sense the word "*shen*" 神 (spirit, essence) is integral to the discourse of both transcendence and surface in Chinese aesthetics. On the one hand, "*shen*" is linked to a spiritual under-standing of higher truths. Thus Yu He 庾龢 said to Dai Kui 戴逵 about his painting, "Walking the Buddha Image," "The spirit and illumination of the image are too vulgar (*shenming taisu* 神明太俗), which springs from the fact that your own worldly passions haven't yet ended (*shiqing weijin* 世情未盡)" (*SS* 21.8). Yu thereby merges artistic achievement with religious enlightenment. On the other hand, "*shen*" can be perceived and apprehended only through the particularities of surface details. For example, when Huan Wen says to his nephew Huan Si 桓嗣, "A constant resemblance is a matter of form; an intermittent resemblance is a matter of spirit (*heng si shi xing shi si shi shen* 恆似是形 時似是神)" (*SS* 25.42), or when Wang Huizhi 王徽之 and Xie Wan debate whether Zhi Dun's lack of beard and hair diminishes his "spirit and illumination" (*SS* 25.43), the emphasis is on how "*shen*" can be perceived and appraised through appearance.[63] The word "*shen*" (in various compounds such as "*shenqing*" 神情, "*shenzi*" 神姿, "*shenming*" 神明, "*fengshen*" 丰神, and "*shenmao*" 神貌) recurs in the discourse on human character in *Shishuo* and encompasses the dual concerns with surface and transcendence.[64] Usually translated as "spirit" or "essence" but actually quite untranslatable, the word "*shen*" may be described as the power to apprehend, appreciate, and transcend sensual reality. For example, He Yan claims, "Whenever I take a five-mineral powder, not only does it heal my illness, but I am also aware of my spirit and illumination becoming receptive and fluid (*shenming kailang* 神明開朗)" (*SS* 1.14). The mental-spiritual state he describes implies heightened powers of perception and association, a more intense enjoyment of sensual reality coupled with a sense of detachment. In evaluating character, *Shishuo* is dominated by ideals of detachment (*xu* 虛), remoteness (*yuan* 遠), reticence (*jian* 簡), purity (*qing*), simplicity (*dan* 淡), style or spirit (*feng* 風), limpidity and refinement (*fengliu* 風流), and openness and clarity (*lang* 朗)—words that also become the standard vocabulary in art and literary criticism. Xu Fuguan observes that these words are all related to "*shen*"—in a sense they chart varying modes of the subject's pleasure in and transcendence of sensual reality, such as obtain in the word "*shen*."[65] When the word "*shen*" appears in later literary and aesthetic thought (notably in *Wenxin diaolong*), it is used to describe aesthetic contemplation and the expansive movement of the spirit in the act of creation, often with echoes of access to essence, philosophical transcendence, or religious enlightenment. At the same time, discussions of art and literature from the fourth and fifth centuries are marked by attention to detail, texture, and form. In some ways we are still confronted with the duality of "*shen*" that informs *Shishuo*.

The discourse of transcendence in literary and aesthetic thought has traditionally received much more attention, in part because of its laudatory and justificatory functions, in part due to seminal works such as Yan Yu's 嚴羽 (early to mid-thirteenth century) *Canglang shihua* 滄浪詩話. Yet we should note that from the time of its first emphatic articulation in the Six Dynasties, this discourse has been accompanied by the fascination with surface.[66] Thus in his *Wen fu*, for example, Lu Ji makes grand claims for poetic creation and links it to Daoist meditation:

> He [the poet] stands in the very center, views deeply and afar [*xuanlan* 玄覽],
> Nourishes feelings and intent in the ancient canons....
> He observes all past and present in a single moment,
> Touches all the world in the blink of an eye....
> He cages Heaven and Earth in fixed shape,
> Crushes all things beneath the brush's tip.

But when he discusses various genres, metaphors of surface and an emotive vocabulary become dominant:

> The poem (*shi* 詩) follows from the affections (*yuanqing* 緣情) and is sensuously intricate;
> Poetic exposition (*fu* 賦) embodies the world of things (*tiwu* 體物) and is clear and luminous.[67]

The phrase "sensuously intricate" (*qimi* 綺靡) refers literally to the texture of fine silk, while "clear and luminous" (*liuliang* 瀏亮) describes the reflective surface of water. Almost three centuries later, Xiao Yi 蕭繹 (508–554) wrote: "As for literature, it needs only to be covered by phrases like finest silks (*qigu fenpi* 綺縠紛被), [and expressed through] delicate and intoxicating musical tones (*gongzhi miaoman* 宮徵妙曼); as [moving] lips gather and close, feelings and spirit sway (*qingling yaodang* 情靈搖蕩)."[68] Metaphors of surface (especially fabric) also feature in the entries on literary judgment in *Shishuo*:

> Sun Chuo 孫綽 said, "Pan Yue's 潘岳 writings are as dazzling as draping brocade 爛若披錦; there is no place in them which is not good. Lu Ji's writings are like gold pieces to be picked out from spreading sand 排沙簡金, there are often treasures to be seen" (*SS* 4.84).[69]

Sun Chuo said, "Cao Pi's 曹毗 (mid-fourth century; not to be confused with the poet and Wei ruler Cao Pi) talent is like bright luminary brocade with a white background 白地明光錦, cut to make breeches for a lowly census-board bearer 負版. Not that there's any lack of color and pattern (*wencai* 文采), but there is definitely no cut or shape (*caizhi* 裁製)" (*SS* 4.93).

We may compare such comments with their apparent opposite, Ruan Fu's 阮孚 judgment of Guo Pu's 郭璞 poems: "One of Guo Pu's poems reads, 'In the forest are no silent trees,/Of streams no still flow.' Ruan Fu said, 'The pure depth, the awesome height, and the sounds of movement—there are indeed no words for it. Whenever I read this, I often feel that my spirit transcends and my bodily form is transported (*shenchao xingyue* 神超形越)'" (*SS* 4.76). At first glance we have here standard components of the discourse of transcendence: poetic appreciation of nature, ineffability, the reader's sense of removal from mundane reality. Upon closer examination, we see a continuum between Ruan Fu's comments and Sun Chuo's—there is a similar attention to concrete details and the palpable, sensuous experience of reading. The mention here in the same breath of spirit and bodily form is typical—spiritual transcendence is experienced as the removal of bodily form. In *Shishuo* as a whole, as in later writings on art and literature, the interest in form, surface, and perceptual horizons is inseparable from philosophical and religious concerns with transcendence.

More broadly, the interest in perceptual horizons, contours of emotions, precise embodiment of things, and felicitous verbal expressions in *Shishuo* is echoed in various models of correspondences, natural continuities, and stimuli-responses in later reflections on writing and literature. As mentioned above, the problem of whether words can exhaust meaning was a much debated philosophical issue at the time. The consequent ruminations on the relationship between intent (*yi* 意) and verbal expression (*yan* 言), emotions (*qing* 情) and aesthetic surface (*wen* 文) in *Shishuo* lead us to central concerns in Six Dynasties literary thought. The problematic link between language and meaning is dramatized in some memorable anecdotes from *Shishuo*: "The monk Gaozuo 高坐 (Srimitra) did not speak Chinese. Someone inquired about the significance of this. Emperor Jianwen 簡文帝 (Sima Yu 司馬昱) replied, 'The purpose is to simplify the tedium of verbal exchange 以簡應對之繁'" (*SS* 2.39). Liu Jun cites "Gaozuo biezhuan" 高坐別傳 in his commentary:

His reverence had a natural distinction, being lofty and luminous (*tianzi gaolang* 天姿高朗), and his style and manner were vigorous and forthright (*fengyun youmai* 風韻遒邁). The moment the Prime Minister Wang Dao saw him, he marveled at him and considered him a like-minded spirit. While Zhou Yi 周顗 was serving on the Board of Civil Office, he once patted him on the back and said, "If in my selections for civil office I could get someone as worthy as this, I'd have no regrets." Sometime thereafter Zhou Yi met his death. His reverence sat opposite his coffin, and recited Sanskrit mantras (*huzhu* 胡祝) of several thousand words, and his voice was resounding and vibrant. Then he wiped his tears and stopped weeping. Such were his grief and joy over rise and decline in human affairs (*aile xingfei* 哀樂興廢). He was by nature lofty and austere (*gaojian* 高簡), and did not learn the Jin language. When the various gentlemen spoke with him, they all relied on translators. However, he grasped the spirit and understood the intent (*shenling yide* 神領意得), in the instant before any words were uttered (*dun zai yan qian* 頓在言前) (*SS* 4.39).

Gaozuo is esteemed despite, or perhaps because of, his foreignness.[70] His ignorance of the Chinese language highlights his intuitive understanding and powerful emotions, conveyed through his appearance, style, voice, and gestures. His encounters with Jin notables are marked by scenes of recognition, which celebrate a profound mutual understanding that goes beyond words. By not knowing Chinese, Gaozuo thus rises above linguistic mediation, averts the tedium and trouble (*fan* 繁) of the social aspects of conversation, and embodies the ideal of a simple, austere, unceremonious (*jian* 簡) existence.

With more self-conscious flourish Yue Guang 樂廣 dramatizes the elusiveness of meaning, the limits of language, and the expressive power of gestures:

A guest asked Yue Guang about the statement "meanings do not reach" (*zhi bu zhi* 旨不至). Yue for his part did not make any further detailed analysis of the words or sentence. He simply used the handle of his sambar-tail chowry and struck it against the low table, saying, "Does it reach or not?" The guest said, "It reaches." Yue then raised the chowry again and asked, "If it reaches, how can it be removed?" With that, the guest thereupon understood and submitted. Yue was sparing with words and yet conveyed his meanings (*ci yue er zhi da* 辭約而旨達)—he was like this in all cases (*SS* 4.16).

The statement "meanings do not reach" is recorded as Hui Shi's 惠施 teaching in *Zhuang Zi*, chapter 33, "Tianxia pian" 天下篇 (All under Heaven) and is also attributed to Gongsun Longzi 公孫龍子 in *Liezi* 列子, chapter 4, "Zhongni" 仲尼. We have here a prototypical anecdote about sudden enlightenment in Chan Buddhism, although Yue Guang had no connection with Buddhism and the rise of Chan was a later development.[71] Like Gaozuo's Sanskrit mantras and Ruan Ji's 阮籍 famous whistle (*xiao* 嘯) (*SS* 18.1), Yue Guang's little performance renders palpable and compelling abstract propositions about the limits of linguistic reference and verbal communication.

In addition to the discourse of transcendence and the discourse of form and surface, there is a discourse of emotions and intensity in traditional literary thought. Characters in *Shishuo* savor emotions (their own and other people's), observing how one can "die from passions" 為情死, "the middle years bring injuries from grief and joy" 中年傷於哀樂, "one cannot help having feelings" 未免有情, and "where passions concentrate is precisely among people like us" 情之所鍾正在我輩. The self-conscious scrutiny of emotions leads to ruminations on the correlation of feelings and language in *Shishuo* that echo the emphasis on the expressive-affective axis in Chinese poetics:

> Whenever Huan Yi 桓伊 listened to unaccompanied singing (*qingge* 清歌), he would always cry out loud, "What is to be done (*naihe* 奈何)!" Xie An, hearing of this, said, "Ziye (Huan Yi) can be said to have the single striving of deep feelings" 子野可謂一往有深情 (*SS* 23.42).

> Liu Ling composed "Ode to the Virtues of Wine" 酒德頌, and he lodged his mind and spirit therein (*yiqi so ji* 意氣所寄) (*SS* 4.69).

> When Sun Chu removed the mourning clothes after the death of his wife, he composed a poem and showed it to Wang Ji 王濟. Wang said, "I do not yet know whether the writing is born of the feeling (*wen sheng yu qing* 文生於情), or the feeling the writing (*qing sheng yu wen* 情生於文). Reading this, I am filled with melancholy, noting more the momentousness of conjugal relations" (*SS* 4.72).

> Yu Ai completed "A Poetic Exposition on Intent" (Yi fu 意賦). His cousin Yu Liang 庾亮 saw it and asked, "Do you have intent? If so, it cannot be fully expressed by a poetic exposition. Don't you have intent? If not, why

then write a poetic exposition about it?" He answered, "I am between having intent and not having intent" 在有意無意之間 (SS 4.75).

Overcome with feelings, Huan Yi can only utter an exclamation or
question that acknowledges his sense of being overwhelmed. Yet this
half-inarticulate cry suffices to convince Xie An of Huan Yi's deep feelings. In the other examples, felicitous verbal expression is celebrated as
a genuine, spontaneous, natural, and adequate expression of thoughts
and feelings. Wang Ji's brief comments on the relationship between
writing and feelings might have inspired Liu Xie's extensive discussion
of the problem in *Wenxin diaolong* (especially in the chapter "Qingcai"
情采). Even the half-serious exchange between Yu Ai and Yu Liang is
not really about ineffability and the confines of language. Rather Yu Ai
is claiming for himself a province of creation that includes his partial
abdication of control. In other words, while *Shishuo* contains anecdotes
dwelling on the limits of linguistic expression and communication, it
tends to treat literature as the art of the possible and affirms the momentum of intent and emotions behind the act of writing. Various combinations of these two aspects reverberate in Six Dynasties literary thought.

Perhaps the most obvious formal connection between *Shishuo* and
the discourses on the arts is the preoccupation with ranking and evaluative statements. Zong Baihua 宗白華 notes how works such as Xie He's
謝赫 *Hua pin* 畫品 (Classification of Paintings), Yuan Ang's 袁盎 and
Yu Jianwu's 庾肩吾 *Shu pin* 書品 (Classification of Calligraphy), Zhong
Rong's *Shi pin*, and Liu Xie's *Wenxin diaolong* share similar conceptual
models and vocabulary as the discourse of evaluating and appreciating
human character (*pinzao renwu* 品藻人物).[72] (Indeed, some *Shishuo*
entries would not seem out of place in *Shi pin*.)[73] In contradistinction
to the traditional ideal of "knowing people" (*zhiren* 知人) by divining
their moral core, the discourse on human character in *Shishuo* is fashioned on the basis of style, appearance, talent, verbal expressions, the
expressive-affective powers of these qualities, and self-conscious ruminations on the evaluative act itself. Stephen Owen begins his study,
Readings in Chinese Literary Thought, with a quotation from *Analects*
2.10: "He said, 'Look to how it is. Consider from what it comes.
Examine in what a person would be at rest. How can a person remain
hidden?—how can someone remain hidden (*ren yan sou zai* 人焉廋
哉)?"[74] He argues rightly that Chinese literary thought "began its devel-

opment around this question of knowledge, a special kind of knowing as in 'knowing a person' or 'knowing the conditions of the age.'"[75] However, it is when this hermeneutics fuses with, or is displaced by, the concern with pleasure, the absorption with surface, or reflexivity on perception and judgment that aesthetic self-consciousness comes into its own.

Anxieties

From the moment of its birth aesthetic self-consciousness seems to be plagued by self-doubt and is driven by the need to apologize. By way of conclusion, I would like to briefly examine how the suspicions of negativity in *Shishuo* reverberate in Six Dynasties literary thought. Qualities that are for the most part praised in *Shishuo*, such as wit, beauty, eloquence, detachment, imperturbability, loftiness, freedom, unrestraint, and emotional intensity (among many others), sometimes also arouse anxieties related to the following two charges: immorality and inauthenticity.

Several entries in *Shishuo* record the view that "pure conversation undermines the polity" (*qingtan wuguo* 清談誤國)—that is, absorption in abstruse philosophical debates detracts attention from government service and affairs of state, even as evaluating character becomes aesthetic appreciation rather than the wherewithal for recruiting employable talent. I cite two of the most famous examples.

> Wang Xizhi and Xie An went up together to Yecheng 冶城. Xie was bemused, his thoughts wandering far, for he had the aspiration to transcend the world (*gaoshi zhi zhi* 高世之志). Wang said to Xie, "Yu of Xia 夏禹 ruled with such diligence that his hands and feet were worn and calloused. King Wen of Zhou had no time to spare even for his meals. Now when 'four suburbs are filled with fortifications,' it is fitting that everybody should exert himself. As for vain talk that causes neglect of duties (*xutan feiwu* 虛談廢務), and frivolous writings that obstruct essential tasks (*fuwen fangyao* 浮文妨要), I am afraid that's not needed right now." Xie replied, "Qin 秦 appointed Shang Yang 商鞅, and perished after two reigns. Was it 'pure conversation' that brought them to disaster (*qingyan zhi huan* 清言致 患)" (*SS* 2.70)?

When Huan Wen entered Loyang 洛陽 (356), he crossed the Rivers Huai
淮 and Si 泗 and reached the northern territories.[76] Climbing to the turret
of his ship with his subordinate officers, he looked out over the Central
Plain, and with deep feelings said, "For causing the Sacred Land to be
engulfed (by barbarians) and to lie waste for a hundred years (*shenzhou
luchen, bainian qiuxu* 神州陸沉百年丘墟), Wang Yan and those about him
can't escape bearing the blame!" Yuan Hong 袁宏 impulsively replied,
"The cycle of fortunes (*yun* 運) on its own brings about rise and decline,
why must it be their fault?" Coloring angrily, Huan Wen looked around
and said to all present, "Have you gentlemen ever heard of Liu Biao 劉表
(d. 208)? He owned a large ox weighing a thousand catties. It ate ten times
as much fodder and beans as ordinary oxen, and yet when it came to bearing heavy burdens or traveling long distances, it wasn't even the equal of a
sick calf. When Cao Cao invaded the Jing 荊 Province (203), he cooked
the ox to feast his officers and men. At the time everyone expressed
delight." Huan meant this as an analogy for Yuan. All present were
shocked, and Yuan too lost color (*SS* 26.11).

Liu Jun cites in his commentary *Bawang gushi* 八王故事 (Accounts of
the Eight Princes): despite his high office, Wang Yan did not trouble
himself with worldly affairs. The baleful, corrupting influence was such
that all in government "admired the principle of folding the hands in
silence, and took the neglect of duties for their ideal." Another quoted
source, *Jin yangqiu* 晉陽秋 (Jin History), tells how Wang Yan blamed
himself when he was about to be killed by Shi Le 石勒 (311): "If our
group had not revered frivolity and emptiness (*zushang fuxu* 祖尚浮虛),
we never would have come to this." It is interesting that both *Shishuo*
anecdotes are structured as dialogues in which opposite opinions are
articulated. Xie An seems to have the last word, as he points to the
complex historical reasons that bring down dynasties. Likewise, Yuan
Hong's dissenting voice appears reasonable, despite (or perhaps because
of) Huan Wen's fury and threatening pose. The affinity between Xie
An and Yuan Hong is celebrated in another anecdote: "After Yuan
Hong had finished writing his *Mingshi zhuan* 名士傳 (Biographies of
Renowned Gentlemen), he went to see Xie An. Xie laughed and said,
'I used to characterize the people and events of the north in the company of others, just for amusement and nothing more. Now you've
come along and written a book about it!'" (*SS* 4.94) Neither Xie An
nor Yuan Hong fits the image of the disengaged, unrestrained famous

gentleman indulging in philosophical speculations. Despite Xie An's stated aspiration to "transcend the world," he was an able statesman, and Yuan Hong was a notable historian, scholar, and poet. They represent a more balanced, judicious assessment of the Wei-Western Jin legacy.

However, what finally gains ground in later historical accounts are the opinions attributed to Wang Xizhi and Huan Wen. In the context of Eastern Jin history, the condemnation of Wei-Jin advocates of Abstruse Learning and Pure Conversation is enmeshed in factional politics.[77] Thus Huan Wen's remark may be in part explained by his enmity for Yin Hao 殷浩 and others who continued the tradition of Pure Conversation at the time. Negative judgments of the Wei-Jin cultural-intellectual legacy, sometimes linked to anguish over recent or contemporary historical crises, are reiterated in Ge Hong's 葛洪 *Baopu Zi* 抱樸子 (The Master Who Embraces Simplicity); *Jin ji* 晉紀 (as cited in Liu Jun's commentary);[78] sections of the *Jin shu;*[79] Sima Guang's 司馬光 *Zizhi tongjian* 資治通鑒 (Mirror for the Aid of Government); and, most famously, Gu Yanwu's 顧炎武 *Rizhi lu* 日知錄 (Learning Accrued Day by Day). Some modern scholars devoted to *Shishuo* are also not free from such biases.[80]

Suspicions of immorality or amorality are hard to dispel in discourses devoted to the delineation and judgment of beauty. Even the most cursory survey of literary thought in the Six Dynasties suffices to draw attention to the rhetoric of self-defense and self-justification. Although the distinctness of literature as a category of significance is first articulated in this period (e.g., in the preface to *Wenxuan*), there are also impressive attempts to emphasize the continuity between literary activities and other spheres of human existence, notably in *Wenxin diaolong*, chapter 47, "Cailue" 才略 (Talents and Judgments), and chapter 49, "Chengqi" 程器 (Measuring Vessels). If there is less emphasis on the pragmatic functions of literature, literature is nevertheless repeatedly praised as the vehicle to higher truths. As noted above, attention to form and surface is supposedly redeemed by appeals to transcendence. All the same, there is enough unease about excessively sensuous and ornate diction to call for a kind of "self-purgation"— negative judgments that prune what is deemed corrupting in order to preserve a more pure, normative, and coherent *wen*.[81]

The charge of immorality is closely related to anxieties over insincerity. There is a great emphasis on naturalness, freedom, and rejection of pretense and conventions in *Shishuo*, and yet these cultural attitudes have to be perceived and delineated from the outside. Precisely because surface, perception, and evaluation are so important, there is fear of a growing distance between self and persona, genuine feelings and assumed pose: "Xie An once praised Wang Shu 王述, saying, 'Lift up his skin, and underneath it's all real (*duopi jiezhen* 掇皮皆真)'" (*SS* 8.78).[82] Genuineness is something to be discovered or verified "underneath the skin." The potential discrepancy between surface and meaning is a recurrent concern in *Shishuo*. Physical beauty may be faked. Cao Pi, Emperor Wen of Wei 魏文帝 (r. 220–226), suspected that He Yan powdered his face to enhance the fairness of his skin: "In the hottest summer month, he (Cao) offered him (He) hot soup and dumplings. After He had eaten it, he broke into a profuse sweat. After he used his scarlet robe to wipe his face, his complexion appeared fairer than ever (*SS* 14.2).

According to Liu Jun's commentary, He Yan was known to be extremely vain and inseparable from his powder puff, so it was quite likely that he did use powder. More to the point, Cao Pi grew up with He Yan within the palace. Why would he need to apply this test? For all its implausibility, however, this anecdote answers the need to unmask and to seek the truth "underneath the skin." This truth becomes more elusive when it comes to moral and spiritual matters. Filial piety, supposedly one of the most natural virtues, still calls for elaborate conventions. One famous anecdote addresses the criteria for evaluating filial piety:

> Wang Rong and He Qiao experienced the loss of a parent at the same time, and both were famous for their filial devotion. Wang, emaciated, could barely support himself on the bed; while He, wailing and weeping, performed all the rites. Emperor Wu 晉武帝 (Sima Yan 司馬炎, r. 265–290) remarked to Liu Yi 劉毅, "Haven't you been visiting Wang and He? I hear that He's grief and suffering go beyond the requirements of ritual propriety, and it makes me worry about him." Liu said, "He Qiao, even though performing all the rites, has not diminished in spirit and vital breath; Wang Rong, even though not performing the rites, is so consumed by grief that he is all bones. Your servant believes that He Qiao's is the filial devotion of life (*shengxiao* 生孝), while Wang Rong's is the filial devotion of death (*sixiao* 死孝). Your majesty should not worry about Qiao, but rather about Rong" (*SS* 1.17).

The "filial devotion of life" implies observance of rites for the sake of the living. There is a social dimension to He Qiao's grief, insofar as he is doing what is expected of him. By contrast, the "filial devotion of death" is an emotion sufficient unto itself, with scant regard for the public or for life itself. Liu Yi thus suggests that Wang Rong's negligence of ritual propriety implies more genuine feelings.[83] Once such standards are acknowledged, however, we can have another type of role playing, the deliberate performance of nonconformity to signify genuineness. The very practice of character evaluation makes for heightened self-consciousness. Even a presumably sincere expression of emotions acquires the dimensions of mediation and performance. Recall Ruan Ji's unconventional mourning: "When Ruan Ji was about to bury his mother, he steamed a fat suckling pig and drank two ladles of wine. Then he attended the last rites, and managed only to utter, 'Alas! The end!' He gave off one long wail, spit blood, and wasted away for a long time" (*SS* 23.9). During the period of mourning, Ruan displayed the utmost equanimity, while his commiserating friend, Pei Kai, wailed. Pei justified this reversal of roles: "Ruan is someone beyond the limits of society (*fang wai ren* 方外人), so he does not respect the rules of rites. The likes of myself are solidly within the bounds of conventions (*su zhong ren* 俗中人), so I have to observe the decorum of behavior" (*SS* 23.11). "Their contemporaries admired both for acting in a fitting manner (*liang de qi zhong* 兩得其中)." Ruan's refusal to abstain from wine and meat and his apparent equanimity are ambiguous—this purports to be his own idiosyncratic mode of expressing his grief, yet it also suggests deliberate control of his emotions. His distaste for the conventional expression of filial piety takes precedence over his need to mourn his loss. In rejecting a prescribed role, he takes up another, newer yet widely acknowledged model, that of "one beyond the limits of society." When the demonstration of difference from social norms becomes the primary concern, genuineness is confused with its mannerisms and effect. This is where accusations of bad faith (*jiaoqing* 矯情) apply.

Other factors contribute to the persistent concern with authenticity: the dictates of certain idealized character traits (e.g., imperturbability) that actually call for a repression of emotions; the need to reconcile ambitions and government service with Daoist and Buddhist disengagement; the fact that nonconformist and unconventional behavior may be motivated by political frustrations or the desire to escape political persecution; and the sense of belatedness (as evinced by Eastern Jin questions as to whether the Zhengshi 正始 model of vibrant wit and philosophical speculation is being properly emulated—e.g., *SS* 2.40, 2.99, 4.22, 8.51, 8.23). The question of genuineness charts an area where evaluation of character merges effortlessly with literary judgment. Sun Chuo, otherwise a major literary talent and discerning critic, is criticized several times for incommensurate expressions of grief in his writings whereby he insinuates that there is a closer relationship between himself and the diseased, when in fact no such ties warrant Sun's display of sorrow.[84]

Six Dynasties literary thought valorizes genuineness and naturalness. As in *Shishuo*, however, this is often expressed as anxiety and nostalgia for something already lost. The moment of innocence and effortless continuity between medium and meaning is often set in antiquity (as in *Wenxin diaolong*), although some Chu-Han works and the Jian'an 建安 masters are admitted into the pantheon (this is true of *Wenxin diaolong* also, but more so of Zhong Rong's *Shi pin*). Perhaps this is the prize of self-consciousness. Once genuineness is upheld as an ideal, it is difficult to be spontaneously fulfilled; the only paradise that can be conceived is paradise lost.

NOTES

1. References to *Shishuo xinyu* are by chapter and entry number. Translations are based on Richard B. Mather, *Shih-shuo Hsin-yü: A New Account of Tales of the World* (Minneapolis: University of Minnesota Press, 1976), with slight modifications. *Shishuo xinyu* is attributed to Liu Yiqing 劉義慶 (403–444), although it is quite likely that Liu Yiqing simply oversaw its compilation. For a general introduction to its nature and significance, see Richard Mather's introduction to his translation, pp. xiii–xxx, and an excellent recent study by Nanxiu Qian, *Spirit and Self in Medieval China: The Shih-shuo hsin-yü and Its Legacy* (Honolulu: University of Hawai'i Press, 2001). For accounts of its textual history, see Wang Nengxian 王能憲, *Shishuo xinyu yanjiu* 世說新語研究 (Nanjing: Jiangsu guji chubanshe, 1992), pp. 1–113, and Fan Ziye 范子燁, *Shishuo xinyu yanjiu* 世說新語研究 (Harbin: Helongjiang jiaoyu chubanshe, 1998), pp. 1–207.

2. Lu Xun, "Wei-Jin fengdu ji wenzhang yu yao ji jiu zhi guanxi" 魏晉風度及文章與藥及酒之關係, in *Eryi ji* 而已集; see *Lu Xun Xuanji* 魯迅選集, 4 vols. (Beijing: Renmin wenxue chubanshe, 1992), vol. 2, pp. 377–405.

3. *Shishuo* contains a handful of anecdotes from the Western Han and the (Liu) Song dynasties, but the vast majority of the entries cover the period from the final years of the Han to the Eastern Jin. For a statistical survey of the distribution of *Shishuo* entries in different periods, see Pu Meiling 朴美齡, *Shishuo xinyu zhong so fanying de sixiang* 世說新語所反映的思想 (Taipei: Wenjin chubanshe, 1990), pp. 5–7.

4. Xiao Ai 蕭艾 points this out in the context of his discussion of the meanings of the term "*wenxue*" 文學 in fifth- and sixth-century writings; see his *Shishuo tanyou* 世說探幽 (Changsha: Hunan chubanshe, 1992), pp. 146–148.

5. The inclusion of *Shishuo* and other *xiaoshuo* 小說 (pseudohistorical, semifictional, or downright fantastic) sources in the *Jin shu* arouses the ire of Liu Zhiji 劉知幾 (661–721); see his criticism in Pu Qilong 蒲起龍 comp., *Shitong tongshi* 史通通釋, chapter 15, "Caizhuan" 采撰 (Taipei: Shijie shuju, 1988), p. 56. The framing and editing of *Shishuo* anecdotes in *Jin shu* narratives sometimes result in significant divergences.

6. Richard Mather's term; see his introduction to *A New Account of Tales of the World*, p. xiv. Lu Xun calls *Shishuo* "the textbook for famous gentlemen (*mingshi jiaoke shu* 名士教科書)."

7. See, among others, Chen Yinke 陳寅恪, *Jinming guan conggao erbian* 金明館叢稿二編 (Shanghai: Shanghai guji chubanshe, 1980), p. 83; Tang Changru 唐長孺, *Wei Jin Nanbei chao shi luncong* 魏晉南北朝史論叢 (Beijing: Sanlian shudian, 1955), p. 290; Mou Runsun 牟潤孫, *Lun Wei-Jin yilai zhi chongshang tanbian jiqi yingxiang* 論魏晉以來之崇尚談辯及其影響 (Hong Kong: Chinese University of Hong Kong, 1966); Lu Xun, *Zhongguo xiaoshuo de lishi de bianqian* 中國小說的歷史的變遷, 2d lecture; Zhou Yiliang 周一良, *Wei Jin Nanbei chao shi zhaji* 魏晉南北朝史札記 (Beijing: Zhonghua shuju, 1985), p. 52; Wang Xiaoyi 王曉毅, *Zhongguo wenhua de qingliu* 中國文化的清流 (Beijing: Zhongguo shehui kexue chubanshe, 1991), pp. 78–89.

8. Fan Ye 范曄, "Danggu liezhuan" 黨錮列傳, *Hou Han shu* 後漢書, 12 vols. (Beijing: Zhonghua shuju, 1973), *juan* 67.2185.

9. For example, Cao Pi refers to Xun Shuang's 荀爽 (late second to early third century) formulation, "How lovable are those who love me, how detestable those who detest me!" as "*qingtan*." See Cao Pi's letter to Zhong Yao 鍾繇; quoted in Pei Songzhi's 裴松之 annotations of Chen Shou's 陳壽 (233–297) *Sanguo zhi* 三國志, 5 vols. (Beijing: Zhonghua shuju, 1959), *juan* 13.396. See also Ying Ju's 應璩 (190–252) letter to Cao Changsi 曹長思, in *Wenxuan* 文選, comp. Xiao Tong 蕭統 (Zhengzhou: Zhongzhou guji chubanshe), *juan* 42.597. He Changqun 賀昌群 mentioned some of these examples in his *Wei-Jin qingtan sixiang chulun* 魏晉清談思想初論 (Beijing: Shangwu yinshu guan, 1999 reprint of 1947 edition), p. 1.

10. For example, *SS* 8.5, 8.6, 8.12, 8.13, 8.14, 8.20, 8.22, 8.29, 8.36, 8.37, 8.65, 8.71, 8.100, 8.104, 8.120, 8.137, 8.152, 9.36, 9.40, 9.42, 9.59.

11. See *Hou Han shu, juan* 66–68.

12. See *Hou Han shu, juan* 68.2227–2231.

13. See Qian, *Spirit and Self*, pp. 1–90. Liu Shao 劉邵 (fl. 240–250) emphasizes the discernment of character through conversation and disputation in *Renwu zhi* 人物志 (esp. chs. 4 and 7, "Caili" 材理 and "Jieshi" 接識). Wang Xiaoyi discusses *Renwu zhi* in this context and also corroborating evidence from the *Sanguo zhi;* see *Zhongguo wenhua de qingliu*, esp. pp. 78–89. For illuminating discussions of *Renwu zhi* in the tradition of evaluating character, see Tang Yongtong 湯用彤, *Wei-Jin xuanxue lungao* 魏晉玄學論稿 (Beijing: Renmin chubanshe, 1957), pp. 5–25; Mou Zongsan 牟宗三, *Caixing yu xuanli* 才性與玄理 (Taipei: Xuesheng shuju, 1962), pp. 43–66; and Qian, *Spirit and Self*, pp. 113–117.

14. Chen Yinke, *Jinming guan conggao chubian* 金明館叢稿初編 (Shanghai: Shanghai guji chubanshe, 1980), pp. 41–47, 180–205. See also Xiao Ai, *Shishuo tanyou*, pp. 257–272.

15. See Paul Rouzer's discussion of how the ties and tensions within the elite shape *Shishuo xinyou* in *Articulated Ladies: Gender and Male Community in Early Chinese Texts* (Cambridge, Mass.: Council of East Asian Studies, Harvard University, 2001). Wang Nengxian discusses the significance of evaluating character in advancing a person's career in the Wei-Jin period in *Shishuo xinyu yanjiu*, p. 139.

16. Zhou Yiliang, *Wen Jin Nanbei chao shi zhaji*, pp. 159–161, 200–202.

17. Terry Eagleton, *The Ideology of the Aesthetic* (Oxford: Basil Blackwell, 1990), p. 1.

18. The *zhuwei* is the inevitable paraphernalia of Pure Conversation, although it might have been used on other occasions. Supposedly used to wave away small insects, it becomes also an accessory to heighten the user's gracious pose. The *zhuwei* apparently originated from the Wei-Jin period; see Yu Jiaxi 余嘉錫, comp., *Shishuo xinyu jianshu* 世說新語箋疏, ed. Zhou Zumo 周祖謨 and Yu Shuyi 余淑宜, (Beijing: Zhonghua shuju, 1983), p. 611. Compare Wang Nengxian, *Shishuo xinyu yanjiu*, p. 133.

19. Yu Jiaxi cites *Guozi* 郭子 (*Taiping yulan* 太平御覽) as the source of this image (*Shishuo xinyu jianshu*, p. 220).

20. One should note that the use of military metaphors is also sometimes playful and tongue in cheek.

21. Of course one may say the same about *Zhuang Zi*, and it is not surprising that exegetical exercises on *Zhuang Zi* feature prominently in Pure Conversation. Xu Fuguan gives an illuminating analysis of how *Zhuang Zi* epitomizes the aesthetic spirit in the Chinese tradition and further surmises that Pure Conversation acquires deeper aesthetic significance when its focus shifts from *Lao Zi* 老子 and *Yi* 易 to *Zhuang Zi*; see his *Zhongguo yishu jingshen* 中國藝術精神 (Taipei: Xuesheng shuju, 1981), pp. 45–143.

22. In the tradition of other early Chinese stories about ugly but wise women, such as those found, for example, in *Lienü zhuan* 列女傳, *Shishuo* tells of prescience and wit belied by plain appearance in chapter 19, "Worthy Ladies" 賢媛 (e.g., *SS* 19.6, 19.7, 19.8, 19.9). There is also interest in the aura of beauty manifested almost as moral authority, as when jealous rivals are awed into submission (e.g., *SS* 19.13, 19.21). But female beauty in the context of sensual attraction and obsessive attachment is disparaged (e.g., *SS* 35.2).

23. In this entry Pei Xia is debating Guo Xiang 郭象 (d. 312). Guo is one of the most famous Xuanxue thinkers from the period; his commentary on *Zhuang Zi* is still widely read. Pei Xia, like his clansman Pei Wei 裴頠 (267–300) (who authored the "Treatise on Actuality" [Chongyou lun 崇有論]), champions "moral teachings" (*mingjiao* 名教). It is interesting to note that the anecdote does not allude to these differences but merely remarks on the difference between Guo's vigorousness (*sheng* 盛) and Pei's subtlety (*wei* 微). Ironically, the commentator on the Daoist text is forceful and engaged, while the champion of Confucian principles is subtle and detached. There is a hint that Pei wins, although external evidence suggests that Guo is by far the superior thinker. Guo Xiang's vigorous style may be linked to his belief in actuality (*you* 有); see Liu Rulin 劉汝霖, *Han Jin xueshu biannian* 漢晉學術編年, 2 vols., 1933 preface (Shanghai shudian reprint), vol. 2, pp. 247–254.

24. See *SS* 4.38. Xu Xun is chagrined by comparisons that rank him with Wang Xiu 王修 and relentlessly defeats Wang in two rounds (when they switch sides) in a debate on Buddhist doctrines.

25. Chapter 10, "Admonitions and Warnings" (Guizhen 規箴), contains many examples of political remonstrances. It is notable for its emphasis on the contexts and performance of remonstrances.

26. There is a very similar anecdote in the same chapter (*SS* 2.4). Another anecdote about Zhong Yu and Zhong Hui share the same structure (*SS* 2.11).

27. Xu Zhen'e 徐震堮 points out that in the tradition of Han *fu* 賦 (poetic exposition or rhyme prose), the rhetorical exchange between a host and a guest is a standard topos; see his *Shishuo xinyu jiaojian* 世說新語校箋, 2 vols. (Beijing: Zhonghua shuju, 1984), vol. 1, p. 107.

28. For example, *SS* 2.2, 2.3, 2.4, 2.5, 2.11, 2.12, 2.27, 2.43, 2.46, 2.49, 2.50, 2.51, 3.3; all the entries in chapter 12.

29. This is one of the three topics upon which Wang Dao 王導 (276–339) loved to expound (*SS* 4.21). The other two are "music has no sorrow or joy" (*sheng wu aile* 聲無哀樂) and "nourishment of life" (*yangsheng* 養生). Liu Jun's commentary to that entry cites excerpts of Ouyang Jian's 歐陽健 (ca. 265–300) "Yan jin yi lun" 言盡意論; see Yu Jiaxi, *Shishuo xinyu jianshu*, p. 211; Mather, *A New Account of Tales of the World*, p. 103. According to Tang Yongtong, the debate on the relationship between word and meaning (*yanyi zhi bian* 言意之

辯) is decisive for the rise of Abstruse Learning in the Wei-Jin period (*Wei-Jin xuanxue lungao*, pp. 26–47).

30. For example, Yin Zhongkan (d. 399–400) described the spiritual and intellectual meanings of *Daodejing* 道德經 (The Way and Its Power) with a somatic metaphor: "If for three days I don't read the *Daodejing*, I begin to feel the base of my tongue growing stiff" (*SS* 4.63).

31. In comparison, the famous Buddhist master Huiyuan 慧遠 (334–416), credited with an important synthesis of Daoist thought and Mahayana Buddhism, appears in only two entries (*SS* 6.61, 10.24).

32. Fragments of his disquisition on *Zhuang Zi* are quoted in Liu Jun's commentary. His Buddhist treatise, "Jise lun," does not survive.

33. Hui Jiao 慧皎 mentioned Zhi Dun's accomplishments as calligrapher in *Gaoseng zhuan* 高僧傳 (Biographies of Exalted Monks). Xiao Ai gives a perceptive comparison of accounts of Zhi Dun in *Shishuo* and in *Gaoseng zhuan;* see his *Shishuo tanyou*, pp. 351–368.

34. Structurally this is similar to *SS* 2.50: Yu Liang 庾亮 (289–340) asks Sun Fang 孫放 (d. 327) about his courtesy name, Qizhuang 齊莊, "With whom do you wish to be equal (*qi* 齊)?" Fang replied, "Zhuang Zhou 莊周." "Why don't you emulate Confucius instead of Zhuang Zhou?" "Since the Sage was 'wise at birth' (*shengzhi* 生知), it would be difficult to emulate him." Liu Jun cites in his annotations "Sun Fang biezhuan 孫放別傳," which specified that Sun Fang was eight at the time and that Yu Liang, well pleased with Fang's rejoinder, commented that even Wang Bi's answer might not be considered superior.

35. The exchange is attributed to Ruan Zhan 阮瞻 (fl. 307–312) and Wang Rong (234–305) in "Ruan Zhan zhuan" 阮瞻傳 in *Jin shu*.

36. See, for example, Tang Yongtong, *Wei-Jin xuanxue lungao*; Mou Zongsan, *Caixing yu xuanli*; Gao Chenyang 高晨陽, *Ru Dao huitong yu zhengshi xuanxue* 儒道會通與正始玄學 (Jinan: QiLu shushe, 2000), esp. pp. 281–368.

37. For various explanations of the Jin vernacular expression "*jiangwu*" 將無, see Yu Jiaxi, *Shishuo xinyu jianshu*, pp. 208–209. Xu Zhen'e notes that "*jiangwu*" is similar to "*dewu*" 得無, another expression in *Shishuo*, and also close to the phrase "*mofei*" 莫非 in modern Chinese (*Shishuo xinyu jiaojian*, vol. 1, p. 112). The term "*jiangwu*" also appears in *SS* 1.19, 6.28, 23.40. Caught in stormy weather while boating on a lake, Xie An obliviously whistles and intones poems. The storm becomes more violent, and Xie finally says, "If it is like this, perchance we should return?" (*SS* 6.28). Unlike Ruan's remark, here the expression "*jiangwu*" does not convey tentativeness. In both cases, however, there is the same sense of poise, equanimity, mastery of the situation, and lofty detachment.

38. See *SS* 4.32 and Chen Yinke's explication in *Jinming guan conggao erbian*, pp. 83–89. Wang Meng compares him to Wang Bi and He Yan: "His

accomplishment in searching after subtleties [*xun wei zhi gong* 尋微之功] is in no way inferior to that of Wang Bi" (*SS* 4.98); "Naturally, this man's a Wang Bi or a He Yan behind an almsbowl" (*SS* 4.110).

39. This common ground is most obvious in Buddhist and Daoist discussions, but note also how entries on Confucian and Daoist exegetes share the same structure (e.g, *SS* 4.1, 4.2, 4.4, 4.5, 4.7, 4.10, 4.17).

40. See *SS* 4.12, on how Wang's arguments are used to challenge Pei. Rivalry also implies affinities: Wang sends inquirers to speak with Pei when he himself is indisposed (*SS* 4.11).

41. Ji Zha was a wise and virtuous Wu prince who refused to accede to the throne. He was famous for his discernment in music and prescient appraisal of characters. For accounts of Ji Zha, see *Zuo zhuan* 左傳 Xiang 29, 31, and *Shi ji* 史記 31 ("The Hereditary Family of Wu Taibo" 吳太伯世家). Zhang Liang was the resourceful and elusive strategist who helped Liu Bang win the empire. Unlike other helpers of the first Han emperor, he managed to escape persecution through disengagement and the art of Daoist self-preservation. See *Shi ji* 55 ("The Hereditary Family of the Marquis of Liu" 留侯世家).

42. Liu Jun claims that this is highly implausible. According to *Yongjia liuren ming* 永嘉流人銘, Wei Jie died only forty-five days after arriving at Yuzhang, and all other sources state that Wei Jie died in Yuzhang. See Yu Jiaxi, *Shishuo xinyu jianshu*, p. 614; Mather, *A New Account of Tales of the World*, p. 312.

43. Another entry records his desolation when he was about to cross the Yangtze River in 311. "As I view this bleak expanse of water, without my being aware of it a hundred thoughts came crowding together. Yet if one cannot help having feelings (*wei mian you qing* 未免有情), who indeed can dispel this [sadness]?" (*SS* 2.32).

44. Two cousins argue over the comparative virtue of their respective fathers (*SS* 1.8).

45. Characters are judged by their ability to evaluate other characters. Yang Huai 楊淮 said of the opposite judgments of his two sons offered by Pei Wei and Yue Guang 樂廣: "The superiority and inferiority of my two sons turns out to be nothing more or less than the superiority and inferiority of Pei Wei and Yue Guang" (*SS* 9.7). Sun Chuo and Xu Xun discussed eminent personalities from the past, and Zhi Dun commented, "You two worthies possess, in your own right, talent and sensibility" (*SS* 8.119).

46. The conventional topos are stories about how one prescient character recognizes the essence and destiny of another character by interpreting details of his appearance and behavior. Such interpretive acts often have decisive historical consequences. See Eric Henry, "The Motif of Recognition in Early China," *Harvard Journal of Asiatic Studies* 47, no. 1 (1987), pp. 5–30.

47. Wang Yan was then sixteen. Shan Tao's approbation is mixed with dire predictions in "The Biography of Wang Yan," in *Jin shu, juan* 43; in *Jin*

shu, juan 34, "The Biography of Yang Hu," Yang Hu gives his negative judgment of Wang Yan when the latter is already powerful and famous.

48. Gu was obviously not painting from "life" since he was born thirty-four years after Wang Yan's death.

49. The only exception I found is an anecdote in "Affairs of State" (*SS* 3.7) that links "*timu*" to political discernment and the proper employment of talent.

50. Xu Fuguan discusses the relationship between Xuanxue and the appreciation of nature in *Zhongguo yishu jingshen*, pp. 232–236. See also Qian, *Spirit and Self,* pp. 179–190.

51. For example, *SS* 2.61, 2.85, 2.91, 9.17, 18.6, and 18.11.

52. When Guo Tai arrived at Runan 汝南, he visited Yuan Hong 袁宏 with great dispatch but took his time when he paid his respects to Huang Xian. Contrary to what one may expect of such haste and tardiness, Guo gave the cited explanation of Huang's superior and unfathomable virtue.

53. Wang Yan contrasts Pei Kai's vigorous spirit with his body's "slight indisposition." In fact, Pei died that year. Qian interprets this anecdote in the light of the rivalry between Wang and Pei, see her *Spirit and Self,* pp. 161–162.

54. According to this anecdote, Wang Xizhi was at first disdainful of Zhi Dun, until the latter proved his mettle with his eloquent disquisition on "Free and Easy Wandering" 逍遙遊 (*Zhuang Zi,* ch. 1). Wang's enjoyment is palpably physical: "In the end Wang threw open his lapels and unfastened his girdle and lingered, unable to tear himself away" (*SS* 4.36).

55. See Xu Fuguan, *Zhongguo yishu jingshen,* p. 235.

56. The image of the pine recurs in evaluations of character. In addition to the above examples, see *SS* 2.67, 2.84, 8.154, 14.5, 17.5, and related metaphors of trees towering aloft and spreading out to describe different styles of personality.

57. Yu Jiaxi, *Shishuo xinyu jianshu,* notes that the images in this entry are clearly inspired by Mei Sheng's "Qi fa" 七發 (Seven Stimuli).

58. Liu Tan therewith compares Huan Wen to founders of states and dynasties, Sun Quan and Sima Yi. We see the same mixture of ugliness and spirit portending greatness in an anecdote about Cao Cao (*SS* 14.1).

59. In another entry involving Yin Zhongkan (*SS* 24.61), Liu Jun cites *Zhongxing shu* 中興書 in his commentary to point out that Yin was blind in one eye.

60. "Emperor Ming asked Xie Kun, 'How would you rate yourself in comparison with Yu Liang?' Xie replied, 'As for "sitting in ceremonial attire" in temple or hall, and making the hundred officials keep to the rules, I am no match for Liang. But when it comes to [enjoying and finding repose in] a hill and a vale, I consider myself superior'" (*SS* 9.17).

61. The term here is *"a'zhe"* 阿堵, a Jin vernacular expression that means "this thing" or "these things." It appears also in *SS* 4.23, 6.29, and 10.9.

62. The two lines are from Ji Kang's tetrasyllabic poem to his brother, "Zeng xiucai rujun shi" 贈秀才入軍詩. According to *Jin shu*, Gu valued Ji Kang's poems and thus painted scenes from them (cited in Yu Jiaxi, *Shishuo xinyu jianshu*, p. 722).

63. Both entries are from the chapter "Taunting and Teasing" 排調. Huan Si resembles his maternal uncle, and Huan Wen baits him with the apparently ameliorative comment that the resemblance is only intermittent, only to reveal his barb with the cited lines. Wang Huizhi and Xie Wan discuss Zhi Dun's appearance in front of him—in part as retaliation for Zhi Dun's haughtiness—and incur his extreme displeasure.

64. See Zong-qi Cai's essay in this volume, "The Conceptual Origins and Aesthetic Significance of *"Shen"* in Six Dynasties Texts on Literature and Painting."

65. Xu Fuguan, *Zhongguo yishu jingshen*, p. 156.

66. I discussed this issue in terms of the ambiguities of *"wen"* in Wai-yee Li, "Between 'Literary Mind' and 'Carving Dragons': Order and Excess in *Wenxin Diaolong*," in *A Chinese Literary Mind: Culture, Creativity, and Rhetoric in* Wenxin Diaolong, ed. Zong-qi Cai (Stanford, Calif.: Stanford University Press, 2001), pp. 193–225, 275–282.

67. Lu Ji, *Wen fu*, in *Zhongguo lidai wenlun xuan* 中國歷代文論選, 3 vols., ed. Guo Shaoyu 郭紹虞 (Hong Kong: Zhonghua shuju, 1979), vol. 1, pp. 136–154. The translation here is based on Stephen Owen, *Readings in Chinese Literary Thought* (Cambridge, Mass.: Council on East Asian Studies, Harvard University, 1992), pp. 87, 110, 130.

68. Xiao Yi 蕭繹, *"Liyan pian"* 立言篇, in *Jinlou zi* 金鏤子, in Guo Shaoyu, ed., *Zhongguo lidai wenlun xuan*, pp. 301–302.

69. In Zhong Rong's *Shi pin*, this remark appears as a comment on Pan Yue and is attributed to Xie Hun. Richard Mather cites Ge Hong's (284–364) opposite judgment in his biography of Lu Ji (Jin shu); see *A New Account of Tales of the World*, p. 136.

70. Indian or Central Asian monks are in general depicted with respect and sympathy in *Shishuo*; see *SS* 3.12, 4.47, 4.47.

71. See comments of Liu Chenweng 劉辰翁 and Wang Shimao 王世懋, in *Shishuo xinyu huijiao jizhu* 世說新語彙校集註, compiled by Zhu Zhuyu 朱鑄禹 (Shanghai: Shanghai guji chubanshe, 2002), p. 180.

72. Zong Baihua, "Lun *Shishuo xinyu* he Jinren de mei" 論世說新語和晉人的美, in *Zong Baihua xueshu wenhua suibi* 宗白華學術文化隨筆 (Beijing: Zhongguo tiedao chubanshe, 1996), pp. 130–151.

73. See, for example, *SS* 4.69, 4.76, 4.84, 4.85, 4.93.

74. Owen, *Readings in Chinese Literary Thought*, p. 19.

75. Ibid., p. 20.

76. According to Cheng Zhenyan 程震炎, Huan Wen invaded Loyang in the twelfth year of Yonghe (356) and crossed the Huai and Si to attack Murong Wei 慕容暐 in the fourth year of Taihe 太和 (370). The two military expeditions are mistakenly conflated here (Yu Jiaxi, *Shishuo xinyu jianshu*, pp. 834–835).

77. See *SS* 7.3 (Liu Jun's commentary), Yu Jiaxi's annotations in *SS* 8.54, and Jiang Fan's 蔣凡 perceptive discussion of this issue in *Shishuo xinyu yanjiu* 世説新語研究 (Shanghai: xuelin chubanshe, 1998), pp. 69–138.

78. See Liu Jun's commentary in *SS* 8.54; compare the passage from *Wenyuan yinghua* 文苑英華; cited by Yu Jiaxi, *Shishuo xinyu jianshu*, p. 454.

79. See *Jin shu:* j. 75 ("Fan Ning zhuan" 范寧傳); j. 82 ("Yu Yu zhuan" 虞預傳); j. 91 ("Rulin zhuan" 儒林傳). These sources are discussed in Jiang Fan, *Shishuo xinyu yanjiu*, pp. 69–138.

80. See, for example, Xu Zhen'e's introduction to *Shishuo xinyu jiaojian*, and Yu Jiaxi's notes in *Shishuo xinyu jianshu*, pp. 171–173. Of course there are also more positive assessments. See the works by Chen Yinke, Tang Yongtong, Xu Fuguan, He Changqun, Tang Changru, Nanxiu Qian, Xiao Ai, Wang Nengxian, and Jiang Fan cited in this chapter (among others).

81. I discussed these issues in Li, "Between 'Literary Mind' and 'Carving Dragons.'"

82. The same metaphor is used in *SS* 25.50.

83. Yu Jiaxi questions the filial piety of both Wang Rong and He Qiao by citing other sources; see *Shishuo xinyu jianshu*, p. 20.

84. See *SS* 26.9, 26.17, 26.22. Sun Chuo for his part claims that character and literary talent can be considered separately. "Zhi Dun asked Sun Chuo, 'How do you compare with Xu Xun?' Sun replied, 'In terms of exalted feelings and far-reaching aspirations, your disciple has long inwardly bowed in submission; but in the matter of intoning a rhyme or chanting a poem, Xu will have to sit north" (*SS* 9.54).

Chapter 9

● ●

Nature and Higher Ideals in Texts on Calligraphy, Music, and Painting

Ronald Egan

Han and Wei Texts on Calligraphy

The first and perhaps most lasting impression made by the Han and Wei period texts on calligraphy is that of the verbal amplitude of their descriptions of the various scripts. These descriptions typically occupy the largest portion of the texts and in most cases are clearly that to which the author primarily devoted his attention and energy.

The world of nature is the primary trope in these elaborate characterizations of the scripts. Both animate and inanimate nature supply the material for the long strings of metaphors and analogies that constitute the bulk of each account. A representative passage is given below from Cui Yuan's 崔瑗 (fl. ca. A.D. 107) "Cao shu shi" 草書勢 (The Configuration of Draft Script). This description of the script follows upon an account of its origins and history. But the description is longer than the history:

> When we observe its models and images, there is propriety wherever we look. The rectangular forms do not match the carpenter's square, the round ones do not accord with his compass. Lowered on the left and raised to the right, from far away it looks like a leaning precipice. A bird

stretches its neck, standing erect, intent on flying off. A wild animal recoils
with fear, poised to race away. Here, there are dots and dabs that resemble
a string of pearls which, though broken, remains intact. With anger and
frustration contained inside, they display themselves with abandon and
create marvelous forms. There, there are tremulous strokes perilously
elongated, like a withered tree that stands on the edge of a cliff. The
slanting strokes and dots off to the side are like a cicada clinging to the
branch. Where the brush stroke ends and the configuration is terminated,
the dangling threads are tucked in and knotted away, it resembles the
scorpion that has inflicted its venomous bite and darts to a crack or
crevices,[1] or a hurtling snake that dives down a hole, its head has disappeared but the tail trails behind. Consequently, when you look at it from
afar it resembles a peak that has collapsed or a bluff that has caved in. But
when you examine it close at hand, you find that not a single stroke could
be altered. Its workings are supremely subtle and its essentials are marvelous, always right yet never the same. Here, I have just approximated its
general appearance; such is its configuration, more or less.[2]

Cui's is the earliest of such descriptions of calligraphy. But his
shares several features with other descriptions in later texts that are,
at first sight, apt to puzzle the reader who turns to these texts for
insights into how calligraphy was perceived and rationalized by its
earliest proponents. The writer seems to be quite satisfied to offer up
one after another extravagant analogy between the brushwork and
three-dimensional phenomena, drawn mostly from the world of nature. There does not appear to be anything analytic in the account.
On the contrary, once he begins his description, the author is as if
carried away by his own genius for generating fanciful analogies. The
tone is inflated, if not bombastic, and seemingly lacking in analytic
thought.

Two other traits of these early descriptions of calligraphy, which
emerge when several of them are read together, are apt to give the
reader pause. They are quite redundant from text to text. The images
may be slightly varied, but the general approach is strikingly similar.
Below, for example, is a comparable passage from Cai Yong's 蔡邕
(132–192) "Zhuan shi" 篆勢 (The Configuration of Seal Script). The
passage given here is the main body of the text. It is framed by a short
introduction and closing:

Its form partakes of the marvelous and its ingenuity enters the realm of the divine. It may be a cluster of needles like the points on a tortoise shell, or it may be teeth on a comb like the scales of a dragon. As it relaxes its torso and unleashes its tail, the long and short strokes envelop its body. Forms hang down like the dangling tips of millet, or are piled on top of each other like tangled mass of burrowing snakes. Or as "waves" arise on the right and slanting strokes are accentuated on the left, the falcon stands erect and the bird of prey stirs. They stretch their necks and gather their wings, ready to rise to the clouds. Or a delicate brush is turned inward, so that the start of the stroke is fine and the ending thick, so that it seems here to be broken and there to be continuous. It resembles dewdrops along a thread,[3] weighing it down at the end. The vertical strokes are as if suspended from above, and the horizontal ones like a transverse tie. Dark and unfathomable, askance and askew, they are neither square nor round. They appear to be walking or flying, as they wriggle and flutter along. Looked at from afar, it is the image of geese and swans cavorting in the sky together or an endless formation that stretches on. When examined from close at hand, the ends and junctures cannot be distinguished and the ideographic components cannot be traced. Even [the mathematicians] Ji Yan and Sang Hongyang could not count the writhing brush strokes, nor [the clear-sighted] Li Lou discern the miniscule spaces between them. Even [the craftsman] Gongshu Ban and Carpenter Chui would bow in deference to this superior skill, and the scribes Zhou and Ju Song would fold their arms and put their brushes away.[4]

Birds, animals, insects, craggy mountains, trees and branches, flowers, flowing waters—these are the staples of the descriptions, and they are invariably present, usually in just the haphazard order that we find in Cui Yuan's passage. The nature images are, again, just as above, ordinarily filled out with an occasional reference to artifacts of human culture. For example, the carpenter's compass and square recur in many passages, as do the teeth of a comb, strings of pearls, and some architectural images. We come also to expect certain rhetorical constructions, structured, as above, around directional complements ("to the left ... to the right," "from afar ... from close up") or historical conceits ("even Exemplar A could not ... nor Exemplar B do ..."). Furthermore, while we might anticipate that the descriptions might at least be tailored to the different major script forms, we find, in fact, that the redundancy between descriptions is quite unaffected by the script form being described.

While a first reading of such passages is likely to yield little more than an overwhelming sense of elaborate metaphorical language, a trait strongly reminiscent of the epideictic rhetoric of the *fu* 賦 (rhapsody) genre, I will argue that there is more to these early accounts than mere description. There is another level of meaning apart from that which initially commands our attention. Moreover, this other level is present not only in the interstices between extended strings of metaphors but even in the metaphors themselves. Finally, I will demonstrate that this mode of thinking about the significance of calligraphy became more fully developed and articulated through time, from the Later Han through the Wei and Jin dynasties, and that by the end of the Jin, thanks in part to the influence of contemporary philosophical currents, it constituted a coherent manner of thinking about calligraphy and justification for it as art.

It is, first of all, essential to understand that such accounts as those by Cui Yuan and Cai Yong translated above are informed throughout by assumptions about the philosophical and, indeed, cosmic significance of writing based upon what we are told about its origins in the *Yi jing* 易經 (The Classic of Changes). It is not that there is some vague and distant relation between calligraphy and the origins of Chinese characters in a way that anything composed with them could be said to belong to the legacy begun by the sage inventors of writing. It is rather that Cui Yuan and others have a very specific and immediate parallel in mind: the calligrapher as he works is replicating, in his way, the action of the sages of antiquity who devised hexagrams first and characters later, both of which were modeled on the forms they observed in nature to convey their intentions. The key accounts of the first stage of this process are these, found in the "Xi ci zhuan" 繫辭傳 (Appended Phrases) section of the *Yi jing:*

> When in ancient times Lord Bao Xi ruled the world as sovereign, he looked upward and observed the images in heaven and looked downward and observed the models that the earth provided. He observed the patterns on birds and beasts and what things were suitable for the land. Nearby, adopting them from his own person, and afar, adopting them from other things, he thereupon made the eight trigrams in order to become thoroughly conversant with the virtues inherent in the numinous and the bright and to classify the myriad things in terms of their true, innate natures.[5]

> The Master said, "The sages established images in order to express their ideas exhaustively. They established the hexagrams in order to treat exhaustively the true innate tendency of things and their countertendencies to spuriousness.[6]

By Han times, it was already conventional to think of the invention of writing, by the legendary Cang Jie 倉頡, as following upon the invention of the trigrams and hexagrams. That is the way Xu Shen 許慎 (ca. 58–ca. 147) explains the origin of writing in his preface to *Shuo wen jie zi* 説文解字 (An Explanation of Phrases and Analysis of Characters): first there was Bao Xi 庖犧 (Fu Xi 伏犧), who created the trigrams by modeling them on the images he observed in heaven and earth, and then there was Cang Jie, who similarly created writing by modeling it upon the tracks of animals and birds that he observed: "According to their category he made images of [the natural] forms, and so called it patterns/writing" (依類象形,故謂之文).[7]

Cui Yuan, launching into his description of draft script, writes, "When we observe its models and images, there is propriety wherever we look" (觀其法象,俯仰有儀). Saying this, he is alluding to and mimicking the *Yi jing* passage that describes Bao Xi's invention of the hexagrams: "When in ancient times Lord Bao Xi ruled the world as sovereign, he looked upward and observed the images in heaven and looked downward and observed the models that the earth provided" (古者包犧氏之王天下也,仰則觀象於天,俯則觀法於地). Likewise, when Cui and Cai Yong present strings of nature images that are said to "resemble" the calligraphic forms, their inspiration is directly or indirectly (i.e., through the accepted notion of how Cang Jie worked) the continuation of the same *Yi jing* passage: "He observed the patterns on birds and beasts and what things were suitable for the land. Nearby, adopting them from his own person, and afar, adopting them from other things, he thereupon made the eight trigrams" (觀鳥獸之文,與地之宜,近取諸身,遠取諸物,於是始作八卦).

If the assumption about what the calligrapher does is so heavily dependent upon the model of the sages and their invention of hexagrams and writing, it stands to reason that assumptions about why and to what end he does so may be similarly related to the older notions. The second *Yi jing* passage quoted above addresses these issues for the "images" (*xiang* 象) and the hexagrams that embody them. It is worth stressing that the ends specified are nonverbal or supraverbal. In fact,

non-
verbal

立象以盡意

the preceding sentence in the classic tells us that "words do not exhaust ideas." It was, therefore, in order to express meaning better than words could do that sages devised the images and hexagrams. There is a parallel here with calligraphy, for although calligraphy does consist of written words, its meaning as art has never been restricted to the verbal meaning of the words that the calligrapher writes. The words function in calligraphy in a nonverbal way, somewhat like the way the images of the hexagrams were believed to function for the sages who devised them.

Discussing these issues in his history of Chinese aesthetics, Li Zehou 李澤厚 plausibly asserts that the *Yi jing* notion of the sages having "established the images in order to express their ideas exhaustively" (聖人立象以盡意) lies just behind and informs in a profound way the early texts on calligraphy under discussion here.[8] Yet those early texts do not speak of any *yi* 意, "idea" or "meaning," being conveyed by calligraphic images. The most one can say, at the early stage of writing about calligraphy, is that the notion of ideas or meaning being communicated in a nonverbal manner by calligraphy is present *by implication* through the parallel with the *Yi jing* passages. It would not be until later times that the notion of calligraphy containing or conveying an idea would become an explicit and central notion in discussions of the art.

What the early texts do explicitly address is the thought that calligraphy and its images have the power to partake of what is divine or numinous. Cai Yong says this directly in "Zhuan shu": "Its forms are essential and marvelous, with an ingenuity that enters the realm of the divine" (形要妙，巧入神).[9] At the end of his essay "Jiu shi" 九勢 (The Nine Configurations), Cai Yong similarly characterizes the aim and ideal of calligraphy: "When the accomplishment with brush and ink is grand, we enter into the domain of the marvelous" (須翰墨功多，即造妙境耳).[10]

We might first be inclined to discount the significance of such statements, viewing them as rhetorical flourishes. In fact, such claims are fundamental to the new awareness of calligraphy as something beyond "handwriting"—that is, a mere medium to convey verbal meaning. Moreover, the early statements about the capacity of calligraphy to enter into the realm of the divine or marvelous are buttressed at every turn by a cluster of other claims and conceits that in various ways all seek to establish for calligraphy a significance that lies beyond what words can express, is independent of any human or natural analogue, supercedes any other human craft, and has the potential to convey a meaning that is transcendent of the mundane world and ineffable. These claims, being interwoven and interdependent, cannot be neatly separated. But let us examine some of the key formulations.

There is, first, the idea that the calligrapher's brush produces forms that *resemble* familiar forms and shapes. But there is a limit to that resemblance. Consequently, calligraphy is suspended between likeness and unlikeness (i.e., it has distinctiveness). We read, for example, that "the rectangular forms do not match the carpenter's square, the round ones do not accord with his compass" (Cui Yuan). This is said of draft script, but the seal script is likewise said to be "neither square nor round" (Cai Yong). In other words, there are shapes to be seen in the traces of the calligrapher's brush, and these shapes are reminiscent of those made with exquisite care by craftsmen, but the calligrapher is not bound by their rules or forms.

This constant variation of the forms produced by the calligrapher's brush is fundamental to his art. This aspect of calligraphy is directly acknowledged by Zhong You 鍾繇 (151–230) when he says:

> It adjusts to circumstance and accords with what is right, so that there is no constant rule. At times it stretches tall and reaches wide, at times it is like teeth on a comb or needles in a row, at times it is as level as a millstone and straight as a rope, at times it wriggles like a snake, all topsy-turvy, at times the verticals slant and the corners lean, at times it has the compass's circle and the square's angles. The elongated and curtailed complement each other, and the disparate forms share a common configuration.[11]

It is to be noted that this passage does not describe different styles of the script under discussion (clerical script). Instead, it describes the constant variation within any style of the script; hence the assertion that "the disparate forms share a common configuration" (異體同勢).

Zhong You's description mixes abstract language, naming geometric shapes, with metaphors. But the point is surely the same as in the writings by Cui Yuan and Cai Yong, where there is a higher concentration of concrete metaphors and analogies. We may say that these descriptive passages invariably present a multiplicity of images or analogies for two reasons: the calligraphic forms are perceived to be constantly changing as the eye views character after character with ever changing compactness or sparseness of strokes and different combinations of verticals, horizontals, angles, curves, etc., and no single analogy, even for a particular character, is felt to be sufficiently accurate or precise. To assert "the disparate forms share a common configuration" is to say that there is a unifying consistency of image and form to each of the script forms (seal, clerical, draft), which is why they are felt to be integral and coherent, each by itself. The separate characters are not as dissimilar as the wildly divergent metaphors in the typical litany might lead us to suppose. If they were, there would be no coherence to the calligraphic inscription as a whole. We may even suggest that the instability of the metaphorical equivalences in these accounts, the way that none is sustained and each immediately gives way to another, usually of radically different tenor and tone, is itself indicative of the writer's keen awareness that none of them is by itself very satisfying. Most readers will naturally read the string of metaphors itself as an approximation of how the calligraphy appears here and there. But another reading is also possible: it is like this; no, it is like that. The writer struggles to come up with an apt comparison, only to conclude that what he presents is inadequate and then to try again. In either case, it is clear that the metaphors and analogies are only approximations, and any one of them is ultimately imperfect, which is why so many are offered.

There is an intriguing dichotomy to the overall impression that calligraphy imparts, as described in these accounts. That impression combines a sense of infinite variation within a consistent manner or thrust. "There is no constant rule" (靡有常制), yet "the disparate forms share a common configuration." We may link the two components of this apparent contradiction to two other frequently mentioned impressions. The first, which springs from the "common configuration," is the sense of "rightness" that the inscription as a whole conveys. "There is propriety wherever we look" (俯仰有儀; Cui Yuan); "not a single stroke could be altered" (一畫不可移; Cui Yuan); "it adjusts to circumstance and accords with what is right" (隨事從宜; Zhong You); "what a spectacle it is, in its perfect balance of outer beauty and inner substance! (粲斌斌其可觀; Cai Yong).[12] And yet this "rightness" contains an element of mystery. It is beyond the power of the eye or mind to fully comprehend or account for it. This is the consequence of the bewildering variety of shapes and strokes that defies the identification of "a constant rule." "When you examine it from close at hand, the ends and junctures cannot be distinguished and the ideographic components cannot be

traced" (迫而視之，端際不得見，指撝不可勝緣; Cai Yong); "its work-
ings are supremely subtle and its essentials are marvelous" (機微要妙;
Cui Yuan); "when you examine it from close at hand, the mind is confused and the eye dazzled" (近而察之，心亂目眩; Zhong You).[13] The
conceits that we have seen about historical exemplars follow from this.
Because calligraphy defies rational apprehension, the greatest mathe-
maticians could never count its strokes, the most discerning viewers
could never follow or fathom its brush strokes, and the greatest craftsmen could never match its technical skill or replicate its forms. The
"rightness" that calligraphy exhibits, in other words, transcends language and, indeed, rational analysis. Naturally, it also transcends the
objects of the physical world that are cited to describe it.

A passage in Cai Yong's essay "Bi lun" 筆論 (On the Writing
Brush) may be used to summarize this discussion:

> Calligraphic forms must partake of worldly shapes and appearances. They
> must resemble sitting and walking, flying and moving, going away and
> approaching, lying down and arising, being sad and happy, insects eating
> the leaves of trees, sharp swords and long halberds, a mighty bow and rigid
> arrow, water and fire, clouds and mists, or the sun and moon. It is only
> when writing presents, this way and that, forms that may be viewed as such
> images that it can be called calligraphy.[14]

There is an expectation—indeed, a requirement—that calligraphic
forms will remind the viewer of forms and actions in the three-
dimensional world. But again, it is just a "resemblance" (ruo 若). Moreover, there is some equivocation evident in the language of the
penultimate phrase: 縱橫有可象者. "Zongheng" 縱橫 ("this way and
that" or even "here and there") suggests that these resemblances are not
exact correspondences and that they may appear different to different
viewers. This is exactly what the preceding list implies. What reminds
one onlooker of "flying" may remind another of "moving," etc.
Depending upon how they are viewed ("this way and that"), the images
are liable to change right before one's eyes. "You ke xiang zhe" 有可象
者, "[presents forms] that may be viewed as such images," likewise suggests a certain ambiguity in the calligraphic forms. To say that they
"may be viewed" as images is to say that they sometimes will and sometimes will not or that some of them will and some of them will not.
Finally, we find here the same key term, "xiang" (images), as found in

the *Yi jing* passage with which we began. A *xiang* is not a picture or replica of anything in the physical world. It is an abstracted construct that somehow captures the essence of the thing but not exactly its physical form. This has been clear from the beginning, inasmuch as it is clear that the "images" in the hexagrams that Bao Xi invented were not pictures of things in the world that inspired him.

For all of these reasons, then, the passage conveys a notion of calligraphy as simultaneously being reminiscent of physical things and independent of them. Calligraphy exists in a realm between representation and abstraction. If it does not call to mind the myriad shapes of the world, it has no power or potential. Then it is just handwriting, not "calligraphy." Yet at the same time, calligraphy lies beyond the worldly forms of which it may remind us. Those forms appear and disappear in the mind and eye of the viewer as he looks at the inscription. They are inherently fluid and unstable, and therein lies their distinctiveness from the things of the real world.

Jin Dynasty Thought on Calligraphy

As writings on calligraphy mature and proliferate—that is, as we move from the initial Han-Wei period to what could be considered the second stage or period, that of the Jin dynasty (265–419)—attention to an underlying *something* conveyed by or embodied in calligraphy escalates. The trope of nature still dominates writings about the art, as critics continue to stress that the calligrapher is inspired by the natural (and cultural) forms in the world around him and mimics them with his brush. But this emphasis upon the "images" *(xiang)* captured in calligraphy subtly yet steadily yields ground to consideration of other modes of meaning that might be discovered in this art of the brush. The argument in the preceding analysis of Han-Wei writings is that both of these aspects of thinking about calligraphy are already evident in the earliest writings. The importance of the "images" of nature to understandings and justifications of the art in Han-Wei thought is immediately obvious. What may be less evident is that even in these first attempts to characterize the art, the analogy with nature was somehow felt to be less than fully adequate. It had to be complemented by acknowledgment that calligraphy was capable of conveying, beyond the "images," a deeper significance or meaning. The model and inspiration for this idea was surely the archetype of the ancient sage, who "established images in order to express their ideas." But with calligraphy, it was not at first easy to make the same claim about "ideas" since the art did not come with a text attached to it, explicating the "ideas" embodied in the "images," as did the hexagrams in the *Yi jing*. And so the earliest theorists on calligraphy were content to refer vaguely to an import that was "marvelous" or "divine" and lay beyond the ability of language to explain.

The situation changes with the advent of the Jin dynasty. We begin to find then explicit references to *yi* (idea) as something that the finest calligraphy attains and conveys: "Then Cang Jie was born, who invented writing. Tadpole characters and bird seal script were modeled on things and represented their forms in images. Later enlightened sages introduced variants on these, giving rise to abundant *yi* and ingenuity (睿哲變通，意巧滋生)" (Suo Jing 索靖 [239–303]).[15] This interest in *yi* as a calligraphic ideal has its clearest articulation, appropriately enough, in the writings of the greatest calligrapher of the period, Wang Xizhi 王羲之 (303–361 or 321–379). In Wang's writings the concept occurs with unprecedented frequency and is given a new level of importance. (I follow Li Zehou in relying upon Wang's personal letters for his views on calligraphy, rather than on the several essays dubiously attributed to him.)[16] Examples are given below:

> I have expended my mind fully on such refined work for a long time. When I examine the ancients, I find that only Zhong You and Zhang Zhi attain real excellence. The others have only minor fine points; their insufficiency lies in *yi* (不足在意). After these two masters, my calligraphy comes next. Recently, I received your calligraphy. Your *yi* has gradually become more profound (意轉深). There is *yi* evident between all the dots and strokes (點畫之間皆有意). It is something that cannot be described in words. In the most marvelous examples, everything is this way.[17]

> Zijing's "flying white" script possesses a great amount of *yi* (大有意).[18]

> The calligraphy that you have learned possesses *yi* (君學書有意); today I'm sending you a scroll in my own draft script.[19]

> I am unable to make my "flying white" script superior, but its *yi* is truly excellent (意乃篤好).[20]

Before examining the concept of "*yi*" as Wang Xizhi utilizes it, we should take note of a parallel usage in contemporary philosophical discourse that likely influenced Wang and facilitated his adoption of the term. That influence is Wang Bi's 王弼 (226–249) famous commentary on the *Yi jing*, a work of paramount importance in the entire Abstruse Learning 玄學 movement of the period.[21] Wang Bi's commentary specifically focuses on the problems of the significance of *xiang* and of their relationship both to language (*yan* 言) and to some deeper meaning, making it readily applicable or transferable to thinking about calligraphy. Although the theorist on calligraphy thinks of these key terms in a different context—that of artistry with the brush rather than the hexagrams of the *Yi jing*—he is concerned with the same terms and relationships. And as we have seen, there is a long and, indeed by Jin times, unavoidable association between rationalizations of calligraphy and approaches to the *Yi jing*.

Wang's thinking about these issues is summarized in his "General Remarks on the *Zhouyi*," which presents an overview of his approach to the classic. The key passage is contained in the essay entitled "Ming xiang" 明象 (Clarifying the Images).[22] Wang's understanding of the "images" in the *Yi jing* marked a radical departure from Han dynasty interpretations, which had insisted upon linking the "images" to numbers (an approach known as *xiangshu* 象數) and then using mathematical operations to combine and recombine the numbers to generate new trigrams and hexagrams. The whole procedure was linked to cosmological and calendrical calculations. By liberating the "images" from such calculations and by understanding them instead as signifying abstract ideas, Wang Bi cleared the way for a reading of the *Yi jing* that was rich in metaphysical, literary, and personal meanings.[23]

For our purposes, what is particularly interesting is the equivocation over the importance and role of the "images" that is evident in Wang Bi's interpretation. He begins by asserting that "images" are capable of "yielding up completely" the ideas behind them, just as words have the ability to convey fully the meanings of those same "images." But this notion quickly gives way to one that is quite contrary. Following *Zhuang Zi* 莊子, he reverts to the thought that the "images" are merely an expedient for conveying ideas and that once the idea has been grasped, the "image" has no enduring use or value. Not content with this, he carries this devaluation of "images" even further in the next paragraph. It is not just that "images" may be dispensed with once the idea has been grasped, but also that keeping an "image" in mind (staying "fixed" on it) ensures that the idea will *not* be grasped. What will be grasped is only the "image" itself or perhaps the wrong idea. Consequently, Wang Bi arrives at his conclusion that "getting the ideas is in fact a matter of forgetting the images" (得意在忘象).

We have already seen something analogous to this ambivalence in the parallel discussions of the "images" presented by calligraphy in Han and Wei period texts. The discovery of "images" of the three-dimensional world in the brush strokes of calligraphy is ubiquitous in the early texts. But the same texts also insist that calligraphy conveys something that goes beyond those images and cannot be approximated adequately by them. That is why, as observed above, it may be said that calligraphy is felt to be both rooted in nature and to transcend it.

What Abstruse Learning and Wang Bi in particular seem to have contributed to this discussion—and what I would suggest is Wang's influence upon Jin period thinking about calligraphy—has two components. The first is Wang's insistence that the "images" of the hexagrams must actually be banished from the mind if it is to grasp the idea conveyed by them; this insistence gives new weight to the contention that there is something beyond the images before the eye. With Wang Bi, there is no longer any doubt about wherein the ultimate value lies. It lies in the "abstruse mystery," the "Nothingness," that is the Dao of his philosophical school. Transposed to calligraphy, this is largely a matter of a new emphasis. With its famous veneration of the unknown and unnamable, Abstruse Learning had the effect of giving more weight and legitimacy to a conception of calligraphy that saw it as something more than the "images" of nature. Under the influence of Wang Bi, it became plausible to begin to think of the traditional metaphors and analogies as *quite* inadequate for a full appreciation of the art. The second, which follows from the first, is that Wang Bi actually gave a name to this elusive "meaning" that lay behind the "images." To be sure, the *Yi jing* had already used the term "*yi*" to designate what the sages sought to convey through the hexagrams. But Wang Bi does not refer just in passing to that term. He makes it a part of his systematic analysis of the *Yi jing* (in the continuum of "idea"—"images"—"words") and indeed gives it primacy even as he insists that words and "images" must be forgotten if the "idea" is to be grasped. This is a singular conception of "idea," that no definitive words can approximate it, and one that obviously lends itself to appropriation by those looking for a term to designate the nonverbal import or "meaning" of art. This is, I would argue, precisely what Jin dynasty calligraphy critics did, jumping at the chance to incorporate into their enthusiasm for calligraphy the philosophical term that had recently been given such currency and weight.

What precisely does Wang Xizhi mean by "*yi*" in the passages cited above? Given the later history of the term's usage in writings about calligraphy, we might assume that Wang is thinking about the "idea" or "meaning" that is originally contained in the artist's mind and that he then "lodges" in his brushwork. This is the sense in which "*yi*" was regularly used in calligraphy criticism in the Song and later dynasties. But Wang Xizhi's understanding of the term is at variance with later usages, and it is precisely because his understanding draws heavily upon Abstruse Learning thought, as shaped by Wang Bi, that this is so.[24] As we have seen above, Wang Xizhi speaks of "*yi*" as something that is either present or absent in the finished work and seems to be quite independent of the calligrapher's intentionality or aims: "The other [ancient calligraphers] have only minor fine points; their insufficiency lies in *yi*. . . . Recently, I received your calligraphy. Your *yi* has become more profound. There is *yi* evident between all the dots and strokes. It is something that cannot be described in words." It does not sound like Wang Xizhi is talking about the calligrapher's intent or personality. He is talking about something that the finest calligraphy attains, that is "profound," that is in the best works evident even in the tiniest dots (or *between* them), and that cannot be captured or described in words. This, then, is not analogous to the poet's "idea," which, in Lu Ji's 陸機 (261–303) formulation, his writing may or may not "capture."[25] Nor is it a quality that simply reflects the calligrapher's inner nature, transferred automatically from personality to brushwork, so that it might be judged to be admirable, fawning, or indifferent. It is rather something that the calligraphy itself, not the calligrapher, embodies and exudes. It is even independent, to a degree, of technical proficiency: "I am unable to make my 'flying white' script superior, but its *yi* is truly excellent." If a work of calligraphy "possesses *yi*," it will be distinguished. If *yi* is lacking, nothing else really matters.

Wang Xizhi's *yi*, his calligraphic ideal, is strongly reminiscent of the "ideas" in Wang Bi's treatment of the *Yi jing* that are conveyed by images and words but also lie beyond them. But there is a crucial difference between the two. Wang Xizhi's *yi* may be, like Wang Bi's, profound and ineffable, but it is also aestheticized, as Wang Bi's "ideas" are not. As important as *yi* itself is in Wang Xizhi's remarks on calligraphy, it is not conceived of independently of the beauty of the brushwork, and so the brushwork itself never becomes dispensable (as Wang Bi's "images" do). Wang Xizhi says, "and so I realize that in your calligraphy every character is fresh and extraordinary, every dot is perfectly turned, so that the beauty could not be greater" (亦知足下書字字新奇，點點圓轉，美不可再).[26] Similar references to the sheer beauty or intricate delicacy (*qi mi* 綺靡) of brushwork are widespread in writings of Wang Xizhi's period.[27] In fact, this emphasis on the beauty and appeal of the brushwork is ultimately inseparable from the conviction that the finest calligraphy embodies a *yi* that transcends language. Wang Xizhi may have borrowed the *yi* of Abstruse Learning, but at the same time he transformed it from a metaphysical ideal to one that has both metaphysical and aesthetic properties.

Texts on Music

Music has a longer history as a recognized expressive form than calligraphy, and writings about music also began long before those about calligraphy. By piecing together the considerable amount of textual material on the subject of music found in the classics and other pre-Han and Han dynasty works, one could reconstruct a history of musicological thought in that period, which is something that could not be done for calligraphy.[28] Despite this venerable history, the great transformation of thinking about music and its elevation to new levels of independence and significance took place at roughly the same time that they took place for calligraphy and the other visual and literary arts—that is, during the late Han and Wei-Jin periods.

Turning from writings of the period on calligraphy to those on music, one is immediately struck by a conspicuous common feature: the preponderance of descriptive language and, in it, the prominence of the trope of nature. Reading Han accounts of music, especially the few surviving rhapsodies on different musical instruments, one is forcefully reminded of the nature images in Han writings on calligraphy. Here, for example, are lines from Ma Rong's 馬融 (79–166) "Rhapsody on the Long Flute" 長笛賦 (in David Knechtges's translation):

爾乃聽聲類形	And then, the sounds that one hears take on various forms:
狀似流水	Their manner is like flowing water,
又象飛鴻	And they further resemble soaring geese.
氾濫溥漠	Like water in flood, broad and boundless,
浩浩洋洋	They flow mighty and vast, powerful and strong,
長彎遠引	Drawing into the distance, as far as the eye can see,
旋復迴皇	Reeling and rebounding, wavering and wandering about....
繁手累發	Intricate cadences sound forth again and again,
密櫛疊重	Overlapping and repeating, close as comb teeth.
踊跟攢仄	Then, pressed and pushed together, compactly clustered,
蜂聚蟻同	The notes swarm like bees, converge like ants.
眾音猥積	A multitude of sounds gather about,
以送厥終	To send off the finale.[29]

Extended descriptions of this kind (much longer than the excerpt given here) may be found in virtually all the rhapsodies on music from the period.

It is not just the music itself that is described in a way that is replete with such images. Even the setting in which the raw material (in this case, bamboo) grows from which the instruments will be fashioned is typically treated in a similar way. A rich cacophony of nature sounds (e.g., the crying of gibbons, rushing of rapids, whirring of breezes, chattering of squirrels, singing of pheasants) is described. These sounds lend to the wood, as it is sprouting and developing, an intrinsic affinity with audible nature that will eventually show itself in the music that the instrument performs.[30]

The parallel between music and calligraphy does not stop with the role played by the natural world in the thinking and description of both arts. There is also an ultimate abstract value posited for music that transcends the art's affinity with nature, much like the concept of "*yi*" in thinking about calligraphy. That value is *he* 和, "harmony." Furthermore, conceptions of this ultimate ideal in music also underwent significant transformation during the Wei-Jin period. The result of this transformation was the establishment of a concept of "harmony" that claimed for music a new order of meaning and independence, much as did the new conception of "*yi*" for calligraphy.

The notion of "harmony" as the supreme value of music was certainly not new. What was new was the sort of "harmony" envisioned. The earlier tradition of writings on music is overwhelmingly concerned with the ability of music to bring about a grand social harmony among persons of different rank and social standing. As the "Record of Music" 樂記 in *Li ji* 禮記 (Classic of Ritual) says, "Music serves to unite people, while the rituals serve to differentiate them" (樂者為同，禮者為異).[31] This is the Confucian vision of the function of music in a well-ordered society, in which music is coordinated with the rituals in bringing about a social harmony and unity that consists, nevertheless, of a thoroughly and rigidly hierarchical structure.

In Han dynasty rhapsodies on music, such as Ma Rong's excerpt above, we already see a change from such earlier "classical" discussions of the subject. The earlier accounts, such as those in *Xun Zi* 荀子 and in the "Record of Music," do not dwell upon descriptions of the sound. They concentrate instead upon discussions of the social effects of good (and bad) music and their ramifications for the orderly rule of the state. Since their focus is not on the aural aspects of musical performance, they do not feature an elaborate descriptive language. The trope of nature as an analogy or inspiration for all the sonorities of music is thus left largely undeveloped.

To be sure, passing reference is made in the classics to the idea that "music is the harmony of heaven and earth" (樂者天地之和也).[32] There is also the observation that "the clear and distinct [musical passages] present an image (*xiang*) of heaven, the ample and grand present an image of earth, the beginnings and endings present an image of the progression of the four seasons, and the circulation and returning [of the actors and dancers] present an image of winds and rain."[33] But such assertions are intended more to posit a cosmic analogue for the harmonies of court ritual music, to evoke cosmic order as an analogy and justification for imperial authority, than they are intended genuinely to explore the idea of a cosmic origin for human music. Actually, the concept of an affinity between music and nature is not so clearcut or well established in pre-Han times as it is with calligraphy. There is no archetype in the field of music so compelling as that of the sage-inventor of the hexagrams and images.

What we detect in the Han rhapsodies is a new interest in strengthening the idea of a correspondence between natural or cosmic music and its human counterpart, so that many aural phenomena in nature are listed as "resemblances" to the sounds that musical instruments produce. Han dynasty cosmological thinking, which developed elaborate schemes correlating cosmic phenomena with human inventions (including musical tones and modes), surely contributed to this new way of thinking about music. No doubt the descriptive conventions of the rhapsody form also encouraged writers to elaborate upon this correspondence once it had been discovered.

These innovations in musicological thought become explicit and self-conscious with Ruan Ji 阮籍 (210–263), who wrote at length on the subject. In addition to his "Yue lun" 樂論 (Essay on Music), several other of his writings—including "Tong *Yi* lun" 通易論 (Analyzing *The Classic of Changes*), "Da *Zhuang* lun" 達莊論 (Comprehending *Zhuang Zi*), "Qing si fu" 清思賦 (Rhapsody on Pure Thinking), and "Daren xiansheng zhuan" 大人先生傳 (Biography of the Great Man)—touch on music and related issues.

Here I will identify three aspects of Ruan Ji's treatment of music that are significant departures from earlier Confucian accounts. The first is his insistence that music is a phenomenon that transcends human invention and human society. Music is cosmically pervasive and it reveals the fundamental unity of all things. This conception is the key to the opening passage in his "Yue lun":

> What we call "music" is none other than the forms of heaven and earth, and the innate natures of all the myriad things. When the forms are united and the innate natures obtained, there is harmony (合其體，得其性，則 和); when the forms are separated and the innate natures lost, there is discord. In ancient times, when the sages created music, they accorded with the forms of heaven and earth (以順天地之體) and brought to fruition the natures of the myriad things.[34]

What Ruan says here about music is remarkably similar to what he says elsewhere about the *Yi jing*.[35] It seems likely, in fact, that Ruan Ji's conviction about the pervasive immanence of music in all things comes from the analogy of the *Yi jing* and its underlying presence in the grand unity of nature.

In any case, comparing Ruan Ji's opening statement about music with that in the "Yue ji" chapter in *Li ji*, we see that the classic presents a radically different orientation:

> Melodic lines arise from the hearts of men. The heart is moved when external things cause it to be so. The affections, thus being moved by external things, express themselves in sounds. As these sounds respond to each other, they are transformed. When these transformations are complete, we have a melodic line. When such lines are combined for the pleasure that they give and enhanced by shields and axes or plumes and ox-tails [in performances representing battlefield scenes], then we have what is known as "music."[36]

The emphasis here is on a concept of music as uniquely human, a product of the human heart-mind as it reacts emotionally to the stimulus of external things. There is no suggestion that those external things contain music, much less that music is their "innate nature." There is likewise no hint of any thought of a commonality between human music and the sounds of nature. Indeed, what is stressed is the divergence between human music and the sounds produced by other animate creatures, and even the distinction between the gentleman's "music" and something lesser produced by the masses: "Melodic lines are produced by the hearts of men. Music brings into communication similar and dissimilar melodic lines. So it is that birds and beasts know sound but do not know melodic lines, and the commoners know melodic lines but do not know music. It is only the gentleman who is able to know music."[37]

The second key aspect of Ruan Ji's conception of music concerns its relation to the emotions. Here too we see Ruan Ji arguing for an understanding of music that divorces it from the purely human and subjective. His views on the subject mark a departure from the classical Confucian understanding of music as something that gives expression to the full range of emotions while serving at the same time to regulate them, and they also break with the Han dynasty emphasis on music and its special affinity to one emotion in particular—that is, sadness or sorrow (*bei* 悲, *ai* 哀). Ruan Ji is very clear in his rejection of this latter viewpoint, which was widespread in his own day, and appeals in his rejection to the authority of the ancient equivalence of "music" with "joy, pleasure," based on the two readings and meanings of the character 樂 (*yue/le*).[38] At the same time, Ruan Ji's understanding of music does not conform to the traditional Confucian understanding of its relation to the emotions either. Elsewhere in "Yue lun" he says:

"Therefore, when Confucius was in Qi and heard the 'Shao' music, for three months he did not know the taste of meat. It means that the finest music causes people to be without desires, making their hearts calm and their 'breath' settled (言至樂使人無欲，心平氣定), so that they no longer find meat tasty. Viewed in this light, we see that music of the sages consists of harmony and nothing more."[39]

He also observes, in a similar vein:

> Qian and kun are easy and simple, therefore the most elegant music is not
> complicated. The Way and Virtue are calm and placid, therefore the five
> tones have no flavor (道德平淡，故五聲無味). Being uncomplicated, yin
> and yang are in perfect communication; having no flavor, the myriad
> things are joyful of their own accord. The empire progresses daily towards
> transformation to goodness without knowing it, and customs become
> increasingly simple as everything shares the same music. This Way of
> naturalness is the beginning of music.[40]

For society and the state, music serves to keep customs "simple" through its flavorless components and induces the "joy" of harmonious unity. For the individual, music has the analogous effect of calming the mind and stabilizing the vital forces, so that there are no longer any desires. Both conditions are part of Ruan Ji's larger vision of social and individual salvation, which are heavily dependent upon Abstruse Learning values. We are reminded of Ruan Ji's image of the Perfect Man as described in his essay on Zhuang Zi: "The Perfect Man is at peace with life and is quiescent regarding death.... His mind and breath are calm and controlled, so they do not dissipate or become sullied."[41] Similarly, there is this description of the personal ideal in his "Rhapsody on Pure Thinking": "With a heart of ice and body of jade, he is purified and retains his thought; being at peace and placid and free of passions, he attains his intent and accords with his feelings."[42] In Ruan Ji's thought generally, the desires or passions are something to be transcended and abandoned. Music may be "joy, pleasure" to him, but what he has in mind when he says this is a serene, philosophical "joy."

The traditional Confucian viewpoint is significantly different. As we have seen, that viewpoint holds that the emotions are absolutely fundamental to music. It is when the heart comes into contact with external things and is moved by them that "sounds" are produced in the first place. This centrality of the emotions to music is pervasive in Confucian accounts. That is not to say that the emotions are always considered positive, for, as we know, Confucian thinking about music is nothing if not obsessed with the danger of music's potential to release uncontrolled and excessive emotions. The function of proper music, in fact, is to ensure that the emotions, "which cannot be avoided," are suitably controlled and regulated, so that they always conform with Confucian virtues.[43] This is the basis of the sage's paradigmatic reaction to correct music: "It is joyful but not wanton, sorrowful without injury"; or "there is worry but not disaffection ... thought without fear."[44] The point is certainly not that there is no emotion, but the emotion is measured and proper. The composure that Ruan Ji envisions, the calmness and flavorlessness of his musical ideal, is distinct from this.

The last point of Ruan Ji's views that is important to us here is an idea that the greatest beauty transcends worldly forms. The idea constitutes the opening statement in his "Qing si fu":

> I maintain that forms that are visible are not the most beautiful of sights, and notes that can be heard are not the finest music (余以為形之可見，非色之美，音之可聞，非聲之善). In ancient times the Yellow Emperor ascended to the realm of immortals from the top of Mount Jing, and performed "Xian Pool" over the embankment of Southern Marchmount. He was like a ghostly spirit in his obscurity, so that the musicians Kui and Ya did not get to hear his tune.[45] Similarly, Nüwa displayed her glory on the shore of the Eastern Ocean, and floated in the air beside the hills to the west. Trees and rocks followed her, dropping into the sea, and consequently she never showed her eminence in Jasper Tower.[46] So it is that only when there is hidden mystery that has no form and utter stillness with nothing to hear that one can perceive true loveliness and purity (是以微妙無形，寂寞無聽，然後乃可以睹窈窕而淑清).[47]

We are accustomed to claims that the highest truth (or the Way) is formless, that it cannot be captured in words, that Nothing is the source of all things, etc. As an analogy for this philosophical position, we are also familiar with the assertion that "the great note is rarefied in sound; the great image has no shape."[48] What is new in Ruan Ji's formulation is the centrality of aesthetics to his statement. He does not refer to "beautiful sights" and "fine music" simply as a way of evoking the Way that cannot be named. What is uppermost in his mind is beauty, for this is the introduction to a poetic account of his encounter with a goddess of unearthly beauty and his frolic with her through the empyrean. Interestingly enough, in this account it is the poet's own zither music that first transports his spirit aloft, "as if ascending Kunlun Mountain and overlooking the Western Ocean." Eventually, in this elevated state, he encounters the goddess of incomparable purity and grace (who will finally elude him). Of course he *perceives* her beauty, *hears* her elegant words, and *savors* her marvelous perfume. But these sensations are presented as unworldly ones. The goddess is, indeed, the embodiment of the highest beauty that has no earthly form or sound. She is testament to Ruan Ji's opening claim; she is conceived on the analogy of the beautiful forms that we know in this world but at the same time leaves them behind.

Ruan Ji here stakes out a position about the nature of beauty that bears directly upon our inquiry into perceptions of the relationship between the arts and nature. His is a more forceful denial of the assumption that beauty is confined to worldly forms than perhaps had ever been made previously. He does not develop the idea with regard to music (since his immediate purpose is to celebrate the ethereal beauty of the goddess he encounters), but he does at least make mention of music. His idea will be taken up and magnified by the next great thinker on music, Ji Kang 嵇康 (223–262).

The first of Ji Kang's innovations that must be discussed is his position that "music has no sorrow or joy." This proposition, radical in its day, constitutes the title of Ji Kang's famous essay on music and the emotions, "Sheng wu aile lun" 聲無哀樂論 (Music Has No Sorrow or Joy). I have discussed the essay at length elsewhere and will here touch only upon aspects of it relevant to the topic at hand.[49]

Ji Kang's position may be understood as a further development of Ruan Ji's claim that "true" music is not sad, nor does it engender that affection. Ruan Ji associates music with "joy" instead, but we have seen that despite the apparent affinity of this position with ancient Confucian notions, in fact Ruan Ji's "joy" is the "calm and flavorless" serenity of Abstruse Learning wisdom rather than the social and moral harmony of traditional Confucianism. Ji Kang is even more daring in the break he makes with orthodox ideas about music, insisting that "joy" as well as "sorrow" are utterly extrinsic to musical sound. Music may release emotions that are already present in the listener's or player's heart, but it does not carry or instill them by itself. In this regard music is like wine: a man who drinks may become very emotional (either "joyful" or "sorrowful"), but that is only because the wine facilitates the expression of pent-up emotion. The wine is not the cause or bearer of that emotion in the first place.

Ji Kang's thesis directly contradicts the equivalence so commonly given in the classics that "music is joy" (a step Ruan Ji had been unwilling to take). His boldness in advancing this thesis is a function of how important it is to him, both intellectually, as an Abstruse Learning thinker, and personally, as an accomplished *qin* player and a believer in the role of music in "nourishing life" 養生. For Ji Kang, music's origins in the cosmos and its natural harmonies elevate it beyond anything that human emotion could influence or alter:

> When heaven and earth bring together their virtues, the ten thousand things are thus engendered. Cold and heat go alternately forth, and the Five Phases are thereby completed. These manifest themselves in the five colors and the five musical notes. The existence of the notes and music is like that of the odors and flavors that permeate heaven and earth. The good and bad among them, though they may encounter corrupting and confounding circumstances, retain their inherent nature and do not change. How could like and dislike alter a tune, or sorrow or joy change its rhythm?[50]

> Emperor Shun ordered Kui to strike stones and chimes, and the eight notes were blended together, thus uniting men and gods in harmony. To judge from this, although the supreme music awaited the sage to first compose it, it did not thereafter require a sage to maintain it. Why? Music possesses a harmony derived from nature and that is not connected to human emotions.[51]

> Today, because we view worthy men as superior, we say that we like them, and because we view foolish men as inferior, we say that we dislike them. The liking and disliking are connected to us ourselves, while the worthiness and foolishness are connected to those other men. Could we, on the basis of our own likes and dislikes, call the first "likable man" and the other "unlikable man"? Or could we, because we happen to enjoy a particular flavor call it "enjoyable flavor" (i.e., instead of "sweet flavor, tart flavor," etc.) and call the one we happen to find offensive "offensive flavor"? To judge from this, inner and outer have different applications,

and objective and subjective [qualities] are named differently. Music
should be evaluated on the basis of good and bad. It has nothing to do
with sorrow or joy.[52]

In Ji Kang's view, to say that emotion is intrinsic to music would be
to demean it. It would make music in some fundamental sense subjective and personalized. As we see here, his understanding is rather
that music is as grand and universal as nature itself and its primal
forces.

Passages found in Ji Kang's "Qin fu" 琴賦 (Rhapsody on the Zither)
lend support both to the separation of the emotions from music and to
the claims about the cosmic and philosophical significance of the art.
The rhapsody's account of an idealized player and setting stresses the
chill of the evening air, the instrument being cool to the touch, and the
repose of the player's mind. The player eventually intones a song about
joining the Daoist Liezi on an immortals' flight through the skies:
"Viewing all things as the same, I am free from worldly cares; / I yield
to fate, go or stay at will."[53] Similarly, later Ji Kang gives this description of ideal listeners to a *qin* performance: "Unperturbed and empty
of care, rejoicing in antiquity, / They abandon worldly affairs and are
oblivious of self."[54]

There are many points in common between these descriptions of
qin music and its effects and Ji Kang's views on nourishing life (detailed
in his several essays on the subject), so many that there is no question
that the two subjects are closely related in his mind. The ideal of the
calm and placid mind; of rising above the emotions of joy and sorrow
(which are not only undesirable, but actually injurious to the mind and
spirit); of nurturing the mind with the "harmonies" of nature; and of
abandoning worldly concerns to gain insight into larger truths—these
are all as central to Ji Kang's teachings on nourishing life as they are to
his writings about the *qin* and music generally.[55]

So important are the spiritual and psychological effects of music to
Ji Kang's views on the subject that there is even a level at which the
music itself finally becomes dispensable (much like the "images" in
Wang Bi's interpretation of the deep meanings of the *Yi jing*). Ultimately, what matters most to Ji Kang the philosopher (if not to Ji Kang
the *qin* player) is the heart or mind as it is acted upon by music, not the
music itself. Consequently, he says the following at one point in his

essay on music and the emotions: "As for the nature of music, what is primary is the mind. Therefore, music that has no sound is the father and mother to the people" (故無聲之樂，民之父母也).[56] Elaboration of this notion is found in one of his essays on nourishing life: "If there is a 'master' within [i.e., in the heart/mind], then the inner gives pleasure/music to the outer. In this case, even if there are no bells or drums, the pleasure/music is complete" (雖無鍾鼓，樂已具矣).[57] We have seen this idea in Ruan Ji, where it is mentioned in connection with his idea that supreme beauty transcends material manifestation. Ji Kang is, if anything, even bolder than Ruan Ji since he puts his claim about "music that has no sound" in his essay on music. Once it had thus been articulated, this idea about the supremacy of soundless music would enjoy a rich and prominent place in Chinese thought on the art. From Tao Qian on, references to the "stringless zither" and superior expressiveness of "silent" music would become commonplace in treatments of music that link it with meditative communication and insight.

Ji Kang leaves us, then, with this interesting conjunction of representations about music. The notion of music as the human analogue of nature's symphony of sounds is very prominent in his writings. The descriptive elaborations of this idea in his rhapsody on the *qin* run to hundreds of lines. This effusiveness of nature language cannot, moreover, be accounted for entirely by the generic proclivities of the rhapsody form. In Ji Kang's thought, musical notes are immanent in the cosmic forces that pervade heaven and earth. For thinkers like Ruan Ji and Ji Kang, in other words, the music in nature is not just a projection or reflection of man's emotive condition or the social and political situation in the empire, as it tended to be in earlier writings, whether classic Confucian treatises or the Han rhapsodies on music. Music becomes, in Abstruse Learning thinking, larger than man. It has an essence all its own, derived from heaven and earth themselves, and is no longer either dependent on or even effected by man's emotions. At the same time, music becomes, in one sense, grander than nature itself. Nature is both the fullest embodiment of the harmonies of the five phases and an imperfect or incomplete embodiment. Given the insistence of these philosophers upon the supremacy of Nothing and its nameless and formless verities, no music, neither that of man nor of nature, could ever compare with the inaudible harmonies of the Way as they intuited it.

Texts on Painting

There is a third art that has similarities to the two dealt with so far. The parallel case of painting must at least be mentioned here, although space does not permit a full treatment of it. It may simply be said that thinking about painting underwent corresponding developments, although at a somewhat later time—namely, the late fourth and early fifth centuries. The primary theorists were Gu Kaizhi 顧愷之 (d. ca. 406) and Zong Bing 宗炳 (375–443). The first great innovation was to establish unequivocally the primacy of something beyond formal verisimilitude as the ideal and end of painting.[58] Such formal likeness had been the traditional ideal in painting, referred to variously with such phrases as "*tuhua qi xing*" 圖畫其形, "drawing [the subject's] form" (Liu Xiang 劉向 [ca. 77–ca. 6 B.C.]); "*fa qi xingmao*" 法其形貌, "replicating his body and face" (Ban Gu 班固 [32–92]); and "*xie qi xingxiang*" 寫其形象, "tracing his appearance" (Huangfu Mi 皇甫謐 [215–282]).[59] As an alternative conception, Gu Kaizhi promotes the notion of "*chuan shen*" 傳神, "transmitting the spirit" (he likewise speaks of "*xie zhao*" 寫照, "tracing the [inner] illumination"). While he also gives attention to formal likeness, he clearly subordinates it to the aim of capturing the inner life-spirit (e.g., in his notion of "*yi xing xie shen*" 以形寫神, "using the formal appearance to trace the spirit").[60]

At first, "*shen*" referred to the "spirit" of the person depicted in the painting. That is, "*shen*" was originally conceived as the liveliness or vitality of the subject in portraiture, a quality that lay beyond the person's physical features. Behind this new painterly interest in a person's *shen* is the general interest in human character and personality that is so widespread in the Wei-Jin period generally, exemplified in its earliest stage by Liu Shao's 劉邵 (fl. 240–250) treatise on character types, *Renwu zhi* 人物志 (Treatise on Personality Types). The fascination with the inner makeup of persons is attested in the wealth of anecdotes collected together in *Shishuo xinyu* 世説新語 (A New Account of Tales of the World), a collection organized around personality traits. Evident in that work is a view of inner qualities as more valuable and meaningful than external and patently visible ones (e.g., "Someone asked, 'How would Du Hongzhi compare with Wei Hu?' Huan Yi replied, "Hongzhi had purity of complexion [*fu qing* 膚清], while Wei Hu, radiantly shining, had gentility of the spirit [*shenling* 神令]).[61] At the same time, there is interest in the possibility of discerning inner qualities through knowing observation of the external. This is then quite logically extended to the issue of how a painter might evoke or capture those inner qualities through depictions of the external appearance. Several anecdotes in *Shishuo xinyu* involving the portrait painter Gu Kaizhi turn on this very issue. In his uncanny mastery of the art, Gu perceives that by adding three whiskers to the chin of Pei Kai he captures his subject's "spirit and intelligence" (*shen ming* 神明).[62] Gu's special attention to the eyes in portraiture, described in several anecdotes, also clearly springs from his desire to get beyond external forms and, through them, "to transmit the spirit."[63]

Later, notably with Zong Bing, the concept of "*shen*" began to be applied unambiguously to the painting of landscape. This change in itself was a key development and prepared the way for the subsequent elevation of landscape to become a major subject of painting. Zong Bing's assertions about *shen* in real landscape, and from there to painted representations of the same, must have been influenced by Buddhist thought of the day (including Zong's own faith in the religion). The idea that Buddhist "principle" (*li* 理) is present in landscape, and especially in mountains and streams that are remote from the corrupting effects of civilization, is reflected in Zong's beliefs about landscape as a material thing that nevertheless embodies "the numinous" (*ling* 靈) and, further, that "landscape through its formations beautifies the Way" (山水以形媚道).[64] Such notions allowed for an appreciation of painted landscapes that was not only aesthetic, but contained as well a degree of religious awe.

Conclusion

As we know, crucial developments regarding the conception and values of calligraphy, music, and painting took place during the late Han and the early post-Han era. Nature was a significant element in the way all three arts were thought of and described. With calligraphy and music, nature was a trope used to characterize the texture and qualities of the artistic media, to root them, as it were, in an analogy of universal familiarity. With painting, nature was not a trope but the subject matter of the art form itself (or at least a major subject matter option, the alternative to portraiture). The parallel among the three arts goes beyond their reliance upon the rhetoric or subject of nature. With all three, there was posited an ultimate meaning or goal of the art that lay beyond nature but was nevertheless intimately connected with it. For each art there was one term and concept, among many, that emerged as the key designation of this ultimate meaning. The key term differed with each art: for calligraphy it was "*yi*" (idea); for music, "*he*" 和 (harmony), and for painting, "*shen*" 神 (spirit). The choice of each term was determined by the circumstances or older ideologies connected with each art and unique to each. For calligraphy the deciding factor in giving special importance to "idea" was the connection between writing and the "images" and hexagrams in the *Yi jing*. For music, it was the ancient notion of a cosmic "harmony" uniting all within heaven and earth. For painting, it was the earlier dominance of portraiture as a subject and the assumption that a portrait might, like a person, possess an inner "spirit."

Different as they may have been, what the three concepts had in common was that each transcended nature as it was used in service of the three arts, and each, indeed, could readily be associated with the Way of heaven and earth. They each also transcended the perceptible forms of the respective art that embodies them: "idea" lies beyond the "images" presented by the written characters; "harmony" (cosmically conceived, not musically) lies beyond the sounds and notes of song; and "spirit" lies beyond the formal shapes and colors of painting. "Harmony" is associated with an extreme degree of this transcendence of form, to the extent that perfect "harmony" is often said to leave the medium behind altogether and consist, in fact, of "silent" music. Regardless, the primary significance of the establishment of the three ideals is that they lifted their respective arts above the formal and representational, so that the replication of nature (its shapes, movements, and sounds) was no longer the highest goal, and they gave to each a spiritual-metaphysical-aesthetic claim and dimension. The impulse to posit these higher ideals may well have sprung in part from an ambivalence over formalism—that is, a sense that art that did not seek to accomplish or capture anything beyond the forms of the world would never be accorded the kind of validation that the new aesthetic thinkers sought for it.

Nevertheless, nature played a special part in this conception of the arts and their ultimate aims. It had the role of an intermediary between the artistic forms and the ideals that came to be articulated. Without nature it is unlikely that the abstract ideals beyond it could have been posited. In what they were doing, the thinkers on these arts were essentially mimicking what long had been asserted about the inverted hierarchy of man, heaven and earth (nature), and the Way—that is, that one proceeds upward from man and civilization through nature (the ten thousand things) to arrive at the Way, the ultimate principle and the "mother of all things." But now, for the first time, it was to account for and validate the arts that such a model was constructed.

The three ideals were each closely associated with the Way, which lurks just barely above each. It is, in fact, the intimate association of "idea," "harmony," and "spirit" with the ultimate and ineffable that lends to each of the three its aura of profundity. Whatever the particular focus and context, whether metaphysical "idea," cosmic music, or the spirituality attributed to landscape, this was not the Way of ancient Confucianism but instead the Way of Abstruse Learning, fused with a new appreciation and validation of aesthetic beauty. In other words, the establishment of the three ideals marks a break with older understandings of music and the visual arts that located each squarely in a system of social-political-ethical values determined by Confucianism and other statecraft ideologies. With the new notions of calligraphic "idea," musical "harmony," and painterly "spirit" in place, writing with the brush was no longer valued solely for the semantic content of the words on the page, music was no longer prized only for its ritual uses or ability to unite persons of different rank and status, and painting was no longer appreciated primarily for its depiction of historical or religious paragons and the lessons they implicitly imparted. Nature and its supplementary ideals developed at this time thus contributed to the freeing up of the arts from their earlier subordination to politico-ethical concerns and prepared the way for further innovations in thinking about the arts that would follow during the later Six Dynasties period.

NOTES

1. Following the variant version of these lines found in the *Quan Hou Han wen* text; see note 2.

2. Cui Yuan's 崔瑗 text is preserved in quoted form in Wei Heng 衛恆, *Si ti shu shi* 四體書勢. I have used the version found in Wei Heng's biography in *Jin shu* 晉書 (Beijing: Zhonghua shuju, 1974), 36.1066. Compare the version of Cui Yuan's text found in *Quan Hou Han wen* 全後漢文 (in *Quan Shanggu Sandai Qin Han Sanguo Liuchao wen* 全上古三代秦漢三國六朝文, ed. Yan

Kejun 嚴可均 [Beijing: Zhonghua shuju, 1965 reprint of 1887–1893 edition]), 45.7a, with minor variations.

3. Reading the textual variant "*yuan*" 緣 in place of "*lü*" 綠.

4. Cai Yong's 蔡邕 essay is also preserved in Wei Heng's *Si ti shu shi;* see *Jin shu,* 36.1063–64, which I have followed. Compare the version of Cai Yong's text in *Quan Hou Han wen,* 80.1a.

5. *Zhou yi* 周易, "Xi ci zhuan" 繫辭傳, B/2; trans. from Richard John Lynn, *The Classic of Changes: A New Translation of the I Ching as Interpreted by Wang Bi* (New York: Columbia University Press, 1994), p. 77.

6. *Zhou yi,* "Xi ci zhuan," A/12; in Lynn, *Changes,* p. 67.

7. Xu Shen 許慎, "Xu" 序, *Shuo wen jie zi* 說文解字, in *Quan Hou Han wen,* 49.2b.

8. Li Zehou 李澤后, *Zhongguo meixueshi* 中國美學史 (Beijing: Zhongguo shehui kexue chubanshe, 1984), vol. 2, pp. 589ff.

9. Cai Yong, "Zhuan shi" 篆勢, in Wei Heng, *Si ti shu shi, Jin shu,* 36.1063.

10. Cai Yong, "Jiu shi" 九勢, in Chen Si 陳思, *Shu yuan jinghua* 書苑菁華 (Siku quanshu ed.), 19.2a.

11. Zhong You 鍾繇, "Li shi" 隸勢; quoted in Wei Heng, *Si ti shu shi, Jin shu,* 36.1065. See Li Zehou's discussion of Zhong You's authorship of this passage in *Zhongguo meixue shi,* vol. 2, p. 407.

12. Cai Yong, "Zhuan shi"; quoted in Wei Heng, *Si ti shu shi, Jin shu,* 36.1064.

13. Zhong You, "Li shi"; quoted in Wei Heng, *Si ti shu shi, Jin shu,* 36.1065.

14. Cai Yong, "Bi lun" 筆論, in Chen Si, *Shu yuan jinghua,* 1.2b–3a, adopting the textual emendations in Li Zehou's version of the text; see *Zhongguo meixue shi,* vol. 1, p. 598.

15. Suo Jing 索靖, "Cao shu shi" 草書勢, *Quan Jin wen* (in *Quan Shanggu Sandai Qin Han Sanguo Liuchao wen*), 84.10b.

16. Li Zehou, *Zhongguo meixue shi,* vol. 2, pp. 414, 418–419.

17. Wang Xizhi 王羲之, "Yu ren shu" 與人書, *Quan Jin wen,* 22.6a (Li Zehou, *Zhongguo meixue shi,* vol. 2, p. 419, whose textual emendations I have adopted, here and throughout these quotations).

18. Wang Xizhi, "Yu ren shu," *Quan Jin wen,* 22.6b, reading the variant character "*yi*" 意 for "*zhi*" 直 (Li Zehou, *Zhongguo meixue shi,* vol. 2, p. 419).

19. Wang Xizhi, "Za tie" 雜帖, *Quan Jin wen,* 23.4a (Li Zehou, *Zhongguo meixue shi,* vol. 2, p. 419).

20. Wang Xizhi, "Za tie," *Quan Jin wen,* 26.3a (Li Zehou, *Zhongguo meixue shi,* vol. 2, p. 419).

21. Li Zehou, *Zhongguo meixue shi,* vol. 2, pp. 420–421; compare his discussion of Wang Bi's treatment of "*yi*" and "*xiang,*" vol. 2, pp. 125–130.

22. Wang Bi, "Ming xiang" 明象, in "Zhouyi lueli" 周易略例, *Wang Bi ji jiaoshi* 王弼集校釋, ed. Lou Yulie 樓宇烈 (Beijing: Zhonghua shuju, 1980), vol. 2, p. 609; translated in Lynn, *Changes*, pp. 31–32.

23. My description of the impact of Wang's understanding of the "images" is derived from the account by Lynn, *Changes,* p. 17.

24. The point about the crucial difference between what Wang Xizhi means by "*yi*" and the sense of the same term in Song dynasty writings on calligraphy has been made by Liu Gangji 劉綱紀, *Shufa meixue jianlun* 書法美學簡論 (Hupei: Jenmin wenxue chubanshe, 1982), p. 90, and further elaborated by Li Zehou, *Zhongguo meixue shi*, vol. 2, pp. 430–433.

25. "[The poet] always worries ... that his writing may not capture his ideas" 恆患……文不逮意; Lu Ji 陸機, "Wen fu" 文賦, in *Wenxuan* 文選 (Hu Kejia, 1809 ed.), 17.1b.

26. Wang Xizhi, "Za tie," *Quan Jin wen,* 26.9a (Li Zehou, *Zhongguo meixue shi,* vol. 2, p. 419).

27. See Li Zehou, *Zhongguo meixue shi,* vol. 2, pp. 432–433.

28. A pioneering effort toward this end has been made by Kenneth J. DeWoskin, *A Song for One or Two: Music and the Concept of Art in Early China* (Ann Arbor: Center for Chinese Studies, 1982; Michigan Papers in Chinese Studies, no. 42), esp. chs. 3–6. See also Lothar von Falkenhausen, *Suspended Music: Chime-Bells in the Culture of Bronze Age China* (Berkeley: University of California Press, 1993).

29. Ma Rong, "Chang di fu" 長笛賦, *Wenxuan,* 18.6a–18.7a; in David Knechtges, trans., *Wenxuan, or Selections of Refined Literature,* vol. 3 (Princeton, N.J.: Princeton University Press, 1996), pp. 269–271.

30. See, for example, Ma Rong's rhapsody, "Chang di fu," *Wenxuan,* 18.2b–3b; in Knechtges, *Wenxuan,* vol. 3, p. 263 (lines 23–50).

31. "Yue ji" 樂記, *Li ji zhushu* 禮記注疏 (*Shisan jing zhushu* 十三經注疏, ed. Ruan Yuan 阮元, 1814), 37.11b.

32. Ibid., 37.16a.

33. Ibid., 38.10b.

34. Ruan Ji 阮籍, "Yue lun" 樂論, *Ruan Ji ji jiaozhu* 阮籍集校注 (Beijing: Zhonghua shuju, 1987), A.78.

35. Ruan Ji, "Tong *Yi* lun" 通易論, *Ruan Ji ji jiaozhu,* A.130.

36. See "Yue ji," *Li ji zhushu,* 37.1a.

37. Ibid., 37.7b–37.8b.

38. Ruan Ji, "Yue lun," *Ruan Ji ji jiaozhu,* A.99; translated in Ronald Egan, "The Controversy over Music and 'Sadness' and Changing Conceptions of the *Qin* in Middle Period China," *Harvard Journal of Asiatic Studies* 57, no. 1 (June 1997), p. 14.

39. Ruan Ji, "Yue lun," *Ruan Ji ji jiaozhu,* A.95.

40. Ibid., A.81.

41. Ruan Ji, "Da *Zhuang* lun" 達莊論, *Ruan Ji ji jiaozhu*, A.144.

42. Ruan Ji, "Qing si fu" 靜思賦, *Ruan Ji ji jiaozhu*, A.31.

43. "Yue ji," *Li ji zhushu*, 39.19a.

44. *Lun yu* 論語, 3/20, and *Zuo zhuan* 左傳; in *Chunqiu jingzhuan yinde* 春秋經傳引得, Harvard-Yenching Institute Sinological Index Series, supplement no. 11 [Taipei: Ch'eng-wen Publishing, 1966, reprint], 326/Xiang29/8.3–8.4 (on the music of Zhounan and Shaonan and Wang).

45. The allusion is to the story of how the Yellow Emperor ascended to the heavens when he performed his musical piece "Xian Pool." Here the point is that ordinary musicians, left back in the world, did not get to hear him.

46. The operative Nüwa story here is that she drowned while on an expedition to the Eastern Ocean and transformed into a bird that was seen atop the western hills overlooking the ocean when she was not filling the ocean with branches and stones. Consequently, Nüwa's beauty, like the music of the Yellow Emperor, was inaccessible to mortals.

47. Ruan Ji, "Qing si fu," *Ruan Ji ji jiaozhu*, A.29.

48. *Lao Zi* 老子, Book 41.

49. See Egan, "The Controversy over Music and 'Sadness,'" pp. 14–30.

50. Ji Kang 嵇康, "Sheng wu aile lun" 聲無哀樂論, *Ji Kang ji jiaozhu* 嵇康集校注 (Beijing: Renmen wenxue chubanshe, 1962), 5.197.

51. Ibid., 5.208.

52. Ibid., 5.199–200.

53. Ji Kang, "Qin fu" 琴賦, *Ji Kang ji jiaozhu*, 2.96; translated in Knechtges, *Wenxuan*, vol. 3, p. 291.

54. Ji Kang, "Qin fu," *Ji Kang ji jiaozhu*, 2.107; translated in Knechtges, *Wenxuan*, vol. 3, p. 301.

55. See Ji Kang, "Yang sheng lun" 養生論, *Ji Kang ji jiaozhu*, 3.143–157, passim.

56. Ji Kang, "Sheng wu aile lun," *Ji Kang ji jiaozhu*, 5.223.

57. Ji Kang, "Da nan yang sheng lun" 答難養生論, *Ji Kang ji jiaozhu*, 4.191.

58. My summary of Gu Kaizhi's and Zong Bing's views on painting in this and the following paragraphs is derived in large part from the analysis in Li Zehou, *Zhongguo meixue shi*, vol. 2, pp. 471–521.

59. For the three phrases, see, in order, the *jijie* 集解 commentary on *Shi ji* 史記 (Beijing: Zhonghua shuju, 1959), 3.94; *Han shu* 漢書 (Beijing: Zhonghua shuju, 1962), 54.2468; and the pseudo-Kong commentary on *Shang shu zhushu* 尚書注疏 (in *Shisan jing zhushu*), 10.1b.

60. Gu Kaizhi 顧愷之, "Lun hua" 論畫, as quoted in Zhang Yanyuan 張彥遠, *Lidai minghua ji* 歷代名畫記 (Siku quanshu ed.), 5.10a. For the ideal of *xie zhao* 寫照 in combination with *chuan shen* 傳神, see Gu's statement

recorded in Liu Yiqing 劉義慶, *Shishuo xinyu jianshu* 世説新語箋疏, ed. Yu Jiaxi 余嘉錫 (Beijing: Zhonghua shuju, 1983), 21.13.722.

61. Liu Yiqing, *Shishuo xinyu jianshu*, 9.42.524; compare Richard B. Mather, trans., *Shih-shou Hsin-yü: A New Account of Tales of the World* (Minneapolis: University of Minnesota Press, 1976), p. 260.

62. Liu Yiqing, *Shishuo yinyu jianshu*, 21.9.720.

63. Ibid., 21.13.722.

64. Zong Bing 宗炳, "Hua shanshui xu" 畫山水序, as quoted in Zhang Yanyuan, *Lidai minghua ji*, 6.3b.

Chapter 10

The Conceptual Origins and Aesthetic Significance of "*Shen*" in Six Dynasties Texts on Literature and Painting

Zong-qi Cai

"*Shen*" 神 is one of the most ubiquitous and polysemous terms in both philosophical and aesthetic discourses of premodern China. In many ways, its ubiquity has obscured its polysemy. As we frequently come across it in texts of all kinds, we become rather unmindful of its polysemous nature. We tend to see it as carrying the same nebulous import no matter where it appears. In translating it into English, therefore, we often choose the catchall term "spirit." This tendency to ignore the polysemy of "*shen*" is particularly conspicuous in literary and art criticism. Scholars of Chinese philosophy often seek to distinguish the meanings of "*shen*" in different texts, but we seldom observe similar efforts in either Chinese-language or English-language publications on traditional Chinese literary and art criticism. So it behooves us to carefully examine the neglected polysemy of "*shen*" in various major texts on literature and the arts.

Here I propose to study the polysemy of "*shen*" in Six Dynasties texts on literature and painting. During the Six Dynasties, "*shen*" began to be used extensively in reference to all major aspects of literary and art criticism. The proliferation of the term is very notable in discussions on authorial qualities, the creative process, the ranking of literary and art works, and the principles of aesthetic judgment. What is more significant is that this term figures prominently in some of the most important tenets or theories of literature and the arts developed during the Six Dynasties. Focusing on these tenets and theories, I shall examine how leading Six Dynasties critics ingeniously adapted different notions of *"shen"* developed by Confucian, Legalist, Daoist, Buddhist, and other philosophical schools to theorize about different aspects of literature and painting. By investigating the conceptual origins of *"shen"* in given tenets or theories, I aim not only to demonstrate the ramifying aesthetic significance of this all-important term, but also to shed some new light on the tenets or theories under discussion. As these tenets and theories constitute the core of Six Dynasties aesthetics, any new interpretation of them could in turn help us to better understand the broad historical development of Six Dynasties aesthetics.

"Shen" as Conscious Supernatural Beings: "Spirits and Man Are Thereby Brought into Harmony"

"Spirits and man are thereby brought into harmony" (*shen ren yi he* 神人以和) is the ending statement in the famous "Shi yan zhi" 詩言志 passage recorded in *Shang shu* 尚書 (The Book of Documents).[1] The word *"shen"* in this statement is used in its original sense of "live supernatural beings."

Xu Shen 許慎 (ca. 58–ca. 147) provides a phonological gloss (*yin xun* 音訓) of *"shen"* in his *Shuowen jiezi* 説文解字 (Explanations of Simple and Compound Words). He considers "𥘆" *(shen)* and "神" *(shen)* as homonymic and identical in meaning. He writes, "魗 *(shen)* is 神 *(shen)*."[2] In the *Shanhai jing* 山海經 (The Classic of Mountains and Seas), 魗 appears and refers to a particular mountain spirit in the Qiyao Mountains: "The Mountain Spirit Wu Luo rules there."[3] If we pursue a graph-based gloss (*xingxun* 形訓) of *"shen"* 神, we will reach the same conclusion about its original meaning. The 示 radical of 神 is used in oracle bone inscriptions and is written as 𥘆. Xu Zhongshu contends "𥘆 represents the shape of a wood symbol or stone pillar fashioned in the image of a divine being."[4] He further explains that "In prognostications made during sacrificial occasions and recorded in oracle bone inscriptions, this graph appears as a generic name for heavenly spirit, earthly gods, the late dukes, and the late kings."[5] In the bronze inscriptions of Shang and Zhou times, the word "神" begins to appear. It is constructed of 示 and a graph like 乙, signifying a man kneeling in worship. It is variously written as 示, 示, 示, and so on.[6] The fact that "示" can denote at once the spirits *(shen)* of heaven and earth and human ghosts (*gui* 鬼) speaks to an inseparable relationship of "*gui*" and "*shen.*" In fact, in the texts about high antiquity, spirits and ghosts often appear together. Sometimes they are distinguished as separate categories. Sometimes spirits are seen as the finest of ghosts.[7] More often they are used interchangeably, and as a result the phrase "*guishen*" 鬼神 (ghosts and spirits) comes into currency.

Sacrificial service to ghosts and spirits constitutes the center of human life from high antiquity through the end of the Shang. What we nowadays call literary and artistic activities are actually parts of sacrificial service. The "Minggui" 明鬼 (Explaining Ghosts) chapter of *Mo Zi* 墨子 speaks of the high religious purposes of writing:

> This is how the sage kings of ancient times, when they ruled the world, put the affairs of the ghosts and spirits first, and those of the people last. . . . Such was their deep concern for the service of the ghosts and spirits. But, fearing that their sons and grandsons in later ages would not understand this, they made a record of it on bamboo and silk to be handed down to posterity. Again, fearing that these might rot and become lost, so that later ages would have no way to learn what had been written on them, they inscribed it on bowls and basins, and engraved it on metal and stone as well.[8]

The "Shi yan zhi" passage tells of a similar use of poetry, songs, music, and dance for the service of ghosts and spirits. "Poetry expresses the heart's intent *(zhi)*;[9] singing prolongs the utterance of that expression. The notes accord with the prolonged utterance and are harmonized by the pitch tubes. The eight kinds of musical instruments attain to harmony and do not interfere with one another. Spirits and man are thereby brought into harmony."[10]

With the rise of humanism in the Zhou, the center of people's life gradually shifted from the service of ghosts and spirits to the governing of human affairs based on the principles of *li* 禮 (ritual). Along with this profound societal transition, poetry, songs, music, and writing were reconceptualized as the useful means of regulating nature's processes, human relationships, and even the cosmic order. Such new views of literature and the arts abound in the *Zuo zhuan* 左傳 (The Zuo Commentary), the *Guo yu* 國語 (Speeches of the States), the *Li ji* 禮記 (The Classic of Ritual), and other texts produced during the later Zhou and the Han. However, the phrase *"guishen"* by no means disappears from discussions on literature and the arts. In fact, it often figures just as prominently. In the *Guo yu*, for instance, Zhoujiu 州鳩, a famous entertainer, speaks emphatically of music's effects on the spirits *(shen)*: "Therefore, we chant with the virtue of the mean, and we sing with the notes of the mean. The virtue and notes are not violated and therefore they bring harmony between the spirits and man. Thus the spirits are put at ease and the commoners are made to listen."[11] In the midst of its discussion on the ethical and sociopolitical functions of *The Book of Poetry* (hereafter the *Poetry*), *"Shi da xu"* 詩大序 (The Great Preface to *The Book of Poetry*) makes a similar statement on the effects of the *Poetry* on the *guishen:* "To move heaven and earth and to win the sympathy of ghosts and spirits, nothing is nearly comparable to the *Poetry.*"[12]

Are the ghosts and spirits *(guishen)* in these two passages the same as the spirits *(shen)* in the "Shi yan zhi" passage? I would say no. In these two passages, there is a conspicuous absence of an ongoing sacrificial service like the one seen in the "Shi yan zhi" passage. Without the context of religious activities, it is difficult for us think of these ghosts and spirits as live supernatural beings who are being worshipped and invoked. What, then, are these ghosts and spirits if they can no longer be conjured up as live supernatural beings?

To answer this question, we must first investigate the new meanings of *"guishen"* developed in the philosophical texts of the late Zhou and the Han. In these texts, we find that ghosts and spirits seem to have gone through a process of naturalization.[13] In other words, they have become less live beings in a numinous world and more of an indwelling force of nature. Chapter 60 of the *Lao Zi* says, "If the Dao is employed to rule the empire, spiritual beings will lose their supernatural power. Not that they lose their spiritual power, /But that their spiritual power can no longer harm people."[14] Explaining this passage, Wang Bi 王弼 (226–249) writes, "If things abide by *ziran*, the spiritual power cannot do anything to them. As spiritual power cannot do anything to them, one does not know that spiritual power is spiritual power."[15] In naturalizing ghosts and spirits, Zhuang Zi went even fur-

ther. He simply regarded them as born of the Dao: "The Dao has its
reality and its designs but is without action or form.... Before heaven
and earth existed it was there. It gave spirituality to the spirits and to
the God on high; it gave birth to heaven and earth."[16] In the *Commentaries to the Book of Changes* (*Yi zhuang* 易傳), the Dao and *shen* (spirits)
are identified as one and the same: "One yin and one yang are called
the Dao"; "The unfathomable change of yin and yang is called *shen.*"[17]
In numerous Han texts, ghosts and spirits are commonly identified
with yin and yang to the extent that they are sometimes used as the
alternate name of yin and yang. For instance, yin and yang are called
two spirits in *Huainan Zi*: "There is the simultaneous birth of two spirits, which govern heaven and earth. So far-reaching [is the primordial
mass] that we do not know where it ends. So great that we do not know
where it comes to rest. Thereupon, it becomes distinguishable as yin
and yang. Further dispersed, it forms the eight utmost points. When
hard and soft complement each other, the myriad things take shape."[18]
In the "Lunsi" 論死 (Explaining Death) chapter of *Lunheng* 論衡 (Balanced Inquiries), Wang Chong 王充 (27–ca. 97) unambiguously states,
"Ghosts and spirits are the names of yin and yang. The breath of yin
traces the course of return of things and therefore it is called *gui.* The
breath of yang leads things and makes possible their growth and therefore it is called *shen.*... Yin and yang are called *guishen.* After their
deaths people are also called *guishen.*"[19]

In view of all these new meanings of "*guishen,*" it is obviously inappropriate for us to automatically think of live supernatural beings when
we come across the words "*guishen*" or, separately, "*gui*" and "*shen*" in
the depiction of literary and artistic activities in a late Zhou or Han
text. Unless we can identify an actual religious activity in the immediate
context, we should not take phrases like "*gang guishen*" 感鬼神 (touching the ghosts and spirits) too literally. More often than not, "*guishen*"
should be taken to mean the mysterious, omnipresent, yet impersonal
indwelling force of the world. This "naturalized" notion of "*guishen*"
attests to the new humanistic understanding of literature and the arts at
the time.[20] In the post-Han writings on literature and the arts, we continue to see a prodigious use of phrases like "*gan guishen.*" However,
such phrases retain little of their erstwhile association with live supernatural beings and are often merely hyperbolic expressions for praising
the power of literature and the arts.[21]

"Shen" as Anima: "To Convey the Spirit and Give a Vivid Portrayal"

"To convey the spirit and give a vivid portrayal" (*chuanshen xiezhao* 傳神寫照), a remark allegedly made by Gu Kaizhi 顧愷之 (ca. 345–ca. 406), has for nearly two millennia been regarded as the cardinal tenet of traditional Chinese portrait painting. The word *"shen"* in this tenet is markedly different from the *"shen"* discussed in the previous section. When *"shen"* occurs in the depiction of poetry, music, or dance in pre-Han and Han texts, it either refers to a certain form of numinous existence or is used hyperbolically to praise certain utilitarian effects of these artistic activities. When so used, *"shen"* does not have much aesthetic significance in and of itself. By contrast, the *"shen"* in Gu's *"chuanshen xiezhao"* tenet, as well as in his writings in general, has little to do with an external numinous existence; nor does it involve a utilitarian judgment. Instead it pertains solely to inner human life and serves to articulate aesthetic judgment. So Gu's use of *"shen"* marks the entry of the word into the nascent realm of aesthetic discourse.

To set the context for my discussion of Gu's new aesthetic notion of *"shen,"* I must first consider briefly the new philosophical notions of the human *shen* in the late Zhou and Han texts. In addition to the yin-yang cosmic principle, *"shen"* is increasingly used in these texts to denote the actuating force inside a man. The divergent theories of the human *shen* developed by pre-Han and Han thinkers fall into two broad schools: one known for its equal emphases on spirit and body (*xing-shen bing zhong* 形神並重) and one known for its privileging of spirit over body (*zhong shen qing xing* 重神輕形). The competing developments of these two schools eventually led to the famous *xing-shen* debate in the later Han. The *"xing-shen bing zhong"* school believes that the *shen* is inseparable from and thus dependent on the *xing*. Once the *xing* perishes, the *shen* must perforce dissipate. To emphasize the mutual dependence of the *xing* and the *shen*, thinkers of this school often codify the two as an inseparable yin-yang pair. So theirs is, in short, a *xing*-bound notion of the human *shen*. The *"zhong shen qing xing"* school stresses that the *shen* is the master of the *xing*, and it can continue to exist even after the latter dissolves. Thinkers of this school, therefore, champion a *xing*-free notion of the human *shen*. Each of these two notions has exerted a profound and lasting influence on the development of Six Dynasties aesthetics. Here, to begin with, let us consider the simultaneous influence of these two notions in Gu Kaizhi's writings on portrait painting.

Gu undoubtedly endorses the idea that "The *shen* is more valuable than the *xing*" (神貴于形), as he singularly emphasizes the importance of conveying the *shen* of the subject in portrait painting. In *Shishuo xinyu* 世説新語 (A New Account of Tales of the World), we are told, "In painting a human portrait, Gu would leave the pupils of the eyes unpainted for years. When people asked him why, he replied, 'The four limbs, however beautifully painted, have little to do with what is miraculous in a portrait. To convey the spirit and give a vivid portrayal, what matters is that place [the eye].'"[22] What Gu Kaizhi said about the four limbs and *shen* seems quite analogous to the *xing-shen* relationship described in the following three passages from *Huainan Zi*:

> If the *shen* serves as the lord and the *xing* follows, it will prove beneficial. If the *xing* is in control and the *shen* follows, it will prove harmful.[23]

> The spirit of vital essence (*jingshen* 精神) is endowed by heaven, and the bodily form (*xingti* 形體) is derived from earth. . . . Therefore the heart is the lord of the body *(xing)*; spirit *(shen)* is the precious [essence] of the heart.[24]

> When the lord of ten thousand chariots dies, his corpse is buried in the wilderness, but people perform sacrifice for his *guishen* in the luminous hall. The *shen* is more valuable than the *xing*.[25]

In these three passages, we can see that the *shen* is valued over the *xing* mainly for its more sacred origin in heaven and for its enduring, metaphysical existence. Unlike the compilers of *Huainan Zi*, however, Gu does not explore the *xing-shen* relationship on an abstract philosophical plane, even though he obviously values the *shen* over the *xing*. To him, the spirituality of the *shen* denotes not so much a *xingshang* 形上 (metaphysical) existence as the innermost part of personality. The Latin word "*anima*," if cleansed of its Western religious meanings of the soul, comes close to this use of "*shen*" by Gu. Apart from "the soul," "*anima*" denotes the inner self of an individual, especially as opposed to the outer aspect of personality.[26]

For Gu, the *anima* or the innermost personality of the subject in portrait painting is revealed, first and foremost, through the eye. His preoccupation with the eye obviously reveals the influence of the *xing-bound* notion of *"shen"* formulated by the *"xing-shen bing zhong"* school. Of course, long before the *"xing-shen bing zhong"* advocates, Mencius paid attention to the inherent relationship between the eye and the *shen*. He was quoted as saying, "What lies inside a man cannot be better revealed than through the eye. The pupils cannot hide what is evil."[27] Annotating Mencius' remarks, Zhao Qi 趙歧 contends that they mean "the eye is the manifestation of the spirit *(shen)* and is where the vital essence *(jing* 精*)* lies."[28] This view of the eye is unequivocally endorsed by Wang Chong, the standard-bearer of the *"xing-shen bing zhong"* school: "The appearance of great writings in the country is the evidence of a world ruled by a sage. When Mencius observed a human character, he focused on the eyes. If the heart is pure, the eyes are clear. What we speak of as being clear are the eyes and writings. To survey the conditions of a state and to observe a human character are one and the same thing."[29] In *Renwu zhi* 人物志 (Studies on Human Abilities), Liu Shao 劉劭 (fl. 240–250) speaks of the eye in the same vein: "In examining the spirit and observing the countenance, [we see that] the feelings issue from the eye."[30] Explaining Liu Shao's remarks, Liu Bing 劉昺 says, "The eye is the manifestation of the heart."[31]

In discussing the importance of the eye, Wang Chong and other *"xing-sheng bing zhong"* advocates do not merely want to confirm our common experience of the eye's revelatory efficacy in person-to-person interaction. More important, they seek to invalidate the *"zhong shen qing xing"* stance of their opponents by demonstrating the dependence of the *shen* on the eye, an organ of the body. Of course, they would have undermined their opponents' stance far more effectively if they had gone one step further to claim that the eye was the home or even the source of *shen*. Qian Zhongshu 錢鍾書 mentions an instance of such a claim made later in the Ming novel *Ping yao zhuan* 平妖傳 (The Suppression of Demons): "The numinous spirits of ten thousand things all gather inside the pupils of the two eyes."[32] In my opinion, such a claim can be traced back much earlier—to the early Han at least. *Huangdi neijing* 黃帝內經 (The Inner Classic of the Yellow Emperor), a famous classic of medicine compiled during the early Han or earlier, gives this description of the eye:

> The eyes are the essence of the five parts and six organs of the viscera. They are where the *ying* 營 (breath) and the *wei* 衛 (breath), the *hun* 魂 (soul) and the *po* 魄 (soul) constantly dwell and where the spirit and breath (*shenqi* 神氣) are born. So if the *shen* is exhausted, the *hun* and *po* souls will dissipate and the *zhiyi* 志意 (intent and will) will be unsettled. Therefore, the pupils or the black part of the eye are modeled on the yin. The white part and red blood vessels are modeled on the yang. Yin and yang combine as one, and so there is the luminous vital essence.[33]

Even though this view of the eye as the source of *shen* does not figure prominently in the Han *xing-shen* debate, it is likely to have been widely known, if not widely held, at the time.

Whether taken as a manifestation or the source of the *shen,* the eye is of paramount importance in the widespread Han-Jin practice of judging human character by physiognomic features. When Gu Kaizhi makes the important transition from judging human character in words to portraying it in portrait painting, it is quite natural that he continues to attach paramount importance to the eye. In addition to the passage cited above, there are other accounts of Gu's overriding concern with the eye in his portrait paintings. When he tried to persuade a friend who was suffering from an eye disease to sit for a portrait, he said, "If I paint the pupils of your eyes with sharp dots and then apply the 'flying white' brushstrokes over them, it will be like wafting clouds covering the sun. Isn't this beautiful?"[34] Similarly, when asked why he left the eyes unpainted in the portraits of Ji Kang and Ruan Ji, he replied, "How can I do that? If I painted their eyes, they would then want to speak."[35] Again, when he did a painting for a four-character-line poem by Ji Kang, he made his famous remark, "[To paint] the hands plucking the five-string lute (*qin*) is easy, but [to capture] the eye sending off the homing geese is difficult."[36] In his essay "Wei-Jin shengliu hua zan" 魏晉勝流畫贊 (Eulogies on Famous Paintings of the Wei and Jin Dynasties), he himself offers a thorough analysis of the eye's relationship to the *shen* in portrait painting:

> Whether in the positioning, size, or thickness of ink, or in the act of dotting the eye, if there is a minuscule flaw, the daemon and breath (*shenqi*) of the subject will be consequently changed.... There is no such thing as a living human holding hands to make obeisance and looking forward and yet not

facing something in front of him. If a painter seeks to depict [a subject's] *shen* by means of the *xing* but leaves out the thing(s) actually faced by the subject, he does not correctly use the living body as the fish trap [for catching the spirit]. What comes out his hand is bound to be faulty. It is a big flaw to leave out the thing(s) faced by a subject. It is a lesser flaw to incorrectly align [the subject's eyes] with the thing(s) being faced. Therefore, one cannot afford not to observe carefully. The shades of brightness and darkness in a portrait are not as important as the communion of the spirit (*shen*) through eye contact.[37]

Here Gu identifies the eye as the most important means, or the "fish trap," for catching the spirit of the portrait subject. To him, it is imperative to correctly align the eyes of the subject with whatever he is actually looking at. If the subject can establish an intense eye contact with concrete things, then the innermost of his personality—that is, his *anima*—will reveal itself. On the contrary, if he has no real eye contact with the outside world, his eyes will look blank and his whole being lifeless. Therefore, Gu declares, "It is a big flaw to leave out the thing(s) faced by a subject." Gu also warns against what he considers a lesser flaw—incorrectly aligning the subject's eyes with the outside world. According to him, the dotting of the eyes does not allow even a minuscule flaw, "whether in the positioning, size, or thickness of ink." Only if a portrait painter dots the eyes of the subject without the slightest flaw can he make his subject come alive. To drive home the difficulty in handling the eyes, Gu constantly repeats his remarks: "To paint the hands plucking the five-string lute is easy, but [to capture] the eye sending off the homing geese is difficult."

Gu Kaizhi's conception of the human *shen* as *anima* seems to have incorporated the two opposite notions of *"shen"* prevalent at the time. As the innermost part of personality, this *anima* signifies a high degree of spirituality. Gu's emphasis on this spirituality reminds us of the privileging of the *shen* in texts like *Huainan Zi*. Yet insofar as it is resident or at least manifest in the eye, a sensory organ, this *anima* can be anything but independent of the *xing*. Therefore it seems to come quite close to the *xing*-bound notion of *"shen"* elucidated by Wang Chong and others. In sum, we may say that Gu's tenet "to convey the spirit and give a vivid portrayal" has crystallized insights from both sides of the Han *xing-shen* debate.

"*Shen*" as Elan Vital: Liu Xie's Theory of Nourishing the *Qi*

In the "Yangqi" 養氣 (Nourishing the *Qi*) chapter of *Wenxin diaolong* (The Literary Mind and the Carving of Dragons), Liu Xie 劉勰 (ca. 465–ca. 521) employs the word *"shen"* five times, each time paralleling it with a *xing*-related word such as *"ming"* 命, *"qi"* 氣, and *"sheng"* 生. This consistent parallel phrasing indicates that the *shen* is even more intimately bound up with the *xing* here than in Gu Kaizhi's works. When the *shen* is bound up with the bodily qualities and functions as the actuating force of the body, it comes quite close to what is called élan vital in French and English. As I shall demonstrate, the *xing*-bound conception of *"shen"* in the "Yangqi" chapter represents a Chinese version of élan vital rooted in the *xing*-bound views of *"shen"* developed in pre-Han and Han philosophical texts.[38] In defining this *xing*-bound *shen*, Qian Zhongshu writes:

> The [human] *shen* has two meanings. The *shen* in the phrase *"yangshen"* 養神 (nourishing the spirit) is the *shen* depicted in the 'Zai You' chapter of the *Zhuang Zi*: 'Do not shake up your essence *(jing)*, and the *shen* will guard the body *(xing)*.' By eliminating the sages and abandoning intelligence, one can keep undisturbed the [heart], the heavenly endowed lord of one's own being.[39]

Based on Qian's definition and categorization, I shall refer to this *xing*-bound *shen* as the primary human *shen*, as opposed to the secondary human *shen* (to be discussed in the next section). Of the pre-Han philosophical thinkers, Guan Zi offers us the most lucid exposition of the primary human *shen*. As if to emphasize its inseparable bond with the body, he refers to it as the *jing* 精 (vital essence), while reserving the word *"shen"* mostly for the *xing*-free *shen*. According to Guan Zi, man is born of the fusion of heaven's *jing* and earth's *xing* 形 (body, shape): "For the life of man, heaven produces his vital essence *(jing)* and earth his body *(xing)*. The two (the *jing* and the *xing*) combine to make a man. When the two are in harmony, there is life. If they are not in harmony, there is no life."[40] How can heaven's *jing* and earth's *xing* combine to make a man? To Guan Zi, there is no problem for the two to blend with each other because both are constituted of *qi*. With regard to the *xing*'s relationship to the *qi*, he says, "*Qi* is what fills the body and action is what actualizes the meaning of rectitude."[41] As for the *jing*'s relationship to the *qi*, he says, *"Jing* is the essence of the *qi*. When the *qi* moves unimpeded, there is life. With life there comes thought, with thought there comes knowledge, and with knowledge, then, there comes a stopping point."[42] Here Guan Zi conceives of two kinds of human *qi*: *xingqi* 形氣 (breath of the body), which permeates and governs the body, and *jingqi* 精氣 (breath of vital essence), which produces and governs mental activities. In saying *"Jing* is the essence of the *qi*," Guan Zi apparently regards the *jingqi* as more refined and by inference more valuable than the *xingqi*. But he is far from setting up the kind of absolute body/spirit dichotomy familiar to Western traditions. Quite the contrary: he stresses that the *jingqi* is dependent on the *xingqi* as much as the other way around. Only when *"Qi* moves unimpeded"—that is, when there is a smooth, mutual flow or permeation of the *jingqi* and the *xingqi*—can the *jingqi* generate thought and knowledge. His remark, "If [the body is] not filled with the *qi* richly, the heart will not obtain its fulfillment," aptly underscores the degree to which he believes the *xingqi* impacts all mental activities, including moral will and intent.[43]

Guan Zi's theory of *qi* exerted an immense influence over the Han *xing-shen* debate. Most *"xing-shen bing zhong"* advocates strive to build their arguments on what Guan Zi has said about the *qi*'s pivotal role in both the physical and mental activities of man. In adapting Guan Zi's theory, they often opt to substitute the word *"shen"* for the word *"jing"* and consequently bring the *xing-shen* pair into prominent use. For instance, when elaborating on Guan Zi's view on the origin and constitution of man, Sima Tan 司馬談 (?–110 B.C.) pairs the *xing* with the *shen* instead of the *jing* as Guan Zi did. Sima writes,

> What gives life to all human beings is the spirit *(shen)*, and what they rely upon is the body *(xing)*. When the *shen* is used excessively it becomes depleted; when the body toils excessively it wears out. When the body *(xing)* and spirit *(shen)* separate we die; when we die we cannot return to life; what separates cannot return to how it was. Therefore the sage attaches great importance to this. From this we can see that the *shen* is the foundation of life, and the physical form *(xing)* is the vessel of life.[44]

In *Lunheng*, Wang Chong not only elucidates Guan Zi's view in *xing-shen* terms, but actually codifies *xing-shen* as a yin-yang pair: "That by which man is born are the *Yang* and the *Yin* fluids, the *Yin* fluid produces his bones and flesh, the *Yang* fluid, the vital spirits. While man is alive, the *Yang* and *Yin* fluids are in order. Hence bones and flesh are strong, and the vital force is full of vigour. Through this vital force he has knowledge, and with his bones and flesh he displays strength. The vital spirit can speak, the body continues strong and robust. While bones and flesh and the vital spirit are entwined and linked together, they are always visible, and do not perish."[45]

In transforming Guan Zi's *jing-xing* theory into their own *"xing-shen bing zhong"* theories, Han thinkers like Sima Tan and Wang Chong display two common tendencies. The first is to attach importance to both the *xing* and the *shen*. They do not merely oppose their opponents' attempts to valorize the *shen* at the expense of the *xing*. Sometimes they even do just the opposite, arguing that the *xing* determines the *shen*. The second is to regard the *qi* as the inherent link between the *xing* and the *shen* and correlate the *xing-shen* with the yin-yang.

The Han *xing-shen* theories had a great impact on the development of theories of literature and the arts during the Six Dynasties. In *Dianlun lunwen* 典論論文 (A Discourse on Literature), the very first Chinese work that discusses literature in its own right, Cao Pi 曹丕 (187–226) advances his theory of literary *qi* (*wenqi lun* 文氣論). This theory is very much a product of thinking about literature through the conceptual framework of the Han *"xing-shen bing zhong"* theories. He writes:

> In literature *qi* is the dominant factor. *Qi* has its normative form (*ti*)—clear and murky. It is not to be brought by force. Compare it to music: though melodies be equal and though the rhythms follow the rules, when it comes to an inequality in drawing on a reserve of *qi*, we have grounds to distinguish skill and clumsiness.[46]

The *"qi"* in the statement "In literature *qi* is the dominant factor" pertains to both the physical and mental conditions of the author and thus may be seen to encompass both the *xingqi* and the *jingqi*. In saying "*Qi* has its normative form (*ti*)—clear and murky. It is not to be brought by force," Cao Pi means that each author is differently endowed with the pure and rising *jingqi* (or *yangqi* 陽氣) and the murky and sinking *xingqi* (or *yinqi* 陰氣) and therefore possesses his own individual character. To Cao, such individual character is an endowment of nature, and "although it may reside in a father, he cannot transfer it to his son; nor can an elder brother transfer it to the younger."[47] When such individual character manifests itself in a literary work, it becomes a certain unique artistic style. Commenting on the *qi*-based styles of some prominent contemporary writers, he notes that "Xu Gan has the sluggish *qi* of the Qi state" and that "Kong Rong's form and *qi* are lofty and marvelous."[48] On the surface, Cao's theory of literary *qi* seems identical with the notion of "Style is the man," developed in Western literary criticism. Upon close scrutiny, we can see that the two are essentially different. To most Western critics, literature and the arts are pure projects of the mind and have little to do with the physiological conditions of an author or artist. By contrast, Cao and most traditional Chinese critics believe that artistic creation is impacted as much by the author's physiological as by his mental conditions. So literary *qi* or style, as meant by Cao Pi, is an embodiment of, among other things, the author's physiological constitution as well as his spirituality.

The influence of the Han *"xing-shen bing zhong"* theories is even more evident in the "Yangqi" chapter of Liu Xie's *Wenxin diaolong*. At the very beginning of the chapter, Liu informs us of the source of his idea of the *qi:* "Wang Chong [of the Later Han] wrote a chapter on the theme of nourishing one's *qi*; it was based on his own personal experience, not just on unfounded speculation."[49] Immediately after this citation, he defines the *xing* and the *shen:* "Ears, eyes, nose, and mouth are organs which serve our physical life; thinking, pondering, speech, and linguistic expression are functions of our spirit" (*WXDL*, 42/5–8).[50] These remarks seem to have been borrowed almost directly from Wang Chong's definitions of the *xing* and the *shen* cited above.

Next, Liu moves on to explore the effects of literary creation on the author's *xing* and *shen* and vice versa. On the one hand, he carefully examines how literary creation may adversely affect the physical and mental conditions of the author. He holds that literary creation is an activity that voluminously consumes both the *xing* and the *shen* of the author. If not properly pursued, he believes that it can ruin an author's health. He points out that "if one works too hard, his *shen* will be worn out and his *qi* will be consumed. This is the invariable law of our disposition and temperament" (*WXDL*, 42/11–13).[51] To drive home this point, he adds, "Now a man's capacity and natural parts are limited, but he may work his mind without limit. There are men who are ashamed of their short 'wild duck' legs and aspire to those of the crane: they will force themselves to write and their minds to function. In so doing, they wear out the vitality within, which fades away as gaunt and emaciated as the trees on Mount Niu" (*WXDL*, 42/40–47).[52] To support his view, he mentions similar lamentations of others over the adverse effects of literary creation: "Master Cao feared the ruining of one's life by literary composition; and Lu Yun sighed over the exhaustion of the *shen* by thinking (*si*)" (*WXDL*, 42/54–55).[53] At its worst, Liu believes that an overexertion by an author may result in the shortening of his life. "If in the process he has to burn up his inner force and dry up the harmonious natural flow of his vitality," Liu writes, "his writing will only serve to shorten his years and do violence to his nature" (*WXDL*, 42/65–68).[54] All these remarks strike us as an elucidation of the above-cited comments by Sima Tan on how the depletion of the *shen* harms the *xing*.

On the other hand, Liu seeks to show how the cultivation of the *xing*—or to be exact, the nourishing of the *qi*—can produce a positive impact on literary creation. He first points out that the emotional state of the author is an immediate factor for the success of literary creation. "When we follow our intent spontaneously and are in harmony with our nature, the principles of things are revealed and our feelings find unobstructed expression.... Therefore, in the art of literary writing, temperance and readiness for expression are of prime importance: that is, it is essential to keep the mind pure and tranquil so that its vitality may find spontaneous expression" (*WXDL*, 42/9–10, 77–80).[55] To attain this kind of ideal mental state, Liu tells us, one must learn to "nourish our native *qi*" and make sure that the *qi* or vitality "may find spontaneous expression." He offers two major suggestions on how to achieve such an optimal physical readiness. The first is to choose the right moment of literary creation and avoid overworking: "As soon as one feels vexed, he should immediately give up thinking, so as not to let his mind become choked. When inspired, give vent to your heart and entrust it to the brush" (*WXDL*, 42/81–83).[56] The second is to take active measures to relieve fatigue: "A pleasant trip is a sure cure for weariness, and talk and laughter will bring restoration from fatigue" (*WXDL*, 42/85–86).[57]

At times Liu seems to suggest that the factors of the *xing* are more important than those of the *shen*. This is shown in his comparison of young and older writers. Liu holds that young writers enjoy an advantage over older ones. Their superior physical strength more than makes up for their lack of experience and insights, and therefore they have greater chances of success than older writers (*WXDL*, 42/34–39). In any event, he has unambiguously embraced the *"xing-shen bing zhong"* stance in the "Yangqi" chapter, as evidenced by his explicit citation of Wang Chong and his exclusive concern with the primary human *shen.* By all measures, this chapter represents a most ingenious appropriation of the *"xing-shen bing zhong"* theories for literary criticism.

"Shen" as Daemon: Lu Ji's and Liu Xie's Theories of "Daemon and Thought"

Liu Xie begins the "Shensi" 神思 (Spirit and Thought) chapter by defining the phrase *"shensi"* itself: "The ancients observed, 'The physical body is by the rivers and lakes, but the mind remains below the gate towers of Wei.' This is what is called spirit and thought *(shensi)"* (*WXDL*, 26/1–4). To underscore the great distance over which the *shen* roams, he adds, "In the thought process of writing, the spirit goes afar. In the state of silence and mental concentration, thought reaches to a thousand years ago. With a slight change of one's facial expression, one's vision may have already crossed ten thousand leagues" (*WXDL*, 26/5–10).

The *shen* described here belongs to what Qian Zhongshu classifies as the second kind of human *shen,* or the secondary human *shen* as it will be called hereafter. If the primary human *shen* is characterized by its inseparable bond with the *xing,* the secondary human *shen* is known for its out-of-body flight, one that defies normal restrictions of time and space. Defining this secondary human *shen,* Qian writes,

> As regards the *"shen"* in "Together one with heaven and earth, the luminous divinity *(shenming)* travels," a remark from the "Tianxia" chapter of *Zhuang Zi,* it does not mean the absence of thought or deliberation, of seeing or hearing. Rather, it means the transcendence of thought and deliberation, of seeing and hearing. It means an affirmation of the miraculous realm and the attainment of the ultimate truth. This is what is meant by these remarks: "The import of the vital essence enters the *shen*" in *The Book of Changes*; "When one is great, one becomes a sage; being a sage, one becomes *shen* (luminous divinity)" in *Mencius*; and "The vital essence of the heart is called sagely" in the *Kong Cong Zi.* The "Daode" 道德 chapter of the *Wen Zi* also writes, "Superior learning means listening with the *shen*; lesser learning, with the heart; and inferior learning, with the ears."[58]

The "*shen*" discussed in this passage is anything but the *xing*-bound, primary human *shen*. It is highly appropriate for Qian to distinguish it from the primary human *shen* and accentuate its *xing*-free character. However, we should not think that primary and secondary human *shen* can be separated from each other in any absolute terms. It is not hard to perceive an inherent link between the two if we carefully observe their common origins in the *jing* or vital essence. As Qian foregrounds the *jing* in his definitions of the two, he is no doubt keenly aware of an important *jing*-based connection between the two. But he does not elaborate on this connection.

To clearly see this connection, we need only compare two statements cited above. The first is "Do not shake up your essence (*jing*), and the *shen* will guard the body (*xing*)." The second is "The import of the vital essence enters the *shen*" (*jingyi ru shen* 精義入神). In the first statement, by Zhuang Zi, the primary human *shen,* as élan vital, is practically identical with the *jing*, vital essence. To keep the *jing* intact in the body and to let the *shen* dwell in the body (as its guard) mean essentially the same thing. As shown above, Guan Zi uses the word "*jing*" exactly in the sense of the primary human *shen*. This demonstrates the fundamental sameness of the *jing* and the primary human *shen*. By contrast, the second statement, from *The Book of Changes,* seems to tell us that the *jing* and the *shen* are two separate but intimately related phenomena. When one's *jing* reaches a certain state, one can enter the *shen*—that is, embark on a daemonic or out-of-body flight along with the *shen* (the numinous processes) of heaven and earth.

Through this brief comparison, we can see that the secondary human *shen* is, at its embryonic stage, dependent on the meticulous preservation and accumulation of the *jing* or the primary human *shen*. So this secondary human *shen* actually demonstrates a conflicting dual nature: its initial residence and hence dependence on the *xing* and its eventual departure from and hence transcendence of the *xing*. Of all the words about human spirituality in Western languages, "daemon" probably comes closest to suggesting this dual nature. As an attendant power or spirit in Greek mythology, the daemon travels between the supernatural and human worlds as it seeks to mediate between gods and men. For this reason, it seems appropriate to render the secondary human *shen* as "daemon" when necessary.

Considering the dual nature of the secondary human *shen*, it is little wonder that its depiction in pre-Han and Han philosophical texts focuses, often alternately, on the concentration of vital essence (*zhuan-jing* 專精) at its embryonic stage and on entering the *shen* (*rushen* 入神) at its fully operational stage.

In depicting the "concentration of vital essence," pre-Han and Han thinkers pay close attention to its miraculous end result. In the *Speeches of the States,* there is a detailed account of a transcendental transformation resulting from the purification of vital essence:

> In ancient times, the *shen* of common people is not impure. Among them are those whose vital essence is clear and free of any alien substance and who could display a serious and upright attitude. Their intelligence was sufficient to discern correspondences between the realms above and below. Their sageliness could shine far and bright. Their luminosity could give light to things. Their power of hearing was such that they could catch the faintest of sounds. Having attained all this, they had their luminous divinity endowed within them. If they are males, they are called *xi*-shamans. If they are females, they are called *wu*-shamans.[59]

The *Huainan Zi* tells of how an ancient blind musician and a commoner's daughter achieved similar suprasensory capabilities through a careful concentration of vital essence: "Now, take this blind music master and commoner's daughter: their rank was lower than that of the Director of Hemp, their authority lighter than floating feathers. Yet by concentrating their essences (*jing* 精) and disciplining their thoughts, discarding all concerns and gathering together their spirits (*shen* 神), they merged with the Nine Heavens above and stimulated their most subtle essences (*zhijing* 至精)."[60] It is noteworthy that even Guan Zi, the founding father of the *"xing-shen bing zhong"* school, talks about how the concentration of *qi* and *jing* can enable ordinary people, not just shamans, to communicate with ghosts and spirits:

> Concentrate your breath of life until you become spirit-like, and all things are complete [within]. Can you concentrate? Can you adhere to the Unity of Nature? Can you know good fortune from bad without resorting to divination?... Think! Think! And again think! As you think and it is still not comprehended, [you may believe] the spirits will make it comprehensible. Yet [it is comprehended] not through the power of the spirits, but through the utmost development of your own essence (*jing*) and breath of life.[61]

In depicting "entering the *shen*," the full operation of the secondary human *shen*, pre-Han and Han thinkers usually strive to show how the human *shen* enters or integrates with the cosmic *shen* or miraculous modus operandi of heaven and earth. This modus operandi, usually called the Dao or yin-yang, is an everlasting process of change and transformation (*hua* 化). Therefore, "entering the *shen*" means nothing but a daemonic flight along with the process of transformation. This daemonic flight of the secondary human *shen* is described by Zhuang Zi as the "roaming of the heart" (*youxin* 遊心): "Just go along with things and let your heart roam freely *(youxin)*. Resign yourself to what cannot be avoided and nourish what is within you—this is best."[62] Commenting on the effects of *youxin*, he writes, "Let your heart roam in simplicity and blend your *qi* with the vastness, follow along with things the way they are, and make no room for personal views—then the world will be governed."[63] The *Huainan Zi* offers an even more elaborate description of the "roaming of the heart." Sometimes, it is depicted as a ride upon the mysterious, invisible cosmic process. At other times, it is depicted metaphorically as a journey of live immortals roaming in the universe: "Wang Qiao and Chi Songzi puffed and blew, expired and inspired; they exhaled the old and took in the new; they left the form behind and pushed knowledge away; they cherished the plainstuff and reverted to the verity—thus they roamed in the somber minuteness and ascended clear through the cloudy heavens.[64]

"Concentration of vital essence" and "entering the *shen*" respectively mark the inactive and dynamic states of the secondary human *shen*. These two states of the secondary *shen* are conspicuously similar to, if not identifiable with, the two major phases of literary creation: the initial quiet contemplation and the ensuing dynamic flight of imagination. When Lu Ji 陸機 (261–303) sought to comprehensively describe the creative process for the first time ever, it was not surprising that he extensively appropriated the descriptions of the secondary human *shen* in various philosophical texts. It is also natural that, approaching the subject shortly afterward, Liu Xie would do the same.

In depicting the initial contemplation, Lu Ji emphasizes the need to suspend the operation of all sensory organs and achieve the utmost quietude: "This is how it begins: perception is held back and listening is reverted."[65] Liu Xie, too, emphasizes the importance of concentrating one's vital essence and attaining complete quietude. "Therefore in shaping and developing literary thought," he writes, "what is the most important is 'emptiness and stillness' (*xujing* 虛靜). One must remove obstructions in the five viscera and cleanse the spirit" (*WXDL,* 26/26–29). Only when one reaches "the state of silence and mental concentration," Liu believes, can one's daemon begin its out-of-body flight.

In depicting the flight of imagination, both Lu and Liu accentuate its transcendence of normal restrictions of time and space. Lu writes, "My essence galloping to the world's eight bounds, /My mind roaming ten thousand yards, up and down ... He observes all past and present in a single moment, /Touches all the world in the blink of an eye."[66] Like the "roaming of the heart" described in the *Zhuang Zi* and the *Huainan Zi,* this flight of literary imagination starts off the well-concentrated *jing* or vital essence, goes through the entire spectrum of temporality, and reaches the ultimate ends in all directions. Liu describes this flight of imagination with almost the same wording: "In the state of silence and mental concentration, thought reaches to a thousand years ago. With a slight change of one's facial expression, one's vision may have already crossed ten thousand leagues" (*WXDL,* 26/7–10). In the meantime, both Lu and Liu have taken note of an important difference between literary imagination and the "roaming of the heart." Unlike the latter, literary imagination is not directed toward achieving a permanent transcendence of time and space and perpetuating the blissful excursion in the Great Empyrean (*taiqing* 太清). Rather, it travels beyond the boundaries of time and space momentarily, only to return to our world for good. Immediately after describing the outbound flight of literary imagination, Lu describes its return flight to the world of emotions, images, and words: "And when it is attained: light gathers about moods (*qing*) and they grow in brightness, /Things (*wu*) become luminous and draw one another forward; /I quaff the word-hoard's spray of droplets, /And roll in my mouth the sweet moisture of the Classics.... Then, phrases from the depths emerge struggling as when the swimming fish, hooks in their mouths, emerge from the bottom of the deepest pool; /And drifting intricacies of craft flutter down, as when the winging bird, /Caught by stringed arrow, plummets from the tiered clouds."[67] Liu describes this double journey of literary imagination in a similar fashion. Having observed its outbound flight over a thousand years and across "ten thousand leagues," he traces its inbound flight along with things *(wu)* from afar toward one's ears and eyes. In saying "the daemon wanders with external things" 神與物遊

(*WXDL,* 26/17), he means one's daemon goes out to course along with things, not aimlessly, but toward a final return along with them to one's own mind. "External things come in toward the ear and the eye, with language controlling the hinge and trigger [for their influx]" (物沿耳目，而辭令管其樞機; *WXDL,* 26/20–21). Here he stresses that the influx of things from afar is filtered through perceptual (the use of ears and eyes) and intellectual (the conscious use of language) processes before those things coalesce into an artistic vision. From the passages just cited, we can see that neither Lu nor Liu regards the transcendence of time and space as the purpose of imagination, as Zhuang Zi and many others would. To them, the transcendental flight of literary imagination is not an end, but a means of selecting the best possible images, words, and designs for an artistic recreation of the world in which we live.[68]

The descriptions of the secondary human *shen* by pre-Han and Han thinkers, once appropriated by Lu and Liu, become the standard source for theoretical formulations about the creative process. Like Lu and Liu, later literary and art critics tended to draw, explicitly or implicitly, from these descriptions. Adapting the descriptions of "the concentration of vital essence," many critics developed various theories of emptiness and stillness (*xujing shuo* 虛靜説). Likewise, inspired by the descriptions of "roaming of the heart," other critics developed various theories of the daemon and thought (*shensi shuo* 神思説).

"*Shen*" and Aesthetic Perception: "Breath Resonance and Lively Animation"

"Breath resonance and lively animation" (*qiyun shengdong* 氣韻生動) is the first of the Six Laws (Liu Fa 六法) of painting established by Xie He 謝赫 (fl. 500–535). In traditional Chinese literary and art criticism, the phrase "breath resonance" (*qiyun* 氣韻) is used interchangeably with the phrase "daemon resonance" (*shenyun* 神韻). Qian Zhongshu observes that "'breath resonance' means nothing but the lifelikeness of human figures in a painting.... What Xie [He] and Yao [Zui] call 'numinous spirits' (*jingling* 精靈) and Gu Kaizhi calls 'luminous divinity' (*shenming* 神明) all refer to this [breath resonance]."[69] Contrary to the traditional explanation of the first law, Qian argues that "lively animation" (*shengdong* 生動) is not an adjectival description of breath resonance. Rather, it is a definition of what "breath resonance" is. The two

particles, *shi ye* 是也, attached to the *"qiyun shengdong,"* seem to lend
support to Qian's new interpretation, as they enable him to punctuate
the first law as 氣韻生動，是也. So punctuated, the first law would
read "Breath resonance is liveliness and animation" instead of "Breath
resonance should be lively and animated."[70]

Qian's new interpretation of the first law aptly foregrounds Xie's
central concern with the rhythmic vitality of painting and introduces a
new approach to the study of the Six Laws as a whole. However, it
seems inappropriate to totally ignore the descriptive elements in the
first law, which reveal a hidden process of aesthetic perception.
Although the word *"yun"* 韻 literally means "rhyme," it often functions, by extension, as an aural metaphor for describing one's subjective
impressions. The *"yun"* in the phrase *"qiyun"* is a good case in point.
Its metaphorical, descriptive function is brought to the fore in a dialogue about Xie He's first law cited by Qian Zhongshu:

> Wang Cheng said, "The ancients spoke about 'breath resonance and ani-
> mation.' May, for instance, the soaring movement in Mr. Wu's brush-
> work be considered an example of 'resonance'?" I replied, "'Animation'
> shows that the daemonic has been attained. If one is talking about the
> 'daemonic,' that achieves it fully. But it is not necessarily an example of
> 'resonance.'" Wang Cheng said, "What about Lu Tanwei's using just a
> few brush strokes to paint a lion? May that be said to have 'resonance'?" I
> replied, "Painting a lion with just a few brush strokes is to be abbreviated
> yet completely capture its underlying Pattern. If one is talking about
> Pattern, that achieves it fully. But it too is not necessarily an example of
> 'resonance.'"
>
>   With that, Wang Cheng asked me to explain the matter, and so I told
> him, "'Resonance' is 'to have more meaning' than what is overtly
> expressed." Wang Cheng said, "Now I understand. I have noticed that
> when a bell is struck, after the initial gong has passed, a residual sound is
> heard. It wavers and undulates in the air, being a note 'beyond the primary
> sound.' This must be the meaning of 'resonance.'" I replied, "You've got
> the gist of it but do not yet grasp its finer points. Where do you suppose
> this 'resonance' comes from?" Wang Cheng did not answer. I said, "It
> comes from 'having more' than what is expressed."[71]

In comparing the animating effects of *yun* (resonance) to the lingering
echoes of a bell, the speaker here intends to underscore that *"yun"* is

anything but a redundant word added to *"qi"* or *"shen."* Rather, it connotes the enduring aesthetic effects produced by the *shen* or the rhythmic *qi* pulsating inside a painting. Once we recognize this element of aesthetic perception in the phrase *"qiyun,"* we can see that *"shengdong"* should be taken as a further elaboration of the effects of aesthetic perception adumbrated by the word *"yun."*

In the Wei-Jin and later discourses of character judgment, there are numerous examples of descriptive statements about *qiyun* and *shenyun*. As shown in the following passages, these statements consist of *"qiyun"* plus a two-character descriptive phrase, a syntactic construction identical with Xie's first law:

> [Xu Qian and others] passionately pursued literature, vying with [Liu] Che [Emperor Wu] of the Han and surpassing Cao Pi. Their breath resonance *(qiyun)* is lofty and far-reaching; their elegant phrases are ingeniously constructed.[72]

> [Zheng Daozhong's] breath resonance *(qiyun)* is tranquil and harmonious; his appearance and manners are gentle and dignified. His mind was not distracted by praise or criticism. His intent did not alter because of glory or disgrace. He paced up and down before the gates of [Duke] Zhou and Confucius and wandered contently in the realm of Lao Zi and Zhuang Zi.[73]

> [Yuan Jun's] display of inner spirit *(fengshen* 風神) was pure and uplifting; his breath resonance *(qiyun)* runs high and unimpeded. He reached heaven-like perfection in the ways of filial piety and friendship, and he was versatile and well versed in learning and the arts.[74]

There seems to be little doubt that Xie has formulated his first law on the model of such statements. To Xie, *"qiyun shengdong"* is an ideal aesthetic effect of an art work as a whole, not of its specific parts. His concern with the overall, unified aesthetic effect seems to be the hallmark of his painting criticism. In his *Guhua pinlu* 古畫品錄 (A Record of the Rankings of Ancient Painters), Xie does not show the kind of meticulous attention to detail that we often see in Gu Kaizhi, especially in his discussion on the eye and the *shen*. In commenting on the twenty-seven painters placed in six different ranks, Xie is consistently preoccupied with the overall features of their works. Indeed, he singles out *geti* 格體 (established form), *huati* 畫體 (the painting form), *tifa* 體法 (form and methods), and *tizhi* 體致 (form and style) as the main objects of his investigation. He tends to praise these overall formal features profusely with phrases such as "refined and subtle" (*jingwei* 精微), "well-rounded" (*zhouzhan* 周瞻), "elegant and enchanting" (*yamei* 雅媚), and "extraordinary" (*bufan* 不凡). In evaluating the twenty-seven painters placed in six ranks, he also makes plenty of pithy, impressionistic comments.[75] Like his *"qiyun shengdong"* law itself, these comments are modeled on the descriptions of human characters in texts like *Shishuo xinyu.*

As an aesthetic ideal, the *"qiyun shengdong"* law displays a distinctly transcendent tendency. As mentioned above, *"qiyun"* and *"shenyun"* are interchangeable in the discourse of character judgment. Both often denote a transcendent quality or tendency physiognomically displayed in a living person. So in his painting criticism, Xie often uses *"qiyun"* interchangeably with the *shen* in reference to the transcendent quality in a given painting: "Zhang Mo's and Xun Xu's [paintings] display breath resonance. They are miraculous and partake in the spirits (*canshen* 參神). They excel in revealing the numinous spirits (*jingling* 精靈) and leave few traces of rules and methods. If one is merely concerned with the representation of actual things, one sees little evidence of excellence. But if one is interested in what lies beyond image, one will then lose interest in richness and opulence and call those paintings subtle and miraculous."[76] Similarly, Xie speaks of the paintings by Emperor Ming of the Jin as "insufficient in representing form and appearance, but quite successful in conveying the daemon and breath (*shenqi* 神氣). The traces of his brushes have a transcendent thrust and at times present a wonderful spectacle."[77]

It is noteworthy that Xie, in the two passages just cited, depicts *"canshen"* and *"shenqi"* with a string of phrases with a distinctly transcendent accent: "ultimately miraculous" (*jimiao* 極妙), "beyond image" (*xiangwai* 象外), "subtle and miraculous" (*weimiao* 微妙), "marvelous spectacle" (*qiguan* 奇觀) and, in fact, the word "transcendent" (*chaoyue* 超越) itself. It is apparent that his notion of the *shen* stands in sharp contrast to Gu's.[78] When Gu talks about the *shen*, he mainly thinks of the lifelike appearance of the subject in portrait painting. For Gu, "to convey the spirit" is to reveal the inner personality of the portrait subject through his eyes, not to lead us to a miraculous realm beyond image. Only when he discusses the portraits of the legendary sages Fu

Xi and Shen Nong and the Daoist Heavenly Master Zhang Daoling does he employ the words *"shen"* and *"shenqi"* with a tinge of transcendent color.[79] Nonetheless, when he comments on the portraits of the Seven Sages of the Bamboo Grove, well known for their quest of transcendence, he does not see the need to capture their transcendent spirit—that is, their *fengshen* or *shenyun*, as it was called at the time.

It is widely accepted that both Gu's *"chuanshen xiezhao"* principle and Xie's *"qiyun shengdong"* law are derived from the Wei-Jin discourse of character judgment. In view of the sharp contrast between Gu's and Xie's notions of *"shen,"* we should raise questions about this commonly accepted view. In expounding his *"chuanshen xiezhao"* principle, Gu largely ignores the issue of transcendence and focuses on the revelatory efficacy of the eye. Furthermore, he examines the eye-*shen* relationship strictly within the conceptual framework of the *"xing-shen bing zhong"* theories. So it is best to trace his *"chuanshen xiezhao"* principle in pre-Han and Han *"xing-shen bing zhong"* theories, not the Wei-Jin discourses of character judgment.[80] Only Xie He's *"qiyun shengdong"* law may be regarded as an example of a bona fide adaptation of those discourses to painting criticism. In establishing the *"qiyun shengdong"* law, Xie has in effect transformed *"shenyun"* from an ideal image of man in those discourses into an ideal vision of art, one that lies beyond word and image. This reconceptualization of *"qiyun"* and *"shenyun"* as a transcendent aesthetic ideal sets a new direction for the development of Chinese aesthetics during the Six Dynasties and later periods. Inspired by his *"qiyun shengdong"* law, his contemporaries and later critics extensively appropriate *"qiyun," "shenyun," "fengshen," "fengbiao"* 風標, and other similar terms from the Wei-Jin discourse of character judgment. Most of them use these terms as the highest aesthetic categories for evaluating or ranking poets and artists, as well as their works. Some even seek to build comprehensive theories around these terms. Wang Shizhen's 王士禎 (1634–1711) *shenyun shuo* 神韻説 (theory of daemon breath) eloquently testifies to the enduring influence of Xie's law.

Conclusion

By way of conclusion, let me synthesize my findings and reflect on the complex semantic transformation of *"shen"* as a philosophical term and its eventual metamorphosis into an equally polysemous aesthetic term.

In the texts about high antiquity, *"shen"* means almost exclusively "ghosts and spirits"—namely, the conscious supernatural beings who were believed by the ancients to rule the worlds of both nature and man. In the works of pre-Han Confucian, Daoist, and Legalist thinkers, *"shen"* often appears as the ultimate cosmological principle as it is used interchangeably with *"tian"* 天, the Dao, and the yin-yang. In the meantime, this cosmic *"shen"* is often regarded as the origin of both the *xing* and the *shen* of man. Some early thinkers like Guan Zi stressed the mutual dependence of the *xing* and the *shen* and developed the *"xing-shen bing zhong"* theories. Others, like Zhuang Zi, considered the *shen* as the daemon capable of roaming outside the body and formulated *"zhong shen qing xing"* theories. During the Han, the ancient notion of *"shen"* as a conscious divinity was reintroduced and incorporated into various yin-yang and *wuxing* 五行 (five phase) cosmological schemes by Dong Zhongshu and his followers and by the fabricators of *chenwei* 讖緯 (augury and apocrypha).[81] To denounce this redeification of the *shen*, Huan Tan 桓譚 (ca. 40 B.C.–A.D. 32), Wang Chong, and others launched the first philosophical debate on the *xing-shen* relationship, giving impetus to the further development of *"xing-shen bing zhong"* theories. Then, in the Eastern Jin, Huiyuan 慧遠 (334–416) and his Buddhist followers reconceptualized the *shen* as the Dharma-nature (*faxing* 法性), Dharmakāya (*fashen* 法身), or Nirvāna, thus turning it into a purely Buddhist notion of the ultimate reality.[82] To invalidate the then widespread quest of the Buddhist *shen*, Fang Zhen 范縝 (ca. 450–ca. 515) and other thinkers launched the second *xing-shen* debate. Like their predecessors in the first *xing-shen* debate, they sought to disprove the *shen* as divine self-presence by demonstrating its inseparability from the *xing*. Thanks to these two debates, the term *"shen"* becomes all the more important, with its range of meanings substantially expanded and its subtle nuances expounded.

Extremely polysemous and fully elucidated by thinkers of all persuasions, the term *"shen"* constitutes a rich source of insights and inspiration for the development of Six Dynasties aesthetics. Indeed, more often than not, Six Dynasties critics embraced one or more notions of *"shen"* as the broad conceptual framework for exploring one particular subject of literary and art criticism. For instance, Gu Kaizhi adopted both the *xing*-free and *xing*-bound notions of *"shen"* for formulating the principle and method of portrait painting. While the former notion inspired him to establish the *chuanshen xiezhao* ideal, the latter helped him develop a down-to-earth method for achieving that ideal. Like Cao Pi, Liu Xie developed a theory of literary *qi* on the basis of *"xing-shen bing zhong"* theories developed by Guan Zi and Wang Chong. It is strictly within the framework of these theories that he explored the dynamic, reciprocal relationship of a literary author's *xing* and *shen* to literary creation. When examining the creative process itself, however, both Liu Xie and his predecessor Lu Ji mainly relied on the daemonic notion of *"shen"* expounded in the *Zhuang Zi,* the *Huainan Zi,* and other texts. In these philosophical texts, daemon is extensively depicted either in its inactive, body-resident state or during its out-of-body flight. These two kinds of description were adroitly adapted by Lu and Liu to characterize two main phases of the creative process—initial contemplation and the ensuing flight of imagination. Indeed, without the help of the daemonic notion of *"shen,"* they perhaps could not have established their views about *xujing* (emptiness and stillness) and *shensi* (spirit and thought)—two core parts of their comprehensive theories of literary creation. In establishing the principles and criteria for evaluating painting, Xie He made use of the *xing*-free notion of *"shen"* in basically the same way as it had been used by the Wei-Jin practitioners of character judgment. While those practitioners most valued the emanation of transcendent spirit in a human character, Xie regarded the revelation of what lies beyond image and word as the highest ideal of painting. Thanks to his formulation of the *"qiyun shengdong"* law, *"shen,"* *"shenyun,"* and other similar phrases evolve into important terms of aesthetic judgment.

In examining the conceptual origins and aesthetic significance of *"shen,"* I am keenly aware of the risk of overgeneralization. In Six Dynasties texts on literature and the arts, the use of the term is so ubiquitous and its meaning is so polysemous and fluid that it can very well be traced to more conceptual origins than generally thought. So it is impossible for anyone to exclusively identify its conceptual origin(s) or determine with absolute certainty its aesthetic significance in a given text. With this qualification, I would argue that the amount of evidence adduced seems sufficient to support my observations about the conceptual origins and aesthetic significance of *"shen"* in various tenets and theories examined. In examining the transformation of *"shen"* from a polysemous philosophical term into a correspondingly polysemous aesthetic term, we have practically reviewed the highlights of Six Dynasties aesthetics. This aptly testifies to the pivotal importance of the term at all the major stages in the development of Six Dynasties aesthetics.

NOTES

1. The "Canon of Yao" is divided into two chapters (the "Canon of Yao" and the "Canon of Shun" ["Shun dian" 舜典]) in *Shang shu zhengyi* 尚書正義, commentary by Kong Yingda 孔穎達 (574–648); collected in *Shisanjing zhushu* 十三經注疏, comp. Ruan Yuan 阮元 (1764–1849), 2 vols. (Beijing, 1977); hereafter *SSJZ*. The "Shi yan zhi" statement appears in the latter chapter in this edition of *The Book of Documents*.

The dating of the "Canon of Yao" chapter, along with some others, is a matter of longstanding debate among scholars. Gu Jiegang 顧頡剛 dates it as early as the transitional period between the Western Zhou and the Eastern Zhou in his "Lun *Jinwen Shang shu* zhuzuo shidai shu" 論今文尚書著作時代書, *Gushi bian* 古史辨, 7 vols. (reprint, Hong Kong: Taiping shuju, 1962), vol. 1, pp. 200–206. Gu's dating is accepted by Zhu Ziqing 朱自清, *Shi yan zhi bian* 詩言志辨 (Beijing: Guji chubanshe, 1956), p. 9, and by Luo Genze 羅根澤, *Zhongguo wenxue piping shi* 中國文學批評史, 3 vols. (Shanghai: Gudian wenxue chubanshe, 1957–1961), vol. 1, p. 36. However, Qu Wanli 屈萬里, "*Shang shu* bu ke jin xin di cailiao" 尚書不可盡信的材料, *Xin shidai* 新時代, 1, no. 3 (1964), pp. 23–25, chooses to date this chapter to the end of the Warring States.

2. In Duan Yucai 段玉裁 (1735–1815), annot., *Shuo wen jie zi zhu* 説文解字注 (Yangzhou: Jiangshu guangling guji keyin she, 1977), 9a, p. 435.

3. See Wang Li 王力, *Tongyuan zidian* 同源字典 (Beijing: Shangwu yinshuguan, 1999), p. 535.

4. Xu Zhongshu, *Jiaguwen zidian* 甲骨文字典 (Chengdu: Sichuan cizhu chubanshe, 1990), pp. 10–11.

5. Ibid.

6. See Rong Geng 容庚, *Jinwen bian* 金文編 (Beijing: Zhonghua shuju, 1985), p. 10.

7. See Sima Qian 司馬遷, *Shi ji* 史記 (Beijing: Zhonghua shuju, 1959), 1/1/12, 41.

8. Sun Yirang 孫詒讓 (1848–1908), *Mo Zi xian gu* 墨子閒詁 (Beijing: Zhonghua shuju, 1986), pp. 214–215; translation taken from Burton Watson, *Basic Writings of Mo Tzu, Hsün Tzu, and Han Fei Tzu* (New York: Columbia University Press, 1963), p. 101.

9. The word *"zhi"* has been translated as "earnest thought" in James Legge, *The Shoo King or the Book of Historical Documents*, vol. 3 of *The Chinese Classics* (reprint, Taibei: Wenxin, 1971), p. 48, and as "the heart's intent" in James J. Y. Liu, *Chinese Theories of Literature* (Chicago: University of Chicago Press, 1975), p. 75. Liu's translation seems to be more appropriate because it avoids the rationalistic connotations of "earnest thought" and yet subtly implies moral inclination. However, the word *"zhi"* can take on a wide range of different meanings, depending on the historical periods and particular contexts in which it is used. For this reason, Liu finds it necessary to render it as "emo-

tional purport," "moral purpose," or "heart's wish" in other contexts (p. 184). Liu's translation has been adopted with slight modification ("heart/mind") in Pauline Yu, *The Reading of Imagery in the Chinese Poetic Tradition* (Princeton, N.J.: Princeton University Press, 1987), p. 31. For a discussion on the translation of *"zhi,"* see Stephen Owen, *Readings in Chinese Literary Thought* (Cambridge, Mass.: Council on East Asian Studies, Harvard University, 1992), pp. 26–29.

10. Kong Yingda, *Shang shu zhengyi,* in *SSJZ,* vol. 1, p. 131.

11. Wei Zhao 韋昭 (204–273), annot., *Guo yu* 國語 (Shanghai: Shanghai guji chubanshe, 1978), *juan* 4, p. 130. In addition to this passage, we can find in "Speeches of the Zhou" another excellent example of the overriding concern with natural processes and forces during the Spring and Autumn period. It is the long speech made by Prince Jin 晉公子 to his father, King Ling 靈王, in 549 B.C., about twenty-seven years before Zhoujiu's comments. In that speech, Prince Jin explains the systematic correlation of human society and natural processes and forces and urges his father not to disrupt the order of nature (*Guo yu, juan* 3, vol. 1, pp. 101–112). For a discussion of the cosmological significance of this passage, see James A. Hart, "The Speech of Prince Chin: A Study of Early Chinese Cosmology," in *Explorations in Early Chinese Cosmology,* ed. Henry Rosemont (Chico, Calif.: Scholar Press, 1984), pp. 35–65. This book is published as vol. 1, no. 2, of the *Journal of the American Academy of Religion Studies.*

12. Kong Yingda, *Mao shi zhengyi, juan* 1, in *SSJZ,* vol. 1, p. 270.

13. While this natualization of *"shen"* represents a significant development in the "high" cosmological thinking of the time, it does not mean that the intellectual elite then suddenly gave up occult religious activities centered on live spirits and ghosts in their real life. Quite the contrary; such activities continued to be popular and vibrant throughout the Warring States and Han periods among many members of the elite, as well as the vast majority of unlettered commoners (see Donald Harper, *Early Chinese Medical Literature: The Mawangdui Medical Manuscripts* [London: Kegan Paul International, 1998]).

In fact, whereas earlier philosophical texts had often naturalized *"shen"* and identified it with the cosmic order, *Taiping jing* 太平經 (The Classic of the Great Peace), *Baopu Zi waipian* 抱朴子外篇 (The Master Who Embraces Simplicity), and other religious Daoist texts redefined the naturalized *"shen"* (i.e., the cosmic order) by integrating conscious divinities within it. This union of the cosmic order with spirits and ghosts is prominent in the grand hierarchy of spirits and ghosts established in Tao Hongjing's 陶弘景 (456–536) *Zhenling weiye tu* 真靈位業圖. See Ge Zhaoguang 葛兆光, *Daojiao yu zhongguo wenhua* 道教與中國文化 (Shanghai: Shanghai renmin chubanshe, 1987), pp. 55–77.

14. Gao Ming 高明, annot., *Boshu Lao Zi jiaozhu* 帛書老子校注 (Beijing: Zhonghua shuju, 1996), pp. 118–120. Translation taken from *Commentary on*

the Lao Tzu by Wang Pi, translated by Ariane Rump in collaboration with Wing-tsit Chan (Honolulu: University of Hawai'i Press, 1979), p. 171. The style of romanization has been changed to the pinyin.

15. Ibid.

16. Guo Qingfan 郭慶藩, ed., *Zhuang Zi jishi* 莊子集釋, 4 vols. (Beijing: Zhonghua shuju, 1961), 1/3/246–247. Translation taken from Burton Watson, *The Complete Works of Chuang Tzu* (New York: Columbia University Press, 1968), p. 81. The style of romanization has been changed to the pinyin.

17. Kong Yingda, *Zhou yi zhengyi* 周易正義, *juan* 7, in *SSJZ,* vol. 1, p. 78.

18. Liu Wendian 劉文典, ed., *Huainan honglie jijie* 淮南鴻烈集解, 2 vols. (Beijing: Zhonghua shuju, 1989), vol. 1, *juan* 7, p. 218.

19. Huang Hui 黃暉, annot., *Lunheng jiaoshi* 論衡校釋, 4 vols. (Beijing: Zhonghua shuju, 1990), 3/20/872.

20. See Zong-qi Cai, "The Making of a Critical System: Concepts of Literature in *Wenxin diaolong* and Earlier Texts," in *A Chinese Literary Mind: Culture, Creativity, and Rhetoric in* Wenxin diaolong, ed. Zong-qi Cai (Stanford, Calif.: Stanford University Press, 2001), pp. 33–59.

21. A notable exception to this is Liu Xie's mention of *"shen"* as live supernatural beings in the "Zhu Meng" 祝盟 (Sacrificial Prayers and Oaths) chapter of *Wenxin diaolong* 文心雕龍 (The Literary Mind and the Carving of Dragons). See Zong-qi Cai, "The Polysemous Term of *Shen* in *Wenxin diaolong,*" in *Recarving the Dragon: Understanding Chinese Poetics,* ed. Olga Lomová (Prague: Charles University Press, 2003), pp. 37–64.

22. Liu Yiqing 劉義慶, *Shishuo xinyu [jiaojian]* 世説新語[校箋], annot. Xu Zhen'e 徐震堮, 2 vols. (Beijing: Zhonghua shuju, 1984), *juan* 21, vol. 2, p. 388.

23. Liu Wendian, ed., *Huainan honglie jijie, juan* 1, vol. 1, p. 41.

24. Ibid., *juan* 7, vol. 1, pp. 219, 226.

25. Ibid., *juan* 14, vol. 2, pp. 487–488.

26. See Anne H. Soukhanov et al., eds., *The American Heritage Dictionary of the English Language,* 3d ed. (Boston: Houghton Mifflin, 1992), p. 72.

27. Jiao Xun 焦循, ed. *Menzi zhengyi* 孟子正義, 2 vols. (Beijing: Zhonghua shuju, 1987), *juan* 15, vol. 1, pp. 518–519.

28. Ibid.

29. In Huang Hui, *Lunheng jiaoshi,* 3/20/868.

30. Bao Wugang 鮑吾剛 (Wolfgang Bauer), ed., *Renwu zhi yinde* 人物志引得 (San Francisco: Chinese Materials Center, 1974), p. 212.

31. Ibid.

32. Qian Zhongshu 錢鍾書, *Guan zhui bian* 管錐篇, 4 vols. (Beijing: Zhonghua shuju, 1979), vol. 2, p. 714.

33. Shi Song 史崧, comp. Lingshu jing 靈樞經 (Beijing: Renmin weisheng chubanshe, 1956), *juan* 12, p. 133.

34. Liu Yiqing, *Shishuo xinyou [jiaojian], juan* 21, vol. 2, pp. 387–388.

35. See Li Fang 李昉 et al., comps., *Taiping yulang* 太平御覽 (Beijing: Zhonghua shuju, 1960), *juan* 70, vol. 3, p. 3133.

36. In Fang Xuanling 房玄齡, comp., *Jin shu* 晉書 (Beijing: Zhonghua shuju, 1974), 8/62/2405.

37. In Shen Zicheng 沈子丞, comp., *Lidai lunhua mingzhu huibian* 歷代論畫名著匯編 (Beijing: Wenwu chubanshe, 1982), pp. 7–8.

38. Whereas Liu deftly appropriated these views to formulate his theory of nourishing the *qi* (*yangqi lun* 養氣論), the religious Daoists of the time did the same to develop their theories and methods of nourishing and circulating the *qi*. Whether Liu also drew from the rich body of contemporary religious Daoist texts on *yangqi* and *yangshen* 養神 (the nourishing of the spirit) is an issue seldom addressed in the studies of *Wenxin diaolong*. Although an investigation of this issue promises to be rewarding, there is no space for it here. On the religious Daoist views on *qi* and *shen*, see Robert Ford Campany, *To Live as Long as Heaven and Earth: A Translation and Study of Ge Hong's Traditions of Divine Transcendents* (Berkeley: University of California Press, 2002), pp. 18–60.

39. Qian Zhongshu, *Tan yi lu* 談藝錄 (Beijing: Zhonghua shuju, 1987), p. 43.

40. Yan Changyao 顏昌嶢, ed., *Guan Zi jishi* 管子校釋 (Changsha: Yuelu shushe, 1996), *juan* 16, p. 406. Translation taken from W. Allyn Rickett, *Kuan-Tzu: A Repository of Early Chinese Thought* (Hong Kong: Hong Kong University Press, 1965), p. 166.

41. Yan Changyao, ed., *Guan Zi jishi, juan* 13, p. 332. See Rickett, *Kuan-Tzu*, p. 169.

42. Yan Changyao, ed., *Guan Zi jishi, juan* 16, p. 400; translation taken from Rickett, *Kuan-Tzu*, pp. 160–161, slightly modified.

43. Yan Changyao, ed., *Guan Zi jishi, juan* 13, p. 332; translation taken from Rickett, *Kuan-Tzu*, p. 169, modified.

44. See Ban Gu 班固 (32–92), *Han shu* 漢書 (Beijing: Zhonghua shuju, 1962), 9/62/2713–2714. Translation taken with modifications from William Theodore de Bary and Irene Bloom, comps., *Sources of Chinese Tradition, vol. 1: From Earliest Time to 1600* (New York: Columbia University Press, 1999), p. 282.

45. Huang Hui, annot., *Lunheng jiaoshi*, 3/22/946; translation taken from Alfred Forke, *Lun-Hêng, part 1: Philosophical Essays of Wang Ch'ung* (New York: Paragon Book Gallery, 1962), p. 249.

46. See Yu Yuan 郁沅 and Zhang Minggao 張明高, comps., *Wei-Jin Nanbeichao wenlun xuan* 魏晉南北朝文論選 (Beijing: Renmin wenxue chubanshe, 1996), p. 14; translation taken from Owen, *Readings in Chinese Literary Thought*, p. 65. The style of romanization has been changed to the pinyin.

47. Ibid.

48. Yu Yuan and Zhang Minggao, *Wei-Jin Nanbei chao wenlun xuan*, p. 13. See Owen, *Readings in Chinese Literary Thought*, p. 62.

49. Zhu Yingping 朱迎平, ed., *Wenxin diaolong suoyin* 文心雕龍索引 (Shanghai: Shanghai guji chubanshe, 1987), 42/1–4 (i.e., chapter 42/sentences 1–4); hereafter *WXDL*. All subsequent references to *Wenxin diaolong* are to the text of *WXDL* included in this book. This text is taken, with minor emendations, from Fan Wenlan 范文瀾, ed., *Wenxin diaolong zhu* 文心雕龍注 (Beijing: Renmin wenxue chubanshe, 1958). Translation taken with slight modifications from Vincent Yu-chung Shih, trans. and annot., *The Literary Mind and the Carving of Dragons: A Study of Thought and Pattern in Chinese Literature* (Hong Kong: Chinese University Press, 1983), p. 429.

50. Shih, *Literary Mind*, p. 429.

51. My translation. Compare Shih, *Literary Mind*, p. 429.

52. Shih, *Literary Mind*, p. 429.

53. My translation. Compare Shih, *Literary Mind*, p. 431.

54. Shih, *Literary Mind*, p. 431.

55. Ibid., pp. 429, 433, modified.

56. Ibid., p. 433.

57. Ibid.

58. Qian Zhongshu, *Tan yi lu*, p. 43.

59. Wei Zhao, *Guo yu, juan* 18, p. 559.

60. Liu Wendian, ed., *Huainan honglie jijie, juan* 6, vol. 1, pp. 191–192. Translation taken from Charles Le Blanc, *Huai-Nan Tzu* 淮南子 *Philosophical Synthesis in Early Han Thought: The Idea of Resonance (Kan-Ying* 感應) *with a Translation and Analysis of Chapter Six* (Hong Kong: Hong Kong University Press, 1985), pp. 103–104, slightly modified.

61. Yan Changyao, ed., *Guan Zi jishi, juan* 16, p. 405; translation taken from Rickett, *Kuan-Tzu*, p. 164, modified.

62. Guo Qingfan, ed., *Zhuang Zi jishi*, 1/4/160; translation taken from Watson, *The Complete Works of Chuang Tzu*, p. 61.

63. Guo Qingfan, ed., *Zhuang Zi jishi*, 1/7/294; translation taken from Watson, *Complete Works of Chuang Tzu*, p. 94, slightly modified.

64. Liu Wendian, ed., *Huainan honglie jijie, juan* 11, vol. 1, p. 361. Translation taken with slight modifications from Benjamin E. Wallacker, *The Huai-Nan-Tzu, Book Eleven: Behavior, Culture and the Cosmos* (New Haven, Conn.: American Oriental Society, 1962), p. 40.

65. Yu Yuan and Zhang Minggao, *Wei-Jin Nanbei chao wenlun xuan*, p. 146.

66. Ibid.; translation taken from Owen, *Readings in Chinese Literary Thought*, p. 96.

67. Yu Yuan and Zhang Minggao, *Wei-Jin Nanbei chao wenlun xuan*, p. 146; translation taken from Owen, *Readings in Chinese Literary Thought*, pp. 98, 101. The style of romanization has been changed to the pinyin.

68. For more detailed studies of Liu Xie's theory of literary creation, see Ronald Egan, "Poet, Mind, and World: A Reconsideration of the 'Shen si'

Chapter of *Wenxin diaolong*," and Shuen-fu Lin, "Liu Xie on Imagination," in Cai, ed., *A Chinese Literary Mind*, pp. 101–126, 127–160. See also Zong-qi Cai, *Configurations of Comparative Poetics: Three Perspectives on Western and Chinese Literary Criticism* (Honolulu: University of Hawai'i Press, 2002), pp. 142–170.

69. Qian Zhongshu, *Guan zhui pian*, vol. 4, p. 1354.

70. See Victor H. Mair's essay in this volume for a detailed and exhaustive discussion of Xie's Six Laws and their Indian connection.

71. Qian Zhongshu, *Guan zhui pian*, vol. 4, p. 1362. Translation taken with a slight modification from Ronald Egan, ed. and trans., *Limited Views: Essays on Ideas and Letters by Qian Zhongshu* (Cambridge, Mass.: Harvard University Asia Center, 1998), p. 110.

72. Li Yanshou, comp., *Bei shi* 北史 (Beijing: Zhonghua shuju, 1975), 9/83/2779.

73. Zhao Chao 趙超, comp., *Han Wei Nanbei chao mu zhi huibian* 漢魏南北朝墓誌匯編 (Tianjin: Tianjin guji chubanshe, 1992), p. 130.

74. Ibid., p. 273.

75. See Shen Zicheng, *Lidai lunhua mingzhu huibian*, pp. 17–20.

76. See Shen Zicheng, *Lidai lunhua mingzhu huibian*, p. 6.

77. Ibid., p. 20.

78. See ibid., pp. 17–20.

79. See his essays "Lun hua" 論畫 and "Hua yuntaishan ji" 畫雲臺山記, in *Zhongguo lidai huajia daguan: Liang Jin Nanbei chao Sui Tang Wudai* 中國歷代畫家大觀：兩晉南北朝隋唐五代, ed. Shanghai remin meishu chubanshe (1998), pp. 27–30.

80. That the *"chuanshen xiezhao"* principle gets cited in *Shishuo xinyu* does not necessarily mean that it is inspired by the discourses of character judgment. Rather, it seems to indicate that it has been appropriated by Liu Yiqing to illustrate his ideal of transcendent character traits.

81. I have discussed the influence of the *chenwei* notion of *"shen"* in Liu Xie's *yuan Dao shuo* 原道說 (the theory of the Dao as the source of [literature]) in Cai, "The Polysemous Term of Shen in *Wenxin diaolong*," pp. 37–64.

82. In the longer Chinese version of this chapter, I have discussed the influence of Huiyuan's Buddhist reconception of *"shen"* in Zong Bing's essay "Hua shanshui xu" 畫山水序 (Introduction to Painting Landscape). See Zong-qi Cai 蔡宗齊, "Liu chao wenyi lilun zhong 'shen' de zhexue yuanyuan he meixue yiyi" 六朝文藝理論中"神"的哲學淵源和美學新義, *Zhongguo wenxue yanjiu* 中國文學研究, ed. Institute of Classical Chinese Literature, Fudan University, vol. 4 (2001), pp. 18–61.

List of Contributors

Susan Bush is an associate in research at the John King Fairbank Center for East Asian Research. She is the author of *The Chinese Literati on Painting: Su Shih (1037–1101) to Tung Ch'i-ch'ang (1555–1636)* (Harvard, 1971, 1978) and co-editor of *Theories of the Arts in China* (Princeton, 1983) and *Early Chinese Texts on Painting* (Harvard, 1985). More recently she wrote the article on Chinese art theory and criticism for the *Encyclopedia of Aesthetics*. Her areas of research and publication include Six Dynasties decorative motifs and Song-Jin painting.

Zong-qi Cai is Professor of Chinese and Comparative Literature at the University of Illinois, Urbana-Champaign. He is the author of *The Matrix of Lyric Transformation: Poetic Modes and Self-Presentation in Early Chinese Pentasyllabic Poetry* (Michigan, 1996) and *Configurations of Comparative Poetics: Three Perspectives on Western and Chinese Literary Criticism* (Hawai'i, 2002). He is the editor of *A Chinese Literary Mind: Culture, Creativity, and Rhetoric in Wenxin diaolong* (Stanford, 2001).

Kang-i Sun Chang received her Ph.D. from Princeton University and is now Professor of Chinese Literature at Yale University. Her scholarly publications include *The Evolution of Chinese Tz'u Poetry* (Princeton, 1980); *Six Dynasties Poetry* (Princeton, 1986); and *The Late Ming Poet Ch'en Tzu-lung: Crises of Love and Loyalism* (Yale, 1991). She is the co-editor (with Ellen Widmer) of *Writing Women in Late Imperial China* (Stanford, 1997). She is also the compiler and co-editor (with Haun Saussy) of *Women Writers of Traditional China: An Anthology of Poetry and Criticism* (Stanford, 1999). In addition, she has published several books and numerous articles in Chinese on literature and society, gender studies, cultural theory, and aesthetics.

Ronald Egan is Professor of Chinese at the University of California, Santa Barbara. He received his Ph.D. from Harvard University in 1976 and has taught at Harvard, Wellesley College, UCLA, and UC Santa Barbara. His research is on Chinese poetry, aesthetics, and literati culture of the Song period. He is the author of *Word, Image, and Deed in the Life of Su Shi* (Cambridge, 1994) and the translator of *Limited Views: Essays on Ideas and Letters by Qian Zhongshu* (Harvard, 1998).

Robert E. Harrist Jr. is the Jane and Leopold Swergold Professor of Chinese Art History at Columbia University. He has published studies of Chinese painting and calligraphy, including *The Embodied Image: Chinese Calligraphy from the John B. Elliott Collection at Princeton University*, co-authored with Wen C. Fong.

Rania Huntington is Assistant Professor of Chinese Language and Literature at the University of Illinois at Urbana-Champaign. She received her Ph.D. from the Department of East Asian Languages and Civilizations at Harvard University. She is the author of *Alien Kind: Foxes and Ming-Qing Narrative* (Harvard, 2003). Her research interests center on the supernatural in Chinese literature and classical language narrative *(wenyan xiaoshuo)*.

Wai-yee Li is Professor of Chinese Literature at Harvard University. She is the author of *Enchantment and Disenchantment: Love and Illusion in Chinese Literature* (Princeton, 1993) and *The Readability of the Past in Early Chinese Historiography* (Harvard, forthcoming).

Shuen-fu Lin is Professor of Chinese Literature at the University of Michigan, Ann Arbor. He is the author of *The Transformation of the Chinese Lyrical Tradition: Chiang K'uei and Southern Sung Tz'u Poetry* (Princeton, 1978) and *The Pursuit of Utopias* [in Chinese] (Tunghai, 2003). He is also co-editor (with Stephen Owen) of *The Vitality of the Lyric Voice: Shih Poetry from the Late Han to the T'ang* (Princeton, 1986) and co-translator (with Larry Schulz) of *The Tower of Myriad Mirrors: A Supplement to Journey to the West (by Tung Yüeh)* (2d ed., Michigan, 2000).

Victor H. Mair is Professor of Chinese Language and Literature in the Department of Asian and Middle Eastern Studies of the University of Pennsylvania. He is the author of numerous books and articles on medieval Buddhist literature, early Sino-Indian and Sino-Iranian cultural relationships, and the archaeology of Bronze Age Central Asia. He is also the editor of *The Columbia Anthology of Traditional Chinese Literature* and *The Columbia History of Chinese Literature*.

François Martin received his Ph.D. in Chinese at Paris 7 University and teaches Chinese history and philology at the École Pratique des Hautes Etudes in Paris. He specializes in Six Dynasties poetry, the history of Chinese prosody, and the social role of poetry in ancient and medieval times and has published papers on these subjects.

Index

Production Notes for Zong-Qi Cai / *Chinese Aesthetics*

Cover and interior design by the University of Hawai'i Production Department

Text in Plantin and display type in Kabel Bold

Composition by ASCO Typesetting

Printing and binding by the Maple-Vail Book Manufacturing Group

Printed on 60# Sebago Eggshell, 420 ppi